FACTORY
Fairy Tales

Ged Duffy

My favourite band that, at the time, I had the least understanding of how important they could be, was probably Stockholm Monsters, who I still love to this day, even though they lost my fucking guitar or burned it or something, 10 or 15 years ago. Stockholm Monsters were scallys, they were the scally band three, four years before the Mondays, before the Roses. Maybe if I'd have understood it more, maybe I would have done better by them"

Tony Wilson interviewed by James Nice in Manchester in 2005.

"I started to get into music early on because all the older guys that lived round our way were into a band called the Stockholm Monsters. They were the first band ever to come from Burnage and I think they had a top 75 hit with a song called 'Fairy Tales'. From there you get into Joy Division, New Order and then it was The Smiths and then the Roses and then the Mondays and then you start your band."

Noel Gallagher talking to *The Manchester Evening News* 1 July 2002.

"Another band that's often overlooked in the telling of the Factory Records story but a real favourite of mine. They always seemed to know how to tug at my teenage heartstrings. I have the 7 inch single with two different sleeves and now, thanks to this album, I have the demo as well. This song doesn't seem to age."

Tim Burgess describing "Fairy Tales" on "Tim Peaks", the compilation album of some of his favourite songs

"When I was 10, I was walking down Burnage Lane with my mum when I saw a guy in front of me with white hair and a big black exclamation mark. He was a punk. I later found out that he was a member of Stockholm Monsters... the first band to come from Burnage... Oasis were the second."

Noel Gallagher talking to Jules Holland on BBC 2 14 May 2021.

First published in 2021

This book is copyright under the Berne Convention. All rights are reserved. Apart from any fair dealing for the purpose of private study, research, criticism or review, as permitted under the Copyright Act, 1956, no part of this publication may be reproduced, stored in a retrieval system, or transmitted, in any form or by any means, electronic, electrical, chemical, mechanical, optical, photocopying, recording or otherwise, without the prior permission of the copyright owner. Enquiries should be sent to the publishers at the undermentioned address:

EMPIRE PUBLICATIONS
1 Newton Street, Manchester M1 1HW

© Ged Duffy 2021

ISBN: 978-1-909360-91-4

Cover photo: 'Some muppet with a bass' - this photo was taken on stage with Lavolta Lakota in 1983. It's my favourite photo of me. I used to have it on the wall of my office at home and during an argument with Janine, she ripped it off the wall and despite requests from me not to damage it, she scrunched it up into a ball and threw it at me shouting "it's not important, it's just a picture of a fucking muppet with a bass!" hence the name.

For Jack, Tom, and Liam

Contents

Foreword ix
Introduction xi
Manchester In The 1970s 1
1. Forbidden love, electric shocks and slave labour 5
2. God's brothers, Noddy Holder and friendly natives ... 12
3. Johnny kicks the doors in 23
4. Robert Leo Gretton - a bitter blue 35
5. The loveable promoter 49
6. Ian Curtis gave me a quid 68
7. Hooky throwing right hooks at the Russell 88
8. An unforgettable night 105
9: Fucking Discharge! 114
10. Let's start a band 120
11. A close encounter with the Angels 124
12. Monsters' first gigs 130
13: Advice to Barney, don't fuck with Slim 140
14. A scrap with Bauhaus 152
15. Scooter in the sky 167
16. Into Europe with New Order 177
17: Leaving a band by mistake 190
18: Several scouse bands with stupid names 204
19: Hooky gave me a speaker cab so I had to play again ... 213
20: Lavolta Lakota - what a shit name! 218
21: Follow the leaf 229

22. Playing the Hacienda at last 232
23: Mark E Smith doesn't share his beer 236
24: Moving out of Hulme by mistake 241
25. How hard can it be to find a fucking drummer! 249
26. Love and marriage 265
27: Twat 273
28: Daddy Duffy goes to Rotterdam and this time it's 2-1 277
29. Champions at last 282
30. Double trouble at home 285
31: Devastating news 289
32: 1999 and all that 294
33: Worst Christmas imaginable 299
34: Single Parent 304
35: American Woman 308
36: Another son 317
37. Moscow and Divorce 321
    A life spent making mistakes? 327
    Acknowledgements 333

Foreword

OUR TRUTH!

One great thing about this Covid-induced retirement that many of us have had to endure this year and last is that some people have finally got round to doing something that they had always promised themselves. To tell the story of their lives!

I was lucky enough to spend a lot of time with The Stockholm Monsters and Ged at a fantastic time in their personal history and in Manchester's. To me each one of these memoirs written is very important and fulfils a vital role. It fills in the missing pieces of the mad musical jigsaw that we have all struggled to complete at one time or another. In the pub, in our heads, even in our hearts. Every one of us has a different memory of the same time or happening. In his 1873 essay *Truth and Lying in an Extra-Moral Sense*, Friedrich Nietzsche argues that we create our truth about the world through use of metaphor and myths. To get closer to our psychological or literary truth: "our truth". I think a big part of our lives are about the art of storytelling. The stories we tell ourselves and the ones that people tell us.

I know for a fact that some of Ged's old band-mates disagree with his story in the same way that my band-mates disagree with my recollections, be it in print or even spoken in interviews or privately. But that is not the important thing. The important thing is telling your story and getting it in print. What an achievement. I'm proud of you Ged!

The Monsters and Lavolta Lakota along with all the other players in their story: Slim, Andy Fisher, even me, need to be laid out for posterity for all to read. The bands wrote some great tunes, did some great gigs (some shit gigs too) but they are a very important part of the Manchester scene of the 80's and 90's. We were all living our young lives to their fullest; adventure after adventure, discovery after discovery, lesson after lesson, some good, some bad but every one was exciting, and I miss them all madly. *Fairy Tales* is aptly named, or is it? Judge for yourself.

One of my best memories of Lavolta Lakota is being in Strawberry 2 Studios with them doing a session. We were mixing at night because

Factory Fairy Tales

it was cheaper, the song 'Prayer' I think, and waiting for the band who were in before us to finish their own session. There were two of them sat at the mixing desk in front of the seats where we sat behind them. As I sat waiting listening to this wonderful brass band music that they were mixing, one by one the members of Lavolta stumbled in: Mikey, Dave Hicks, Ged, all taking a seat next to me at the back, then they all started skinning up, almost all at once, all of them with the necessary equipment of skins, tobacco and Marijuana laid out neatly on their laps. They were nearly finished and almost ready to start smoking the resulting joints when for some reason I thought I could do with hurrying the Brass band players up. So striding to the mixing desk I said, 'This music is great what's the band called?'

Without turning round one of the guys said, 'Thank you Hooky, what a compliment! We are The Stockport Police Brass Band, my name's Sergeant Gilfoyle. Pleased to meet you.' As he turned to shake my hand you should have heard the gulps and kerfuffle behind me as the lads jumped out of their skins and hid their shit as fast as they could. I was laughing my dogs off for hours!

Whenever Lavolta played I used a copy of that tune as their intro music to remind them of the lucky escapes we all had.

Great days.

Peter Hook
September 2021

Introduction

It's 1978, and a fledgling 15 year-old Gary *Mani* Mounfield is beginning to spread his musical wings - sneaking out of his bedroom window in Failsworth, meeting Kaiser, cadging a lift to gigs off the older kids from across the street. I was introduced to the Russell Club and my life changed forever. A place populated by a total mish mash of subcultures, lunatics and general outsiders from all areas of Manchester and beyond. Friendships that were made in this club as young gig goers and hanging out at Discount Records in the Underground Market after school and on Saturdays that still last to this day. Ged Duffy is one of these guys… a guy who was at the same school as I was, albeit a couple of years above me. Ged, Slim and 'Dot Dash' Derek were the first people to meet us at the Russell. We were a great crew who looked out for each other when out and about in the war-zone that was Manchester city centre in the 70's. When the Russell closed we moved on to Rafters, Deville's, The Poly and The Mayflower.

Subsequently Ged and his band, the Stockholm Monsters, become the first people who we actually knew to get a record deal. Myself and my North Manchester mates proceeded to follow the Monsters around the UK as they embarked on their first tour opening up for New Order. Gigs that spring to mind are ones at Derby Blue Note Club, Imperial Cinema on Moseley Road in Birmingham, Sheffield Poly and North London Poly. These gigs very often degenerated into wild west brawls but the touch paper was lit in me, my path was chosen for me at these gigs. I owe Ged, Slim, Stockholm Monsters and all those mad fuckers at the Russell Club a debt of gratitude for turning this young 15 year-old scoundrel on to it!

Cheers Ged, I'm eternally grateful for being a part of your tale, however small. Your story deserves to be told.

Mani
September 2021

Manchester In The 1970s

When you look at Manchester nowadays with its trendy wine bars, kerbside café bars and glass-fronted skyscrapers, it's hard to believe what the city was actually like in the 1970s. Nowadays it's been re-branded as Manc-Hattan, whereas in most people's eyes it was a slum in the seventies.

The city still had extensive war damage and was full of Victorian buildings caked in over 100 years of dirt, soot, and grime from the factories and mills around the city. Some of these buildings were in serious disrepair and needed money spending on them. If you look at the buildings near Piccadilly Gardens, such as the old Woolworths and Debenham's buildings, you can see the grandiose architecture and back in the early part of the 1970s Market Street was lined with the same quality of building. The Council could have sandblasted the grime off these buildings, spent money on repairs and instructed developers that they could turn the interiors into whatever they wanted, on condition that the external walls remain intact – had they done this then Manchester would have a great architectural heart today. Instead they built the Arndale Centre – known locally as the biggest toilet in Europe.

This new shopping centre consisted of 210 shops over two floors, a market with 200 stalls over two floors, 60 apartments were built on the roof, there was a bus station underneath, a multi-storey car park and the Arndale Tower which was a 21-storey office block yet it looked awful as the huge external wall was tiled in a vile yellow which resembled the wall in a public convenience. Originally the architects wanted to allow the shops to have glass-fronted areas where they could display their goods, but the Council refused to allow this, hence the toilet wall was built instead. There were other problems: the bus station didn't open as planned, and when it finally opened the new double-decker buses made by Leyland Coaches were about two inches too tall to get into it, although the council denied this.

Manchester was a very tribal city in those days. You were either in a gang, or you were an outsider. Everything was black or white; you're one of us, or you're one of them. You did what you had to survive. In school you made friends with the 'cock' (the hardest lad) in the year and then you ran with his gang dishing out the beatings rather than receiving them. In Burnage we would fight with other gangs from Levenshulme, Withington and Fallowfield and you defended your area at all costs. Cutting across these district allegiances were football allegiances - you were either a Red or a Blue. It was mad going away with United in those days. You got carried away with the rush of taking over a football ground and in some cases whole towns. The feeling of being part of an army gave you a tremendous high. Being part of the football crew gave you the skills needed to survive in Manchester City Centre at night, especially if you looked different to the norm. It was a complete war-zone around Piccadilly Bus Station every weekend.

Life was completely different in the 1970s. A lot of these differences stemmed from the relatively primitive technology at our disposal. For a start there were only three TV channels and each one of them shut down at midnight apart from New Year's Eve, when they showed little men in kilts, singing and dancing in the New Year for an extra hour. One constant was that the top-rated TV show, then as now, was *Coronation Street*. The top comedy shows at the time were *Love Thy Neighbour*, *Benny Hill*, *On The Buses*, *Steptoe and Son*, *The Dick Emery Show*, *The Goodies*, *Dave Allen*, *Morecambe and Wise*, and *Monty Python's Flying Circus*. The last two are probably the only ones that would be allowed to be shown nowadays as the rest would be classed as racist, sexist or both.

Most pubs had two rooms: the men went in the vault to smoke and drink and couples went into the lounge. Some pubs had a takeaway section with a separate entrance, and you returned the empty bottles when you had finished to get a few pence back per bottle. It was rare to see a lone female in a bar unless she was a lady of the night. Pubs opened between 11.30am and 3pm, and then from 5.30pm till 11pm, except on Sundays when it was noon till 2pm and 6pm to 10pm. These drinking hours had remained pretty much unchanged since the First World War!

When I left school it was still the case that if you left one job, you could get another one almost immediately. There was little unemployment as full employment was government policy. Flats and bedsits to rent were always available and cheap. References and all that nonsense weren't needed.

Sweet shops were everywhere and a 10p mix would last a couple of days. Burnage had three sweet shops that I can recall. Every area

Ged Duffy

had its own cinema. It was the Concorde in Burnage and the Scala in Withington. Before the internet, if you wanted to find something out you went to the library and borrowed a book or looked it up in the reference section. Every town, however small, had a library.

There were no computer games, so you hung around on the streets, played football or became a joy rider. If you wanted a burger then it was table service only at your nearest Wimpy Bar. That is unless you were a single woman, then service would be denied to you because you might be a prostitute touting for business. I kid you not. The first McDonald's to open in Manchester was on Market Street in 1983. The only KFC in the whole of Manchester was on Oxford Road.

If you were out and about and needed to call someone then there were red public phone boxes on every other street corner. Finding your way meant using a road map or A to Z; banks were only open between 10 and 3pm Monday to Friday and there were no cash machines so most people kept their pay packets at home and took money with them as needed; there was no home delivery, so you had to go to the shops and buy it yourself (unless you were ordering stuff from Kay's catalogue); in place of emails you had to write a letter and post it or call someone on their land line.

The FA Cup Final, European Cup Final, and the England v Scotland game were the only ones shown live on TV, occasionally they would show a World Cup qualifier such as England's disastrous draw with Poland in 1973 that saw us fail to qualify for the World Cup. During the season there would probably be only four or five games per season shown live, but we had two different highlights shows – *Match of the Day* on BBC and *Kick Off* on Granada. All league games kicked off at 3pm on a Saturday and mid-week games kicked off at 7.30pm on a Wednesday unless there was fixture congestion or some other crisis. All European Cup, UEFA Cup, and Cup Winner's Cup games were played on a Wednesday and kicked off at 7.30pm. Most football matches were pay at the turnstile, so you got there early and queued to get in.

In many ways modern life seems much better nowadays, but one thing that we did far better back in those days is that there were very few places where you could buy a ticket for a gig, so you usually went along on the night and paid on the door. Nowadays a whole tour is sold in five minutes on the internet.

Factory Fairy Tales

It's about 11pm on the evening of Thursday 25th February 1982, and we are just about to hear the finished mixed version of our second single 'Happy Ever After' played through the speakers at Strawberry Studios. Tony Wilson and Rob Gretton have both turned up so that they can hear it too. Hooky turns the tape on and the song starts to blast through the studio's high-quality speakers. Gretton is sat in the corner with a spliff in his hand nodding his head, whist Wilson is up on his feet dancing and singing along as the melody floats through the air.

As soon as it finishes Wilson proclaims, "Well darlings, that's a massive pop hit but unfortunately you're on Factory and it'll sell fuck all" and with that he turned away and floated off into the Stockport night.

In time, Gretton looks up and says, "He's right, you know". We decided then and there to talk to Rough Trade Records but that's another story.

By the way Wilson was right on both counts - it was a great pop song and it sold fuck all.

Looking back on it all now, nearly 40 years later, I realize that I was so lucky to have been friends with Tony, Rob, and the rest of New Order, and being part of the Factory family. So how did a skinny red head with poor eyesight and a slight speech impediment, the son of Irish immigrant parents, end up being involved with the coolest record label of all time and find himself living in the best city in the world?

To find out, we have to go back to when my life began.

Hope you enjoy reading my story.

1. Forbidden love, electric shocks and slave labour

I was born on 27th December 1960 in St Mary's Hospital in the heart of Manchester. This old Victorian hospital is sadly no longer there as the new St Mary's was opened in 1970. My Mum was due to sail back to Ireland the first week in January to have me but these plans changed when she fell ill on Boxing Day and was rushed to hospital. The following day she had to have an emergency C Section as both of our lives were in danger. Mum nearly died after having me and she was in hospital for a few weeks following my birth. She always seemed to be ill when I was growing up and I used to blame myself for this as she was 42 years old when I was born, which was very old for the medical facilities in 1960. Yet despite being in constant pain, she would always have a smile for me. I was baptised in the nearby Holy Name church a few weeks later. The Holy Name has now got its own place in Manchester musical folklore thanks to The Smiths song 'Vicar in a Tutu'. Last time I looked the lead was still on the roof.

My Mum and Dad both came from County Mayo in Ireland but from completely different social backgrounds. Mary Murray (my Mum) had four brothers: Paddy, John, Paul, and Mick. They were originally mountain folk, farming sheep and growing crops out in the wild, mountainous bogland of Mayo. Someone in their village contracted Tuberculosis (TB) and as a result the whole village was evacuated and demolished. Mayo Council gave a house to the family to move into in a small coastal village called Castlelacken. The two-bed single storey stone cottage came with a large field at the front for hay growing, a side field for growing vegetables, and two fields at the rear for cattle. These two fields backed onto the beach and the Atlantic Ocean. As a result of the TB, the house was marked with a big black cross on the gable wall to show that the family living there had come into contact with it, even though no one in the Murray Family had ever had it.

My dad, Jack Duffy, had an older brother called Tom and one-half brother called Joe. His Mum died young, and his Dad remarried. When his half-brother was born his stepmother decided that they could not afford to raise three children, so my dad ended up living with his three spinster aunts and his bachelor uncle in a large house

Factory Fairy Tales

in nearby Carrowmore Lacken. His aunts and uncle owned the local shop and petrol station and as a result they were quite well off. He earned money doing deliveries for the shop and had quite a good time growing up there.

When Dad met Mum he was banned from seeing her by his aunts as Mum's family had been involved with TB, and anyone associated with that disease were regarded as low-class scum. Dad ignored his family and married Mum in secret. They had to live apart and see each other in secret, but when mum got pregnant the truth had to come out. Having been disowned by his family Dad left for England with my Uncle Mick to become a navvy, one of McAlpine's Fusiliers, and worked on the construction of the M1 between Nottingham and Derby. In his absence my sister Margaret was born in November 1952.

Mum and Margaret stayed in Ireland for another seven years until Dad had managed to save enough money to get them over to join him. They came over in 1959 and moved into a two up, two down mid-terrace in Holstein Street, which was a couple of minutes' walk away from the Apollo Theatre in Ardwick Green. As you could imagine Margaret was not pleased, as she was now seven and had spent all of her life by the sea in a rural environment, and she was now living in smog covered, industrial grey Manchester. Things got worse for Margaret as she contracted meningitis a couple of years later and would have died without a local doctor spotting it and rushing her to hospital in his car. Whilst she was recovering Mum took her back to Ireland and Margaret stayed there for a couple of years and reluctantly returned around 1964.

During our time in Ardwick Dad had got into a little bit of bother with the police. The people who lived on Holstein Street were all poor and had nothing worth stealing except for the lead on the roofs. Several roofs had been targeted so Dad wired his to the electric supply! One night the family were awoken by a loud yell. It turned out that a guy had got on the roof to steal the lead and had been thrown off it by the electric shock, he was knocked out the second he hit the back-yard. The police came and just told Dad to unhook the roof from the electric supply and not to do it again. When the guy regained consciousness he was arrested, and the police ignored his claims of being electrocuted, the police were so different in those days. On another occasion Dad wired the back door to the electric supply as the guy living next door discovered when he tried to break

Ged Duffy

in a few weeks later, but this was not reported to the police as he was a known offender.

In 1963 Manchester City Council compulsorily purchased the house in Ardwick so that they could build the Ardwick Medical Centre and a parade of shops. Dad purchased a three-bedroom semi-detached house in Burnage for £2,500 on the corner of Glendale Avenue and Mauldeth Road, and this became our family home. Margaret still lives in the house to this day. Growing up in Burnage in the 1960s was quite good. Most of the people living there were either Irish or of Irish descent and there was a good community spirit around the place. It was safe to walk around and there was little crime. The other great thing about Burnage was that when the wind blew in a certain direction you could smell the beautiful aromas coming out of McVitie's biscuit factory in nearby Levenshulme.

Coming from a strict Catholic family it was mass every Sunday and every Holy Day as well. We didn't eat meat on a Friday, and we gave up something every year for Lent. From the age of seven it was Confession every fortnight and even though I turned my back on being a practising Catholic at the age of sixteen, I am still plagued to this day with Catholic Guilt at certain times.

Mum and Dad's relationship was very cold - I can never remember them kissing each other. Mum was very warm, talkative and generous whereas Dad was quiet, kept himself to himself, appeared to have a cold personality but basically, he was just very shy around people. Dad would come home from work around 6pm to find his tea on the table waiting for him. Once he had eaten he would fall asleep on the sofa in the living room. Whilst he was doing this Mum would sit in the kitchen and knit (I was never short of jumpers growing up). At 10pm Dad would wake up and watch the news. If Margaret or I were watching something he would just turn the telly over. Once the news had finished he would turn the telly off and go to bed. We would turn the telly back on once he was safely upstairs.

Mum and Dad both lived a simple life, and they were not interested in flash things or fancy holidays even though Dad earned good money on the building sites. Even our meals were simple and followed a pattern of the same meals on the same day every week.

Sunday: Roast Lamb.

Monday: Leftovers from Sunday.

Factory Fairy Tales

Tuesday: Bacon and cabbage.

Wednesday: Fried mackerel.

Thursday: Fried steak.

Friday: Colcannon (mashed potato and cabbage) or as a treat fish and chips from the chippy.

Saturday: Pork chops or liver.

All meals were served with boiled potatoes and vegetables except Colcannon which we had sometimes with swede. The meals were wholesome and filling, but the house stank of fish from Wednesday till Monday because of the mackerel.

Every summer for six weeks Mum and I would fly to Ireland to stay at the farmhouse in Mayo. Six weeks by the sea might sound amazing but a typical day for me was as follows:

5.30am: get up and have breakfast.

6.30am: Milk the cows, feed the calves and get the eggs from the hen house. There were no milking machines, so it was all done by hand. I discovered very quickly that you had to tie the cow's tail round one of her legs, since if you didn't you were likely to get a severe clout round the head from her tail which invariably would be covered in cow poo. Not a nice experience but one that would only happen to you once.

8am: Get the milk ready for the dairy wagon collection.

9am: Work in the field or go to the bog and cut the turf.

Noon: Lunch and then back in the field or in the bog.

2pm: Free time. If we were cutting the turf, there was no free time.

6pm: Milk the cows and feed the calves.

7pm: Put the hens back in the hen house and leave the milk at the gate for evening collection followed by tea which was the main meal of the day.

This was a typical routine every day and the only deviations from this

MUM AND HER BROTHERS...
Left to right: Mick, Mum, Johnny, Paddy and (front) Paul

were on Sunday when we went to morning mass and didn't do any work in the field and once a fortnight when my Uncle Paddy would have to go into the nearest town, Ballycastle, to sign on for his social security.

The only transport available to Paddy for the eight mile ride to Ballycastle was the donkey and cart. This involved the dangerous procedure of getting the bridle onto the donkey without him kicking or biting you. Once he was out on the road he was generally okay, and easy to control most of the time, but he did still have his moments where he refused to move and would snort at us both and kick the cart. After signing on we would tie the donkey to a lamp post and go in a local pub. Paddy would have a couple of pints of Guinness, and I would have two glasses of red lemonade and two packets of Tayto cheese and onion crisps.

The farmhouse was extremely small and basic. When I was a small child there would be six people living there, but as the years passed it would end up with just Paddy, Mum, and me and then it was tolerable. There was a main room which acted as the living room and dining room with a bedroom off it on each side. There was a tiny kitchen and a bathroom. Paddy slept in a bed in an alcove in the main room which had a curtain across it for some privacy. The cooking was done on the range which was next to the open fire in the living room. The house

Factory Fairy Tales

was freezing cold every morning, but within a few minutes of the turf going on the fire it quickly warmed up.

During my free time I would go down to the beach and play football with Johnny who lived next door. The beach was always deserted and was not on any tourist map and we had hours of fun down there. This beach was known as Lacken Strand and it's now on a tourist route known as The Wild Atlantic Way. Nowadays there's a car park built next to the beach, and it's signposted for a few miles around so it's not as quiet and deserted as it used to be.

From an early age I was taught that you had to be respectful to the priests in Ireland because they would think nothing of giving you a slap whenever they felt like it. If you have ever watched the TV show *Father Ted*, then Father Jack is a good portrayal of the local priest in Castlelacken. The people were terrified of the priest and treated him like a God. When he visited your house he got the best food and best whiskey all served up in the best china and we would sit there watching him eat and drink whilst we had nothing. However there would be no Poitín given to the priest. Poitín is an illegal moonshine made in a small pot with fermented potatoes, malted barley and sometimes with crab apples and it was about 90% proof. My Uncle Tom was the local brewer and he used to leave the bottles to ferment in the field where we used to cut the turf. When someone ordered one he would cycle off to the bog and come back with it. Tom passed away in 1978 and no one knows where his stash is buried but if someone opened one of these bottles now, I guess the fumes would be enough to kill you. When his Stepmother asked Dad and him to leave the family home, Tom stowed away on a ship to America. During the voyage he was discovered, and instead of arresting him the Captain offered him a job as a Steward. He worked for Cunard Shipping for many years. One day he got off the ship in America, decided to leave his job and went to Chicago, where he ended up getting a job as a Police Officer. Unfortunately, he got shot and was invalided out of the force. He returned to Ireland and settled back in Dublin, where a few years later he was awarded the Fáinne badge. This is an award that bestowed on someone who could tell a story in Gaelic for 30 minutes in front of their peers. This is a very prestigious award with honourees including George Bernard Shaw, James Joyce, Oscar Wilde and Brendon Behan. While they were all great writers, Tom was not but he was a great storyteller. The Fáinne badge was a small pin badge of the letter *F*, very much like the Factory pin badge that I used to wear in the early 1980s.

The view I woke up to every morning from the farmhouse

He wore it with pride until he passed away.

Tom looked like he was a member of the Irish folk group The Dubliners with his long grey hair, a long grey beard, a black shirt, black trousers, and a black suit jacket. He lived in a small cottage that was run down with one habitable room in it and had no electricity or running water. He used to get up late afternoon and be out all night on his bike. People used to think that he was a mental case, so they were afraid of him, but he was harmless.

2. God's brothers, Noddy Holder and friendly natives

My first school was St Bernard's RC in Burnage but after a few months and many visits to the Headmaster, Mum took me out of there. I had a really bad speech impediment when I was very young, and no one could understand what I was saying. I was getting bullied constantly. Over the next two years I attended speech therapy twice a week, and gradually learned how to talk. I still have issues pronouncing my R's, but I live with it. During these two years I attended a school in Chorlton.

At the age of seven I started at St Anne's Prep in Fallowfield which meant that I had to get the No 50 bus every day to and from school. St Anne's was the prep school for Xaverian College and the school's sole purpose was to get you to pass your 11 plus exam and then go to Xaverian. Most of the teachers were brothers or nuns and these people of God did not mind dishing out God's punishment by way of a belt on the hands or the backside at any given opportunity.

During my first couple of months at the school all the first year pupils were taken on a day trip to Old Trafford to meet the Manchester United players. Paddy Crerand and Nobby Stiles had sons going to the school and the visit had been arranged via these two. We were greeted at Old Trafford by Sir Matt Busby who took us all on a tour of the dressing rooms and the stadium. Then we went out onto the pitch and broke up into separate groups to train with the players. My group of pupils trained with Paddy Crerand, Brian Kidd and George Best, which consisted of passing the ball one touch between us all for about half an hour. We then had lunch with the players and staff followed by a group photo of some of the players, staff, us kids, Sir Matt, and the European Cup. It remains one of my most treasured memories. Most of my classmates had a United shirt to wear but my Mum and Dad did not know where to buy one from, so I had to wear my school uniform. As I got older, I started to question whether this had ever happened or not as there was no photograph of it and Mum and Dad couldn't remember it happening. I discovered that it was true in 1996 but that's another story.

Around this time I went into the Royal Eye Hospital for a routine operation on my right eye. I wore glasses because I had a squint in

Ged Duffy

SCHOOL TRIP TO OLD TRAFFORD, 1968
I'm in the third row, second from the right
with the lovely National Health glasses.

that eye and the operation was to correct it. Somehow the operation went wrong and as a result I have had blurred vision in my right eye ever since.

School carried on and I discovered that apart from art, history, and English literature, I was not interested in any of the other subjects. Every day was a drag apart from the football games in the playground. I kept my head down until I shocked myself and most of the teachers by passing my 11 plus exam and gaining admission to Xaverian. St Anne's is no longer there and was replaced by a housing estate several years ago.

Xaverian College was a public grammar school, and the complex was split into buildings on two sides of Lower Park Road, Rusholme and it was a big daunting place compared to St Anne's. The first and second year pupils were on one side of the road and the rest of the school on the other. Once again a few of the teachers were brothers and they enjoyed dispensing God's justice whenever they could. There was a small church built near the entrance of the school and we were forced to spend a lot of time in there. I had to wear a school blazer, shirt, tie and grey flared pants to school. I hated this uniform. My only act of rebellion was a pair of black 18 hole Dr Martens boots which led to the nickname *Docker Duffy*.

Factory Fairy Tales

When I was 12, I fell in the playground whilst playing football and broke my wrist. It took nearly ten weeks to heal and since it was my writing hand, I was off school. I never caught up with the lessons that I missed and as a result, I gave up on a lot of subjects. While I was off with my right arm in plaster up to my elbow, I started to listen to the radio during the day. One day I heard 'Gudbuy to Jane' by Slade and it suddenly woke me up. My Mum and Dad did not listen to any music apart from having the radio tuned to an Irish music station. Margaret listened to James Taylor, Cat Stevens, Joni Mitchell, so my house was hardly a hotbed of music.

My Dad brought me a Dansette record player with its own built-in speaker, and I bought 'Gudbuy to Jane' as my first single. I played it to death, and I still love it to this day. I started listening to the radio under the covers every night discovering all these amazing bands that I had never heard before: The Beatles, The Rolling Stones, The Who and then glam rock emerged. I started buying singles by Slade, Sweet, T Rex, Mud and Bowie. I started watching *Top of The Pops* every Thursday evening. I remember watching Bowie do 'Starman' on the show and it blew my mind. He looked so different to everyone else and that was the start of my Bowie craze. Sometimes I would be able to watch *The Old Grey Whistle Test* and I remember seeing New York Dolls and Roxy Music on there.

During October and November 1973, we had power cuts which came without any warning and could last for days. Candlelight became the main source of lighting for a lot of the time that winter and television shut down at 10.30pm to preserve electricity. As a kid it was exciting as it would become pitch black in an instant. Businesses could only open three days per week until everything went back to normal in March 1974. Petrol was also rationed during this time.

I attended my first game at Old Trafford with a friend called Jimmy Connell from school. I got the 22 bus down to Stretford Arndale and met Jimmy there and we walked down Chester Road with the hordes of singing fans and turning onto Warwick Road and seeing the ground for the first time is a memory that I have never forgotten. We queued up and went into the Stretford Paddock which was next to the Stretford End.

Man United 1 Newcastle United 0 was the result and Jim McCalliog scored the winner. The other thing I remember from this game is that Malcolm MacDonald rounded Alex Stepney and passed the ball into the empty net and ran off to celebrate with the travelling Geordies in the Scoreboard End behind the goal. When he got there they were screaming at him to turn round - the ball had stuck in the mud and Stepney had got back up, picked it up and cleared it down the pitch. The Geordies gave him some merciless stick. I came home from the match absolutely buzzing with excitement. The size of the ground, the atmosphere, the constant swaying of the crowd in the Stretford End, the smell of the Bovril, pies and stale beer at half time, the crush getting out of the ground, being carried over the bridge at Railway Road by the crowd and the singing... I loved it all and I was hooked.

A couple of weeks later I saw us relegated to the Second Division when City beat us 1-0 at Old Trafford. This is a game infamous for Denis Law scoring and immediately walking straight off the pitch, and the fact that the match never actually finished, as the Stretford Enders invaded the pitch to attack the City fans in the Scoreboard End. This was my first glimpse of the Red Army in action.

I had come to the realization that most of the kids in my year wanted to be doctors, lawyers, or architects whereas I had no idea what I wanted to be, and I didn't think I was on the same level as some of them intellectually, I was a drifter and definitely not University material. The teachers realized this as well, so I wasn't one of their priority students. Occasionally there would be a fight between Xaverian and the local comprehensive St Pius X and it would be a bit risky for a few days afterwards coming to and from school as I had to walk past St Pius X to get to my bus stop and there would be kids from both schools on the bus. Sometimes there would be some scuffles on the bus. They looked upon us as easy meat, someone they could bully, and they would be shocked that some of us would fight back and give them a kicking sometimes.

Most of the teachers were okay but geography was the one subject where everyone paid attention. The teacher would be writing on the blackboard and would suddenly turn round and throw the board duster in one complete movement at whichever pupil was talking. He would hit you straight between the eyes and I don't think I ever saw him miss. I can tell you that it hurt like hell as I was the recipient of this gift a couple of times. I think his name was Mr Hunter, but I'm not completely sure.

Miss Whitelegg, the French teacher, was completely different. She used to wear short skirts, stockings and suspenders and liked to

Factory Fairy Tales

walk up and down each row. The number of lads who kept dropping their pens or rulers as she walked past was uncountable. She knew what was going on, but I think she liked the attention. We all had a serious crush on Miss Whitelegg.

I hated the PE teacher. I had no interest in jumping over a stupid horse or climbing a rope as I just wanted to play football. Over time he would pick on a few of us who were not following his instructions, he would throw heavy medicine balls with force at each of us so that it would hurt us when we tried to catch it, but his favourite trick was to have everyone hang by their arms on the side bars which were situated on all the walls of the gym. Then he would let everyone get down apart from our chosen little crew and we would hang there for a full lesson sometimes. What a twat he was!

By now I was going to every United home game and most of the aways in the Second Division and it was a blast. United took thousands to every away ground and smashed up everywhere they went. It was like a war zone outside each ground and Manchester was in the area. There were riots at Millwall, Cardiff and several other grounds. The Millwall one was mental as a red had stuck a kung fu star into a police horse's arse and it lost control running and kicking in the middle of the fighting fans. The policeman riding the horse got thrown off in the middle of it all and took a kicking off both sets of fans.

The Cardiff riot, which occurred inside and outside Ninian Park, was probably the most violent game that season. The walk from the train station to the ground was okay with the usual police escort. Once inside we had been given one complete side of the ground. This area was next to their main end and was only separated by a piece of thin wire. The police tried to form a No Man's Land but failed. Both sets of fans attacked the police and some broke through into the others area and got involved in some serious fighting. They were singing about the Munich Air Disaster, where eight United players had died in 1958, and United were singing about the disaster that had happened outside Aberfan, where a landslide had killed 116 children and 28 adults in 1966. Both sets of fans attacked each other with slabs of concrete and bits of wood pulled from the terracing.

Normally fighting stopped during the game and might resume if a goal was scored, but at this game it carried on for the 90 minutes and during half time. Every Welshman must have come down from the valleys to fight United that day. Afterwards it was complete mayhem.

Ged Duffy

The fighting was crazy and non-stop with people getting the absolute shit kicked out of them. The police were in the middle of it all.

Suddenly, without any warning the fighting stopped, and the crowd parted. It turned out that a lad was lying on the floor bleeding heavily from several stab wounds. The police carried him away and then the fighting resumed! There were running battles all the way back to the train station. The front page of the papers the next day showed an old man leaving the ground wearing his Second World War army helmet, to protect himself from the hail of missiles raining down.

Later that season I remember coming out of Boundary Park after Oldham had beaten United 1-0 and we walked down a street of terrace houses. Every window was going in and every car was getting damaged except one house. The guy that owned this house was sat outside his house with his rottweiler and a shotgun.

On 26 April 1975 we lifted the Second Division Title after beating Blackpool 4-0 in front of a packed Old Trafford. The atmosphere that day was electric. We couldn't wait to get into the stadium as it was a complete day of celebration as we were going back to where we belonged... the First Division. The singing that day was non-stop. After Martin Buchan had lifted the trophy there was a massive pitch invasion and I dug up a lump of God's Acre and buried it in our side garden. I was so pleased with myself for doing that. The grass is still there to this day so I know a piece of Old Trafford will forever live in Burnage. I had witnessed the lows of relegation and the highs of becoming champions all within the space of about 15 months and I never guessed, when I walked out of Old Trafford that day, that it would be 17 years before I experienced that high again.

On Thursday 2 January 1975 a new TV show aired on ITV at 9pm called *The Sweeney*. It was a cop show based on the infamous Flying Squad of Scotland Yard. The two lead characters, DI Jack Regan played by John Thaw and Sergeant George Carter played by Dennis Waterman, quickly became icons. It was the first cop show that showed beatings, violent robberies, drinking and shagging and the cops were portrayed as being only slightly less dodgy than the villains – it was realistic. The robbers always had Mark II Jags to drive round in whereas The Sweeney had a Ford Consul GT. Soon everyone at school wanted to be Jack Regan and every Friday it was important that you had seen both *Top of The Pops* and *The Sweeney* from the

Factory Fairy Tales

previous night as all the conversation that day would be about both.

Other favourite shows at this time that were talked about in the playground were: *Budgie* starring Adam Faith, *The Avengers* with John Steed who was played by Patrick Macnee and Emma Peel. Emma was played by the beautiful Diana Rigg (I had a crush on her) and then *The New Avengers* with John Steed and Purdey, who was played by Joanna Lumley (another crush). *The Saint* with Roger Moore playing Simon Templar, *The Benny Hill Show* (sorry I know it's considered sexist nowadays, but it wasn't back then, and the sight of a suspender belt and stocking top was very excitable to a teenager). Talking of Benny Hill, who can ignore his hit single 'Ernie (The Fastest Milkman In The West)' - absolute classic.

On 29 April 1975, I went to my first live gig with my mate Jimmy from school - Slade at the Kings Hall, Belle Vue. The Kings Hall had a capacity of 7,000 seats and was a large, cavernous building with a good sound. It was a memorable night and Slade were amazing. The place was packed with screaming girls, fans dressed like Slade and a few skinheads who looked very menacing in their Dr Marten boots and short hair cuts. It was all seated and we were sat near the back, but it didn't matter where you were seated because as soon as Slade hit the stage everybody swarmed to the front.

When the show finished and the house lights came on you could see the damage caused as at least the first 20 rows were gone with just bits of wood left lying on the floor. It was a great gig as nearly every song played had been a big hit and they were easy to sing along to.

This was also the year I got my first job, at Bostock's newsagents on Burnage Lane, as a paper boy. I was up at 6 am to do the morning shift and straight after school to do the afternoon run. This gave me a regular income and then Jimmy's dad, who owned the New Ardri Irish dancehall in Hulme, gave me a job as a glass collector for his Sunday afternoon slot. The New Ardri was packed every Sunday and he would put an Irish showband on as entertainment. To this day I still like live Irish music, a bit of a fiddle or tin whistle still gets the old legs to move. I have spent many hours sat in pubs in Ireland listening to local musicians who just walk in, sit down, and start playing.

With the spends that my Dad gave me every week, and the money I was earning, it now meant that I could keep going to see United home and away but also start adding to my record collection. I had always just bought singles but now I was buying albums. Bowie's *The Man who Sold The World*, *Hunky Dory*, *Ziggy Stardust*, Slade's

Ged Duffy

Slayed, Slade in Flame, Old, New, Borrowed and Blue, Roxy Music, The Rolling Stones and The Beatles were all soon added to my collection.

I decided to get my hair cut in a David Bowie fashion so armed with a photo I went to Tony the Greeks Barbers on Burnage Lane. Tony studied the photo and gave me a short back and sides! I should have known better as Tony also owned the grocers next door and I think he did the barber bit just for extra money.

Going away with United was like watching a military operation as around 15,000 to 20,000 reds were going to every away game and taking over most grounds. There were fights everywhere and the Football Specials put on by British Rail were getting back to Manchester Piccadilly or Victoria every weekend smashed and torn apart. Every young fan dressed the same; a long white butchers coat covered in United patches, parallel flared jeans or Oxford bags cut off and turned up over 18 hole Dr Marten boots, and a scarf tied around each wrist - a combination of Clockwork Orange and skinhead.

27 September 1975 was my first visit to Maine Road for the derby. Maine Road was a weird ground both inside and out. It was surrounded by streets of terrace houses with alleyways running between them and it was always dangerous for away fans outside. Inside, three sides of the ground were all-seater and the one standing terrace ran the whole length of the pitch and was called the Kippax after the street it was built on, Kippax Street.

United were allocated the away section of the Kippax and the whole of the Platt Lane Stand behind the goal which was next to our section. There was a small No Mans Land area between us and the City fans. We were packed in like sardines in our section, and City must have let in as many people as they could to make more money. As soon as the game started snooker balls and darts were thrown from the City section into our section. We couldn't move as there was no space, so you just had to hope that they didn't land on your head. There would be cries from the reds who had been hit, such as "Fuck, what was that" or "Fucking blue scum" and then the ball or dart would go back over to claim a blue victim. This carried on the whole game and made it impossible to actually enjoy watching the game which finished 2-2.

To get out of the Kippax, you had to go down some external stairs and at the bottom you ended up meeting the blues coming out of their section, it was a fight just to get out of the gate. Once

Factory Fairy Tales

outside I turned onto Yew Tree Road and then onto Platt Lane past the stand where thousands of reds, who had been sitting, joined the swell of people. More fights broke out and the police were fighting a losing battle. I dived into Platt Fields Park and removed all my United colours and walked on to Wilbraham Road. This area was Fallowfield and proper blue bandit country, but I didn't see any of the blue crew knocking about as I walked up Egerton Road onto Mauldeth Road then through Withington which was another blue territory before I made it safely home.

On 11 October I went to Elland Road for the first time on the Football Special and it was like a war zone from the moment we got off the train. The police escorted us to the ground but along the route Leeds fans jumped in among the United fans and fights were breaking out and the police weren't doing much to stop it. Once inside the ground it felt like being back in the Roman Colosseum as the sheep shagging natives vented their inbred fury towards us. I think we made them even angrier by beating them 2-1. Outside it was like Custer's Last Stand as the rabid Yorkshire hordes attacked us en route to the station. After one long constant running battle we made it inside and when the train finally pulled out of the station, minus a few windows, I made a vow that next time I would get the coach.

Liverpool (Bin Dippers) away on 8 November was another spicy away day. As soon as we got off the coach in Stanley Park we were met by a scouse welcoming party and the fighting started. Inside the ground there was a definite feeling of hatred towards us and once outside it was non-stop fighting all the way back to the coach park. I saw a red get his face slashed by a scouser just as he was lining up to board his coach. Needless to say, the scouser took a severe kicking from about ten reds who grabbed him. We were instructed by the police to lie on the floor of the coach until we reached the East Lancs. They were right as the majority of the windows on the coach got smashed by locals standing by the roads leading away from Anfield.

At the end of this season I went to Wembley Stadium for the first time to see United win the 1976 FA Cup Final. Unfortunately, no one had told Second Division Southampton this news and they won the cup. I was absolutely gutted after the match and the journey back to Manchester was so quiet. We'd been so confident of winning the cup that the council and the club had arranged a victory parade the next day through Manchester and a civic reception at the Town Hall. The civic reception couldn't be cancelled so it went ahead as planned.

Ged Duffy

Over 250,000 reds gathered in Albert Square to hear United manager Tommy Docherty promise us that we would be back next year and win it, I felt better when I left the Albert Square after hearing all the speeches and being involved in all the singing and I was optimistic but can you imagine a quarter of a million supporters turning out after a defeat today?

By now I was buying the *NME*, *Melody Maker* and *Sounds* every week and reading them cover to cover and back again. I had stopped buying my favourite comics, *The Beano*, *The Dandy* and *Tiger*. So no More Bash Street Kids, Dennis the Menace, Gnasher, Roger the Dodger, Billy Whizz, Minnie the Minx, Desperate Dan, Korky the Cat, and Roy of the Rovers as they were replaced by the likes of David Bowie and Alice Cooper. I was like a sponge soaking up music and learning about new (to me) bands. Albums by The Small Faces, The Who, Velvet Underground and Lou Reed were now added to my collection. By this time my friend Jimmy had moved back to Ireland and I had not been to any gigs since seeing Slade over a year earlier. I was now nearly 16 and I had been so lucky growing up in such a stable household, with no money worries, home cooked meals, being able to get away from smog covered Manchester every Easter, summer and Christmas and go to Ireland where I could breathe fresh air. I always had new clothes when needed, my laundry was always done, and I used to get spends every week.

I have two memories of my childhood that have stuck with me for ever. One I can remember myself and one which Mum and Margaret told me about many times. In 1961 Mum and Margaret went to the local corner shop in Ardwick, and they left me outside asleep in my pram. I was about six months old. When they came out the pram had gone, and they saw a woman pushing it away. They didn't panic or scream, Mum decided to follow her from a distance. They followed the woman to a street in nearby Longsight where the woman knocked on a door and went inside leaving the pram and me outside. Mum rushed forward and ran off with the pram. I have often wondered what my life might have been if Mum wasn't lucky enough to have caught a glimpse of the lady pushing the pram. How would I have grown up? What would my name be?

Dad used to own a light blue Mini van and Uncle Paul had made a bench in the back of the van for people to sit on. I was about five when we got held up in traffic one day outside the Apollo. Dad and Uncle Mick were in the front, and I was in the back. There had been a bad accident. There was a flat-bed wagon which was carrying sheets of glass and these sheets overhung the rear of the wagon by a lot, without any safety markings to show traffic travelling behind. This wouldn't be allowed nowadays, due to heath and safety, but this was 1966. Anyway, the wagon had come to a stop at the roundabout but the motorbike rider behind him hadn't seen the glass and was decapitated. His body was on the ground, his head was inside his helmet a few feet away. Dad shouted at me not to look but it was too late. This vision stuck with me for a long time afterwards and I would have nightmares for many months afterwards.

3. Johnny kicks the doors in

By now the *NME* and *Sounds* were starting to write about a new movement which had started in London called punk. It was spearheaded by Sex Pistols and The Clash, but it was still a small movement. I was 15 and looked about 12, and so I *never* went to the two famous Sex Pistols gigs at the Lesser Free Trade Hall.

My first taste of punk was watching Sex Pistols on *So it Goes* on Granada TV. I think it was around August 1976 and I remember Johnny Rotten shouting "Get off your arse" as they started 'Anarchy in the UK'. As the song finished the camera caught a great image of Rotten just staring with wild eyes into the camera. Years later this image was the one that closed each evening at the Hacienda on the giant video screens. Johnny watched you as you left the building. Tony Wilson presented the show and over the next few months Patti Smith, Buzzcocks, John Cooper Clarke, Elvis Costello, Penetration, The Clash, New York Dolls, Steel Pulse, Magazine, The Jam, XTC, The Stranglers, and most famously Iggy Pop all appeared on the show. Tony deserves great credit for having the balls to get Granada TV to allow him to show these types of bands on their station when the media establishment were against punk. These bands were not shown on TV outside of the North-West which is a big reason why Manchester took to punk so readily and it led of course to the reinvention of the city over the next 20 odd years.

I was now hanging out around Burnage every evening and I became great friends with Derek and Slim. Slim was over six-foot-tall and not slim whereas Derek was about six foot three and looked a real hard nut, they never backed down in a brawl and would both have my back when called upon. We ended up in many a scrape over the next few years. I was wearing Budgie shirts with penny round collars, striped or checks in bright colours, Tank tops, Oxford Bags, denim jacket and red 18-hole Dr Marten boots. The black ones were for school. I honestly thought that I was the dog's bollocks, cool as fuck… looks hideous now thinking back! My image would change for the better over the next few weeks.

One away game that does stand out was Newcastle United away on

Factory Fairy Tales

11 September 1976. Slim and I went on the Football Special train from Victoria Station, and I remember that the train wasn't as full as usual. When we were a few miles from Newcastle there was an announcement over the Tannoy telling us that we were being diverted to a small station in Newcastle due to the massive welcoming committee at the main station. When we arrived at this small station we were met by a large group of Police and the commanding officer told us that we were not to show any colours, not to talk and we were to walk in small groups of two or three spread well apart as they were trying to walk us unnoticed to the ground. It failed.

When we got to the ground it was a shithole and nothing like the great stadium it is nowadays. We were in The Leazes End behind the goal. It was an open end with crumbling steps and concrete. The game finished 2-2 and we were told to wait inside, which is standard procedure nowadays, but back in 1976 everybody always left the ground at the same time. Looking out of this open terrace we could see the concourse outside was full of Newcastle fans fighting with the Police who were trying to disperse them so we could leave.

After a long wait we were matched across the pitch and then up through the Gallowgate Stand which was behind the other goal and then out into the concourse at the other end of the stadium. The idea was to sneak us out without the hordes outside finding out. It worked for a few minutes but as we were walking back to the station we were attacked by a gang of Newcastle fans. It was a pitched battle for about five minutes until more Police came and contained the situation.

When we got to the station there was a mob of Newcastle fans waiting for us and once again it kicked off. After a few minutes, the Police cleared the station and we got on the train. As soon as the train left the station the windows started going in as it was attacked all along the line by local youths on both sides of the track. The journey back to Manchester was freezing as nearly every window in our carriage had been broken.

One of my friends at school, Wayne, was interested in music and since we both had no one to go to gigs with, we decided to go together to see Iggy Pop at the Apollo on *The Idiot* tour in March 1977. Iggy was brilliant on the night and David Bowie played keyboards for him. I started to buy Iggy records after this gig.

The Apollo was originally a cinema and started putting bands on from the early 1970s. It had an upper tier of seats and then a

Ged Duffy

The Underground Market on Market Street

larger seated area on the ground floor. It had great acoustics and was a great place to actually hear bands. It was built next to Ardwick Green roundabout and had a large patch of empty land next to it. I saw several fights on that land over the years, as nobody could hide when they came out as it was all open plan outside with the roundabout and the four roads off it.

A few days later we went to see T Rex at the Apollo. When we got there I discovered that The Damned were supporting them and they were one of the punk bands from London that I had read about. The place was practically empty with about 500 in there out of a capacity of 2,500. When The Damned finished their set the singer Dave Vanian left his microphone on the ground causing a loud feedback while the drummer, Rat Scabies, kicked his drum kit over and then all of the band jumped off the stage and ran through the hall to the back. The gig was great and even though I love T Rex, in my eyes The Damned stole the show.

I went to Virgin Records on Lever Street in Town a couple of days later and I brought 'New Rose' the debut single by The Damned. The great thing about Virgin was that they had listening booths, so I asked them to play it for me before I bought it. It cost me the princely sum of 70p and a few days later I returned to buy their debut album *Damned, Damned, Damned* which I played to death as it was brilliant. I also picked up a copy of The Ramones debut album and this also spent a lot of time on my turntable.

Factory Fairy Tales

I was still going home and away with United, and the Red Army were causing chaos at nearly every ground. The basic footy uniform had changed by now - the white butchers coat and the cut off Oxford Bags had been replaced by short denim jackets and full-length flares with a scarf round your neck or tied to your wrists. My version was to wear straight leg drainpipe jeans as I considered myself to be a punk. Most of the fans still had long hair whereas mine was cut into a short spike style, I wore Dr Martens or Monkey boots.

For a typical home game Slim (pictured above) and I would get to the ground around noon and join the massive queue for the Stretford End. It cost about 70p to get in. Sometimes the gates would close as it had reached capacity and then we would run to join the queue at the Stretford Paddock, Scoreboard Paddock or United Road. We could always get in, even if it meant paying a bit more and going in the Stretford End seats. This area was at the back of the Stretford End and was made up of rows of wooden seats. Once inside we would jump over into the Stretford End. If we went in the Paddock to the side of the Stretford End we would climb the fence and get in the Stretford End. Away games were the same hence you got United fans on all four sides of a ground.

The violence reached new levels when United visited Norwich City on Saturday 2 April 1977. When we got to Old Trafford to get on the coach we were told that our coach was going to have a TV reporter travelling on board with us. *Nationwide* was a daily news show on BBC and they were doing a full show on the notorious Red Army. Some people on our coach were interviewed and filmed for the show. When they came to talk to Slim, they were told very nicely to "fuck off". We were encouraged to sing and act like animals for the cameras. Back in those days you could bring beer on to the coaches and there seemed to be a good supply of it available that day all of it free…

When we got to the stadium something didn't feel right. Something bad was going to happen and the mood of the United fans was more heightened than usual. There were also fans going around

Ged Duffy

outside and inside stoking up the crowd and these were not the normal faces that went away with United. The main body of United were behind the goal in the Barclay Stand in three sections with the remaining section being Norwich fans. There were also Reds in the home end at the other end of the ground and trouble broke out a few times there during the game.

Near the end of the game a United fan got on the roof of the Barclay Stand and started pulling bits off it and throwing them into the Norwich fans below when he fell through the roof, and landed among them and they started attacking him. This was the signal for United fans to jump the fence and attack the Norwich fans inside the Barclay Stand and a pitched battle broke out.

When the game finished United fans started pulling the wooden back wall of the Barclay Stand apart and a few climbed onto the roof to attack the Norwich fans and the Police with as much debris as they could pull off the roof. They then set fire to the perimeter wall of the stadium and started to engage in a pitched battle with the Police who were being pelted with everything that was getting pulled off the back of the stand. The end result was the back wall of the Barclay Stand had basically gone and there were several sections of the roof missing. I think that the stand had to be shut for a while whilst it was repaired.

When we finally got back to the coach the reporters had gone. I guess that they had got the story that they wanted. To this day I am convinced that it was all organized and pre-planned and I find it such a massive coincidence that this should all happen on the day the TV cameras were sent to follow us. I had never seen anything like this level of violence and destruction before or since and it was like a rent-a-mob had just turned up. The following week the Government announced that from that day forward all Manchester United away games had to be all ticket.

Later that month United played Leeds at Hillsborough in the FA Cup semi-final. United won an exciting game 2–1 but before and after it was chaos around the stadium with fans fighting and jumping the turnstiles. Hillsborough had a weird set up as United had the Leppings Lane End and about a third of the Kop end at the other side of the stadium. This meant that many Reds had to walk past the Leeds fans at one end and we had an enormous crush at our end just to get inside the stadium. The police had no idea how to control the crowd or ease the crush. The same issue had arisen the previous year when United had played Derby County at the same ground. Unfortunately, the stadium staff and the Police had still not learnt their lesson by 1989 when 96 Liverpool fans died at the same ground and despite the hatred between Liverpool and United no one deserves to die going to watch a football game.

Now I had another FA Cup Final to look forward and this was against our old enemy, the Bin Dippers When the day arrived it felt a lot more exciting compared to the final the previous year. The United coaches were ordered to only stop at one nominated service station on the M1 on the way down and the same one on the way back. When we got to the "Man United Fans Only" services (as the sign in the car park stated) we noticed that there were a couple of Bin Dippers coaches parked up, and so there was a bit of trouble inside the services and in the car park. The Police came and escorted their coaches away.

The game itself was boring as a spectacle and all three goals were scored within a five-minute period early in the second half. When the team were parading round the pitch at the end with the cup, I remember seeing a message on the Wembley scoreboard from Slaughter and The Dogs congratulating United on the win. The journey home was rowdy and I didn't see any further trouble when we stopped at the services.

The following month I sat my O levels; I was taking ten in total. I passed five in English, English Literature, History, Geography and Maths. My parents thought that I should have done better but, in my mind, I had excelled as I did not think that I would pass more than two. I suppose they were right as my revision had consisted of hanging round outside Slim's pub or playing football in Cringle Fields every evening and weekend, instead of staying in with my face in a textbook.

The one subject that I really enjoyed at school was English Literature and for 'O' Level exam we studied Shakespeare's *Macbeth*, Barry Hines's book *A Kestrel for a Knave* or *Kes* as its commonly known and the poems of William Wordsworth... *I wandered lonely as a cloud* and all that. Who can forget Brian Glover leading out his rag tag team of unwilling PE students in his United kit telling everyone that he was Bobby Charlton in the film *Kes*. As part of the course we had a school trip to Wythenshawe Forum to see *Macbeth* performed live. It was awesome with the music, the lights and the whole drama and suspense of the story. We were taken to see it so that we could

Ged Duffy

understand it and it made a lot more sense after seeing the play. During lessons we would act out the story and the teacher would explain what was being said in modern English, so we all had an understanding of the meaning of the play

Besides going to see *Macbeth,* we also went on three other day trips during my time at Xaverian. First one was to Belle Vue Zoological Gardens. Belle Vue had been opened in 1836 and was the first theme park in the world. The zoo featured an Aquarium, a Monkey House with a chimps tea party, Snake Pit, Hippopotamus Pool, Giraffe Feeding Area, Elephant House, a Sea Lion show area and your normal animals such as lions, tigers and zebras. Second one was to see *Ben Hur* at the Odeon cinema in Manchester and the third was a day trip to Trentham Gardens near Stoke.

I enjoyed school but not the lessons. It was great hanging round with my mates, playing football in the school yard, or tormenting the younger kids. My mates all said that they weren't going to revise. They lied as they all passed their exams and stayed on to join the Sixth Form. I was the idiot as I kept my word and didn't revise and so didn't pass all my exams.

After sitting my final exam I left Xaverian College in the summer of 1977 and that year they decided to stop being a grammar school and become a sixth form college. The kids that came into the first year later that summer would be the last. I couldn't wait to get out of the place. The one main thing I would miss, apart from my mates, was the school dinners. They were great; jam roly poly, apple pie and custard, pie and chips, sausage and mash, fish and chips on a Friday. I never saw anyone from my school again until I was sorting out my divorce years later – the solicitor who was dealing with it was an old mate from school. We had a few good chats, about school and old friends and I used to look forward to seeing him. Then one day I went in to his office for a meeting to be told that he had been arrested for misappropriation of clients' funds. He was a thief. I would never have guessed!

Outside school Derek and I both had chopper bikes and we set up a nice little earner modifying them for people. We would put cow horn or bull horn* handle bars and chopper seats on their bikes and get paid for it. Half the bikes that came to us were knocked off since we

---

* *Cow horn handlebars turned upwards towards the cyclist whereas bull horns were much wider and turned away from the bike on each side.*

Factory Fairy Tales

were asked to spray them different colours. Derek's Gran's back garden was our workshop. Having a chopper back then was an important status symbol. I had a red Raleigh Chopper Mark II, and it was a tidy piece of kit. The chopper had an unusual frame, big padded high back seat, bull horn handlebars, T Bar style five-gear shifter, a 16 inch front wheel and a 20 inch rear wheel. It was a great bike.

One day, whilst walking to get the train to town, Slim and I noticed that a record shop had just opened that morning on Mauldeth Road. It was called Sifters Records and was run by a guy called Pete Howard. Pete was a Red like us and he had a lot of good albums, so we became good customers. Pete is now famous throughout the world after Liam Gallagher sang the words "Mr Sifter sold me songs when I was 16" in the Oasis song 'Shakermaker'. His shop is now on Fog Lane in Didsbury and people come from all over the world to get their photo taken in front of his shop.

Around this time a really important album was released The Clash - *The Clash*. This was a proper album full of fast powerful songs with lyrics that actually meant something. Songs like 'I'm so Bored with the USA', 'Career Opportunities', 'London's Burning', 'Janie Jones', 'White Riot', and a great cover of Junior Murvin's 'Police and Thieves'. They were songs that resonated with us about having no future job prospects and living in boring times. I soaked this album up like a sponge and my love affair with The Clash had begun. The bonus was that there was a red sticker on the cover and once I peeled this off and cut out a coupon printed in the *NME* and sent them both off I received a free Clash *Capital Radio* EP.

I signed on for the first time in July 1977 and they immediately sent me for an interview for a clerical job. Within a few days I started work as a Clerical Assistant at The Equal Opportunities Commission on Quay Street. So much for having the summer off! The major downside about the job, apart from the fact it was boring, was that it was a large open plan office with about 20 people working there and about 80% of them were women. When men get together, they can be crude and rude, but a group of women are just as bad if not worse. The young girls were great, and all they wanted was to find older boyfriends, get married, have kids, and have a nice house but the rest were just bored housewives living in loveless, sexless marriages and most were not backward in showing me their intentions: grabbing my arse when I walked past and telling me what they would do to me if they got me alone. I was a young naïve 16 year old and not worldly

Ged Duffy

wise, the constant chatting up bugged me in the end. If I had been just a few years older then I could have had some serious fun as some of the women were proper tasty and well up for it.

The Underground Market in town had 100 stalls including a Northern Soul record shop, Teddy Boy record shop, Collectors Records selling bootleg albums and second-hand vinyl, Stolen from Ivor sold jeans, lots of clothes stalls, a punk store called Roxy where I brought my first motorcycle leather jacket and belt buckles, Habeas Corpus which sold World's End clothing such as Vivienne Westwood and Malcolm McLaren, a café that did a great cheap chips and gravy and Discount Records.

The main entrance was on the corner of Brown Street and Market Street, where the Tesco is nowadays, with another entrance in Spring Gardens. The entrance I used to use was the one on Norfolk Street which was situated directly opposite the side door into Boots the Chemist. This took you straight to Discount Records which was the third or fourth stall up on the right-hand side. Discount Records was owned by a lovely hippy couple called Sian and Nigel. Even though Nigel looked like Neil from *The Young Ones* and them liking hippy music such as The Grateful Dead and Neil Young, they mostly sold punk and Bowie/Roxy records. You could get any record played in the shop before you bought it, so you didn't have to waste your money on something you didn't like.

The shop itself was just a small unit and every available space on the walls was covered with singles hung with Blu-tac. Mark Farrow used to nip in the shop during his lunch break and worked there on Saturdays. I got to know Mark very well and he used to say that he would love to have the chance to design a record sleeve. In a few years he would feature greatly in my life but not yet.

I also started going into Rare Records on John Dalton Street and got friendly with a young lad working downstairs in the Pop Department called Ian Curtis. Ian worked behind the counter for about a year or so and used to sell me bootleg albums from under the counter. Buzzcocks' *Times up*, *Iggy and Ziggy*, and the Sex Pistols' *Spunk*, were three that I brought off him. He seemed a nice guy, had a good sense of humour and was knowledgeable about music. We'd have a cup of tea sometimes and talk about football. He was a blue but didn't go to the matches, so he wasn't as fanatical as Slim, and I were.

He told me that he was in a band called Warsaw and in June 1978

Factory Fairy Tales

when the *Ideal for Living* 7 inch EP was released I got it from Discount Records. I went in Rare Records one day and was told that he had left but I would see a lot more of Ian over the next couple of years. The ground floor of Rare Records was jazz, blues and folk music. The first floor of Rare Records was classical. Ironically Rare Records did not sell any rare records! HMV, Paramount Books and Records and the newly opened Piccadilly Records were also regular ports of call. There were a few more record shops in Town but these were the main ones that we visited on a regular basis. None of them were a patch on Discount Records. My other main point of call then and for several years to follow, was the Magnet Café at 140 Deansgate, next to the Sawyers Arms. The food was good in there even though it was basically a greasy café like the one in *Only Fools and Horses*.

The new season started and United played both City and Leeds away in the first month. City was exactly the same as last season but this time I stood near the Platt Lane stand in the open section of the Kippax, and I had no problems with the flying snooker balls or darts this time. I went to Leeds on the coach and thanks to the police escort back from the ground I had limited contact with our inbred, sheep shagging friends this time.

Wayne and I went to see Iggy Pop once again at the Apollo in September as part of his *Lust for Life* tour but unfortunately David Bowie was not on the keyboards this time. This was the tour with the famous Horse Tail sticking out of his pants and it was filmed for Tony Wilson's *So it Goes* show. He was supported by The Adverts who were amazing and I purchased their single 'One Chord Wonder'.

This was followed by The Stranglers at the Apollo in October, with the magnificent JJ Burnel on bass. He was so cool and what an amazing sound he got from his bass. Great songs, wild crazy night of fighting with the bouncers. October also saw the release of Never Mind The Bollocks by Sex Pistols. The whole window of Virgin Records was covered in copies of the album cover and the shop had promotional displays. The cover was so different to anything I had ever seen before. I played it constantly for the next few days and to this day I still think that it is a masterpiece. My highlight of the album was the song 'Bodies' which was written about a crazy girl that kept contacting them after she had an abortion.

Slim, Derek and I went to see The Clash supported by Siouxsie & The Banshees at the Elizabethan Ballroom at Belle Vue in November. It was a wild night and as we were queuing up to pay our 90 pence to get in, a large gang of punks charged the doors and smashed their way in, so we just followed them in. Slim and I got the taste for free gigs after that. The Clash were brilliant, a total visual three-pronged attack of Jones, Strummer and Paul Simonon. The Banshees were such a cool band and musically were so different than any other band around at that time. This gig was filmed for So it Goes, and clips have been shown several times on tv over the years. The Spit was flying freely that night so we stayed away from the front of the stage.

In December I handed my notice in at work. One or two of the ladies had progressed from grabbing my arse to grabbing my balls. I was not comfortable working there any longer. I was dreading the Christmas Party when they would be drunk. 12 months later I would have been opening my flies to let them have a feel, going outside with them, and I would have loved working there with all that pussy on offer, but it was wrong Place, wrong Time. Ha, the story of my life!

My 20 Favourite Singles Of 1977

The Clash: 'White Riot', 'Complete Control'

Buzzcocks: 'Orgasm Addict'

Sex Pistols: 'God Save the Queen', 'Pretty Vacant', 'Holidays in the Sun'.

The Damned: 'Neat, Neat, Neat'

Slaughter & The Dogs: 'Cranked Up Really High', 'Where Have All The Boot Boys Gone?'

Chelsea: 'Right To Work'

David Bowie: 'Heroes', 'Sound and Vision'

The Jam: 'In the City'

999: 'I'm Alive', 'Nasty, Nasty'

The Stranglers: 'Peaches'

The Lurkers: 'Shadow'

The Adverts: 'One Chord Wonders', 'Gary Gilmore's Eyes'.

The Ramones: 'Sheena is a punk Rocker'

EPs

Buzzcocks: *Spiral Scratch*

The Drones: *Temptations of a White-Collar Worker*

The Clash: *Capital Radio*

Alberto Y Los Trios Paranoias: *Snuff Rock EP*

My 20 Favourite Albums Of 1977

The Clash: *The Clash*
Sex Pistols: *Never Mind the Bollocks*
The Damned: *Damned, Damned, Damned, Music for Pleasure*
The Drones: *Further Temptations*
Iggy Pop: *Lust for Life*
Iggy & James Williamson: *Kill City*
David Bowie: *Low, Heroes*
The Ramones: *Leave Home, Rocket to Russia.*
The Stranglers: *Rattus Norvegicus, No More Heroes*
Kraftwerk: *Trans Europe Express*
Ultravox: *Ultravox, Ha,Ha,Ha.*
The Saints: *I'm Stranded*
Talking Heads: *Talking Heads 77.*
Wire: *Pink Flag*
Suicide: *Suicide*

4. Robert Leo Gretton - a bitter blue

I started my new job as a Post Boy at The Union of Shop, Distributive and Allied Workers (USDAW) in Fallowfield at the start of 1978. This job was later glorified by Phil Daniels when he played the character of Jimmy in the film *Quadrophenia*. The only good thing about this job was that I could walk there from home every day and not spend money on bus fares. The job was awful and involved a lot of walking around this old, cavernous, two-storey, Victorian building for eight hours a day.

Twice a day Royal Mail delivered to the post room and I had to sort all this delivered mail and then go on my round across both floors of the building dropping it all off at the right departments. I would also collect external mail and internal mail during these rounds and then end up going backwards and forwards, up and down stairs, between the departments getting it all delivered. Every department would be in panic mode from 3.30pm onwards, demanding that their external mail be collected, franked, and put into sacks to be given to the post man at 5pm. If he was late I had to stay behind to make sure that he collected all the bags of mail.

I had been there about six months when I quit. That morning had

ROB GRETTON: *This is exactly how I remember meeting him the first time, with his feet in the air! Definitely a bitter blue.*

been the same as usual, I was constantly up and down the stairs, getting abuse off some people and thanks off others. During my lunch break I received a call to collect something from an upstairs office at the far end of the building. I told the guy that I was on my lunch, but he demanded that I come to collect this piece of mail as it was especially important. So I made my way upstairs to collect it, and without any thanks he gave it to me. I looked at the name on the folder and it was for a guy in the office next door to his. I asked him why he made me give up my lunch and walk to his office when he could have dropped if off on the right desk and be back at his own desk within 60 seconds. He looked at me, laughed and said, "because I can". I threw the file back in his face, told him to go fuck himself, walked downstairs to the post room, put my coat on and walked home. That was the end of me and USDAW.

This happened at the beginning of June, so let us go back to the start of 1978 when the film *Star Wars* finally opened in Manchester. I went to see it and fell in love with it, and I think that I ended up seeing it around 20 times during its run at the Concorde Cinema Hall in Burnage. This was the start of my love affair with *Star Wars,* and I still watch every new film or show which comes out in the franchise. A footnote is that the Concorde Cinema Hall is now a supermarket.

For home games we would go into town in the morning, spend a few hours in Discount Records before getting the match bus from Piccadilly around noon. One day we were walking up Market Street to get the bus when we saw a commotion building up in front of us. In the distance there was a guy running and he was being chased by a woman who was shouting to stop him as he had stolen her bag. As he approached us Slim threw his arm out and clothes-lined him. The guy went up about six foot in the air in a horizontal fashion and then hit the deck. It was a move that anyone from WWE would have been proud of.

Within seconds two coppers arrived and jumped on him and told us both to get out of there immediately. Their exact words were "thanks for doing that, now fuck off" We did as we were told and went to the match.

Most evenings were spent hanging round outside the Victoria pub with Slim, Derek, Karenne Chadwick, Karen Pennington and Wendy Clarke as the rest of our crew would be off in a stolen car or two and we would only see them for a short period each evening. All three of these girls were well fit and up for a bit of fun but I wasn't bothered at this time. If I had my time again, I would have gone out with all of them and then stuck with Karenne (right) as she had a great figure, a great sense of humour and was a very pretty brunette but I wasted a great opportunity there. Wrong decision.

Even though we were doing no harm we would get harassed every night by a copper who we called Spooner (after a cop on a TV show) He would stop his car, get out and search us. I think he just wanted to cop a feel of Karenne. He would ask us what we were doing and tell us to move away from the pub. Slim would point to the name above the door and tell him that he had no intention of moving as it was his dad's pub. Slim would suggest that it was Spooner who should move away as no one inside the pub had asked him to get involved in anything and he was on private land, Spooner used to hate this, but he had no other option than to get in his car and drive off. We would all wave at him as he drove down the road. Fucking knob he was.

I would try and get home most weekday nights around 10pm so I could listen to John Peel on Radio 1. Peel played a session of three or four unreleased songs every evening by a band, and I would try to tape these each night. There was no internet in those days so the only way you could find out about new music was via John Peel or the weekly music papers.

One Sunday Slim, Derek and I jumped on the 169 bus over to Belle Vue to visit the Amusement Park. When we got there we went on a few rides, including the wooden Roller Coaster, and then went over towards the waltzers. As we approached it we could hear 'Complete Control' by The Clash blasting out of the speakers. We saw that there was a group of punks on the platform round the ride and we went over to talk to them. They said that every Sunday, if the punks got to the ride first then the music was punk all day, but if a Teddy Boy got there first then it was Elvis and Eddie Cochrane all day, so every Sunday for the next few months we would be in Belle Vue and would have great fun riding the waltzers non-stop listening to our music.

Factory Fairy Tales

Sometimes there would be a few scuffles with the Teds and with the locals outside but nothing serious. Belle Vue is now a housing estate, a cinema complex, and a massive road junction. What a waste. It would have been a massive tourist attraction nowadays.

In February it was our annual trip to Anfield. Same as last year, there was trouble in Stanley Park. As we were queuing up to get on our coach a scouser ran at Slim and threw a punch. He missed, but Slim connected and knocked the guy spark out. We got on the coach and saw the coppers pick him up off the ground and then nick him. The windows on the coach got smashed again. We always enjoyed our days out in the land of the Bin Dippers.

On 9 March 1978, Slim, Derek and I went to Rafters for the first time to see 999. Rafters was a club on Oxford Street in town directly opposite a huge night club called Rotters which was full of flare-wearing beer monsters and over the next few years we would have many a run in with these knobheads. It was called Rafters due to the ceiling having exposed rafters and I saw quite a few singers swinging from those beams during gigs. Rafters was an L shaped club, situated in a cellar with a capacity of about 500 with Fagins Cabaret Club directly above it with a capacity of 1,000 and bigger bands played there.

Rafters was carpeted, and over time your feet would end up sticking to it. The walls were dark wooden panelling topped with painted white walls. The bar was on the left-hand side of the longer section of the room with the DJ Booth next to the bar and the stage was at the far end of the room. It was dark and dingy with a great sound, a perfect venue.

When we got in we saw a few of the Belle Vue punks and sat down with them. During the evening I went to ask the DJ to play anything by The Clash and he told me to fuck off adding that he wouldn't play that shit. As I came back to my seat I wondered what all that had been about and thought what a weird prick he was. 999 came on and they were brilliant, and they played 'I'm Alive', 'Nasty Nasty' and their new single 'Emergency'. Their debut album came out the following week and I immediately purchased it in Discount Records and to this day I still play it and love it as much as I did back then. We had a great night down at the front going crazy.

A couple of days later we went to the Free Trade Hall to see Devo who were supported by a local Manchester band called Alberto

Ged Duffy

Y Lost Trios Paranoias who were amazing. We could not make out whether they were serious or not, but they were such a great act. I saw them a few times more over the next few years and their shows were always entertaining with a mixture of punk, comedy, and drama. They did a gig a few years later at the Poly about Sid Vicious and the killing of Nancy which involved toy puppets if memory serves. By the way Devo were great as well, crazy but great. Devo were probably the strangest band around at this time with their white boiler suits and straight stage dances. They played 'Uncontrollable Urge', 'Mongoloid', 'Jocko Homo' and a brilliant version of Rolling Stones '(I can't get No) Satisfaction'.

The following Wednesday evening Slim and I were at Old Trafford to see United draw 2-2 with City. There was some trouble in town before the game and a bit outside the ground before kick-off. After the game there was a mass brawl on Warwick Road and the Police dispersed the crowd and we ended up in a group of Reds walking down Railway Road when we encountered a gang of blues and there was a violent scuffle which lasted a few minutes before the Police arrived to break it up. During the encounter I had traded punches and kicks with a Blue who I was sure I had seen before.

The following evening we were back in Rafters to see Generation X who were promoting their debut album which was released that day. We were sat in the small section of the L with the Belle Vue punks when I decided to go and ask the DJ to play 'Nasty Nasty' by 999. He looked up at me and we both said the exact same thing at the same time "oh it's you, you cunt". He was the blue I had been fighting with! He pushed his glasses up his nose with his middle finger, grinned and said, "I'm Rob you alright?" - this was how I met Robert Leo Gretton, one of the greatest blokes that I have ever had the honour to know. However, when I went back to tell Slim that it was the DJ that we had been fighting at the match, he was up for fighting him again!

When you watch 24 Hour Party People you will see that Shaun Ryder was supposed to have been the one fighting Rob. I don't know Shaun, but I would guess that it was probably more box office for the film for it to be him and not someone out of Stockholm Monsters to have met Rob in that manner. Shaun has said in interviews over the years that he was not into going to the football and Tony Wilson later admitted that most of the stuff they showed of him in the film was made up and did not happen.

Slim, Derek and I carried on going to Rafters and over the next

Factory Fairy Tales

few months we saw a lot of bands including Slaughter & The Dogs, Adam and the Ants, Subway Sect, V2, Ed Banger, XTC, Alberto Y Los Trios Paranoias, Elvis Costello, Wreckless Eric, X Ray Spex, The Fall, and many more whose names have escaped me. We had got to know Rob well and one night he told me that he had just agreed to manage a band called Joy Division and that they had a single coming out in a few weeks.

Getting home from Rafters was always a challenge. Piccadilly Bus Station was a battleground every Thursday, Friday, and Saturday night, once all the clubs had emptied and the tanked-up beer monsters arrived they were ready to fight anyone. Beer monsters who had got lucky with a young lady would guard their precious night-time companion and stay away from any trouble, but the rest were game to fight the punks. Add to this scenario, Teddy Boys, Northern Soul boys, and Heavy Rockers, it made for an interesting journey home.

Beer Monsters wore shirts, ties, jackets and flared pants. They were not interested in music really. They went to clubs to drink, fight and cop off with women. They had respectable jobs, didn't do drugs, led boring lives and only had the excitement of getting drunk, laid or getting in a fight at the weekend.

Teddy Boys liked old time rock 'n' rollers and were very fashion conscious. They wore long, bright coloured drape jackets with skin tight jeans or straight leg pants with luminous pink or green socks but any colour would do, and crepe soled shoes known as Brothel Creepers. They had greased back hair with the back cut into a DA shape. It was called a DA as it looked like a duck's arse. They were violent and often carried bicycle chains, flick knives, cut-throat razors or knuckle dusters.

Northern Soul Boys were not as common round town at night time as they all went to Wigan Casino some 30 miles away but the ones that did come to town wore 40 inch parallel flared pants, Ben Sherman shirts, braces and boots. Some of these guys were ex-skinheads from the 60s.

Heavy Rockers wore leather biker jackets with chains and patches on, jeans, biker boots and had long hair. They liked bands such as Deep Purple, Black Sabbath and Led Zeppelin. They were always tooled up with something, usually a knife or a chain.

Ged Duffy

The Hippies were into bands like Grateful Dead or Rush. They stank of josh sticks and dope. They were peaceful, wanted no trouble and yet everyone battered the Hippies.

At this time in my life neither Slim nor I were drinking or doing any drugs, but we made up for that later down the road. Unfortunately, Derek was drinking like a fish and when he got drunk he wanted to fight everyone and anyone. Since Slim and I were used to going away with United we could look after ourselves and knew when it was best to retreat but Derek did not. The late night 50 bus was on the hour every hour after 11pm so we had to survive in Piccadilly usually for about 40 minutes or so before we could get on the bus. We had a few fights, but the physical size of Slim and the fact that Derek had bleached hair with a black exclamation mark dyed on the back of his head and looked like a complete lunatic cut down the amount of shit we could have got in. A lot of the Beer Monsters would think twice about having a go, weigh us up and then decide to forget it and batter some hippies instead.

Once we could board the bus there would always be Beer Monsters from Adswood on it and they would sometimes give us stick when we came upstairs. One night they were seriously taking the piss out of us when Derek suddenly jumped up and ran at them smacking about five or six of them before they even knew what was going on. Slim and I followed him, and we managed to get most of them trapped in their seats at the back of the bus. They backed down and the rest of the journey went smoothly. We found the bus journey home a lot easier moving forward.

At the beginning of June I was in Discount Records when a box of records got delivered and the first one out of the box had an unusual sleeve. It had a picture sleeve showing a German World War 2 drummer boy. I saw the name Joy Division and I remembered that this was the band that Rob Gretton was involved with so I bought it. When I got it home I recognized Ian from Rare Records and played it. The four songs were different to anything else around at that time as in, it was punk but not punk, if you see what I mean.

A few days later the *Live at the Electric Circus* 10-inch mini album came out and I bought it on electric blue vinyl. I got it because of The Fall, John Cooper Clarke, Buzzcocks and Joy Division. When I read the inner sleeve notes I discovered that Joy Division had changed their name from Warsaw and that explained why Ian was in this band

Factory Fairy Tales

and not Warsaw as he had told me in Rare Records.

Virgin Records used to sell concert tickets and coach travel for out-of-town concerts and one of the girls working there had been let down by a friend and asked me if I would be interested in going to see Bowie. I am sorry to say that I cannot remember her name so if she reads this I apologize. On 25 June 1978 the two of us got on a coach from Chorlton Street Bus Station to Stafford Bingley Hall to see David Bowie on the *Stage* Tour. The gig was brilliant, and I remember he started off with 'Warsawa' which blended into 'Heroes' which I put in my top five songs of all time. He also played 'Ziggy Stardust', 'Be my Wife', 'Five Years' and finished off with 'Rebel Rebel'. The sound was amazing, the light show was superb and the connection between the crowd and Bowie was like being in the presence of a God. He was supported by Generation X who were great on the night. I saw them a few times over the years, but this was the best time that I ever saw them.

July 1978 started with The Clash playing the Apollo supported by Suicide and The Specials. The Specials were the first band on and the reception was mixed. I thought that they were great as they were different to any band around at that time with the Ska beat mixed with punk guitar and their movement on stage was great to see. Within a few months they would be massive and known by everyone. Next on were Suicide and I already owned their debut album so I was really looking forward to seeing how a Clash audience would take to them. Within a few seconds of the opening song starting the audience were booing and shouting at them. After a couple of songs the two guys in Suicide were shouting back at the crowd and sticking the V sign up to them. The crowd then launched an endless attack of bottles and cans at the stage until Suicide did a runner off stage which was greeted with massive cheers.

The Clash started with 'Complete Control' and 'Tommy Gun' and the Apollo went wild with people standing on the seats on the ground floor. Seats were getting broken and there were some scuffles with the bouncers in front of the stage. They did 'Clash City Rockers', 'White Man in Hammersmith Palais' and finished with 'White Riot' and 'Guns on the Roof'. The one thing I will say about The Clash is that if you were lucky to see them live, they never let you down and always put on a great show. The following night they played a secret word-of-mouth gig at Rafters. During the day I had gone to town and walked

Ged Duffy

The band at the front of the procession to Alexandra Park

past Rafters and there was a handwritten sign outside saying, "The Clash Live here tonight". When we got in we had missed Suicide, so I have no idea how they went down or how long they managed to stay on stage for but since there were only about 80 people there, I think they must have been okay. The Clash were amazing in a small venue and played a great set. I remember they had a banner that said FUCK behind them on the stage and Joe Strummer climbed up onto the rafters and hung from them during one song.

England in the 1970s was a much different place than it is nowadays. There were a lot of Trade Union strikes. During 1977 and 1978 the Ford workers, the miners, the bin men, and even the grave diggers were all on strike at different times. At one stage the whole country seemed to be a mountain of refuse with bin bags piled up on street corners and there was a major infestation of rats round most major city centres. The National Front blamed immigration for the lack of jobs and were actively targeting young people to join their party so a new movement started up called Rock against Racism to try and combat the rise in race hate crimes which were happening round most of the country.

On Saturday 15 July, Slim, Derek and I attended the Rock against Racism march and concert in Manchester. We got to Strangeways Prison about 11am to join the march to Alexandra Park. There was a small stage set up outside the prison and there was a rally held where a

Factory Fairy Tales

couple of speakers made speeches about the movement and the threat of the National Front and basically got the crowd built up into a united unit. The vibe was amazing, there were punks, skinheads, students, Hippies, Beer Monsters, and normal folk all coming together with one common goal, to tell the NF to do one. There were several flat bed wagons with generators on board so that bands could play as we marched. At noon, the march started, led at the front by a calypso band and we got in behind the Leeds wagon. The Leeds wagon consisted of Gang of Four and The Mekons. Each band would play two or three songs and then sit down to allow the other to play and occasionally they would just jam together. Gang of Four were totally different than any other band around at this time with a superb rhythm section built round one of the great guitarists of his time, Andy Gill. The other band, The Mekons, were another unique sounding band and they were great as well on the day. Their debut single 'Never Been in a Riot' had just come out and that was a really good single as well and their follow up single 'Where Were You' which is an all-time classic if you ask me.

We intended to drop back or move forward to check out some of the other wagons, but we stayed with this wagon since the music was so good. Deb Zee and two of her punkette mates were on board this wagon and Mick Hucknall was matching alongside us. Before the march rumours were rife that the NF would infiltrate the march and start fights from within and that there were various points along the route where they were gathering to attack us. We marched through the city centre and onto Moss Side and never saw any trouble at all.

The atmosphere during the march was like a carnival with people chanting against the NF, holding up the lollipop style Rock against Racism wooden signs (which became their trademark and were seen at all the later rallies), people were hugging each other and the noise was incredible. There were wagons containing Manchester bands, Reggae bands, Funk bands and there was a Liverpool wagon as well. Even the police who were walking alongside the march seemed happy and a few of them were dancing along to the various sounds coming out of every section of the march. The march took over two and a half hours to arrive at Alexandra Park since over 15,000 took part in it. There was a crowd of over 25,000 already in the park waiting for the bands to appear on the main stage. We were greeted with applause and cheers as we got there, and it was an emotional moment showing Manchester coming together for a great cause which is something the

Ged Duffy

city did again in May 2017 after an Islamic Terrorist killed 23 people leaving an Ariana Grande concert at the MEN Arena.

Jilted John was the compère of the event and the first band on was a Reggae band from Moss Side called Exodus. They were good but nothing special. A few months later they changed their name to X-O-Dus and in 1979 they released a single called 'English Black Boys' on Factory Records. Buzzcocks came on next totally unannounced to the sound of John Maher playing the drum intro to 'I Don't Mind', this was a shock to the crowd as they were supposed to headline the event, but they decided to let Steel Pulse do that instead. Buzzcocks were amazing and the whole 40,000 crowd were jumping up and down and singing along to them. I remember that they played 'What do I Get?', 'Ever Fallen in Love' and 'Love you More'.

They got the party atmosphere going but the next band, China Street, brought it crashing back down again. They were a white reggae band from Lancaster and they were shite. Steel Pulse were brilliant as they played songs off their debut album *Handsworth Revolution*, dressed up as Klan members for 'Ku Klux Klan', and got Buzzcocks on stage with them for the encore 'Overall', it was a great day and I feel blessed that I was able to experience the whole event. I am so glad that we decided to do the march and not just turn up for the concert. The only downside was that the PA system was not great and at times the bands sounded like they were on a tinny radio especially as the wind blew the sound away.

A couple of days after the march I was in Discount Records and Nigel told me that he had been given a small number of tickets for an invitation only gig at the Lesser Free Trade Hall and he had tickets for Slim, Derek and me. The gig was to celebrate the fact that Buzzcocks had played their first ever gig exactly two years earlier supporting Sex Pistols and Slaughter and The Dogs, at the same venue and it was to be filmed by Granada TV. The gig was due to take place on Friday 21 July, but we had something else planned before this. The night before turned out to be an important date in our musical education as the three of us went to the Russell Club in Hulme for the first time. This was the start of a whole new adventure and the making of some amazing memories and friendships.

Rafters had eased up on the number of gigs being held there and to be honest nothing really happened there again until August 1980 and in the meantime the Russell Club had opened in May for a series

Factory Fairy Tales

of gigs on Thursday Nights run by Tony Wilson under the name The Factory. These first few gigs featured unknown Factory acts and were poorly advertised and attended. The first gig to be properly advertised there was the one we were now going to which was Siouxsie & The Banshees.

The Russell Club was situated on Royce Road in Hulme just next to Charles Barry Crescent and opposite the Grants Arms pub. The area had a reputation of being a mugger's paradise and not exactly a safe place to be walking round. We got off the 50 bus at Oxford Road and walked past Cavendish House (the Polytechnic venue and bar) down past Clyne's Wine Bar, along Hulme Walk past the flats, and approached Hulme Walk Bridge. Ahead of us on the bridge we could see a gang of lads standing round staring at us and we knew what was coming. We had faced many such experiences already on nights out and with United, so we were ready. Derek would dive into them and hit as many as possible, Slim would take out the biggest one and I would take out the mouthiest and normally the rest would have run off by then. They moved to block the bridge, but we just spread out and carried on walking towards them. As we got near to them, one of them stepped forward and told us to give them our money. Derek told him to "fuck off" and we carried on walking. Another one came forward and told us again to give them our money. Slim told him that if he took one more step towards him, he was going to throw him over the side of the bridge. This obviously scared them as they moved aside, and we just walked straight through them with no problems. Over the next few years we saw them many more times and even if it was just one of us on our own, they never bothered us again.

The Russell was a large stand-alone building and I guess it must have held at least 900. When we got to the door the two West Indian bouncers on duty were pretty laid back and friendly. We had a laugh with them and found out that one of them was called Tex. We always made a point of getting to know the bouncers by name if possible as it always led to the possibility of getting in for free in the future. Once inside we saw that the walls were painted black and there was a mural painted on one of the walls downstairs which read "Relax Sister, this is a real friendly club". There was also a sign that said, "No Tams Allowed". I never quite worked this one out, but it must have referred to the woolly hats that the Rastas wore.

There was a bar on one side and the stage was directly opposite with the DJ booth just behind it. There was a staircase at each end of

Ged Duffy

the building to go to the upstairs section which had its own bar which was directly above the ground floor bar. This upstairs area was behind glass, and you could watch the bands from there if you wished. There was also a small selection of food available up here. The one thing I noticed straight away was that the sound system in the club was good and the DJ played some great music. It was a mixture of punk, Reggae, and Heavy Dub. The place was full of a mixture of punks, Rastas, students, skinheads and a few normal gig goers. As we got more used to going to the Russell, this diversity of clientele was the main feature of the place, anyone was welcome as long as they didn't act like a dick by spitting or throwing beer at the bands.

By the time Siouxsie came on the place was nearly full which is testament to what a great live band they were since they had still not released any music up to that point. The debut single 'Hong Kong Garden' was released a few weeks after this gig. This was a great line up with Kenny Morris's tribal drumming, Steve Severin with his melodic bass lines, John McKay with his unique guitar style and then there was Siouxsie Sioux who sounded and looked great. They were brilliant that night and we left the Russell Club on cloud nine and then walked back to town to get the late-night bus.

One quick tip to anyone going to a gig, take some time to read the posters advertising what's coming up in the future. The following week Suicide played at the Russell, and they were supported by Joy Division. This gig was plastered all over the external walls of the Russell and I never saw it. I only found out after the gig, when someone came into Discount Records to buy their album and told me how good they had been. I was gutted. I remember the day I saw the cover to the Suicide album, and I asked Sian to play it for me. I had never heard of them, but the cover looked good. As soon as the first song 'Ghost Rider' had finished I bought it.

Anyway, the following day was the Buzzcocks and Magazine gig (see poster), so we went to town in the morning and hung round all day and met Derek outside the Free Trade Hall later that evening. The Lesser Free Trade Hall was above the main theatre and was a small room which held about

Factory Fairy Tales

The Russell Club

200 or so. The TV cameras were all set up and we were all told to stand at the front for the two bands who were introduced by Tony Wilson. Magazine came on first and I was looking forward to seeing them as I was playing their debut album *Real Life* to death. John McGeoch was one of the best guitarists from this era. Magazine did not disappoint as they were on fire with every musician at the top of their game and Devoto held the crowd in the palm of his hand as he climbed up and down his specially made mike stand with built in steps so he could tower over his captive audience. 'Motorcade', 'The Light Pours Out Of Me' and 'Shot by both Sides' were great songs. Buzzcocks came on and just rocked the place as they played a fast-paced set full of singles and songs that everyone knew. When you watch the clips on TV you can see Slim in his red coat, which he wore everywhere for years, right up against the stage with Derek and me just behind him. I was wearing a mohair jumper. The audience were going crazy, it was a great gig. Buzzcocks finished their set with 'Moving Away From The Pulsebeat'. For the encore Steve Diggle picked up the bass, Pete Shelley came on and stood to the other side of the stage and Devoto walked on to cheers from the crowd as we all realized that we were about to witness the original Buzzcocks back on stage together again. They did 'I Can't Control Myself'. It was such a great moment and an emotional one as well. What a gig!

5. The loveable promoter

The 1978/79 season kicked off and we were still going to all the home games but now only going to certain away matches such as Leeds, Liverpool, Chelsea, Spurs and City. This season was the beginning of the end for flares and long hair at football and fans were now wearing Fred Perry shirts, straight leg jeans or Lee cords, Kicker boots or Adidas Samba trainers and more importantly no team colours. Hair was now short around the ears and back but with a long wedge cut fringe that you would keep flicking out of your eyes. This was the rise of the Perry Boys.

We went to see Skrewdriver at the Mayflower Club. This was our first trip to the Mayflower which was off Hyde Road in Gorton. We got the 169 bus over to Belle Vue and did the short walk to the club. It was an old, converted cinema with the original name Corona still in big letters above the door and it was covered in weeds growing up the exterior wall. It was a dump inside and the upstairs section was blocked off as it had been condemned by the local council. The toilets were like a lake to get into, and they stank. The bar was a temporary structure which only sold tins of beer and there was a pie inside a glass cover on display to prove to any visiting heath inspector that food was sold on the premises as this was a requirement of having the alcohol license. I discovered weeks later that this pie was over two years old and no food was available at the venue. In fact, the whole venue should have carried a health warning. To be honest it was the sort of place that you needed a vaccine jab before you went in, and you wiped your feet before leaving the place. Pretty apt that it was called Corona! It was may have been a shithole but it was our shithole.

Skrewdriver had just moved from Blackpool to live in Manchester, they were a skinhead band led by vocalist Ian Donaldson. The songs were basic punk and this version of Skrewdriver survived until the end of January 1979. Ian reformed them in the early 1980s with a new line up and returned as neo-Nazis but back in '78 they were still okay. In late 1977 they had released an album called *All Skrewed Up* and their set was mostly made up of this. I loved them and we saw them several times before they broke up and we became friends with Ian.

At this time we were spending nearly every day hanging round town listening to music or plotting to start a band in the Magnet Café over pie and chips with a cup of tea. There were quite a few of us hanging out and occasionally there would be fights especially on a Saturday when people would come in from other areas of Greater Manchester to have a go at us but they would get sorted out and dispatched quickly. There would also be the odd bit of trouble with the Teddy Boys and the Northern Soul mob in The Underground Market but nothing major ever happened.

The first gig in September was Tom Robinson Band and Stiff Little Fingers at the Apollo. There was the normal shit with the security and a few scuffles during Stiff Little Fingers set. They had some great songs and were a great live band, 'Alternative Ulster' and 'Suspect Device' were powerful songs that summed up life in Northern Ireland at that time. Tom Robinson Band did a great set, and it was only afterwards that it dawned on me how political the songs were. They finished off with a Velvet Underground song 'I'm Waiting For My Man'. The following day I picked up their debut album *Power in The Darkness* and it was a strong album with tracks like 'Up Against the Wall', 'Too Good to be True', and 'The Winter of 79'. This was another guy who wrote great rock songs with powerful lyrics.

On 14 September we were touched by the presence of beauty. We went to see Blondie at the Free Trade Hall and I (and I suspect every other male present) never took my eyes off Debbie Harry during the show. My God, I had a poster of her on my bedroom wall and here she was in all her glory. Chris Stein must have been the luckiest guy in the world to be with her. She changed into a mirrored suit for the song 'Fade Away And Radiate' and it was amazing as the lights reflected off her suit and back into the hall. They played all the hits and finished off with two cover versions 'Get it On' by T Rex and 'Jet Boy' by New York Dolls.

We saw Skrewdriver again that week as they played with local bands over two nights at the Mayflower before a crowd of maybe 300 each night. There was a bit of fighting inside the club and some fighting outside with local Perry Boys. Skrewdriver had a barber with them, set up next to the stage, so that anyone could get a skinhead done free of charge and quite a few of the people there became skinheads on those two nights.

One of these nights at the Mayflower, after fighting with the Perry Boys, we ran into a gang of Levenshulme lads whilst walking home. They chased us and we went garden hopping to escape them.

Ged Duffy

Derek and I must have jumped about 30 fences and Slim took out about 20 fences where he just ran through them before we managed to lose them. It always turned out to be eventful coming back to Burnage from the Mayflower.

The following week we went to see Skrewdriver again at the Squat on Devas Street. This building used to be the old Manchester University of Music until it was replaced by a new building built on Booth Street which opened as the Royal College of Music. The University were going to knock down the old building, but it got taken over by students who squatted there until the University backed down and let them turn it into a music venue with some rehearsal space as well. Skrewdriver were good again and several students unwillingly joined the skinhead ranks that night.

Every weekday I would watch local news show *Granada Reports* as I was eating my tea as host Tony Wilson would slip the odd band on unannounced and Joy Division made an appearance on 20 September playing 'Shadowplay'. This was their first TV appearance and the song sounded great.

A few days later we went to see The Stranglers supported by The Skids at the Apollo on *The Black and White* album tour. The Skids were good that night and I would buy their debut album a few months later based on what I had heard and seen at this gig. I always liked the Stranglers because they were not a run of the mill punk band and they had JJ Burnel on bass, who I would rate as one of the best three bass players that I have ever seen live alongside the bass monster Hooky and Mani. My other favourites are John Entwistle, Steven Severin, Lemmy, Jim Glennie, Dave Allen, Youth, Simon Gallop, Bruce Foxton, Paul Simenon, Steve Garvey, Barry Adamson and Tracey Pew. Hooky wrote some unbelievable bass lines over many years whilst over two albums Mani was brilliant. I couldn't choose between these two. They are both Manc legends.

There was always trouble with the bouncers at the Apollo whenever a punk band played there and tonight was no exception. At one of The Stranglers gigs I remember the bouncers fighting the fans and JJ stopped the band and offered out any of the bouncers who were willing to fight him and that stopped the trouble. The Stranglers started off playing some early stuff and then played a few songs from *Black and White* and it was turning into a great gig. When JJ kicked his bass into that amazing bass-line of 'Nice and Sleazy' the strippers walked on and started their act. The crowd went crazy and pushed forward to be repelled by the bouncers. Then some of the crowd started to rip up the seats and attack the bouncers, and try and invade the stage and this carried on for a few minutes until the band were forced to leave the stage and finish the gig early. The fighting with the bouncers continued for a few more minutes. I'm not sure whether this is the gig where some of the PA stack fell over into the crowd, but I think it might be.

The following night it was The Ramones at the Free Trade Hall. This was an amazing gig as they were only on stage for about 45 minutes but played about 20 songs. As each song was finishing Dee Dee ran forward and shouted "1,2,3,4". I think they did about ten songs before they took a break. They were amazing and I felt so happy afterwards that I had finally seen them.

By now, Derek and I had enrolled on a twelve-month 'Introduction to Brick Laying' course at Salford Technical College. I'd had enough of working in offices and Dad had earned a good living out of the building trade, so I decided to go for it. I told Derek my plans and he decided to do it with me. We were in a class of 15 guys made up of 13 trainee beer monsters, and us two. We looked so different to everyone else in the group with our leather biker jackets, drainpipe jeans, Dr Marten boots, and Derek's black exclamation mark on the back of his head. From the first day there was tension toward us but we just ignored them as we knew they were just knobheads. When we went to the cafeteria at lunchtime we stood out like a sore thumb, but we didn't care, because whenever anyone said anything to us Derek would tell them to fuck off, and when you see it from their point of view, would you really want to mess with a guy who has a black exclamation mark on the back of his head? After a couple of days we got talking to a few girls who were doing a clerical course and we used to sit with them at lunchtime. One of the girls was a very pretty, long-haired brunette called June Fellowes and we got on like a house on fire. She used to wear sensible blouses and long skirts to college as she had to look professional in class, but she was a proper rock chick and she dressed differently when she came out to gigs at the Poly and the Russell Club. If I had to compare her to anyone, she had a look of Chrissie Hynde from The Pretenders; tall, slim, classy with a hint of naughty. She had an amazing pair of legs and when she wore short skirts, she looked a million dollars. We got to know each other a lot better over the next few years and even though we were never officially boyfriend/girlfriend we were so close I suppose you would call it friends with benefits nowadays.

Looking back on it now I can say that I loved June but just never got round to telling her. We should have become a full-time item but I was immature and not ready to settle down. Wrong decision again.

October started with Ultravox at Cavendish House, which was part of Manchester Polytechnic. This was the last tour that Ultravox did with John Foxx as he left them shortly afterwards to embark on a solo career. Musically they were at the peak of their powers then and their last album with him, *Systems of Romance,* was a masterpiece and, in my opinion, far superior to anything they did later with Midge Ure. This was a standout gig in my musical education. Ultravox were such an inventive, powerful band. The sound, the lights, the vocals all added up to a special night, and John Foxx was one hell of a frontman; great bass, great drums, great keyboards, great guitar and a touch of electric violin thrown in to create a wonderful sound. This band were so good and it's a shame that they broke up after this tour.

The following day we went to see Buzzcocks at Middleton Civic Hall supported by Subway Sect. Middleton is a small town near Rochdale that had a reputation as a rough place, as it bordered the huge Langley council estate. I was looking forward to seeing Subway Sect as I had bought their debut single and had heard a John Peel session which all sounded good. The gig was good as both bands played well and there had been a few fights inside the hall during the gig but nothing serious. We went backstage afterwards to talk to the band as they recognized us from the Lesser Free Trade Hall gig, Slim's red coat came in handy. By the time we came out most of the crowd had gone and the place was quiet, so we started walking back towards the main bus station to get back to Manchester. As soon as we reached it we were approached by a gang of about 15 Perry Boys, they were led by a right mouthy bastard. We took off running and after a few minutes we were knackered and like the scene in *The Warriors* movie, where they stop and turn to fight the Baseball Furies, we decided to do the same, and put down as many of the fuckers as we could before the inevitable kicking took place. At that exact moment, an "out of service" bus pulled up next to us and the doors opened. The driver shouted to get on and we couldn't move quick enough, the doors shut, and he drove off. He had seen what was about to happen and he was our saviour that night. He dropped us off in town and we got the bus back to Burnage.

A couple of weeks later Slim and I were in The Stretford End and Slim went to for a piss at half time. The second half started, and he had not turned up, so I went to look for him. He came walking back and I noticed his hand was bloody. He told me that he had gone to the toilet and the mouthy leader of the Perry Boys who had chased us in Middleton, had walked into the toilet on his own. I asked Slim what happened, and he smiled, telling me that he probably wouldn't be watching the second half. Justice served.

The next gig we went to was The Pop Group at the Russell. They hadn't released any music yet and the magnificent 'She is Beyond Good and Evil' single was a few months off release. The music was a fractured beat with a brilliant bass and drums, topped off by some wild feedback-driven funky guitar. The singer was singing and screaming, and his lyrics were definitely political. I loved them. It was an absolutely wild stage show and a great night. A couple of nights later it was Wayne County and The Electric Chairs at the Russell. They were notorious at the time for having a single called 'If You Don't Want To Fuck Me Baby, Fuck Off'. Wayne was halfway through his transition to becoming Jayne and he played this gig as Jayne. Apart from the shock value of this band, it was not a memorable gig in my opinion, and I thought that he/she sucked.

Next up at the Russell was the magnificent Wire and this was a great performance. They played songs from the *Pink Flag* album and the new album *Chairs Missing*. No fancy stage show, no gimmicks, just short, sharp and to the point songs with great lyrics and melody. Wire were such an underrated band. The following day Public Image Limited's debut single 'Public Image' was released. The whole of the punk world was waiting to see what Johnny was going to do after the demise of Sex Pistols and he did not let us down. The single was so different from anything around at the time with the sound of the bass and the guitar and the packaging was unique as well with it being a folded-up newspaper.

Friday 20 October 1978 proved to be a life-changing day for me for several reasons. First off because we went to see Joy Division for the first time and more importantly Rob introduced me to Tony Wilson and Alan Wise. Everybody knows the part Tony and Rob played in the history of Manchester music, but Alan is often forgotten and his

Alan Wise: Top Bloke, True Gentleman

part in it was immense. A tall, bespectacled Jewish guy with a receding hairline, Alan always wore a shirt, tie and a dark 1950s style suit like the character Cousin Avi in Guy Richie's film *Snatch*. Alan ran a music promotion company called Wise Moves with his business partner Nigel Baguley and they promoted most of the gigs round Manchester. The company operated from an office next door to Fagins on Oxford Street. Over the years I discovered that no one could ever get truly angry with Alan, he was the lovable promoter. He was one of the funniest men I have ever met, had a brilliant sense of humour, a great smile and laugh. It was always a pleasure to be around him, and I am proud to say that he was a mate. Alan sadly passed away in June 2016 but I'll always remember him as a top bloke even if some of the strokes he pulled with certain bands were outrageous!

A few days prior to the gig Joy Division had released a 12-inch version of 'An Ideal for Living' that I had bought at Discount Records.

Factory Fairy Tales

It sounded a lot better than the 7-inch version, so I was looking forward to seeing them live for the first time. For Factory fans this gig had its own Peter Saville designed poster with the catalogue number (FAC 3).

First up on the night were The Tiller Boys, "an experimental trio with Krautrock/Eno tendencies". This was how Factory Records described them. They were a side-project for Pete Shelley to be active whenever he had some time off from Buzzcocks. As far as I could tell there was no one onstage just a backing tape of noise. They were pretentious shite. This was how Ged Duffy describes them.

Cabaret Voltaire came on and 'played' a set of industrial background noise. There was no real stage presence and it seemed that all the songs sounded the same and just blended into one. The three guys from The Cabs looked so bored behind their synths, bass guitar, and backing tapes with their flashing lights in sync with the drum machine. In time they would develop into a great band but they were not that night. They were three great guys off the stage and were nothing like the dour image they portrayed on it.

By the time Joy Division came on there were about 350 in the club. They sounded so tight as a band with the drums to the fore in the live sound. Ian danced like a demon and the bass seemed to lead most of the songs. As far as I can remember they didn't play any of the songs off *An Ideal for Living*. The crowd gave them a good reception, and you could tell afterwards that they were a band to keep an eye on. I managed to say hello to Ian afterwards, and tell him that I was shocked that he could be like that on stage, compared to the fella I got to know in Rare Records. I also had a few minutes with Rob and he was so pleased with how the gig had gone but not so pleased when I took the piss out of his new beard.

28 October: The Lurkers and Skrewdriver at the Mayflower. The Lurkers were like the English version of The Ramones except that the songs were slightly longer. They were great on the night, playing songs off their album *Fulham Fallout* as well as their four singles. Skrewdriver did a great set which went down well with the punks. When we came out at the end of the night there was a gang of Perry Boys waiting for us so there were a few fights outside. The walk home from Belle Vue up through Levenshulme to Burnage was a bit hairy to say the least. Meeting the Perry Boys outside the Mayflower would become an annoying habit.

Two legends: Tony Wilson and Alan Erasmus

By now my life had developed into a routine; I was going to college weekdays with Derek, hanging round Burnage every evening, going to see United, hanging round town most Saturdays, going to lots of gigs, buying records weekly, and still had not touched any booze or drugs. The college course was going well, and I was enjoying talking to June at lunchtimes. The only issue arose every Friday as we finished the course at noon and the lads all went to the college bar until it closed at 3pm. I would rather have gone back to town but I had to make sure Derek didn't do anything stupid. Occasionally a couple of the trainee Beer Monsters tried to out-drink Derek, but they would fail ridiculously. There was always a tense atmosphere but nothing had happened, so far...

At the start of November we went to see Penetration at the Russell followed by The Vibrators at the Mayflower a couple of days later. Both were good gigs and passed off without issue. On the 10th the second Clash album *Give Em Enough Rope* was released. I loved it from the first listen. The production had polished up their sound to be suitable for mainstream US radio, but the songs were powerful and when played live they proved to be great songs. 'Tommy Gun', 'Safe European Home' and 'Stay Free' became Clash classics. Later that evening we went to the Mayflower to see Skrewdriver again who played another great set. I remember that there was a hippy at the gig

Factory Fairy Tales

and he got pulled up onto the stage and held down against his will and lost his long locks that night to great cheers from the crowd. There was a decent size crowd at this gig and when we got outside the perry boys moved on when they saw so many skinheads. This was the last time that we saw Skrewdriver, they split up just after Christmas.

A couple of days later it was Buzzcocks and Subway Sect at the Apollo which was just as good as the Middleton Civic Hall gig but without any knobheads wanting to kill us afterwards. The following night it was back to the Apollo to see The Jam. It amazes me how a three-piece band can be as loud as they were (please note this was before I saw Mötorhead live). This was an amazing show with lots off *All Mod Cons* and they played about 20 songs and did two encores. Around this time they were just getting to the peak of their powers, and they could put on a great show. Bruce Foxton was one of the most underrated bass players of all time and his bass lines in most songs were important to the sound of The Jam even though Weller took all the credit. Even to this day I cannot work out how people can run and jump about in suits for 90 minutes. The support for this gig was The Dickies and they were brilliant. They did covers of 'Eve of Destruction' and 'Paranoid' at about a thousand miles an hour. They later released these two songs as singles. There were the usual fights with the bouncers inside, but outside multiple fights broke out as there were skinheads and Perry Boys fighting each other and all of them fighting the punks – just another friendly night in Ardwick.

Three days later it was The Skids at the Russell. Good songs with a brilliant guitarist. The following night it was back to the Russell again to see Gang of Four, The Mekons and The Scars. The Human League were advertised as the main act on the poster, but I don't think that they played on the night and if they did, I can't remember it. Three great bands, all different from each other and all great live. Another great night at The Russell. Andy King was something special on the guitar.

By now we had developed a big crew that used to meet at the Russell on a regular basis. Whichever gig we went to, there would be some of the guys at it. Danny O'Sullivan was the DJ and he was always assisted by his mate Pete McKay and these two were the coolest guys in the place. No matter what they wore they looked good, and they played some great music as well. Tex on the door was a top bloke. Alan Wise was a lovable rogue. His partner Nigel Baguley was the organized one of the two and was forever sorting out the messes that Alan would get in.

Our crew were, in no particular order: Kaizer, Mani the Mod, a lad called 'Fourteen', Ozzie, Lee Pickering, Mark Hoyle, Shan, Lita, Muppet, Andy Outatunes, skinhead Paul, Barney, Andy Warbourne, Spenna, June Fellowes, Bob 'the Burger Man' Fellowes, John Rhodes, Paul Kershaw, Anthony Bearon, Deb Zee and Dotty. There was a rasta known as Black Jack who was a cool dude, and another guy called Nasty who was a fucking nutter. Mark Hoyle went on to play with a band called Vibrant Thigh and later on with Dub Sex who were big on the Manchester indie scene. Lee Pickering played bass for a while in Dub Sex before forming Thirst with Karl Burns and Martin Bramah, both ex-Fall members. They released the *Riding The Times* EP on Rough Trade which was really good and worth buying in my opinion. 'Fourteen' ran a gang of pick pockets, muggers, and football hooligans, Ozzie came from Flixton and had two older brothers - the eldest was Vice President of the North West Chapter of the Hells Angels, his other brother owned OZ PA Hire who supplied the PA for New Order and also did the live mixing at their gigs for several years. In winter Alan Wise would put a couple of hot air heaters near the stairs and we would stand there keeping ourselves warm. Ozzie developed a new way to inflict pain on people as he would stand with his back to the heater whilst warming his chain in front of it which he would then pass to someone to hold, and he would laugh as the person received third degree burns to their hand.

Mani was only 14 or 15 when he used to come to the Russell, and he was known as Little Mani as he was short and skinny. The payment hatch at the Russell was pretty high up the wall so he used to crouch down behind people and sneak in. Tex would laugh when he saw him and just let him in. Of course he would go on to join the Stone Roses and was part of the North Manchester crew who came from Moston and Failsworth and they were hard as nails. There was Kaiser, Paul Kershaw, John Rhodes, Nicky Lomas (who was in a great band called Beach Red) and Andy Warbourne (who was in another great band called Deli Polo Club). There was another guy who hung around with them who only had one arm, but he was a nutter and I once saw him put down three people in a fight one night. Thanks to Mani for reminding me recently that his name was Spasi Macca.

Dotty came from Didsbury, so he used to come home on the bus with us, it was handy to have one more mate in case any of the Beer

Factory Fairy Tales

Monsters wanted to start again. He used to wear a distinctive leather jacket with The Clash on the back. Barney was a weird fish. He was short, stocky, was a wild punk but he was a born-again Christian. We used to go back to his flat in Ardwick sometimes after gigs and play music. His favourite album was Sex Pistols *Never Mind The Bollocks,* but he had the song 'Bodies' completely scratched off the album as he could not accept a song about abortion. Barney ended up hanging round Market Street in town with a gang of young mohawks for several years afterwards and I would spot him occasionally. He ended up wearing a leather jacket which was covered in metal studs with Discharge sprayed on the back, tartan bondage pants and 18-hole Doc Martens.

Sometime in 1978 Wire released their single 'Dot Dash', a typically brilliant Wire track of two and a half minutes of pure pop so, since Derek had a black exclamation mark on his head - he now had his nickname: Dot Dash. Spenna soon got the nickname 'Butter Beans'. One night a fight was just about to break out in the Russell and this cunt was squaring up to him. To distract him Spenna shouted at him "where's the fucking butter beans?" The guy stopped in his tracks and stared at Spenna as if to say 'what the fuck you on about' when Spenna duly twatted him in the face to end the fight, so "Butter Beans" became his moniker.

The rest of us came from all over Manchester but mainly Salford, Burnage, Didsbury, while June and Bob the Burger Man both came from Prestwich. We were all punks but none of us wore the designer gear that the London punks wore apart from Pete McKay and Deb Zee and they had either stolen it when they visited London or made it themselves. There were no bondage pants or leather trousers. We wore drainpipes, cheap shirts, and jackets. No studs or Chelsea boots - it was Dr Martens or monkey boots. Slim used to wear sweatshirts and his red coat.

Next up was Sham 69 at the Apollo and there was the usual trouble with the bouncers. Sham played well and did 'Borstal Breakout', so I was happy. Two nights later and back to The Apollo to see The Clash and The Slits. Two great acts and a great show again. The Clash never let you down live with an all action in your face show, although there was more trouble with the bouncers down the front.

David Johansen played the Russell Club towards the end of November.

Top: Me and Ozzie in the Russell (below) Derek, Deb Zee and Ozzie... you didn't mess with these guys!

His guitarist Sylvain Sylvain had been the rhythm guitarist in the New York Dolls. We chatted to the pair of them before the gig and then later that evening Jones, Strummer and Simonon from The Clash turned up to see him play. They had dashed over from a theatre gig in Derby. I spent a few minutes talking to them backstage. David Johansen was really good and played well past his allotted time. Good time, Stones-style rock 'n' roll.

26 November caused me a major headache. Slade were playing at the Mayflower with Skrewdriver supporting them, but Joy Division were playing at the Venue, or to give it its full name 'The Venue at

Factory Fairy Tales

The New Electric Circus'. Slade were the first band I fell in love with but by '78 they were no longer at the peak of their powers hence the smaller venue. Slim, Derek and I had never been to the Electric Circus – the council and police had shut it down at the end of 1977 but it reopened and Joy Division were playing. Nowadays it would be a no brainer, but they were not a big band back then and had not achieved the Godlike status they have now. The Electric Circus was in a rough part of town called Collyhurst. The venue was an old converted cinema and a dump inside and out. You went down some steps to the main room and the stage was at the far end where the old cinema screen would have been. There was a bar to the right of the room and there was an upstairs balcony that we didn't go near.

As soon as we got in we found Lee Pickering at the bar, and he joined us at a table. Most of the Russell crew were over at the Mayflower watching Skrewdriver but a couple more came in before the bands started. There wasn't a big crowd, but Joy Division played a good set, and it was another tight, emotional gig. Once again Curtis was star of the show, and his dancing was becoming more and more part of the act. Rob Gretton came over and had a chat with us afterwards and it was nice to see him again. Alan Wise promoted the gig, and had a chat with us as well. The head bouncer was a guy called Giant Haystacks who was a wrestling superstar – Giant Haystacks versus Big Daddy was the main event at every big wrestling TV event in the 1970s. The New Electric Circus only stayed open for a few more weeks, and we went back to it twice more to see A Certain Ratio (ACR) and The Fall before it shut again. I remember hearing at the time that the police had raided the place for selling beer outside of licensing hours but the writing had been on the wall for some time following the gigs of 1977 which had caused outrage in the national media with clergymen claiming punk was the Devil's Spawn!

The following evening it was Generation X at the Russell supported by Private Sector, an R & B band in the Dr Feelgood mode but not as good. The singer said "if you want an encore you are going to have to ask for one" no one did, enough said. Generation X started with 'Ready Steady Go', which is a great single, but it went downhill from there. Billy Idol spent the whole gig posing in his leather pants to the girls at the front.

The Russell was owned by a guy called Don Tonay who used to turn up some evenings and sit upstairs drinking. I spoke to him a few times and he seemed a nice guy. You knew to behave around him as he was said to be a gangster. The one story that circulates to this day about Don was that every evening he would leave the Russell and climb into the back of a waiting van where there would be two beautiful semi-naked prostitutes waiting for him on a mattress, and he would be driven off. I never saw this happen but it's a nice story.

On 1 December Slim and I went to Birmingham with a girl called Karen who knocked about with us in the Russell. She'd had a relationship with Billy Idol when she'd lived in London. We got the National Express down to the centre of Birmingham and then a bus to Aston University where Generation X were playing. While she went in to see Billy, Slim and I took a walk over to nearby Villa Park and found a café. The Cure were the support band that night and they were still a three-piece at that time. Their first single came out three weeks after this gig and I got it the day it came out. They were brilliant and 'Killing an Arab' and '10.15 on a Saturday Night' stood out. They went down well and played an encore. Generation X were much better on the night than they had been at the Russell but still nothing special. When the gig finished we went back in the tour bus to their hotel. Billy must have knocked back half a bottle of whiskey at the bar and then we were told where we were sleeping. Billy and Tony James were sharing a room so Slim and I slept on the floor of their room whilst Billy spent the night drinking and shagging Karen, and Tony was shagging some bird from the gig who was up for having Billy as well but that did not happen.

In the morning we had breakfast in the hotel with the band and the crew and they drove off to the next show with Karen whilst Slim and I got the coach back up north and went to see The Fall and John Cooper Clarke at the Russell later that evening - both were really good.

The Adverts played the Russell a few days later, they were great - Gaye Advert looked even better in the flesh. They were such an underrated band having made a great debut album *Crossing the Red Sea* and several punk anthems such as 'One Chord Wonders', 'Gary Gilmour's Eyes' and 'No Time to be 21'. Next gig we went to at the Russell was to see The Doomed which was the name that The Damned now played under after ex-member Brian James had threatened legal action if they used the name The Damned. This all got resolved the following month and The Damned could operate again. They were incredible that night and played a lot of the old Damned stuff and some new songs that would end up on the classic *Machine Gun Etiquette* album. There was the usual mosh pit where everybody kicked the living daylights out of each other, and it could be a dangerous place when Ozzie was swinging his chain about especially if you got too near to him, as the scar I have above my right eye can testify. Alan Wise spoke to Slim and I that night to see if we could help out with the stage and become his stage crew and we accepted.

The Boomtown Rats played the Apollo early December supported by The Vipers. The Rats had released five singles and two albums by this time and were reaching the peak of their powers – great set, not much crap from the bouncers and a good night overall. The audience was made up of a lot of pop fans as opposed to punks hence there was less trouble.

Working at the Russell was not going to affect my bricklaying course as we finished at 3pm daily and at noon on a Friday, and my services would only be needed at the Russell from 4pm onwards. On Friday 15 December we broke up from college for Christmas at noon and, having passed our first exams, we went to the bar. We met up with a couple of lads who we had got to know over the last few weeks. These two both liked the same music as us but didn't feel comfortable changing their dress sense at college. We went to the bar where we saw the trainee Beer Monsters were already drinking. We went over to join them and for some reason two of them decided to have a go at Derek. They both said that they could drink him under the table.

First round Derek got two pints and they got one each. Derek necked the first in one go and then drank the second. They copied him the next round. By the fourth round they were getting louder and very insulting to Derek who was still sober at this point. The other trainee Beer Monsters were egging these two on and then one of them finished a pint and threw the glass at Derek's head. Derek jumped up and knocked him clean out of his seat. The other one jumped him from behind, and one more of them joined in to attack Derek. I stepped in then put one of them on the ground, and held off the other. A couple more joined in, and our mates jumped in and started smacking them. I put one of them down with a kick to his bollocks and Derek, having sorted out the one who attacked him, knocked the other one out. Next thing the police arrived, and Derek and I were taken away. They were going to charge us with assault, but no one was willing to press charges. We were called to the Dean's Office and despite telling him that we did not start the fight, we were both expelled with immediate effect with no right of appeal.

We went along to the Russell Club Xmas Party on the 22 December, and the surprise band was Buzzcocks who played a short set with all the singles. Afterwards Alan Wise asked Slim and me to go to the bar upstairs and meet Steve Diggle's brother Phil who was an artist and had been asked to paint a mural on the wall next to the bar upstairs, so the pair of us stood in front of the wall for about 20 minutes while he sketched us on a pad.

There is one more gig to talk about and I can't remember what date it occurred, but I think that it was around summertime, and it was Slaughter & The Dogs at Maxwell Hall, Salford University. They were supported by The Drones and V2 who gave great performances on the night. The venue had a balcony running round three of the sides, and when Slaughter came on there was no sign of singer Wayne Barrett. Suddenly a spotlight shone towards the balcony stage right and Wayne is stood there on the ledge of the balcony with his blue hair shining in the light. He jumps into the crowd below who catch him and feed him above their heads onto the stage. What an entrance and the whole gig matched it. They were amazing on the night and the crowd were like a rabid mob from the first guitar chord to the last. 'Cranked Up Really High' could sum up the audience that night. 'Boot Boys' got an airing as well. One of the best gigs of the year.

1978

Singles

Public Image Limited: 'Public Image'
Siouxsie & The Banshees: 'Hong Kong Garden'
The Clash: 'Clash City Rockers', 'White Man in Hammersmith Palais'
999: 'Emergency', 'Homicide'
Generation X: 'Ready Steady Go'
Magazine: 'Shot by Both Sides'.
Gang of Four: 'Damaged Goods'
The Mekons: 'Where Were You?'

Factory Fairy Tales

Human League: 'Being Boiled'
Buzzcocks: 'What Do I Get?', 'Love You More', 'Ever Fallen in Love'.
The Stranglers: 'Nice and Sleazy'
The Jam: 'Down in the Tube station at Midnight'.
Sham 69: 'Borstal Breakout', 'Angels with Dirty Faces'.
Adam and The Ants: 'Young Parisians'
The Normal: 'Warm Leatherette'
Stiff Little Fingers: 'Alternative Ulster'
Blondie: 'Picture This'
Rolling Stones: 'Miss You'
Sid Vicious: 'My Way'
Patti Smith: 'Because the Night'

EPs

Joy Division: *An Ideal For Living*
The Undertones: *Teenage Kicks*
The Cramps: *Gravest Hits*
Cabaret Voltaire: *Extended Play*
Ultravox: *Retro*
The Fall: *Bingo Master's Breakout*

Albums

Public Image Limited: *First Issue*
Siouxsie & The Banshees: *The Scream*
The Clash: *Give Em Enough Rope*
999: *999, Separates.*
Generation X: *Generation X.*
Magazine: *Real Life*
Buzzcocks: *Another music in a Different Kitchen, Love Bites.*
Ultravox: *Systems of Romance*
The Stranglers: *Black and White*
The Lurkers: *Fulham Fallout*

Ged Duffy

The Jam: *All Mod Cons*
Slaughter & The Dogs: *Do it Dog Style*
Kraftwerk: *The Man Machine*
The Ramones: *Road to Ruin*
Wire: *Chairs Missing*
Penetration: *Moving Targets*
Devo: *Are we not Men? We are Devo*
Johnny Thunders: *So Alone*
Blondie: *Parallel Lines*
Rolling Stones: *Some Girls*
Lou Reed: *Street Hassle*
Boomtown Rats: *Tonic for The Troops*
Patti Smith: *Easter*

6. Ian Curtis gave me a quid

It was a year of change – most punks seemed to be at a crossroads: Sex Pistols had split, The Clash had become radio friendly, Buzzcocks had become a Pop band, The Jam had become a mod band, The Stranglers had become weird with talk of the 'Men in Black' and aliens, Slaughter & The Dogs had split and a lot of the other bands like The Lurkers, Sham 69, and 999 were chasing hit singles and appearing on *Top of The Pops*. By 1979 punk had now split into tribes such as mods, skinheads, Perry Boys and the 'Tribe with No Name' – these were people that started to dress like Joy Division and early ACR with second-hand suit trousers, shirts, and long overcoats. The media could never come up with a name for this fashion.

Punks who stayed loyal to the ethos got into bands like Crass, Angelic Upstarts, Discharge, The Exploited and the flag bearers of them all, UK Subs. These guys now had mohawk haircuts or grew long hair which was fashioned into long spikes.

I had got a skinhead back in November at one of the Skrewdriver gigs but never had any intention of wearing any of the skinhead clobber apart from my Dr Martens. By the start of the year my hair had grown back and since Skrewdriver had split up I was not getting it done again. A couple of the lads in the Russell also got a skinhead and one of these guys, Kaiser, is still a skinhead to this day, even though nature takes care of his haircut nowadays. He married a skinhead girl, and both still go on scooter runs all over the country as well as DJing at these events playing a mixture of punk, ska, and soul. Mani the Mod attends some of these as well with them both.

On 2 January, whilst hanging around Discount Records, a delivery arrived and in among the many records there were some copies of *A Factory Sample* (FAC 2), resplendent in its unique packaging. It had just been released. Sian played a copy immediately and the two Joy Division tracks 'Digital' and 'Glass' were the standouts. I liked the Cabaret Voltaire tracks as well. I purchased my copy and played it a lot over the next few days. These songs sounded more like the band that I had seen a couple of times now, and it was noticeable how much they had changed from their debut *An Ideal For Living*.

We were looking forward to working at the Russell as the great thing about doing the stage was that we would get to meet the bands before they did a sound check and see how they interacted with each other. Well, most of them anyway. The only issue that we would have was when United played at home. We arranged that on these occasions we would get there as soon as possible after the game, but sometimes Derek, Dotty and Steve O'Donnell would step in for us and then we would give the money to those guys.

The first time we worked at The Russell was when 999 played two shows there on 5 January: an under 16 show at 5pm and then the normal show later so we had to be there early to get everything set up. I loved 999, in particular the way they dressed, so I was shocked when they arrived looking nothing like their on stage persona. They were dressed like Beer Monsters with semi-flares and normal shirts, except for Jon Watson who looked like he did on stage. When they came on they were dressed like 999 again but it didn't sit well with me as in my head proper bands look the same standing in the supermarket queue as they do on stage. Jon Watson spent a lot of time talking to Slim and I and he told us that he had family living in Burnage and that he went there a lot. He was a top bloke. The first show for the under 16's was wild with the mic being passed round the kids and there was a mass stage invasion at the end. The later show was nearly full, and they played all of the singles and a lot of songs off both albums. There was a bit of trouble near the front but overall, it was a great gig. Phil Diggle had finished his collage upstairs so Slim and I were now plastered on the wall of the Russell for the world to see.

Next evening, we were back at the Russell to see Armed Force. V2 were supposed to headline but pulled out at the last minute. Our friend Muppet was one of the singers in Armed Force, and they released their only single a few weeks later on their own label. The two songs on the single were 'Popstar' and 'Attack' and it's worth getting hold of if you can They finished the gig with a version of 'Wild Thing' and by that time there were about 40 people on stage. Once again we had to walk home thanks to a strike on GM Buses.

The next couple of gigs we worked at were Teardrop Explodes and then Bette Bright and The Illuminations. At the Teardrops gig we met a lad from Liverpool called Bernie Connor, he was a well-known character who was mates with all the scouse bands. Teardrop Explodes were good on the night and I remember thinking that this Julian

Factory Fairy Tales

Cope bloke could really sing. The only thing I can recall about Bette Bright was that her bass player was ex-Sex Pistol Glen Matlock. We managed to talk to him a few times during the evening - great bloke.

Next up was The Factory Sample Launch Party and since this was a gig promoted by Factory, Slim and I were not working it but we went along to see Joy Division. Factory were still occasionally putting on bands on a Friday and Alan Wise had all the other days apart from Sunday, which was Reggae night. During the evening Rob Gretton told us that we could do the stage at their nights as well. Joy Division played a good set and I reckon that the crowd had gone up to over 400 that night. The Russell was a very dark and dingy club and every band that played there used lots of coloured and flashing lights, but Joy Division just used plain white light, and this made them look different to everyone else. Ian was getting more and more confident with his dancing and the whole band started to sound professional. Their song writing had improved as they were sounding less punky.

The Russell opened at 7pm and closed at Midnight. Since a lot of our mates used to walk back to town afterwards they would help getting the PA and back-line out of the door so we would be finished around half past midnight and then all walk back to town. Sometimes we would run into a gang of Beer Monsters en route and get involved in a battle.

At the beginning of February, Human League and The Scars played at the Russell – I loved both bands despite them being so different. This was before Human League became a massive pop band and they played 'The Path of Least Resistance', 'Almost Medieval' and 'Being Boiled'. The best way I can describe the two bands is Human League were industrial pop whilst The Scars were fractured pop. The Scars played 'Adultery' and 'Horrorshow'. Fast Records had some great bands like these two such as The Mekons and The Gang of Four.

The following day it was The Damned doing two shows. This was the first of four gigs that The Damned would do this year at the Russell. The afternoon show was mad as the kids and Captain Sensible tore up the place. After this gig we went across the road to the Grants and had a drink with The Damned and their road crew. They were the first band to play the Russell that made a point of talking to Slim and me. They were so down to earth and real sound guys. As some fans started to come into the pub, Sensible switched into loon mode, and became the life and soul of the party.

The gig itself was wild. There was the usual fighting at the front mainly against some dickhead punks who turned up and just wanted to spit and throw beer at the band. The Damned finished off with their version of 'Ballroom Blitz' by The Sweet done in their own style as 'Girl with Big Tits'. They invited a girl up on stage from the audience and Dave Vanian carried her on his shoulders as he sang. At one stage Rat Scabies left his drum kit and stood behind the girl and grabbed her tits from behind. She didn't mind. Sensible got half naked down to his y fronts. This was to develop further over the next few visits.

Next up was The Gang of Four. This was another Factory promoted gig. There was a decent crowd in to see Andy Gill's band. I loved them around this era. They had everything; a great rhythm section, an unbelievable guitarist, and a singer whose lyrics meant something. This was another great night at the Russell.

A week later it was Stiff Little Fingers, and this was a memorable gig. The Russell was full, and it was like the wild west down at the front. There were some dicks there causing problems and Ozzie went steaming into them with his chain swinging madly round everyone's heads. At one stage Jake Burns stopped the band and asked the crowd to stop fighting. He got a load of abuse off them, said "Fuck it" and just started playing again. Stiff Little Fingers were awesome on the night.

The following evening it was The Cure. Such a contrast from the carnage of the previous night; a medium-sized crowd and the three-piece played a set of great Pop. When you listen to their debut album you would never guess that they would become the kings of Goth within a couple of years.

Next gig we worked was Cabaret Voltaire and Orchestral Manoeuvres in the Dark (OMD). The two extremes of what a synthesizer can offer. The Cabs were very dark and extremely miserable in their musical style at this stage of their career and their stage show included video film as a backdrop and a good light show in contrast to OMD who were a brilliant Pop band. 'Electricity' must be one of the best Pop songs ever written. Both acts put on a good show to a half-full venue.

Public Image Limited played the Kings Hall at Belle Vue on 23rd

Factory Fairy Tales

February and this caused Slim and I a problem. We got in free to most gigs away from the Russell, as we either knew the promoter or the door staff, but we knew no one at Belle Vue. When someone played at the Apollo we would get there early afternoon and get in with the band's crew by helping carry the gear in or ask the band to put us on the guest list. This usually worked.

This Public Image Limited gig was causing us a problem because it was £3.50 for a ticket and that was astronomical. It was £1.50 for a gig at the Russell. We tried it on with the bouncers to let us in for £1 apiece, money in your pocket, but they said no. Since we didn't have that much on us, we decided to beg for money! People arriving started giving us anything from 10p to 50p. The money soon started mounting up and then a familiar voice asked me "what the fuck are you doing?" I looked round and it was Ian Curtis. I told him I was skint, and he gave me a quid towards our target. He stood around for about ten minutes talking to us and he encouraged passing people to give us some money so we could get in. After about half an hour we counted our money and we had over £10 collected so we paid and went in.

We got in to see Linton Kwesi Johnson reciting his Reggae poetry followed by John Cooper Clarke reciting his Salford poetry. Both would have been good if it weren't for the dreadful PA which was not set up for the spoken word. I loved John Cooper Clarke: 'I Married a Monster from Outer Space', 'Never see a Nipple in the *Daily Express*', 'Twat', 'Kung Fu International' and the classic 'Beasley Street'. He was always great live with his weird appearance and machine gun delivery. There was a long wait after John Cooper Clarke until Public Image Limited came on and Lydon was dressed in a tartan suit and wearing a dicky bow. The stage lights were green, and Wobble sat down the whole gig. They had a stand in drummer that evening, Eddie from the Vibrators, and he was the weak link. Lydon introduced themselves by saying "No gimmicks, no theatre, just us. Take it or leave it." They played most of the songs off *First Edition* as well as a Sex Pistols song 'Belsen Was a Gas' and after about 40 minutes they had finished. They came back on and played 'Annalisa' for the second time that night and then they were gone.

The sound had been poor and Lydon's vocals were lost in the mix. Maybe this was because the hall was vast and the PA wasn't large enough for the size of the room. Lydon prowled the stage in his usual scary manner and put on a great show. Everyone agreed that they had witnessed something special, and I didn't hear any dissenting voices as we left. A footnote to this gig is that UK Subs played at a deserted Funhouse at the same time. The Funhouse was a five-minute walk from Kings Hall. One quick note about this gig. The King's Hall was built right next to the funfair, and it was so sad to see most of the rides had been taken down including the waltzers and the big rollercoaster. The funfair had just closed down a few weeks earlier and this was basically the end of Belle Vue. A famous Manchester intuition had bitten the dust.

March kicked off with The Undertones at the Russell. I had a great time talking to the Derry lads during the afternoon and early evening. John Peel turned up to see them as they were his favourite band and we managed to have about 20 minutes talking football and music with the great man. He was a living legend. This was the second time that The Undertones had played here and they were great on both nights. We got paid at the end of the night by Tex the bouncer as Alan Wise had disappeared before the end of the night. We found out afterwards that he had done a runner without paying The Undertones!

On 16 March The Fall released their debut album *Live at the Witch Trials* on Step Forward Records. This was another game changing album for me along with the Public Image Limited debut that had come out in December 1978. The Fall were unique; the keyboards played by Una Baines were a key part of the sound and they sounded like a sixties garage band. They also dressed differently to any other band and this anti-fashion image ironically became their image. Over the next few years The Fall would develop into a pivotal band, constantly changing and reinventing themselves.

Next up at the Russell were The Skids and I was looking forward to seeing them or should I say, hearing Stuart Adamson. It was packed and knowing Alan Wise there were more inside than the fire safety limit allowed. The Skids were at that stage of their career where they were too big for the Russell but not quite big enough for the Apollo. It was a really good gig. Stuart Adamson was an amazing guitarist and a top bloke. Spent quite a while talking to him after the sound check, and he told me that he was born in Stretford and lived there until he was four, and he still had family in Manchester.

The following day, we were in town hanging round Discount Records before going off to see United play Leeds, when we heard a commotion outside. On Market Street there were a bunch of Reds fighting some of our Leeds friends. We went steaming in and during the fight Ozzie was swinging his chain and hit me above my right eye. I went back into Discount Records, and they patched me up and off we went to the game. I woke up the next morning and my eye had bled overnight. It didn't look good, so I went to the Royal Infirmary and ended up having six stitches in the cut above my eye. I have a scar to this day.

The FA Cup semi against The Bin Dippers. This game was held at Maine Road and both teams had agreed to play in their away strips. United had the Kippax stand from the halfway line, The North Stand and the Main Stand up to the halfway line. Dippers had the other half of the ground. It was a really exciting match which ended in a 2-2 draw. The Replay was on 4 April and this time it would be held at Goodison Park. Once again both teams wore their away strips. The stadium was split in two again, and once again it was an exciting match which was won by a brilliant Jimmy Greenhoff header. United were on their way to Wembley again to face Arsenal in the Final. I can't recall any major issues before or after both games as the police presence at both was large.

A couple of days later we were back at the Russell for another Factory Evening with Teardrop Explodes, OMD, and ACR. Bernie was over from Liverpool with the Teardrops and we spent most of the time in the dressing room and the banter with the scousers was great following our cup win. The two lads from OMD had a good sense of humour. Slim and me already knew Martin from ACR as he lived in Burnage, and he introduced us to his singer Simon Topping. It turned out that Simon was a sound lad and was nothing like the image he projected on stage.

Ged Duffy

The next day was The Damned, The Ruts, and Armed Force. Ozzie was coming to this gig, and he said that he would come across to Burnage and hang with us lot and then go to the gig with us. He was due at noon, and I was in my room playing music. Dad was outside digging up the rear garden so he could flag it as a play area for my nephew Kevin. I kept looking out the front window to see where Ozzie was and at around 2pm I went downstairs to get a drink. I could hear Dad talking to someone so I went outside and there's Ozzie stripped to the waist digging the back garden with Dad. The pair of them were laughing and joking. Every one of my mates that came to the house got on great with the soft spoken, flat cap wearing Irishman.

As soon as I found Ozzie we knocked on for Slim and jumped on the 50 bus as we had to be at the Russell to load the gear in: full house, crazy audience. Another wild night thanks to The Damned. We spent a couple of hours with them again in The Grants. Muppet's band, Armed Force, was good as usual. The Ruts were brilliant. What a great band they were, and their debut album was an absolute cracker. Both bands warmed the crowd into a frenzy for The Damned. There was a bit of trouble when some dicks started spitting but Ozzie and us lot sorted it out quickly. Sensible stripped off totally at this gig and at one stage lifted his guitar and asked if any girl wanted to suck him off. Judging by the number of girls backstage afterwards, I guess that he got his wish.

A couple of days after The Damned had taken over the Russell it was the turn of Girlschool to grace the stage and I really enjoyed them. We spoke to them during the day, and they were top girls. They could drink and curse for England and they could play as well. I don't think the dressing room ever smelt as nice as it did that night with the hairspray and make up. Bit of a different crowd in the Russell that night with a few bikers and metal heads. A couple of days later I was diagnosed with chickenpox and had to miss the one gig that I was so looking forward to seeing which was Iggy Pop at the Russell. As soon as it was announced, it was all our crew could talk about. Everyone who went told me that he was amazing, and the Russell was that packed that moisture was running down the walls. I'm still annoyed to this day that I missed him. Upon my return Slim and Derek raved about how good he was which didn't help! If missing Iggy was bad, then things couldn't get much worse, could they? Well, they did.

Factory Fairy Tales

A couple of days later, whilst I was sick, my mate Mark Silcock knocked on and asked if I wanted to go to London with him the next day. Mark lived in the house opposite on Mauldeth Road and his Dad was a limousine driver. He was taking Kate Bush to London and back and he had room in the front of his car for the two of us. I loved Kate and had a poster of her on my bedroom wall next to Debbie Harry, but I had to decline due to illness. I think that he took Steve O'Donnell instead.

They picked her up at 8am from a hotel in town and she said that it was okay for the lads to sit in the back with her and they spent the whole journey talking to her! When they got to London they dropped her off at the hotel where the event was taking place. Her management had booked a room for her so she could get changed. The three guys got invited into the function room and ended up sitting next to Kate for the meal.

After they had eaten the awards presentation began, and Kate won an award. When they left the venue, she invited the lads to travel in the back of the car with her. When they got to the Apollo, she insisted that all three come in with her, stayed backstage and watched the show from the side of the stage. I'm still jealous to this day!

One day in Discount Records Nigel asked me if I was looking for a job and I replied yes, so 20 minutes later I'm outside SP&S Records on Bengal Street, just off Great Ancoats Street. I go in, get offered the job and started the following Monday 7 May. SP&S were a distributor who sold deleted albums. Once a record company had decided to delete an album from their roster they would sell all their stock to SP&S. The company had two branches in London and Manchester, and they sold to record stores throughout the UK.

The Manchester branch employed two salesmen who sold records out of the back of their vans, and they would come to the office every couple of weeks to restock. My job was to stock their vans, pick post, fax, and telephone orders get orders posted out, do local deliveries in town and invoice everyone. My hours were 8am to 4pm but it was agreed that when required at the Russell I could work through lunch and leave at 3pm.

I still didn't have a driving license so whenever I had to do a local delivery in town, I would walk and then spend some time in the record shops that I was delivering to. My first day of deliveries was on Tuesday 8 May. I delivered some albums to Discount Records, came back to the office, and took seven albums into the record counter at Woolworths at the top of Market Street. I left there about 11am, and just around noon a fire broke out which killed ten people and completely gutted the store. I was lucky that day.

This was a dream job – there was no dress code, and I could take home up to five albums per week free of charge as part of my contract. During my first week I checked and discovered that all six Doors albums were deleted so I got them all for nothing. They let me take all six the first week. The success of *Apocalypse Now* later that year prompted Electra Records to reissue all six albums later this year so that was a result. Over the next few months, I picked up albums by Lou Reed, Ian Hunter, Mott the Hoople, T Rex, Johnny Cash, The Kinks, The Who and several others. Even if there was nothing I wanted, I would still take five albums every week and after a few weeks would take all these albums into Sifters and sell them on to him.

My first gig back after my illness was on 11 May, and it was the Factory First Birthday Party with Joy Division, ACR, OMD, and John Dowie at the Russell Club. ACR were such an unusual band when they first started as they didn't have a drummer or a drum machine. They played a Velvet Underground type wall of noise and I loved them. Later on they got really pretentious and up their own arses with all the whistles, shorts and all that bollocks. OMD had blue lighting set up and it gave off a psychedelic vibe – great pop songs and a great sound. Once again Joy Division had paid for a decent PA so 'Electricity' sounded great. John Dowie came on and wasted everyone's time until Joy Division came on. He wasn't offensive but he wasn't good either. This was probably the best that I had seen Joy Division play so far. I now knew a lot of the songs that they played, and they were so tight. The rhythm was hypnotic, and the music intense. Curtis danced and jerked and was the centre of attention. They played an encore as well, so the large crowd were pleased.

The following night was The Dickies at the Russell which I didn't go to, as I was at Wembley watching United lose the FA Cup Final to Arsenal. How can I sum the cup final up? 85 minutes of shite, three minutes of absolute pleasure and ecstasy followed by a swift kick in the balls. If you remember the match, then you will know what I mean. I should have saved my money and worked at the Russell instead. I planned to get there at about 10pm but when I got off the coach at Old Trafford I wasn't in the mood to be sociable, so went home instead.

Granada TV booked the Russell to film a special show on 14 May featuring Buzzcocks. This was a word of mouth gig with an admission price of £1. The stage was set up like a TV studio with special lighting and a special backdrop. John Cooper Clarke was on first and did a set of his poems. He had to contend with a cameraman shoving his camera up under his nose during his set. I loved him. Great set, made me laugh a lot. Tony Wilson introduced Buzzcocks but as soon as they come on they were told to wait whilst the camera crews and the sound engineers got themselves sorted. Buzzcocks played a long blues jam whilst waiting which sounded good and nothing like their regular songs. Then they played a greatest hits set which was very polished and tight. I remember at one point Steve Diggle got so fed up with the cameraman being so close to him that he suddenly lurched forward and stuck his face into the camera, and this caused the cameraman to retreat quickly and fall over to great cheers from the audience.

A few days later Throbbing Gristle played, or should I say turned up, at the Russell. It wasn't music as I know it. They were a strange band. I know people that absolutely worship them and think that they are one of the greatest bands of all time and the rest just think that they are pretentious art school shite. I sit firmly in the second camp. This was a strange audience for the Russell as it was made up of students, hippies, bikers, Bryan Ferry lookalikes and curious punks. Lee Pickering was the only one of our regular crew who turned up that night. The club was barely half full, and most people stood around for the 40 minute set not understanding what they were watching.

At least I was guaranteed a good time at the next gig which was The Damned. Once again we spent a few hours in the Grant's with the band. Dave Vanian told us that their management were talking to the owners of the Russell about the possibility of buying the club as they enjoyed playing there and were interested in owning a club. Sad to say it never happened but it would have been great.

I got talking to a hippy who was there with them, and he turned out to be Rat Scabies's drum roadie. During the gig I watched him stand at the side of the stage and he was doing all the drum patterns that Rat was doing on stage. On a couple of occasions during the gig Rat jumped off his kit and went walkabout at the front of the stage,

The Damned at the Russell. Another crazy night, this was taken early doors as Sensible is still dressed.

and this guy ran on, jumped behind the kit, and carried on where Rat left off. When Rat returned to the kit, he booted him off and carried on. He came on twice that night, and if you weren't watching closely then you wouldn't have seen him jump behind the kit. There was the usual chaos down at the front of stage, another girl got her tits felt up during 'Girl with Big Tits' and Sensible got naked again. A typical Damned night: fights, tits and swinging dicks!

The next night was Link Wray. I was not looking forward to this at all but was pleasantly surprised at how good it turned out. Link was such a lovely guy who made time to talk to you. It was good time Rock and Roll with plenty of power chords and a few Rockabilly riffs. Everyone at the gig ended up dancing and he put on a great show. Absolutely great gig.

Factory Records issued two great singles in May. 'All Night Party' by ACR (FAC 5) and 'Electricity' by OMD (FAC 6). Both singles were brilliant and unique in their own way. 'Electricity' was, is and always will be the ultimate Pop song and 'All-Night Party' was a tuneful, atmospheric drone which I still think is the best thing that ACR ever did apart from 'Shack Up'. Around this time, I decided to get rid of

Factory Fairy Tales

the Dansette built-in stereo that Dad had bought me and invest in a Technics stereo system with radio, cassette deck, amplifier, record deck and Wharfedale speakers. It was the bees knees at the time and my music had never sounded so good.

June kicked off with Simple Minds and The Distractions. I saw The Distractions several times over the years but I never got into them at all, and tonight was no exception. They were really good at what they did, but what they did didn't float my boat. I was looking forward to seeing Simple Minds as I had bought their album *Life in a Day* and liked it. They sounded like Magazine but not as good. They turned up for the sound check, spent a long time getting the sound right and then left to go and eat. They turned up just before going on stage and stopped anyone coming backstage afterwards so I never got a chance to talk to them. The club was about half full and there were a lot of students in the crowd. They were very tight as a group and played 'Chelsea Girl' which is a classic single.

The following night it was The Only Ones, which I was really looking forward to. Unfortunately I never got the chance to speak to them; they came in, sound checked, left, came back, played and left. There was a fairly decent sized crowd and they played 'Another Girl, Another Planet' – they sounded good.

June continued with The Tourists, who were just an average poppy band. Didn't impress me much and then a couple of days later it was the turn of The Lurkers. The English Ramones were back in Manchester. It was a pretty full gig. There was lots of mad dancing at the front with fists swinging and they played well, it was a good night. We managed to talk to them before the gig and they were decent lads, for cockneys. They were followed on 15 June by Human League. Another good gig from them. Had a good light show and impressed a half-full club. The Human League were a very interesting band at this stage, they wrote some great electronic songs and of course Phillip Oakey had a great voice and great hair! They were really good characters with a typical Yorkshire dry humour and we always enjoyed it when they played. Top lads. I was really pleased when they made it.

Joy Division's debut album *Unknown Pleasures* (FACT 10) was released on 15 June. I heard a few songs off it in Discount Records, but I wasn't impressed on first listen as it sounded nothing like the

Ged Duffy

band that I had seen live, so I didn't buy it. The following night it was The Specials at the Russell, and this was a great gig. Slim and I spent a lot of time talking to Jerry Dammers before the gig and what a top bloke he was. We also talked to Terry Hall and found out that he was a United fan and that he spent a lot of time in Manchester as his brother-in-law was the manager of the Virgin shop in Town. He told us that he got to see United whenever he was up here.

The Russell was rocking, and the dancefloor was full. Can't find anything on the internet to confirm who supported them that night but I'm fairly sure that it was Madness and The Selector. I have this image in my head of NF skinheads causing problems when Madness were on and the band taking their side when they were getting battered by Ozzie and our crew.

A couple of days later, I was at home watching *Granada Reports* when towards the end of the show Tony Wilson introduces Public Image Limited and they play 'Death Disco', which is followed by an interview with Lydon, Levene and Wobble. Towards the end of the interview Lydon asks Wilson if he still ran that club of his. Wilson replied that he did to which Lydon says, "We want to play there tonight so we can get some money for the train fare back to London". Five minutes later the phone rings and it's Rob Gretton asking me to get hold of Slim to sort the stage out for PIL.

ACR played their usual gig: a wall of noise with no drums. They were really good. There were about 200 or so in the audience by the time Public Image Limited came on. Lydon came on and told the crowd "I don't know what you expect but this is just a rehearsal". They started with a new song called 'Chant' and Lydon had a lectern set up so he could read his lyrics to all the new songs. Slim and I were sat on the front of the stage and Slim kept asking them to play 'Fodderstomf' and Lydon kept looking at him and couldn't make up his mind whether to take the piss out of him or not.

They played another three songs off *Metal Box* which all sounded good. One of these was 'Death Disco'. They played 'Public Image' after two false starts. Lydon put this down to the fact that this was the new drummer's first gig with them, and he said, "We admit our mistakes, we know we have many". Afterwards Rob Gretton, Tony Wilson, Slim, a couple of Rob's mates and me spent some time talking with John where we were taking the piss out of his love for Arsenal, and he was moaning at Slim asking for 'Fodderstomf'. It was a great night!

Factory Fairy Tales

On 20 June we went to see Echo and The Bunnymen at The Tingle Tangle Club. This was the first gig to be staged at a new venue in the cellar under Geatano's Restaurant on Back Piccadilly off Tib Street. £1 to get in and free egg and chips thrown in - what a deal! The Bunnymen's debut single 'Pictures On The Wall' had come out the previous month and I was playing it to death at this time. They played eight songs, and the crowd loved them and demanded that they did an encore. Ian McCullough told the audience that they didn't know any more songs, so they played four of the eight again. They were begged to come back on again and they did and played the other four songs that they knew so they did their complete set twice!

Next gig was The Mekons. Every time I saw them I walked away afterwards wondering why they never got as big and as famous as they should have, they were another totally unique band. This was followed by a great event - The Cramps at the Russell - the place was full of Goths. This was a band like no other, B Movie Rockabilly without a bass player. Lux Interior was one of the best front men around and his wife, Poison Ivy, was stunningly beautiful and an amazing guitarist. The drummer Nick Knox looked like Eddie Munster (a character in the TV show *The Munsters*) and the other guitarist, Bryan Gregory, just looked like a weird fucker who played a Flying V guitar. The songs were short, sharp, sleazy, and proper Psycho-billy punk garage. They were really sound people as they spoke to Slim and me a lot during their soundcheck. I fell in love with Poison Ivy that night and I still remember her in her tight pants. What a babe!

Next it was the return of Teardrop Explodes at the Russell. They were becoming a really tight band with a set of great songs, there was a small crowd in with a few over from Liverpool including our mate Bernie. We had a good laugh with the band before and after; proper Manc/Scouse banter. After that it was back down to earth with Chelsea at the Russell. I was looking forward to seeing them, 'Right to Work' was a good single but they didn't back up that promise with tonight's gig. It was half full and most of our usual crew were in tonight. They had an arrogant attitude from the start - typical Cockney twats.

July opened with a great set by The Cure on *The Three Imaginary Boys* album tour, the place was almost full - this was the best I had seen The Cure, probably helped by the fact that I knew all the songs. Nice guys

Ged Duffy

as well and we had a laugh with them, definitely not the moody Goths at this time in their development. Sometime around this period The Pretenders played the Russell. There was nothing flash about them, just well-written, tuneful rock songs. Chrissie Hynde looked good, a proper tasty rock chick with a great attitude. They were another band that were easy to get on without massive egos.

13 July: Joy Division and Crispy Ambulance. This was probably the first time that Joy Division had decided to play a gig in Manchester without a Factory band supporting them but guess what Crispy Ambulance went on to become a Factory band! Slim and I thought that there was a much bigger PA that night than normal and the sound was better for it. 444 people were in the club that night and this was the largest number so far to see Joy Division there. I think that the crowd was bigger than that, but they were getting paid on audience size and Alan Wise was counting! Once again Joy Division gave a great performance with Curtis stealing the show again with his dancing.

A week later Mark E Smith brought The Fall to Hulme supported by Echo and The Bunnymen who still had the drum machine, and it would be a few months before they found a drummer. They played much the same songs that they had at The Tingle Tangle Club a month earlier. The Fall were radically different in both personnel and sound from the band that had just issued their debut album Live at The Witch Trials. The keyboards, so important on the album, had gone and they were just about to go into their Rockabilly phrase. This new line-up sounded fresh and original tonight in front of a loving crowd which was about the same size as Joy Division's the previous week. One footnote is that John Peel was at this gig, and he had his photo taken with the three Bunnymen and this was the photo that they used in 2020 for the cover of their John Peel Sessions double album. Once again John Peel found time to speak to Slim and me - top bloke!

The next day we went to see Adam and The Ants at the Funhouse (the Mayflower under a new name) - it was still the same shithole though! This gig was supposed to be at the Russell, but it got moved and Alan Wise wasn't promoting this one so we weren't working. Slim and I loved The Ants and this was the original line-up six months before Malcolm McLaren took the other three away to form Bow Wow Wow leaving Adam Ant on his own to go on to become a global

Factory Fairy Tales

mega-star. Their single 'Zerox Machine' had just been released and was one of my favourite singles of the year. This was the period before Adam Ant started dressing like a Red Indian and he was dressed in a leather jacket and leather pants underneath a tartan kilt. He was such a cool dude, and they were such a good band. They played a lot of the songs off their debut album, *Dirk Wears White Sox*. The place was full, and it was a wild night down at the front of the stage as there were a large number of people from London who were following The Ants around the country. It was quiet outside afterwards as I think the Perry Boys stayed away as they must have known that there would be a large audience.

MAYFLOWER CLUB
Birch Street, Gorton, Manchester

'STUFF THE SUPERSTARS SPECIAL'

on SATURDAY, 28th JULY, 1979
2 pm till Late (Doors open 1-30)

The Fall, Joy Division, The Distractions
Jon the Postmans, Psychedelic, 5 Skinners
Frantic Elevators, Armed Force, Elti Fits
The Liggers, The Hamsters

Compere: Gordon the Moron

Tickets £1-50

Saturday 28 July turned out to be another one of those great multi-gig nights which cropped up occasionally. We went to the Funhouse for *Stuff The Superstars*. The show started at 2pm and the doors opened at 1.30pm. 11 bands and Gordon the Moron compering all for the sum of £1.50. This was a fund raiser for the local fanzine *City Fun*. The bands who played at this gig in order of appearance were as follows:

Elti Fits – A local band who appeared several times at the Russell as support. Actually did a John Peel session later this year. I quite liked these guys.

Ged Duffy

The Hamsters - They came from Denton, East Manchester. Saw them several times at local gigs round Manchester. A really good band who never made it but are part of Manchester music history. Played a great set at this gig.

Armed Force - Muppet's band were great again.

Foreign Press - Weren't advertised to play but nevertheless played. I didn't like them as I thought that they were just bland. Signed to EMI a couple of years later and both Rob Gretton and Bernard Sumner produced a single each for them.

Frantic Elevators - Fucking brilliant on the day. Saw them a few times. This was Mick Hucknall's band before he became a world superstar with Simply Red. They did a couple of brilliant singles including the original version of 'Holding Back the Years'.

Joy Division - The review of this gig in the next edition of *City Fun* fanzine was as follows: "THEY WERE BRILLIANT. I MEAN BRILLIANT". This is exactly as they wrote it, using capitals so there's no point in me adding anything to it.

The Funhouse pulled in a large crowd for the event but without doubt the majority of people were there to see Joy Division and The Fall, and I felt that it was stupid planning to put Joy Division on as the sixth band and The Fall on as the ninth. These two should have been the headliners. I spent a bit of time with Rob Gretton during the gig, and I can remember him sitting at a table with a can of beer, reading a book whilst some of the bands were on. He was a character.

We left after Joy Division finished, so we missed Ludus, The Liggers, The Fall, The Distractions, and John The Postman. We decided to go to the Russell to see another band without a bass player - The B52s. The Cramps had managed to pull it off and I have to say that The B52s did as well. The place was packed with people wearing Hawaiian shirts and shorts which was definitely not the normal attire you would see around Hulme. I wonder what all the local muggers must have made of these strange people coming into their territory.

I had never heard anything by the B52s prior to this gig and after hearing the first song and seeing the energy that was coming from the stage I was hooked. They never stopped dancing and the lack of a bass wasn't apparent. The girls must have used some heavy-duty hairspray

Factory Fairy Tales

to keep their do's upright for the entire show. The crowd loved them and were all dancing and I don't think that I had ever seen the Russell like that before. There was no trouble or punch ups either. A great night. The place was full as well. Next time I was in Discount Records I bought the two singles 'Rock Lobster' and 'Planet Claire' and the debut album as well. They had a new fan.

Next up at the Russell was OMD - this was the last time they played there as they were just on the verge of becoming major pop stars and they would move over to the Apollo from now on. They were great again and they were one of the few bands that spent money on a good lighting rig for their shows, so they stood out from the norm. A few days later Slaughter and The Dogs and Victim played. Wayne Barrett had left the band back in March but had re-joined them prior to this gig. He was a brilliant front man and Mick Rossi was a proper guitar hero and their show tonight was great. They should have been massive but they just didn't make it. Two great bands.

The next couple of gigs attracted a wholly different audiences. First up were Purple Hearts and Secret Affair. Thanks to the success of The Jam and the excitement generated in anticipation of the upcoming release of the film *Quadrophenia,* there had been a mod revival. These two bands were at the forefront of this new movement, and both played 1960s type R&B. I thought that both bands were good, but I'd rather listen to The Faces. The Russell was full and there were a few parkas in attendance. The following evening it was Selector. The most underrated of the big three Two Tone bands and I think that these should have made it as big as Madness. The Russell was full and bouncing as they played a great set. Top folks as well as they were sound with Slim and me. Bit of bother down the front with some skinheads during the gig though.

Zoo meets Factory Halfway was a one-day festival held in Leigh featuring Joy Division, Teardrop Explodes, Echo & The Bunnymen and ACR on August Bank Holiday Monday. I planned to go to this but when I got up in the morning, I discovered that there was a bus strike, so it was going to be a major pain to get there. It would have meant getting a train to town, then another to Leigh and then having to walk to find the site of the festival. Getting home would have been impossible due to the trains stopping at 10pm. I had seen these bands a lot in the previous few months, so I decided to stay at home instead.

Ged Duffy

Depending on who you believe the audience ranged from between 82 and 200.

The bus drivers were working again the next day when our mates, The Damned, were back again. They absolutely loved the Russell, it was their fourth appearance there this year and probably their worst - I don't mean musically or anything like that, I just mean that it had become predictable. Scabies would jump off his drum-kit and grope a girl, Sensible would get his cock out, Vanian would be mega cool and there would be widespread fighting down the front during the set. They had managed a couple of big hits with singles off the *Machine Gun Etiquette* album but the sudden fame had not changed any of them. A quick footnote about The Damned: at one of the gigs Captain Sensible needed to have a piss and since he was naked at the time, he had a piss on stage. He took some dog's abuse off the crowd, but he loved it. During another of the gigs Rat Scabies pulled his pants off and climbed on his drum kit and mooned everyone whilst Dave Vanian smacked his arse.

The month ended with Teardrop Explodes and Echo and The Bunnymen. Both bands put on a good show. Ian McCulloch got a lot of stick off the crowd as he was wearing black slip-on shoes and white socks - he didn't like that. By this stage in their development, Echo were a long way behind Teardrop both in their stage show and their song writing but that would change moving forward. Teardrop Explodes played a great set of danceable pop songs and the one thing about both of these bands is that both had a singer that could actually sing and I'm glad that both found success. The following night it was Madness and The Modernaires. A full house at the Russell with lots of skinheads and Perry Boys in attendance. Madness were brilliant on the night but there was a lot of fighting down the front. I remember Suggs getting punched in the face afterwards by a Perry Boy who we used to see at United games. There was a big brawl outside between the band and their crew and these lads due to Madness having an allegiance with Chelsea FC.

7. Hooky throwing right hooks at the Russell

The *Futurama Festival* at Queens Hall, Leeds was held on 8th September spread over two days, but we were only going to the first. A few of us including Lee, Slim, Derek, Spenna, and Ozzie went over on the National Express coach. When we got to Leeds we found an off licence and Slim and I sat outside on a bench whilst all the rest went inside. Within minutes, they were racing out of the shop being chased by a couple of staff. When we caught up with the guys it turned out that they had grabbed as much booze off the shelves as they could and did a runner.

The Queens Hall looked like an old tram depot, which is exactly what it was. As we approached the venue we saw that there were a lot of Nazis milling around outside, waving National Front flags and banners with some of them actually dressed as Nazis and seig heiling everyone arriving at the venue. This was causing problems near the venue with some pushing and shoving taking place and verbal threats being exchanged. There were few security staff and those that were there were staying out of it.

Inside it was a large, cavernous building which held about 5,000. The rear of the hall was taken up with people sitting on sleeping bags and this was the area where people would be sleeping overnight. During the day we witnessed several couples getting inside their sleeping bags and in between songs you could hear the moaning as climaxes were reached.

The floor was grey and sticky, and we soon found out that once you sat on it then the your clothes would turn grey as a result of the many years of petrol, diesel, and engine oil leaking onto the floor from the trams and associated machinery. The filled in tram lines were visible all over the hall.

There was no direct daylight coming in the place, no clean air, no refreshments, and no seats. It was smokey, smelly, sweaty, and full of the great unwashed. It was basically a shithole. When we got in we saw that the stage was at the far end of the hall and there was a band on, and either the PA was too small or the acoustics not right for music, but the sound was awful and could only be heard properly if you were in the vicinity of the PA stack. This didn't bode well for

'The World's First Science Fiction Music Festival'. If the building has a history of poor acoustics, then at least hire a PA that can go some way to resolving this issue. The only Sci-Fi link I saw were two guys walking round dressed as robots for no apparent reason, but I suppose I should acknowledge that this was Yorkshire...

We found a spot, sat down and watched a lot of unknown bands play during the afternoon. Each band had a 30 minute slot and then the later bands had a 45 minute slot. No body interested us enough to actually make us get up and venture down to the front. The guys were drinking and having a spliff when a few skinheads came up and started causing shit. Spenna and Slim got up and started talking to them and a couple of minutes later, three of them were on the deck and the rest had run off to bully someone else. Everyone got back to drinking and Spenna was laughing at me for not drinking, so to shut him up I had a drink of white wine from a bottle. I wasn't mad keen on it, but I drank every time a bottle was passed round during the afternoon. He passed me a spliff and once he had shown me how to smoke it and inhale it, I had a smoke. This was something I liked. I was feeling very mellow

Factory Fairy Tales

and happy. All Slim and I had tried before that day was poppers or to give it its correct name alkyl nitrites. We would sniff it straight from the bottle and it would give us a head rush which lasted for a couple of minutes and a sense of euphoria. Our drug taking and drinking started that day. By about 6pm the toilets had completely overflowed, the floor of the hall was full of beer cans, plastic glasses, fanzines and other assorted shite and the place stank of weed and glue.

Spizz Energi came on and a few of us went to the front to see them. Good set, great frontman, and they gave a run out to 'Where's Captain Kirk' which would be a massive hit when released a few months later. ACR came on and they've got a drummer. No, I'm wrong they've got a fucking brilliant drummer who's a human funk machine. Their set was amazing with a lot of the old wall of noise sound completely reformed with a funk drumbeat. Cabaret Voltaire were next, and we sat down again, and I was happy as I can have some more of these spliffs. The Cabs were really good and had a fascinating film show playing behind them. They played 'Nag, Nag, Nag' and a Velvet Underground song 'Here She Comes Now'. There were a few Skins and punks shouting at the Cabs to "Get off, Yer Shit" but they carried on. Sometime after ACR finished, Lee went to the toilet and never came back. We paid no attention to it, as we knew that he loved the Cabs and would have been down the front watching them. After they finished, he still hadn't come back so we all split up and went searching for him. We couldn't find him, so we decided to sit down during OMD's set and wait for him to return. We knew what Lee was like with the women and we thought that he had probably copped off and was screwing someone inside a sleeping bag at the back of the hall. OMD were the first band to get a decent sound out of the PA so far today.

Tony Wilson got on stage and introduced "The Awesome Joy Division" and they were truly awesome. They started off with 'I Remember Nothing' a slow atmospheric number whose drums and bass echoed round the vast hall building up behind Barney's fractured guitar. The set was brilliantly paced with this slow opener then moving up a few gears until a few songs later came 'Transmission' a standout track to be followed up with four classics at the end of the set - 'Shadowplay', 'She's Lost Control', 'Atrocity Exhibition' and 'Dead Souls'. The whole set was so well planned and executed by four guys who had transformed into a tight, well-rehearsed and creative beast. They made the bad PA sound good, and they had won

Ged Duffy

over the whole crowd.

We sat down again and still no sign of Lee, so we split up go looking for him, but we still can't find him. Next up were Punishment of Luxury who were a weird bunch who had definitely listened to Devo. They had the hard task of following Joy Division who had completely blown every other band away. They played well and I enjoyed their set, but they should have gone on before Joy Division.

Still no sign of Lee, and we're now getting concerned for him but there's nothing we can do, so we carry on sitting down and wait for Public Image Limited to come on. Thanks to everyone over running, it was around 2am by the time they came on. By this stage in the day, most of the audience were feeling tired, some had left to catch trains and buses, and Lydon came on with the wrong attitude. The sound was awful and most of Lydon's words couldn't be heard over the band. Lydon had his back to the crowd for most of the gig and spent a lot of time couching down. After about eight songs, Lydon was so fed up with the audience constantly shouting out for him to play Sex Pistols songs, he just walked off and the rest of the band followed him. This was the third time that I had seen Public Limited Image this year and this was the worst out of the three. I put this down to the audience as they didn't understand the band unlike the previous two times in Manchester when the band and audience were in tandem.

We had planned to just attend this first day, but we had now seen how slack the security was, and we could just kip in the hall overnight and stay on for the second day without paying. We had a discussion, but a couple of the guys had things planned for the Sunday, so we went home. We still hadn't found Lee by the time we left the venue to get the coach back to Manchester and it was a couple of days later before we discovered what had happened. Lee had gone to the toilet after watching ACR and he was beaten up in the toilet by five or six skinheads. They battered him that badly the security called for an ambulance and Lee was kept in hospital in Leeds until the following morning and then returned to Manchester alone.

★

Our next gig at the Russell was The Chords - another mod band who played basic sixties rock. The place was full and there were a lot of parkas in attendance tonight, fancy wearing a big winter coat in a

Factory Fairy Tales

packed gig. The following night Joy Division appeared on BBC2 show *Something Else* and played 'Transmission' and 'She's Lost Control'. The Jam also played 'When You're Young' and 'Eton Rifles'. John Cooper Clarke recited 'Chickentown' and there was an interview with Tony Wilson and Stephen Morris (Joy Division's drummer) as well.

Around this time Gang of Four released their brilliant debut album *Entertainment*. It's one of those rare albums where every song is good and there are no filler tracks. In my opinion it's as good as Joy Division's *Unknown Pleasures* and Stone Roses debut.

21 September: The Revillos. Great gig! The Revillos had formed out of the demise of The Rezillos. They were space-punk Pop, it was a fun night. They were so bright and colourful, and their stage show was energetic with lots of dancing both on and off the stage. They were a bundle of fun, and we had a great time talking to them backstage even though we struggled to understand what the fuck they were saying with their thick Scottish accents, but it seems that we laughed in the right places.

The following evening it was the turn of Dexy's Midnight Runners, Swell Maps, and Ludus. Swell Maps were an interesting band who sounded like a cross between early Buzzcocks and early Fall: chainsaw guitar, weird lyrics, and great drums. After seeing them I bought their debut album *A Trip to Marineville* in Discount Records a few days later. Dexy's were headlining but hadn't released any records at this time. Their magnificent debut album *Searching for the Young Soul Rebels* was still a few months off release. They were such a powerful band with the brass section sounding so good live. They were able to go out on a headline tour due to the fact that they were associated with Two Tone and, like the other Two Tone acts that had played at the Russell, trouble seemed to follow them. Skinheads and Perry Boys were in attendance and the front of the stage was a bit tasty at times. Afterwards there was a fight outside with some of the band and the locals and I saw Kevin Rowland get punched in the face.

A few days later we went to see Gary Numan at the Apollo. The stage set was brilliant with everyone set up in boxes and Gary at the front on his own. Two members of now-defunct Ultravox were in the backing band. He played 'Cars', 'Down in the Park' and 'Are Friends Electric'. He was dressed in black with blond hair. I thought that he looked so cool, so robotic, so Germanic. He had such an unusual voice as well and I wanted to be him. Great show, great songs, and no shit outside afterwards.

A few weeks earlier Alan Wise had put a message out in *City Fun* fanzine saying that the trouble that was happening on a regular basis in the Russell had to stop. It was causing him problems with the owner who in turn was having problems getting his license renewed. Alan spoke to Slim and me prior to the Joy Division gig, to tell us that he was stopping promoting gigs at the Russell. He said that because of the hassle over getting the license renewed the owner had told Alan that the cost of him hiring the club for gigs was going up by about 50%. Alan said that he could not make any money if this happened. He also told us both that he still had gigs to do this year but they would be in different venues, and he was working on getting another permanent place to put gigs on.

28 September: Joy Division, Foreign Press, and Teardrop Explodes at the Russell. Teardrop Explodes were not due to play at this gig but turned up in the afternoon and asked Alan Wise if they could and he said yes. Rob Gretton was not happy about it and told them that they were first on before Foreign Press. Teardrop played and I think that most of the crowd didn't recognize them, but I liked their set. Foreign Press played and went down well with the crowd.

Backstage Ian Curtis had a seizure and Alan wanted to cancel the show, but Ian decided that everything would be okay and he wanted to play. By this time the club had filled up and there was a crowd of 800 in to see them and this was the largest that they had drawn so far there. There was a bit of tension in the air and prior to Joy Division coming on there had been a bit of a punch up down near the front of the stage involving a few of the knobheads who caused the trouble later on.

Joy Division came on and they were magnificent with Ian giving a great performance considering what had happened to him only minutes earlier. The way he danced it was like a man possessed. They started with 'Atmosphere' and finished with 'She's Lost Control'. During the gig these same knobheads were causing trouble down the front and there was a massive mosh pit going on which was definitely not the norm at a Joy Division gig. As soon as they came on for the encore and started to play 'Transmission' a fight broke out and Hooky swung his bass at one of the guys fighting and it made a massive feedback sound as it hit the stage. Hooky then jumped off the stage and into the crowd and started fighting with this guy. What Hooky didn't know at the time was that the guy he swung his bass at was Andy Outatunes* and he had been fighting the dicks who were causing the trouble. After a few moments Andy's mates, who had come to the Russell with him to see Joy Division, saw Hooky hitting Andy so they attacked Hooky, and he went down, and they started kicking him. Joy Division's roadie Twinny jumped in to save him and got him out of there. Tex, Slim and I jumped in to stop the fight. Whilst this was going on the band had carried on playing. The trouble then carried on near the mixing deck and Tex, Slim and I grabbed a few of the troublemakers and threw them out. If Ozzie had been in the Russell that night these knobheads would have been battered without doubt.

The remaining band played 'Atrocity Exhibition' without Hooky who climbed back on stage. Hooky shouted some abuse at the rest of the band before finally storming off to the dressing room. The rest of the band carried on and the place erupted when they walked off stage. What a great performance by the band and what a great night. One of the Russell's great nights.

24 hours after the excitement of a brilliant Joy Division show we had the joys of Original Mirrors and John Dowie. This turned out to be the last night at the Russell for a few months and after the previous night's events this was a damp squib. The music was awful, the attendance was low, and it was a nondescript event apart from The Hamsters turning up unannounced and playing, so at least one good band played on this final night. The Russell deserved a better send off. The Russell carried on as a drinking club with Reggae bands on at the weekend, but Wise Moves had decided to move on. The Russell had been a massive part of my life and I was so sad to see it go. When I think of the characters I met there… everything about the Russell was great; the location, the design of the place, the staff and most importantly the venue had great acoustics both for Danny the DJ and for the bands. But it was now time to move on and Alan Wise was trying to put bands on anywhere he could.

Some punks had moved into Burnage and were living near the library. We never saw them until one day we saw one being chased up Burnage Lane by some knobheads. Slim and I intervened and fucked

---

So called because he was in a band called The Outatunes from Salford.

Ged Duffy

them off and found out the lad was called Mark France or "Bollock" on account of the shape of his head. He introduced us to his brothers John, Tony, and Karl. Tony became a great friend of ours and started hanging round with us on Burnage Lane in the evening and we started going in each other's houses to listen to music. Tony started coming to some gigs with us. The first time I met Tony I thought that he was the coolest looking dude that I had ever met - perfect band material.

Wise Moves' first promotion away from the Russell was on 6 October when The Undertones and The Freshies played at the Apollo. The last time The Undertones played at the Russell, Alan had disappeared without paying them. The deal he arranged now was The Undertones were to be paid for both gigs out of the money from this gig. They were amazing on the night, and I felt so sorry for them when Alan disappeared halfway through their set with all of the door money. The lovable promoter strikes again!

The following Monday two records featuring Joy Division were released. Their debut Factory Records single 'Transmission' and 'Novelty' (FAC 13) came out alongside the Fast Records *Earcom 2: Contradiction* EP. As soon as I finished work, I went to Discount Records and picked them both up. 'Transmission' and 'Novelty' were both favourite songs of mine from their live shows. The single was a classic and still is to this day. A couple of years later, when I became good friends of Hooky, he told me a story about the track 'Novelty'. Barney and him had seen AC/DC when they played at the Electric Circus in March 1977 and this song was them trying to write an AC/DC song. When you listen to it, this song has the heaviest metal type guitar on it and is nothing like the rest of Joy Division. He also told me that it was the first song they ever wrote together. The two songs on *Earcom 2*, 'Auto-Suggestion' and 'From Safety To Where?' were both slow burners but I got there in the long run and absolutely love them nowadays.

The following night it was The Ruts at the Funhouse promoted by Alan Wise rearranged from the Russell. The Ruts were great lads. I ended up in a taxi with their manager and singer Malcolm Owen directing them to a dealer in Charles Barry Crescent, Hulme so Malcolm could buy some smack which he injected backstage at the Funhouse on our return. The manager gave me £10 as a thank you as Malcolm would not have been able to go on without it. The Ruts were brilliant that night and they should have been as big as The

Factory Fairy Tales

Clash if you ask me. There was the normal welcoming committee outside the Funhouse at the end, and it was tough getting back to Burnage again.

26 October: Psychedelic Furs at the Poly. We used to go here for the Friday disco and around this time I met Big Stuart and Dave Hicks there and we became great friends. They were both in Manchester as students. Anyway back to the gig. We met up at the Salisbury on Oxford Road, which was next door to A1 Music, the premier musical equipment shop in Manchester. The Salisbury became a regular for us all for the next few years as it had a proper jukebox with a mixture of Rock and punk. I was really looking forward to this gig as I'd heard them on John Peel and I had just bought the great debut single 'We Love You'.

When they came on, they created a wall of noise with two guitarists, saxophone, bass and drums and I had never heard a singer sing so many words. The light show was so simple, and they were just unbelievable. They were like a modern-day Velvet Underground. I have bought every album they ever made since. Butler Rep, the singer, broke three mike stands during the gig. The Poly was packed, and the reception was great. Lee Pickering had a chat with me after they had finished and asked me if I wanted to move into a flat with him, in the centre of Manchester. I had a think for about 30 seconds and said yes.

27 and 28 October: Buzzcocks and Joy Division at the Apollo. I was curious on the first night to see how Joy Division would sound in such a large venue. Buzzcocks were promoting their third album, *A Different Kind of Tension,* released in September. The Apollo wasn't sold out either night this time, as Buzzcocks' popularity had been on the wane for a while and Joy Division were not yet a household name.

Joy Division played a thirty-minute set on the first night which was the norm for a support act at the Apollo. They put on a good show and sounded great. When they finished, the crowd started booing because they didn't come back on to do an encore. This was the first time that I had ever heard 'Love Will Tear Us Apart' and the song stood out from the rest of the set due to Barney playing the keyboards and Ian playing the guitar. I was looking forward to hearing it again the next evening, but they didn't play it.

The following night Joy Division played a different set to the previous night's show and when they went off at the end the audience shouted for an encore. After several minutes, they re-emerged and played for another 15 or 20 minutes. Both nights they were good, and I noticed that some of the crowd left on both nights after Joy Division played. Buzzcocks were good on both nights, not as electric as they used to be but still better than most. Went backstage both nights and had a beer with Rob Gretton and Pete Shelley. This had been an amazing three days: Psychedelic Furs, Joy Division twice and Buzzcocks twice. We were so lucky living in Manchester at this time.

November started with The Specials, Madness, and The Selector at the Apollo. There was wholesale violence between the audience and bouncers - normally the bouncers would just have to act like animals when the main band was on but tonight was different as there were three big bands on the same bill. When The Specials came on, the bouncers had to concede defeat as the amount of people who rushed the stage overwhelmed them. Terry Hall didn't help matters by telling the crowd to "Do the fucking bouncers". Madness were on the verge of becoming mega Pop stars and they put on a great show. The Specials were great and, like The Clash, their lyrics meant something. Outside afterwards there was the usual trouble with the Perry Boys and skinheads.

The following day, The Damned released their new album Machine Gun Etiquette - the cover was great with Sensible wearing the now famous pink mohair jumper and yellow mohair pants. When I played it I was amazed at how different it sounded compared to the first two Damned albums. I had seen them four times this year already, but I was still shocked by how good it was. This is another album that I still play today, and it has never lost its sparkle.

One day I was in the Virgin Megastore* and the girl who I had gone to see Bowie with asked me if I fancied going to see The Who with her. I jumped at the chance, I loved The Who. So on 16 November we got the coach from Chorlton Street Bus Station and went to see The Who at Stafford Bingley Hall. They started off with 'Substitute' and the crowd went wild. Highlights for me were watching Entwistle's fingers when he played and sang 'Boris The Spider' as they resembled a spider

---

The Virgin Megastore had opened up sometime during the early part of the year on Market Street and the old Virgin store closed. There were no listening booths in this one and it had no character compared to the old one.

Factory Fairy Tales

with their movement, the beauty of 'Behind Blue Eyes', the power of '5.15' and the majesty of 'Won't Get Fooled Again'. Townsend was pissed and he fell over a couple of times during the show. At the end of the show, he picked up a shoe that someone had thrown onto the stage and bit it like a dog and then started barking down the mic and walked off.

Over the previous couple of months I'd had the odd drink or two when I was out, but I decided that this was the night that I would start drinking and my guest introduced me to Pernod and blackcurrant which I fell in love with as it was sweet. I had a few drinks during the evening, and I felt good. This was a great gig, but it was bloody freezing coming back on the coach. Later that night I discovered why Pernod and black is also commonly known as purple puke!

After seeing The Who it was time to see their protégés, The Jam, at the Apollo. Once again they put on a very loud professional show full of hit singles. They were an immensely powerful live band.

One other notable event in November was the release of *Metal Box* by Public Image Limited, initially as three 12-inch records which played at 45 rpm, all contained within a circular metal box. The first 10,000 were in this format and once they were sold out in February 1980 it was re-issued as a double album under the title of *Second Edition*. I purchased it from Discount Records. This record is still regarded nowadays as a game-changer as nobody sounded like them in 1979. The way they put guitar, bass, drums, and vocals together was unique, it's still a great album.

After spending an evening listening to *Metal Box* I was back to see Mötorhead at the Apollo. Slim and I worked this one and God were they loud. My ears were still ringing five days later. There was a report in the *Manchester Evening News* that a Noise Abatement Officer at the gig confirmed that Mötorhead were as loud as a jet engine taking off. They had a Lancaster Bomber stage prop which was lowered down so Lemmy could stand on it whilst singing 'Bomber'. The show was great, and they were supported by Saxon who went on to have a few hits as well. Two great bands, two great set of people. No airs or graces just down to earth beer-drinking men. Lemmy was a bass monster with his Rickenbacker and his huge stack of Marshall amps. It was amazing watching what he played: bass chords totally distorted to make a sound, truly memorable. Mötorhead were not Heavy Metal in my opinion but good time loud rock 'n' roll. We spoke to Lemmy for a few minutes backstage prior to the gig and what a top bloke he was. RIP Lemmy, you're sadly missed.

Sometime in November I moved into 24 Len Cox Walk with Lee Pickering. This was a small row of council maisonettes just off Tib Street smack bang in Manchester City Centre. It was Lee's mum's place, but she was having a 12 month enforced break from her preferred employment as a professional shop-lifter. I was still working at SP&S Records and this flat was about five minutes' walk away which was great for me. It was a two storey, three-bedroom maisonette which was above a one-bedroom single storey flat. Lee had his bedroom and I had mine with the spare there for anyone to stay over - on the lower floor there was a living room and a kitchen.

When I moved in, I left my stereo system and all of my records behind at home and brought a cassette player with me. I had taped several of my albums so I had something to listen to in my room. Lee had a cheap stereo set up in the living room and this is what we played our records on.

We settled into a routine of working and going out each night. We would have a couple of spliffs and then venture out to any of the following: Deville's, the Salisbury, Corbieres Wine Bar, City Road Inn, The Briton's Protection, Poly Disco, Peveril of the Peak, or see bands in little venues in the immediate vicinity - now known as the Northern Quarter. We would go to the Cyprus Tavern on a Sunday evening to see whatever local bands would be playing as part of the Manchester Musicians' Collective. My drug taking was a daily thing now and I now understood about the different types of dope such as black, leb, skunk, grass, and Moroccan.

I would take my laundry home on a Sunday and Dad would give me a lift back in the early evening. Mum used to buy two or three bags worth of food for me, and we would eat this during the week. If we were hungry we would call to see Bob the Burger Man in his van on Market Street near Piccadilly Gardens and have a burger. Bob was the brother of June Fellowes who I had met at Salford College the previous year. I had not seen much of June since Derek and I got kicked out, but Bob kept me up to date with her.

Alan Wise was promoting gigs at Deville's now and Slim and I were doing the stage for him. Deville's was a small club over on Lloyd Street near the Town Hall. It was a cellar venue; small and painted black. It became one of the best Goth clubs in Manchester a couple of years later. Next door was its sister bar Lazy Lils which was American themed with bench seats and a bucking bronco.

We had already worked gigs by Foreign Press, Frantic Elevators, and a few more local band nights there before Echo and The Bunnymen played with U2 as the support in early December. The *Manchester Evening News* claimed a few years later that U2 played in front of 11 people at the Poly in May 1980, but I know people who were at that gig and the Poly was full that night as they played with Wah Heat, so it has to be this gig at Deville's. I guess that this must have been U2's first ever appearance in Manchester as they did not have any records out and their debut single did not come out until May 1980. We knew the guys from Echo well as they had played the Russell a few times, and our friend Bernie was with them.

Within 30 seconds of U2 starting their sound check I knew that I would like them. I'm a bass man through and through but I like guitarists that are different: McKay from the Banshees, McGeoch from Magazine and The Banshees, Gill from Gang of Four, Levene from PIL, Barney from Joy Division, Sergeant from the Bunnymen and this guitarist sound checking in front of me was different and he played a Thunderbird to boot. When they had finished I started talking to The Edge and I asked him how he got such an unusual sound and he showed me what effect pedals he used. By the time they went on to play the crowd had grown to the massive figure of 12 people, but they still played a solid set for around 30 minutes. I must point out that this dozen included Slim, Lee, Bernie, and me. Bono was throwing himself round the stage and at one point took his shirt off. Lee shouted at him "Who the fuck do you think you are? Iggy Pop?" and Bono put his shirt back on a few moments later!

The Bunnymen came on and they had improved so much now that they had a drummer. They were getting more confident on stage and the song writing was getting better. They played a great set.

London Calling was released on the 14 December. This was the long-awaited third album by The Clash and it was well worth the wait. It turned out to be a masterpiece. The cover has become one of the most iconic images of all time with the picture of Paul Simonon smashing his bass guitar. I got it from Discount Records and was so excited to play it. This is another album that I still play a lot.

On Saturday 15 December, SP&S Records were having their Christmas do in London so at noon on the Friday we shut the warehouse and got in the coach provided. Everyone had their partner with them, but I was on my own. We got to the hotel in Islington around teatime and checked in. The plan was that we would go out for a meal around 8pm and then meet the rest of the company the following evening. I went for a walk and found The Hope and Anchor and went in for a couple of pints. It was great seeing the place where so many bands had played. There were three floors and the bands played downstairs in the cellar. The barman let me in downstairs so I could see the famous sign behind the stage. I was well chuffed when I met the rest of my work mates at a nearby restaurant. When I told them what I had done they were jealous as they were all serious musical people, and they would have been interested in doing that.

The following morning I got the tube to Camden Market where I bought a couple of bootleg albums of The Clash and some live cassettes of 999, PIL, and Joy Division. I also got a couple of belt buckles and a new leather jacket. I had a burger in McDonald's - it was amazing. Remember we didn't have a McDonald's in Manchester, the first one in town opened in 1983 on Market Street. After having a proper burger, (it was a proper burger as well not like the tiny bland ones they sell nowadays) and a knickerbocker glory (served in a glass bowl), it was back to the hotel and then on the coach to the banks of the River Thames where we met the London staff. En route a couple of the lads told me that they had gone for a beer during the day at the Hope and Anchor as well. The company had booked a booze and food boat trip up and down the Thames. It was an enjoyable night. The only downside was having to get up early on Sunday morning as the coach was leaving the hotel at 9am to take us back home to God's Country but at least I was able to go to the Cyprus Tavern that night.

After Lee playing it on repeat, I finally went to Discount Records and bought Joy Division's *Unknown Pleasures* album. It's a record that has never let me down now for over 40 years. The album had been out for six months, and my copy was still a first pressing. The first pressing of 10,000 had been split between two pressing plants. 5,000 were pressed in black vinyl which when held up to the light had a red tint to it. This was because somebody at the pressing plant hadn't cleaned the machine and the red vinyl still left in it from the previous record pressed mixed with the black causing the red effect tint. The other pressing plant pressed their 5,000 copies in black. The album was not a great seller and the first 10,000 were only finally sold out just a few weeks before *Closer* came out in 1980. After Ian's death, the record sales started.

In late December, we saw Echo and The Bunnymen and Teardrop Explodes at The Tingle Tangle Club. Two of my favourite bands both playing great sets in a small venue with egg and chips as well at a cost of £1 - happy days. A belated birthday present to myself was a first-hand view of a goddess, Blondie, at the Free Trade Hall. What more can I say? Debbie Harry for Xmas. Shame I didn't find her under my Xmas tree. I loved them again. Have to say Clem Burke what a magnificent drummer he was, a modern-day Keith Moon. Great songs, great stage show and Debbie… What more could you wish for?

1979

Singles

Public Image Limited: 'Death Disco
Siouxsie & The Banshees: 'Playground Twist'
The Clash: 'London Calling'
Teardrop Explodes: 'Sleeping Gas', 'Bouncing Babies'
Echo and The Bunnymen: 'The Pictures on my Wall'
Psychedelic Furs: 'We Love You'
The Pop Group: 'She is Beyond Good and Evil'
Joy Division: 'Transmission'
The Cure: '10.15 Saturday Night', 'Boys Don't Cry'
Orchestral Manoeuvres in the Dark: 'Electricity'
The Jam: 'The Eton Rifles'
A Certain Ratio: 'All Night Party'
Adam and The Ants: 'Zerox Machine'
Bauhaus: 'Bela Lugosi's Dead'
Spizz Energi: 'Where's Captain Kirk?'
Blondie: 'Heart of Glass'
Fad Gadget: 'Back to Nature'
The Damned: 'Love Song'
Suicide: 'Dream, Baby Dream'

Ged Duffy

Human League: 'Empire State Human'
Cabaret Voltaire: 'Nag, Nag, Nag'
Killing Joke: 'Nervous System'
Tubeway Army: 'Down in the Park'

EPs

Various: *A Factory Sample*
Various: *Earcom 2*
The Clash: *Cost of Living EP*
Killing Joke: *Turn to Red*
The Lurkers: *Out in the Dark EP*
Slaughter & The Dogs: *It's Alright EP*

Albums

Public Image Limited: *Metal Box*
Siouxsie & The Banshees: *Join Hands*
The Clash: *London Calling*
The Pop Group: *Y*
Gang of Four: *Entertainment*
Magazine: *Secondhand Daylight*
Human League: *Reproduction*
Joy Division: *Unknown Pleasures*
The Stranglers: *The Raven*
The Lurkers: *Gods Lonely Men*
The Fall: *Live at the Witch Trials*
The Jam: *Setting Sons*
The Skids: *Scared to Dance*
The Ramones: *It's Alive*
Wire: *154*
The Ruts: *The Crack*
Adam and the Ants: *Dirk wears White Sox*
Stiff Little Fingers: *Inflammable Material*
Iggy Pop: *New Values*

Factory Fairy Tales

David Bowie: *Lodger*
The Specials: *The Specials*
B52'S: *B52'S*
The Damned: *Machine Gun Etiquette*
Crass: *Stations of the Crass*
The Cure: *Three Imaginary Boys*

8. An unforgettable night

Life in Len Cox Walk was great; we were out every night drinking, getting stoned or watching bands. Every weekend was eventful as we always ended up having people stay over. Some weekends Andy Outatunes would stay over and then around 4am he would disappear for a couple of hours only to return with a couple of bin bags full of stuff that he'd stolen. One night it could be a bag full of Fiorucci designer straight leg jeans, and the next it could be boxes of Kicker boots. He robbed a café one night, so we had food to eat for a couple of months. I lost track of him about two years later. Wonder if he's around or locked up? Andy was always joined in his night time adventures by a couple of the North Manchester lot who shall remain nameless. Sometimes we'd have a knock at the door during the week and a member of the North Manchester crew would leave some stuff to be collected later.

Lee had a way with the ladies and came home with several pretty young things over the months we lived together. Sometimes these girls would turn up with their friends and I struck lucky a few times just by having a bed to sleep in. There was a beautiful punkette from Stockport who worked behind the bar at Deville's and later on the Reception at the Hacienda. She would sometimes spend the night at our flat whilst Lee would be upstairs with her friend. We all tried it on with her to no avail. She went on to become a famous Hollywood actress and ended up marrying Val Kilmer, her name was Joanne Whalley.

Most weekends Slim would plonk himself on the floor and skin up for hours. The room would be a cloud of smoke and the music would keep on playing. If anyone missed their bus or decided to stay out, they would knock on and spend the night. It was a great time to be in the City Centre.

Every Sunday we went to the Cyprus Tavern as there would be at least two or three bands on at a cost of 50p entry. We saw so many local bands there such as Frantic Elevators, Biting Tongues, The Fall, John Cooper Clarke, The Things, Crispy Ambulance, Dislocation Dance, The Hamsters, Dr Filth, Private Sector and many more. We got to meet some interesting people at the Cyprus such as Mark the Ted,

Factory Fairy Tales

Frank the Hippy, Don from Dr Filth, Rocking Dave Holmes, Nigel and John Bidet and I have stories to tell about all these people later on. Shan Hira and his twin sister Lita used to go to the Russell, and we had got to know them a little bit from there, but they were regulars at the Cyprus, so we became good friends. They came from Didsbury, and introduced us to four lads that they knew from Fallowfield; Danny Ram, Paul, Jim, and Gavan and we all became great mates. These guys had just started a band called Model Team International (MTI). Mani, Kaiser and some of the North Manchester guys would be there most weeks. It was a great vibe.

I told Shan that I wanted to be in a band, and I was going to be the singer. He told me that he had just bought a drum kit and was learning to play. We decided that we would form a band, but would allow him time to learn basic drumming, before looking for people to join us.

The first gig of the year was Angelic Upstarts and Armed Force at the Poly. I loved the Poly as the sound was great, there were always lots of student girls hanging around and the beer was cheap. During the day Slim and I were in Discount Records when Upstarts singer Mensi walked in and started looking at the wall of single covers. We had a chat with him, and he put us on the guest list. We spent most of the early evening in the Salisbury smoking and drinking so we were well gone by the time we got there. Once inside we found out that Muppet's band was on as well, so happy days. The place was packed, and it was a wild crowd that went crazy when the Upstarts came on. Can't remember much about the gig but they were loud, fast - really good. Mensi clocked us at the bar beforehand and said hello.

In early March, The Clash played two nights at the Apollo supported by Mikey Dread on the 16 Tons Tour. We went both nights and the first thing we noticed upon entering was that they had taken out the front ten rows of seats downstairs. In most punk gigs these seats would get trashed and then used as weapons against the bouncers. Mikey Dread was great and did a mixture of Reggae and Dub interlaced with backing tapes. He went down well on both nights. The lights went down, and the song '16 Tons' started to play over the PA before The Clash exploded onto stage and launched into 'Clash City Rockers' and the crowd went mental. The set was one of the best that I ever saw them play and included 'London Calling', 'Guns of Brixton', 'White Man in Hammersmith Palais', 'Police and Thieves', 'Stay Free', and

Ged Duffy

'Complete Control'. For the encore they came on and played a long version of 'Armagideon Time', 'English Civil War' and finished off with 'Garageland'.

On Tuesday 5 February Lee and I watched Public Image Limited perform 'Poptones' and 'Careering' on *The Old Grey Whistle Test* on BBC2. Lydon sang 'Poptones' whilst wearing a full-length red overcoat and he made such a visual statement. Wobble sat down through both songs. Lydon took the coat off after finishing the song to reveal a yellow suit jacket. Keith Levene played guitar and hit the keys on his synth at the same time. The performance was immense, and afterwards the presenter Ann Nightingale declared it "the most powerful performance I've ever saw on *Whistle Test*". I agreed with her. I think that this is one of the greatest live TV performances from a punk or post-punk band. It was unreal, intense.

Thursday 7 February turned out to be the best night I have ever had watching music. Slim, Tony and I were going to watch Iggy Pop and Psychedelic Furs at the Apollo. We weren't working so had a few beers and jumped on the 192 to the Apollo. The Psychedelic Furs came on and were fucking brilliant. Butler Rep broke a couple of mike stands and they were in great form. They played most of the songs off their debut album and got a great reception from the crowd and came back to do an encore.

Iggy Pop came on and put on a typical Iggy show throwing himself around, stripped to the waist and giving abuse to the crowd. I was really disappointed that he never played 'Lust for Life' or 'The Passenger', but he did play 'Sister Midnight' and 'Five Foot One'. He was great on the night and the audience loved him. As soon as he finished we were out the door, pushed our way thought the dickhead Perry Boys outside and headed towards town trying to flag down a cab taking us to the New Osbourne Club where Joy Division, ACR, and Section 25 were playing. This used to be a roller disco and was now a nightclub. It held about 1,000 and was a bit of a dump. Like the Mayflower it was situated in a rough part of the city. It later became a massive Acid House club called The Thunderdome and the Thunderdome sign which hung above its door is now owned by my mate Colin Gibbins who has collected every Factory catalogue number which it is physically possible to own, and he has each release in every format in which it was released. He has written a book about how he got the

Factory Fairy Tales

collection together called *Manchester Music and M9 Kidz*. Do yourself a favour and get hold of a copy as it's a great read. Anyway, I digress, let's get back to the gig.

Lee had left the Apollo gig early so he could see ACR. We got to the Osbourne, went in, and got a beer from the bar and met up with him. Within a few minutes Joy Division came on and I remember walking out afterwards thinking that they had been brilliant. We stood directly in front of Ian so that we could experience the full power of the band. When they played 'Love Will Tear Us Apart' the hairs on my arms and the back of my neck stood on end. I told Slim and he said that he felt the same. It was a weird moment, but I felt that I was in the presence of something spiritual and was witnessing something special. I remember them playing 'Atrocity Exhibition' and 'Transmission' for the encore. We had a beer with Rob afterwards, and told him that it was a great gig. I told him what had happened to me during 'Love Will Tear Us Apart' and he looked at me and said "Ged, Don't be a fucking dick" - typical Gretton, no bullshit. He passed me his spliff.

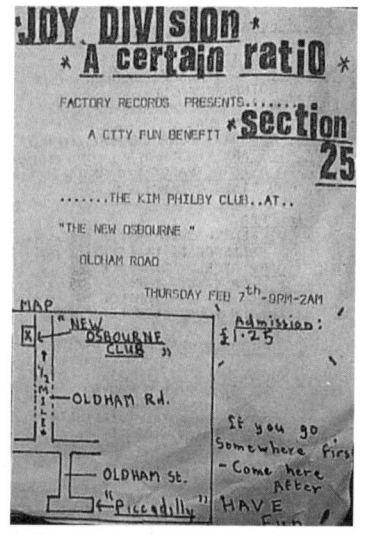

Alan Wise managed to get hold of Deville's again and at the end of the month he had Cabaret Voltaire play there. After the sound check Slim and I sat backstage with the Cabs. They were drinkers and football boys. Top blokes and nothing like the image they portrayed on stage and in the media. I had seen the Cabs a few times, but this was the best gig so far. I think playing in a small, dark club suited them better than the bigger venues like the Russell.

Sometime towards the end of the month Sian from Discount Records rang me at work and told me to drop in after work as she had something for me. When I got there she showed me the Sordide Sentimental recording of 'Atmosphere' and 'Dead Souls' which had been dropped off by Rob Gretton that morning. He had dropped off five copies and had told her to save two for Slim and me. She also

Ged Duffy

told me that Alan Wise had been in and urgently wanted to find us. I walked up to Rafters and called in to Wise Moves office and Alan told me that the Russell was reopening, and he needed Slim and me back for the stage crew.

Psychedelic Furs were the first band to play there – great gig. It was the same door and bar staff at the Russell and it felt like being back home. Another amazing show from the Furs, I never saw them play a bad gig. We had a few beers backstage with them.

A couple of days later it was the turn of UB40 at the Russell. I desperately tried not to like these guys, but they were top blokes (despite the accent) and musically they were incredibly tight and played to a pretty full crowd so Alan was happy. He asked me at this gig if I could do the DJ job when required as well as the stage. I said, "yeah no problem".

Sometime around this period I got my first tattoo. I got a swallow with Raw Power written across it as my favourite song at the time was 'Raw Power' by Iggy and The Stooges. It cost me £7. I felt so rock 'n' roll.

Next gig I can remember is Killing Joke at the Osbourne which was an all-out assault on your senses. This was the tour to promote their single 'Wardance' which was an absolute classic tribal chant. This was my first time seeing Killing Joke and we stood right near the front of the stage. It was like a warzone as people threw themselves into other people and fists were flying and people were getting thrown on stage. It was like this every time I saw Killing Joke over the next few years. Everything about the band clicked. Youth played a heavy bass line on every song, Big Paul was the ultimate powerful tribal drummer, Geordie's guitar sound was unique and then Jaz made noises on his synth and growled his vocals. They were an intense band and made some great music, their first three albums are all classics.

11 April. Joy Division played the Russell with Mini Pops, and Crawling Chaos, this was the last time I ever saw them. I DJed that night and the place was packed with 900 in, but I think that there were a few more than that as Alan was never known to turn anyone away. Due to the trouble at their last gig here, Rob had hired some Hells Angels from Wythenshawe to do the security. These guys were rough and caused a lot of tension with the crowd all evening.

Factory Fairy Tales

Crawling Chaos were absolutely shit. Minny Pops were good – a bit quirky, a bit industrial, a bit pop. They were Dutch and their singer, Wally, was a great laugh. I was loving being the DJ and The Furs, The Bunnymen, Teardrop Explodes, The Banshees, Killing Joke, and The Doors all got a blasting on the night.

Gretton told me that they would be on in 15 minutes, so I lopped on 'Sister Ray' by The Velvet Underground, all 17 minutes of it. Rob immediately turned round and said, "you twat" and I said, "Give us three or four songs in its place". In due course they came on and played the best I ever saw them. Included in the set were 'Shadowplay', 'Love Will Tear Us Apart', and a few songs off the soon to be released *Closer*. They finished with 'She's Lost Control'. Slim and I watched them from the DJ Box at the rear of the stage, so I was stood directly behind Barney and saw first-hand what an amazing drummer Stephen Morris was. I was fascinated by Barney playing the synthesiser on some of the songs and it was weird watching Ian dance from behind as opposed to being in front of him. It was such a brilliant gig and I still recall it at times when I'm listening to *Closer* or *Unknown Pleasures*.

As soon as they went off Gretton walked on stage and grabbed the mike and said "Joy Division will not be coming back on again tonight and if any of you bastards throw a bottle at me there definitely will be hell. I'll come and kick you all in." At this he got bombarded with bottles and ran off the stage with a big grin on his face. They came back on to the sort of cheers that a gladiator might expect, the audience erupted. I looked at Slim and said, "These fuckers have finally made it, they're going to be fucking massive". They played 'Atrocity Exhibition' and sent the crowd wild.

As they went off Rob nodded to me to put a song on as they were not coming on again so since my Velvet Underground album was still on the deck I played 'Pale Blue Eyes'. I'm actually welling up as I write this as they were so fucking good and it's such a shame what happened a couple of weeks later. I've recently read that 'Pale Blue Eyes' was one of Ian's favourite songs. I don't know if that is true or not but if it is then he would have been pleased walking into the dressing room listening to it ringing out in the Russell on the night that Joy Division finally conquered Manchester.

A couple of days later I ended up unemployed again. On the Monday morning I went to work as usual, and was loading the vans of the two sales reps when we got called into the office. The boss told us that the family who owned the company had decided to close the Manchester office and were just going to concentrate on the London one. We were due to close the following Friday.

The sales reps had their van keys taken off them, were given money to get the train home and had a promise of having their expenses paid at the end of the week. The following day a wagon came and started to take away the stock, so my job was to box everything and leave it for the guys to collect. They took some of the stock that day and came back on the Friday to collect the rest. My boss told me that if anything caught my eye as I was packing, I was to put it to one side for me to take home. I walked away with about 60 albums.

I went into Aytoun Street Dole Office and signed on. I'd decided that I was not going to get another job until I had at least given myself the opportunity to become a musician. I stuck to my word until 1986 but at least now, with my new found freedom, I could hang round Discount Records again. Happy Days.

On Wednesday 16 April The Beach Club opened, and it ran every Wednesday until the end of February 1981. The plan was to have two bands on, and show a cult or banned film as well, all for the entrance fee of £1. It was opened and run by Buzzcocks' manager Richard Boon, who ran the New Hormones record label and *City Fun* fanzine.

The Beach Club was in Shudehill, just off Piccadilly, in the City Centre and it was originally a gay bar owned by the famous drag artist Foo Foo Lamarr, and in recent years it had been a strip club called Oozits. Back in those days Shudehill was full of sex shops whose windows were permanently boarded up to stop break ins or being torched by offended citizens. It was a firetrap and you entered via an unsafe flight of stairs, walked past a disgusting toilet, and went up another flight of stairs to the room where they showed the films and had the bar. The room above this was where the bands played and that could hold about 100 people. Over the next ten months I saw a lot of bands and films there, and to be honest I can't remember a lot of the gigs or films because we were normally stoned by the time we got in, but I remember seeing *A Clockwork Orange*, *Birds* and Divine in *Female Trouble*.

The following day Lee received a letter from Styal Prison saying that his mum was getting released early on account of her good behaviour. This meant that I had to get out, so I went back home to sunny Burnage. I'd had a wild five months living in the City Centre and I knew that I wouldn't be in Burnage long. Well, that was my plan but within a couple of months that had changed.

When I moved back home I told Dad that I wasn't looking for a job but that I was earning a little bit from the stage work. He was ok with that, and he said if I needed any extra money I could do the odd day on the building site with him. I did a few days with him on the sites, and it was great fun. He was a real character at work and nothing like he was at home. Every morning on the site we would have steak for breakfast. Dad would clean a spade, put it in the tarmac fire, and fry the steak on the spade. Great memories.

Things had changed a bit in Burnage since I had been away. Some of the lads I used to hang about with were banged up for joy riding, Derek had a job as a labourer and had to be out of his house at 6am so he used to go to bed early, and Karenne had really developed into a pretty girl with a great body. She oozed sexuality and behind her beautiful dark eyes there was a hint of naughtiness. I still didn't try it on with Karenne as I had no intention of staying in Burnage long. Another stupid decision.

Next gig we went to was ACR at the Beach Club with the film *Freaks*. ACR were really good, and this was the first time that I had seen them since Futurama 1 in Leeds. *Freaks* was a film about real life freaks who starred in a circus, and I enjoyed it. It was made in the 1920s and was finally passed for release in the 1980s, a few days afterwards we saw The Cure and The Passions play the Osbourne. The Passions were nothing special and Simon Gallop had joined The Cure on bass. Some of the great pop songs from their debut album were still in the set but they were starting to become the Goth band they ended up.

Magazine and Bauhaus at the Russell promised to be a great gig after the disappointment of the previous two nights of Purple Hearts and Martha and the Muffins, and it lived up to its promise. Bauhaus had released two great singles so far - 'Bela Lugosi's Dead' and 'Dark Entries' and I was looking forward to seeing them live. Bauhaus were brilliant on the night with Pete Murphy prowling the stage, Daniel Ash providing a wall of feedback and the rhythm section of the two brothers providing a steady backbeat. Murphy had his face covered in talcum powder and he looked amazing in the light show they had set

Ged Duffy

up. Sometime during the show he mentioned the word "Baldy" in connection with Howard Devoto and after Bauhaus had blown the audience away and left the stage, Howard refused to come on.

Alan Wise had the quick idea to stage a talent contest with a £20 prize to the winners whilst waiting for Howard to grow a pair. A couple of people got up and sang songs, told jokes and then we decided to do something. Slim picked up a chair and sat on it pretending to be a drummer, Outatunes played air guitar, I played air bass and Muppet decided to mime the words to Buzzcocks 'Boredom'. We were miming along to the song when Muppet switched the mic on and sang "Baldy, Baldy" instead of "Boredom". When we finished people started cheering. We won the £20 but since what we had just done had made Howard Devoto even madder than before, Slim and I had to go backstage and say "sorry" to him.

Magazine eventually came on and they were awesome with McGeoch on guitar, Adamson on bass, and Formula on keyboards. They released three songs from this gig on the 12 inch *Sweetheart Contract* EP a few months later. They played songs off both of their albums, and some new ones that ended up on *The Correct Use Of Soap* which was released a couple of days later. I bought it as soon as it came out and it was as good as the previous two albums.

Next up for us was The Monochrone Set and Ludus. I loved the Monochrone Set's first two singles and they played them both tonight before a small crowd. They were a quirky band and I naturally assumed that they would be a pretentious bunch of art school types with their heads up their arses, I was so wrong as they turned out to be funny normal guys, apart from being cockneys. Ludus were just too arty for me, and I never got them at all. Must have seen them about 20 times supporting people all over Manchester. The singer, Linder, has to be complimented for her artwork for Buzzcocks, so she has a place in Manchester musical history.

A few days later we went to see Section 25 at The Beach Club. This was the first time that I ever listened to Section 25 properly. Every time I had seen them before they had been supporting Joy Division or were just another band on a Factory Night. Tonight they were the main band, and I really enjoyed their atmospheric drone.

9: Fucking Discharge!

On 17 May: Slaughter & The Dogs played the Russell. I think I DJed at this one. After the sound check Slaughter's manager Ray Rossi came over to Slim and I and asked a favour of us. They were going to have something to eat and he wanted to leave his case with us to look after. He told us that on no account were we to open it and look inside. We said we wouldn't. They left. We looked inside... well it's human nature isn't it. There must have been about £30,000 in it which was obviously the money earned by the band during the tour to date although this is a guess as we didn't count it. This suddenly gave Slim and I a dilemma. The Rossi's were a tough family from Wythenshawe, and they would surely find us if we took off with the cash. Nevertheless we thought about disappearing to London to stay with our mates in a squat on the Fulham Road and having a great time for a few weeks. Then we discussed fucking off to Dublin and setting ourselves up as promoters but we didn't know anyone over there. Or perhaps a drug-binge tour of Europe and see where we end up? That sounded like a good plan...

All too quickly Ray returned and we just said "Oh hello Mr Rossi your case is over here. No, we never looked in it."

With our problem now resolved we watched support band Victim. They were okay and I saw them a few times round town and they were always a decent band who didn't make it. Slaughter came on with Ed Banger on vocals as Wayne Barrett had left them again. They weren't as good as the other times I had seen them. They could have been as big as The Clash, but they just never seized the opportunity, Mick Rossi was an amazing guitarist and deserved to be a star.

The first I heard of what happened was two days later. I tuned into the John Peel Show as usual and he announced that Ian Curtis had died the day before. It hadn't been in the papers or on Granada TV (as per the legend) - it was a massive shock. I had just seen him and his mates conquer Manchester a couple of weeks earlier. The first thing that came to mind was, why? He had a brilliant album waiting to be released which would have catapulted Joy Division up to the next level. 'Love will Tear Us Apart' was about to be released and it was the perfect pop song. The world was at his fingertips, but he had his own reasons for doing what he did. As a fan I just wish he had sought help. I had got to know Ian a bit when he worked at Rare Records, and he seemed a normal lad full of life and if you had told me then that he would become a worldwide icon and that Joy Division would be still selling thousands of records a year some 40 years later, I'd have had you admitted into Prestwich Mental Hospital.

Don't forget that only a couple of months earlier Factory had finally sold out of the first pressing of 10,000 copies of *Unknown Pleasures* and had just ordered a second pressing. When I look back on it there were at least another ten gigs of Joy Division that I could have gone to, but I just couldn't be arsed. All these gigs were played in Greater Manchester and all just a bus ride away. I regret this decision nowadays.

Joy Division were a great live band and I'm happy to say that I was lucky enough to have seen them several times whereas there are thousands of their fans all round the world who never got the chance to see them once and I guess that's why Hooky's doing so well with his band nowadays.

Our next gig was Teardrop Explodes at the Russell. It was a strange night with the news of Ian still circulating and a sense of loss hung over proceedings. Teardrops were great as usual. Pop songs sung with passion and played well. Bernie was over from Liverpool, so we had a laugh with him. The following day we went to see Adam and The Ants at the Poly. This was the new look Ants with two drummers providing the Burundi beat. They came on and started with an immensely powerful version of 'Physical' which is my favourite Ants song of all time. They then played their new single 'King of the Wild Frontier', 'Ants Invasion', 'Kick', 'Press Darlings' and 'Cartrouble'. The first encore was 'Zerox', and the second encore was 'A.N.T.S.'. They came back on again for a third encore 'Plastic Surgery'. What a brilliant gig; the lights, the two drummers, Marco on guitar and of course Mr Ant himself - just what we needed to get over the gloom and depression floating round the city over the last few days.

I was looking forward to seeing Gary Glitter and Victim at the Russell. I was so disappointed when Gary Glitter turned up with a backing band and not the Glitter Band, he only had one drummer. The songs didn't have any power to them without the two drummers.

Factory Fairy Tales

It was like watching a cabaret act and we never got the chance to speak to him.

31 May is a night etched into the history of the Russell Club as this was the night that got the place shut down for good. UK Subs and Discharge were on the bill. Discharge turned up with two coaches of fans from Stoke to see them. They were all mohawks and proper unwashed, glue-sniffing bastards. They were intent on taking over the club. I was the DJ that night and the only records I had bought with me were punk ones like The Damned, Pistols, Clash, Buzzcocks, Upstarts, Sham 69, 999, Lurkers, Slaughter, Crass and bands like that. Before the bands came on there were scuffles on the dance floor and the atmosphere was getting bad.

Discharge came on and the Stoke mob went absolutely mental down in front of the stage and were having their own mini battle between themselves hitting and kicking each other. Then they started branching out into the rest of the audience who responded and it just kicked off big time. Ozzie was in the middle whacking as many Stoke heads as he could with his chain. Slim and I were smacking every mohawk we saw. There was a full scale wild west bar room brawl going on at the front. It was like being back in Leeds with United again with everyone involved in the brawl. There was no hiding place.

Discharge went off and the sides retreated to opposite sides of the hall, over turned all the tables to create a large No Man's Land between them and a standoff developed. Bottles and glasses were thrown from either side. I went behind the DJ booth and started playing music. Alan Wise begged me to tone it down the music but I didn't have anything else to play apart from punk.

Next thing I remember was seeing Ozzie starting the charge on his own. He went and stood in the No Man's land between the two sides and was challenging the Stoke lot to fight. This big mohawk stood up and came forward to face up to Ozzie. Ozzie just tore into him and absolutely fucking leathered him. The Stoke lot charged at our lot to save their guy and it went off again big time. This time I stopped the music and Slim and I jumped into the middle of it all with Tex the bouncer trying to stop it all. It was a full scale brawl again with fists and weapons flying. It was carnage.

A few minutes later, about 20 big Rastas turned up and came in to keep the peace. Tex had rang the Reno, a Rasta drinking club in

Ged Duffy

nearby Moss Side and asked them to send some of their guys down. These guys steamed into the Stoke mohawks and after a while the fighting stopped. They stayed there and kept the Stoke lot apart from the Mancs.

UK Subs came on and despite all the stuff they were saying in the dressing room about hitting anyone who came near them with their guitars, they played a good set and managed not to get the crowd worked up any more than they were already. When the gig finished there were police vans parked outside and they escorted the Stoke mob back onto their coaches and away from Hulme. It had been the wildest night I had ever seen at a gig, and it was a total warzone, but it was to have major consequences. There was broken glass all over the floor and all the tables and chairs had been broken and used as weapons.

I had seen lots of mass brawls at gigs before, but this was the worst that I had ever seen. There were lots of people with cut heads especially on the Stoke side and I would assume Ozzie's chain had inflicted a lot of that.

When we got to the Russell the next night Alan Wise told us that the owners were stopping the gigs so the next three gigs booked were going to be the last, as they couldn't have the kind of trouble that had happened at the UK Subs gig happen again or they would definitely lose their license. Bad Manners played and were shite. They were followed the next evening by Toyah. The crowd weren't getting into her, so she threatened to strip if they didn't start dancing. They didn't and she didn't. Pity cos she had great tits. The Beat were the final band to play the Russell to a large crowd but mostly mods, Rude Boys, and a few Skins. The Beat were fucking good on the night. What a tight band and Ranking Roger was a great laugh during the afternoon. None of our normal crew turned up and it was a sad night. I never went in the Russell again after this. I never got to say goodbye to our crew as some of them were never seen at gigs again or in Town, so it was the end of an era.

Alan Wise rang me at home to tell me that he had secured Rafters for his gigs and that Slim and I were needed and the first gig was on 10 July, and it was Cabaret Voltaire. It was great to be back in Rafters and it was nice to see our old friends from The Cabs. Some of the old Russell crew came to Rafters: Mani, Kaiser and the North Manchester lot, Shan, Lita, Derek, Tony and Lee. Once again we had a great scene

Factory Fairy Tales

going at this place.

27 June 'Love will Tear Us Apart' by Joy Division (FAC 23) was released. I took it round to Tony's house and we sat and listened to it nonstop for about 2 hours. It was amazing. It had two versions of 'Love Will Tear Us Apart' and another song called 'These Days'. I honestly thought that it was the best single that I had ever bought in my life. The synthesiser, bass and drums were so perfect together. We couldn't get the tune out of our heads for weeks and even today, whenever I hear it on the radio, I have to stop what I'm doing and listen to it. It gives me the same joy as 'Laid' by James or 'Heroes' by Bowie.

In early July Dexy's Midnight Runners released their debut album *Searching for the Young Soul Rebels*. This was a brilliant album with the attitude of punk mixed with an unbelievable brass section. 'Geno' and 'Burn It Down' were two good singles. This was followed on 14 July with the shock news that Malcolm Owen from The Ruts had died. The Ruts were a fucking great band and their debut album *The Crack* was great. It was a drug overdose in the end that killed him. What a waste of life that was.

On 18 July *Closer* by Joy Division (FAC 25) and *Crocodiles* by Echo and The Bunnymen both came out. I was in Discount Records to buy them both. Sian played them for me in the shop, so I could hear them as I wouldn't have time to hear them when I got home. She also gave me a copy of *Komakino* (FAC 28) which was a free Flexi Disc by Joy Division. These two albums have never faded to me, and I play both of them on a regular basis even now some 40 years later. Good music never dies.

The reason that I wouldn't have time to play them when I got home was because Slim and I were due at Rafters for the visit of Echo and The Bunnymen. Bernie was over again. I loved The Bunnymen, and I got to know them even more when they started showing up at New Order gigs as fans. The great thing about Rafters as opposed to The Russell was that it was only a five minute walk to Piccadilly Gardens to catch the bus. We usually stopped off en route at Angels and ordered a three piece chicken and chips.

Wednesday 30 July turned out to be a Red Letter Day in Manchester musical history as ACR and The Names were supposed to play the Beach Club and the film *Metropolis*. Rob Gretton phoned me the previous evening to tell me that the three remaining members of Joy Division planned to play a short set and he wanted me there to see them. He said that he was calling a few select people to witness the event.

We were at the bar having a beer when Rob looked over, nodded and pointed upstairs. We went up and Bernard introduced themselves as "Our mates couldn't make it. We're the only surviving members of crawling chaos" and started to play. The room was about a quarter full and during the seven song set it slowly filled up as word spread downstairs. All three of the band sang at some point in the set and there were long instrumental passages. They used a backing tape with a synth and drum machine on it. No one knew any of the songs, but we all realized that they had witnessed history in the making that night. There were probably about 90 people there that night as the concert room in the Beach Club could only hold 100. We sat around later, after watching the film, and discussed it all with Rob. He was so pleased that they had done it.

July finished with The Fall at Rafters. They were brilliant, playing great songs like 'Fiery Jack' and 'Totally Wired', they were a great live band, and this was before they got the second drummer. Great gig. I was so much in love with The Fall around this time, they were so unique.

One day, as I was walking past Hunt's Motorbike shop, I saw a 1965 light blue and white Lambretta Li150 scooter for £60 and for some unknown reason I went in and bought it. I was not a mod, not interested in any of that shit but I liked the style of the Mods with their scooters. I had it for a couple of weeks and one day I made the rookie mistake of banking it on a bend which resulted in me sliding into Cringle Fields and the scooter sliding across the road and into the gates of the factory opposite. I rode it home and sold it for £60 to my mate Colin the Mod. I should have put it in Dad's garage and left it. It would be worth at least £6,500 now. Another bad decision!

10. Let's start a band

Sometime in July we finally decided to try and get a band together. Shan was feeling more confident about his drumming, and we had found a bass player called Nigel who Shan knew from the Cyprus Tavern – he was playing in a couple of bands that played there regularly and we were just another one on his list. Tony was going to play guitar as he knew a couple of chords and I was going to sing. Shan came from a well-off family as his father was a surgeon and also had a private practice which he ran from home. He lived in Didsbury and we were going to rehearse in their house which was later featured in the 'Soft Babies' video. The house was so big that we used to rehearse in the attic and Shan's parents could watch TV downstairs without us disturbing them.

The first rehearsal arrived and it soon became very apparent that I couldn't sing. They were jamming and I couldn't put anything to the music that would work with it. I agreed to write some lyrics and see what happened. The second rehearsal came and I hadn't written any proper lyrics. I just couldn't come up with anything that didn't include the line "I just wanna die" or "I just wanna kill". Ha, you could write a whole report on the workings of my mind just by reading those two lines.

During our stage crew work we had acquired a bit of equipment, most of it by foul means, effect pedals such as flange, chorus and distortion. We had a band meeting and decided that Tony would have a go at singing, and I would have a go at playing guitar. Tony would play a few chords on his guitar, and I would play the other guitar through a couple of effect pedals, and just make a weird noise over the song. The next couple of rehearsals went well and we soon had a couple of songs written 'Catch me in Confusion' and 'A Room in a Tower'. Nigel was a bit of a funky bass player and since he was the only person in the band that could actually play he held it all together. Shan would struggle at times to keep the beat and I didn't have a fucking clue what I was doing apart from making a noise!

On the Stockholm Monsters web site there is a story about how the name came from Bowie's 'Scary Monsters' and Ultravox's 'Vienna'. I don't recall it happening like that. This is my version: we

Ged Duffy

were sitting round the dinner table in Shan's kitchen when Nigel read an article from the *Manchester Evening News*. It was about a monstrous fungus that had grown on the walls of a council flat, and the fumes from it killed the elderly lady who lived there. So we came with Monstrous Fungus as the name. A couple of days later Tony came up with Stockholm, so we became Stockholm Monstrous Fungus. Then this got shortened to Stockholm Monsters.

Shan and his twin sister Lita introduced us to speed. Slim and I soon started getting speed off a couple of dealers we knew, and we would have a line or two when we were working at the clubs doing the stage. Speed would be a major part of our life for the next few years. Quickly we had written a third song called 'We are Nation', which was a primal type of song, which had a warriors chant playing as part of the backing. It was now time to get a demo done so we could hear what we sounded like.

Frank the Hippy was a living legend around Didsbury in those days. He was a proper stoner, who lived in a flat off Burton Road. Frank had a four-track studio set up in one of the rooms in his flat and he made some money from doing demos for bands which helped him buy drugs. Frank would bounce the tracks together to make it up to eight track. Many famous Manchester bands recorded their first ever demos at Frank's. He had shelves lined up with these cassettes and the names that jumped out were Simply Red, MTl, and The Fall. So we went to Frank's and recorded three songs in his studio. A couple of days later Nigel decided to leave. Was it a coincidence?

By now I was buying clothes from numerous charity shops round Burnage, Didsbury, Fallowfield, Ladybarn, and Withington. I would get collarless Granddad shirts, Aran jumpers, shirts, and fifties suit pants. I was listening to The Doors and Jim Morrison was my hero, and I was so made up when I got a sheepskin jacket for £1.50, which was like the one he wore on the inside cover of *Morrison Hotel*. Shan later wore this on the 'Soft Babies' video. I was still wearing my Dr Martens, but my motorbike leather jacket got put away for a couple of years.

On 6th August Minny Pops played the Beach Club. The Film was *Pink Flamingos*, and I was looking forward to seeing it as it was banned everywhere. It was written by John Waters and starred Drag Queen Divine, who played a criminal called Babs Johnson. Babs claimed to be "the filthiest person in the world", and she lived in a trailer with her mum "The Egg Queen" and her son Crackers. The characters engage in several crude and sick activities and the only thing missing from the film is that The Cramps would have written the perfect soundtrack to accompany it. Get to see it if you can. It's great – a cult classic.

The Monsters and I had now decided that I was going to the bass player. It had only four strings, so it was bound to be easier to learn. We still hadn't found a guitarist but that would change soon. There was a music shop in Cheadle, so I went there to buy a bass and an amp. I had money saved up from when I was working. I bought a Fender Musicmaster bass and a H/H bass combo amp.

We had started to go into the United Road Paddock this season as it offered a better view of the pitch with it being along the side as opposed to being behind the goal like the Stretford End. It cost a few pence more at £1.20 so it didn't break the bank. We discovered that Big Stuart was a regular in that section so we would go together to the games. We didn't bother with away games anymore. The Perry Boys had taken over football by this point and there would be gangs of 300 or 400 on each side running at each other and fighting. They all dressed the same, had the same flick haircuts so how the fuck did they know that the person they were punching was one of the opposition or one of their own?

They also had their own secret language which was a form of rhyming slang with a Manc or Scouse slant on it, so you never knew what the person you were walking next to was saying so we decided to bin it off. The money saved could be spent on beer, blow or speed. We considered this a better use of our resources.

20 August: Bauhaus play Rafters with a film as support. Bauhaus were amazing again and they suited a small venue. They played 'Bela Lugosi's Dead' as the encore. We spent some time talking to them and they were cool guys. Having a film play as the support was pretentious but at least it meant that Slim and I had less gear to hump around.

Sometime in August MTI played at the Cyprus Tavern. This was their second gig under this name as I think they had played a gig in their local scout hut in front of their mates. It was great seeing your mates up on stage. It gave a big kick up the arse to us to do likewise. Musically I liked Jim's melodic bass playing, Gavin's jerky drum patterns and Gibba's folky guitar. Over the next year or so, I

Ged Duffy

must have seen MTI play at least 30 times at the Cyprus Tavern. They supported everyone from Orange Juice, Aztec Camera, The Fall, The Passage, Private Sector, and The Freshies. The Fall put bands on every Thursday at the Cyprus Tavern and MTI were the resident support act. They were always pissed when they played and the main problem they had was that lead singer Danny had a tendency to jump in the crowd and attack anyone who shouted anything dismissive towards him or the band. I witnessed many of these attacks and was involved in the aftermath of several. Some of these stage exits ended in full scale brawls.

I bumped into June one day on Market Street. She had just finished work and she looked great in her tight blouse, short skirt and stockings. We went for a pint in Seftons which was built on the side of the Arndale Centre. This became our pub over the next few years, and we had many a drink in there watching the video jukebox and playing table top Space Invaders. She told me that she was now living in a bedsit in Didsbury, and I started to see her after rehearsals and stayed there on a few occasions.

2 September: Joy Division release 'Atmosphere' and an extended, remixed version of 'She's Lost Control' on (FACUS2/UK). It was a 12 inch single with a beautiful sleeve. I got my copy from Discount Records and went round to Tony's to play it. This is Joy Division's best song in my opinion – an amazing record. 'She's Lost Control' was so different from the version on *Unknown Pleasures*. This song was danceable, had a disco feel to it and had an extra verse. I absolutely loved it. 'Atmosphere' was such a piece of beauty and what a beautiful song with the most perfect synthesiser pattern that I have ever heard on a song. Listen to Hooky's bass-line on it as it is probably the best bassline he has ever written, as it weaves in and out with the synthesiser. Steve's drumming is so right for the song and Ian's vocal just topped it off.

11. A close encounter with the Angels

Nigel Baguley picked Slim and me up early on the Saturday morning and drove us to Leeds. When we got there, we parked in the car park next to an old 52-seater coach. Nigel pointed at it and said, "that's where you're sleeping tonight". Nigel took us into the hall, and we met the rest of our crew who were four local guys who worked for John Keenan at the Fan Club.

The previous Futurama Festival had little or no security and there had been a lot of fights. Lee had been savagely beaten up and we had been involved in a few scuffles as well. This year they were taking no chances and had hired local Hells Angels to provide on stage and in-house security. You didn't want to fuck with these guys and gals, but that story comes later.

The stage was split into two separate stages separated by a curtain. Behind the hall there was a compound of portacabins erected to act as dressing rooms for the bands and there were a few portable toilets, so we wouldn't have to use the horrific bogs in the hall.

As we got in Siouxsie &The Banshees were sound checking, so we sat down on the edge of the stage and watched them run through a few songs. As soon as they finished our work began. Before they left the stage I got to say hello to John McGeoch and told him that I loved his work with Magazine. He gave me a hug and said thanks. He was a top bloke. We jumped up on stage and helped the Banshees road crew push all their gear to the back of the stage and pulled the curtain back across the middle.

Our role would be to load in a bands gear up the ramp and onto one side of the stage which would be in semi darkness. This would be done as a band was playing on the other side. As soon as their road crew had set everything up, we would move the flight cases off to a designated area which was guarded by a couple of angels. When they had finished their set we would move their flight cases up onto the stage. Whilst they were breaking down their gear we would unload the next band and move their stuff to the side of the stage. Hopefully by this time the road crew would have done their job and we would take their gear off stage and into their van and away they would go.

As one band finished on side of the stage, there would be a break

Ged Duffy

FUTURAMA 2
Queens Hall — Leeds 1980

Under the circumstances it's difficult to inform you of an accurate time for the appearance of any one band — but here's the running order. Working from 12 o'clock (noon):—

SATURDAY 13th SEPT.
... OR WAS HE PUSHED?
EATEN ALIVE BY INSECTS
SOFT CELL
the DISTRIBUTORS
the B*o*B*o*BoS
Y?
the MIRROR BOYS
MUSIC FOR PLEASURE
Acrobats of Desire
ALTERED IMAGES
GUY JACKSON
I'm so Hollow
MODERN ENGLISH
Clock DVA
Blah Blah Blah
WASTED YOUTH
U2
ECHO and the Bunnymen
THE LEAGUE OF GENTLEMEN
(BARRY ANDREWS–ROBERT FRIPP)
SARAH LEE – Johnny Toobad
and
Siouxsie and the Banshees

SUNDAY 14th SEPT.
HOUSEHOLD NAME
Naked Lunch
artery
VICE VERSA
BOOTS FOR DANCING
THE flowers
FRANTIC ELEVATORS
DESPERATE BICYCLES
NOT SENSIBLES
BRIAN BRAIN
Classix Nouveaux
TRIBESMAN
BLURT
Durutti Column
the SOFT BOYS
YOUNG MARBLE GIANTS
4"62"
HAZEL O'CONNOR'S
MEGAHYPE
THE PSYCHEDELIC FURS
ATHLETICO SPIZZ 80
GARY GLITTER

Take into consideration that the earlier groups will play for approximately 30mins while the later groups will play for about 45 minutes to an hour—there may be one or two additions!
Thank you for attending this year—let's hope there's room for another one next year!
P.S. ALL THIS IS BEING IMMORTALISED ON FILM— WATCH THE PRESS FOR FURTHER DETAILS!

of about ten minutes before the band on the other stage would start to play. We ran our bit like clockwork, and we missed maybe only the first five or ten minutes of each act, but we heard them. We would stand at the opposite side of the stage to the curtain, so we were ready to move without having to cross the stage.

Doors opened at noon and the first band was due on at 12.30pm. The first two bands, Or Was He Pushed, and Eaten Alive By Insects, were already parked up outside so we had both bands set up before the doors opened. The third band turned up at noon and they only had one amp, a tape deck and a synthesiser and they didn't need any help off us at all, so we were off to a great start. I paid little attention to the first two bands who were both local but once we had sorted out the fourth band's stage, I watched the third band who were a duo from Leeds called Soft Cell. This was their first-ever gig and I was interested in them because the singer looked different, and he could really sing. They went down well with the locals, and I put their name in my memory bank as someone to look out for. They did a cover of the Black Sabbath song 'Paranoid' and it sounded amazing. The next couple of bands passed me by until Y came on. They announced that they were no longer called Y but were now called Dance Society. The singer had his face covered and after a couple of songs he revealed his face to show that he was a vampire. The crowd fell about laughing, so much for making an impression. They were followed by Mirror Boys, Music For Pleasure and Acrobats of Desire before a girl from Glasgow stole the show…

Altered Images were the first of the early bands to get a great response from the crowd. I think Claire Grogan captured the hearts of the crowd with her shy girl demeanour and her good looks. I think that every male in the audience wanted to take her home with them. The songs they played were very early Banshee-like songs, as opposed to the pop they became famous for. Songs that stood out were 'Dead Pop Stars' and also their version of the T Rex song 'Jeepster'. Next up was Guy Jackson, a solo artist who spent most of his set trying to avoid a stream of beer cans directed at him! I'm so Hollow were a Sheffield band, and they had a bit of a Fall vibe going on. I liked them. Modern English were good as well. They sounded a bit like Joy Division, and I had heard them already on John Peel. Clock DVA were another band from Sheffield who were mates with Cabaret Voltaire that played industrial music. Blah Blah Blah came on dressed in Elizabethan costume. Enough said, there's no need to see this lot - "Slim, skin up mate". For these type of bands we stayed backstage and had a spliff or another line of speed or a can of Red Stripe or all three.

Next on were Wasted Youth, and I wanted to see these guys as I had heard them a few times on John Peel. We got Blah Blah Blah packed up and gone quickly but then we went to unload U2. They had a fucking drum riser that had to be put together on stage and also a massive backdrop. It took about eight of us to put their backdrop up and as a result I only got to see the last song of Wasted Youth. U2 were the first band to have a 45 minute time slot and they made use of it. It's become fashionable to hate them nowadays but early U2 were amazing live. They played most of the songs off their album *Boy* as well as '11 O'clock Tick Tock'. They went down well, and I only missed the first song. I was stood on The Edge's side of the stage, he's a great guitarist.

There was a gap of about 20 minutes until Echo and The Bunnymen came on and I can tell you that the U2 backdrop came down a lot quicker than it went up. We got their gear out quickly and then we set up Robert Fripp. We got to the side of the stage just as the Bunnymen were coming on. I had a tap on my shoulder, and it was our mate Bernie who had come over with the band. The Bunnymen were brilliant this evening and the contrast between Bono and Ian McCulloch was remarkable. Bono tried every rock front man trick in the book to make himself look cool. McCulloch just messed up his hair, drank a can of beer and smoked a roll-up and that was enough! They played most of the *Crocodiles* album and *Read it in Books* as well.

Robert Fripp's League of Gentleman. The atmosphere in the hall was so up and then the king of Prog Rock comes on and kills it dead. We had another spliff and a beer. We got his gear out the door in record time, pulled the Banshees back-line forward, and decided to go out in the hall to watch them. The Banshees came on about 1.30am and they were brilliant. Siouxsie came on wearing a white leather jacket with tassels and a cowboy hat. She was the perfect cowgal. They played 'Happy House', 'Christine', 'Playground Twist', 'Switch', and 'Helter Skelter'. Siouxsie played a second guitar on a couple of the songs. They announced a new song called 'Voodoo Dolly' and this was amazing. John McGeoch's guitar playing was out of this world.

We helped take the gear out to the Banshees truck and then we went outside to get on our coach. As far as we were concerned we were going to be the only ones on the coach but when we got on we found the Hells Angels had taken over the back section of the bus. We sat at the front and Slim skinned up and we had a couple of beers which we had taken from the stage with us. The leader of the angels asked us to come down the back and sit with them. We didn't want to join them, but we felt that they would have taken it as an insult if we didn't so reluctantly we did.

There was about 15 guys and 6 girls. The leader said, "we've got blow, speed and beer so join us". He then pointed out three of the girls and told us that they were "old ladies", and they couldn't be touched but if we wanted to have a good time with any of the others then they wouldn't say no. He said, "They will do anything you want, so enjoy yourselves". One of the girls was beautiful, with long black hair, a great body and when she passed me to go to the toilet, her ass looked great in leather pants. Slim and I decided that we were not going to go anywhere near any of these girls as we didn't know where they'd been. Well, we did, and that was why we didn't. During the night a couple of the angels had some fun with her.

We stayed up all night drinking, smoking, and doing speed and we

Factory Fairy Tales

were well racing by the time we had to be inside the venue around 10am. It had been a great night, and we had built up a great rapport with the angels which carried on through the second day. Before I went inside the hall, I went to the toilet and when I came out the beautiful angel girl came over to me and asked if I wanted a blow-job. I explained that I would love to have one, but I was speeding that much there would probably be no movement down below. She smiled and told me to find her if anything changed during the day. I didn't. I knew where her lips had been, and they were not getting on me.

The second day started with the Glitter Band sound checking minus Gary. One of their road crew sang instead. As soon as they were done we pushed their back line to the back of the stage and loaded in the first two bands. First up were Household Name, another local rock band that sounded okay. Then Naked Lunch, another electronic band - not too bad on the ears. Artery from Sheffield - new wave rock - not bad. Verse Versa from Sheffield - electronic pop, later became ABC and M People. Boots for Dancing - bit like the Gang of Four. The Flowers - now I'd heard these guys on John Peel, they came from Scotland and were on Fast Records - fractured rock, loved them. Frantic Elevators with our mate Mick Hucknall on vocals, brilliant set, went down well with the crowd. Desperate Bicycles - punk band with a giant singer, really good. Not Sensibles - from Burnley. A punk band who played a great set, had the audience up dancing. Brian Brain - punk band from London featuring Martin Atkins out of PIL.

Everything was going like clockwork for us guys doing the stage. We had it off to a tee now and we were setting up and breaking down in a matter of minutes until the knobheads Classix Nouveaux came on and set off some smoke bombs which filled the stage and hall with smoke. This made it so hard for us to break down and set up the adjoining stage because we could see fuck all. After a while it cleared, and we got the stage sorted. Classix Nouveaux were shite, but their laser show was good. Tribesman came on, they were a Reggae band. They were good and gave a great vibe. We went backstage and had a spliff. Well, when in Rome and all that. Next up were Blurt followed by Durutti Column, so we stayed backstage. The Soft Boys came on and they were a basic rock band in the mould of the Stones, and they went down well after the previous two bands. Next up was Young Marble Giants, they were too quiet and soft for this type of gig, then 4 B 2 – a punk band from London featuring John Lydon's brother

Jimmy, they went down well with the crowd. Hazel O'Connor was next up. She was in all of the music magazines around this time as the film *Breaking Glass* was just about to be released and she was the main character in the film. She did a lot of her robot dancing during her set. She went down okay and a few months later she would have a massive hit with the song 'Will You?' which I think is a great song with some beautiful saxophone on it.

It was past midnight when Psychedelic Furs came on. To me, they should have been the headline act. They put on the best show of all of the bands that were on that day. They started with 'Soap Commercial', 'Susan's Strange', 'Dumb Waiters', and then also played 'Sister Europe', 'Pulse' and finished with 'We Love You'. Athletico Spizz 80 were next up. Highlight of their set was 'Soldier, Soldier' and the classic 'Where's Captain Kirk?'. We got the stage cleared and set up for Gary Glitter and went inside the hall to see him. He put on a great show and had the crowd singing along with him. To be honest the whole set was made up of hits.

After two solid days of seeing some great bands, some experimental bands, and some absolutely shite bands, Gary Glitter was a triumphant, fun act to finish it all with some good time, foot stomping rock 'n' roll. We went back on stage and cleared everything up. We dismantled the main PA and loaded everything up into the wagons and it was around 5am when we had finished. The second day had been amazing as we kept getting given spliffs, beer and speed from the angels. Maybe I should have taken up the angel girl's offer, she was stunning. When I think about it now, what's the worst that could have happened, catch a dose and go to Liverpool Street Clinic and take some antibiotics for a couple of weeks.

12. Monsters' first gigs

We went to the Cyprus Tavern the following Sunday and Shan told us that he had someone in mind to become our guitarist. His name was John Bidet, Tony and I had some major concerns because although he was an amazing guitarist, he played in several bands at the same time, and since we were basically all beginners and pretty shit, how would he cope with our lack of ability? For me the most important aspect was that his image was totally wrong, he was never going to fit in with us lot. He would wear green trousers, a yellow shirt with a frilly collar, a red dicky bow and think he looked cool! He looked like Coco the fucking Clown. His hair was based on *The Hair Bear Bunch* - Google it and you will see what I mean.

Anyway, we decided to give him a go. Since he sometimes sang lead vocals or backing vocals in his other bands, he had a proper mike, and some quality equipment which we could make use of.

Towards the end of the month Bauhaus played Rafters. Another great gig by these guys. Rafters was full but a lot of people were unhappy that they didn't play 'Bela Lugosi's Dead'. This was followed by Revillos and Fast Cars at Rafters - a fun night and the Revillos were as quirky as the Rezillos had been – a decent crowd but not full.

We were hanging round Didsbury a lot with the lads from MTI and Dr Filth, and this is where I met a drummer called Guy Ainsworth. He had played on the Dr Filth single 'Slaughterhouse'. Don, the singer from Dr Filth, had a shaved head, always wore John Lennon type sun glasses and had a blue goatee. He worked as a porter in Withington Hospital and one of the lines in the song was "I work in the slaughterhouse". Don used to say "I wheel them in alive and then wheel them out dead. It's a legalized slaughterhouse". Most of these guys would end up in the attic at Shan's house and hang out with us smoking and doing speed. One day someone turned up with some acid tabs and we all dropped one. Shan's parents were away for a couple of days, so we were going to stay overnight.

My first trip was really mellow, and I was smiling and laughing about absolute nonsense for about ten hours. Slim on the other hand had a few issues. Shan got hold of Slim's left hand and counted his fingers from ten back to six. He then counted the fingers on Slim's right hand from one to five. He asked Slim to add the five and six together and tell him how many fingers he had. Slim said eleven and his face dropped. Slim spent the next ten hours trying to understand where he had got the extra finger from. For most of the next day, I would see shapes and the area around my line of vision was still not 100% right. I enjoyed the experience and was already looking forward to doing it again.

It seemed that every week in Didsbury there would be a student party, usually in a house in Rathen Road, Westholme Road, or Old Broadway (where Tony Wilson lived), which were all roads off Wilmslow Road. These parties would be full of students who always had plenty of dope, booze and speed. There were always loads of girls at these parties and we would stagger home to Burnage in the early hours of the morning, having had a good time. Some of the girls were very friendly indeed.

The beginning of October saw The Fall and MTI play at the Poly. We met the lads from MTI and had a beer with them before they played a great set, in front of a responsive crowd. Danny was well behaved and stayed on the stage for the entire gig. They had four songs that stood out from the rest and all four went onto become James songs but with different lyrics. They were: 'Just Hip', 'If Things were Perfect', 'What's the World', and 'Withdrawn'. The Fall came on, and I have to say, they were getting better every time I saw them. For the next two years or so The Fall were at their peak.

Two days after witnessing The Fall we were back to the Poly to see Dead Kennedys. A wild night – at this time a typical punk was wearing studs and sporting a mohawk like the Discharge mob from the Russell, but these guys looked nothing like punks but that all changed when they started playing. Singer Jello Biafra, showed the crowd how to stage dive. It had never been done in this country before. They played both of their singles 'California über alles', and 'Holiday in Cambodia'. They were one of the best punk bands ever and their album *Fresh Fruit for Rotting Vegetables* was a classic when released.

Slim and I made our third visit to the Poly in the space of 10 days to see U2. We spent the day hanging round Discount Records and sometime during the afternoon Bono and The Edge walked in. They recognised Slim from both the Deville's gig with The Bunnymen, and from Futurama. We had a moan at them about missing Wasted Youth due to the time it took putting up their backdrop. They took our names and put us on the guest list. The Poly was packed and U2 were absolutely amazing. This was the *Boy* Tour, and they had a new backdrop behind them this time and they played the same set as at Futurama. We hung around afterwards and went backstage to talk to them.

In early October, Teardrop Explodes' debut album *Kilimanjaro* was released, and I got it from Discount Records. This was a good debut as it contained some great songs like 'Sleeping Gas', 'Treason', 'Poppies in The Field', 'Bouncing Babies' and 'Reward'. Julian Cope had a great voice and the mix of bass, guitar and keyboards really suited them. Sometime in October Killing Joke played at the Poly. I know that they started off with 'Pssyche' which must be one of the best B sides ever. They played 'Wardance' and 'Change' to a full house. Great gig, wild night. Just your typical Killing Joke gig.

19 October: Crass and the Poison Girls at the Funhouse. The scum of the earth turned out in their droves at the Funhouse to see Crass. They were determined to get pissed and destroy as Johnny Rotten had instructed them to in 'Anarchy in the UK'. By the end of the night the toilets had been trashed and were under three feet of water. People were standing on the steps pissing into the dark. I saw a few pissed-up punks not notice the steps and end up floating in the water. When Crass came on the crowd invaded the stage and kept jumping on and off for the whole gig. The spit was flying nonstop, and I don't think I ever saw as much spitting as I did that night. Fights were breaking out all over the place and we smacked several people for spitting and throwing beer near us. Bottles were getting thrown at the stage and amongst the audience.

The singer, Steve Ignorant, was completely covered in spit and green blobs of it were all over his face, hanging from his chin and I saw several direct hits in his mouth as he was singing. The place was totally trashed and thinking about it now this was the last gig ever at this venue. It was like a fucking war zone. Once outside there was a lot of fighting round Gorton with Perry Boys. It was a crazy night. Slim, Derek and I were fighting most of the way back to Levenshulme as we kept running into small groups of them, and we would fight or garden hop depending on how many there were.

The following day U2 released their album *Boy* - this is a brilliant

Ged Duffy

debut album with no bad songs on it. 'I Will Follow', 'A Day Without Me', and 'An Cat Dubh' are the stand-out tracks. This was the start of my love affair with U2. I already had their great debut UK single '11 o'clock Tick Tock' which had been produced by Martin Hannett and even he couldn't ruin a great song like that!

25 October: New Order, Durutti Column, and The Renegades play the Squat. The Renegades were brilliant. Fronted by Burnage's answer to Gene Vincent, "Boppin Brian" on vocals, Tot on guitar, Big Dave on drums and two of our friends from the Cyprus Tavern, Mark 'The Ted' Coley on bass and 'Rocking' Dave Holmes on guitar. They played good time Rockabilly and never failed to entertain every time I saw them. They went down well with the crowd. Next up was Durutti Column with Vinny Reilly on guitar and Bruce Mitchell on drums: Classical guitar, no vocals, haunting melodies but bloody boring after the crowd stomping rock of the Renegades. Thankfully, they only played five songs.

New Order had been advertised as "Special Guests", but the Manchester jungle drums had gone into overdrive and by the time they came on the place was full, I reckon it held about 600 or so. This was Gillian's first gig and they only played for about 20 minutes. Can't remember what they played but they were a lot better than the Beach Club gig. I seem to recall that the crowd seemed to give them a cold reaction as I think that they were expecting to see Joy Division Mk II.

Around this time, Alan Wise fell out with the people who fly-posted for him around town and he got Slim, Tony and me to do it for him. We used Derek as the driver in his Ford Capri 2.8 speed machine and it was a nice little earner. We pasted a copy of the Renegades' Squat gig on the front door of Rocking Dave Holmes' house. He never mentioned it to us. Another trick we had was to follow a bus and stick a poster on the rear engine cover. Alan got so many complaints about his posters ending up in strange places that he switched back to his old poster people to take it over again. It was nice whilst it lasted.

A few weeks after we got sacked from our fly-posting position Derek damaged his car. We had been drinking in town and we went back to the Arndale Car Park to get it. We were parked on the top level and there were two routes out of the car park; one that involved driving down and along each level or the other which was to use the external spiral ramp. This ramp was a complete circle from top to bottom and it was bolted onto the side of the external wall. Derek chose the spiral ramp, and he approached the opening bend at the wrong angle which caused the car to scrape along the barrier. The Capri had a front bonnet that went on for ever and Derek started laughing and just let the car follow the same line all the way down to the ground level. He had to replace his front passenger side wing and get a new bumper.

Alan Wise was back promoting again. Gigs had been lean over the past few months, so we were working again when Simple Minds played Rotters. This was our first venture into the home of our deadliest enemies, the Beer Monsters. This was their palace, their Mecca, their safe haven and here we were. It was an old cinema which had a very plush upstairs section accessed by a massive staircase. The stage had been built at one end of the downstairs dance floor. Walking round the place I could see why it was popular with the Beer Monsters as there were many secluded little corners where you could take a girl to cop a quick feel. I think that I must have been completely stoned at this one as I can only remember two songs from the gig; 'I Travel', and a Velvet Underground cover 'White Light / White Heat'.

Sometime in October we played our first-ever gig at the Cyprus Tavern. We played on the same bill as our mates from North Manchester, Beach Red and Deli Polo Club. I know it seems stupid that I can't remember the date of our first gig, but I think that it was 29 October.

We had invited lots of people to see us and the place was full. Bob the Burger Man, June, MTI and the North Manchester crew were there as well. Tony Wilson and Alan Erasmus were driving past and, seeing the queue outside, decided to see what was happening. Tony saw Slim and he told him that we were playing, and he looked at me and said, "so, you've finally got a band together then". The line-up at our first gig was Shan on drums, John Bidet on guitar, Tony on vocals and me on bass. We played four songs which were 'Catch me in Confusion', 'A Room in a Tower', 'Future', and 'We Are Nation'. Beach Red were a really good band and they should have made it big. Deli Polo Club were the same, should have been massive. Wilson told me that he would get Rob Gretton to call me about him seeing us and if he liked us, then they would talk to us about doing a single.

Ged Duffy

There were few gigs in November aside from The Jam at the Apollo. It was another superb performance: 90 minutes of great songs and a great stage show. The front rows of seats had been removed again so there was no fighting with the bouncers. The Damned released their *Black* album and Adam and The Ants released their *Kings of the Wild Frontier* album – both great and still played by me today. 'Curtain Call' by The Damned showed just how far they had progressed from 'New Rose'. The Ants had some great songs as well such as 'Ants Invasion' and 'Killer in The House'.

Sometime during this month Shan's twin sister Lita joined the Monsters. She was a classically trained pianist and at the level where she could be a teacher if she wished. She had been at every rehearsal we had ever had but she had never shown any signs of wanting to join us. One day we were messing about jamming whilst waiting for John to turn up and she plugged her electric organ in and started playing. It sounded so good that she was instantly part of the gang. She gave us a Doors vibe and that really impressed two Jim Morrison fanatics like Tony and I. Lita *was* the Monsters sound - she was such a gifted musician.

Early December, Throbbing Gristle played Rafters. Definitely a night to get stoned. Thinking about it now, this would have been the perfect night to drop a tab of acid. I have a feeling that acid and Throbbing Gristle would work well together. Next up was Generation X at the Poly. They had a new line up with the guitarist and drummer both leaving to be replaced by ex-Chelsea guitarist James Stevenson and ex-Clash drummer Terry Chimes. They had also changed their name to Gen X. Billy Idol lost it with a member of the audience who spat on his T Shirt. They played a few unknown songs which ended up on the *Kiss Me Deadly* album the following year, but it was an average performance with Billy sulking. This was followed the night after by Classix Nouveaux at Rafters. I had the pleasure of telling their manager that if they wanted to fill the place full of smoke, the machine would be deposited very quickly up the singer's arse. They didn't use it. They complained to Alan Wise about it, and he just told them that if Slim and I had said no then there was nothing he could do.

16 December: Adam and The Ants at the Apollo. This gig should have been at the Poly but the band had become massive and it was moved to satisfy demand. Once again it was another amazing show but Adam had started to play up to the crowd and was on the way to becoming

Factory Fairy Tales

Two sad young men... Tony France and Lee Pickering

a different front man than the one we had been used to seeing. This was the last time we ever saw Adam and The Ants, we left them in the hands of the teeny-boppers. Adam was very clever as he made a habit of recording rare old Ants songs as the B sides of his poppy singles ensuring that old Ants fans like me would carry on buying his singles.

A couple of days later, it was supposed to the turn of Revillos to play Rafters. I worked the stage at Rafters, and I'm positive that this gig didn't happen. I think I only saw Revillos once at Rafters and that was back in September with Fast Cars. On the Stockholm Monsters website it states that we supported the Revillos at this gig and also met Rob Gretton and Peter Hook and asked Hooky to start mixing for us. I don't think that this is right...

As I remember it sometime in early December we played at the Cyprus Tavern and the line-up was Shan on drums, Lita on keyboards, John on guitar, Tony on vocals and me on bass. After talking to Tony Wilson, Rob called me at home and I told him where and when we were going to play. Rob turned up with Hooky but we didn't ask Peter to mix for us that night, as we only said a few words to him. We played the same four songs that we'd played at our first gig, but we had now added a new song called 'Reflected in Violence'. Rob said he would call me the next day and he did. He offered us a support spot at the New Order gig at The Fan Club in Leeds on 4 January. Now we had two weeks of rehearsal to write some new songs and get ready for this gig.

Sometime during this year, Tony and I were round at Mark the Ted's place in Didsbury and were enjoying a spliff or two when a guy turned up to give Mark a copy of a book he had just written. I'd seen the guy there before a couple of times, but this was the first time that Tony had been there when he was there as well. The guy looked like a student, wore an Afghan coat, and was totally nondescript. He spent the whole time staring at Tony and when he went to the toilet, Tony asked Mark "what the fuck's wrong with him? He's creeping me out staring". Mark said, "I've noticed that as well, I don't know what's up with him".

His name was Steven Patrick Morrissey and the next time we saw him he was dressed in the same style as Tony and had his hair cut. He even ended up going in all of the same second hand shops as him and was buying the clothes before Tony could get there!

One other thought, I'm sure Stockholm Monsters were putting 1950s movie stars on their record sleeves before The Smiths were even formed. And people say that he influenced a generation with his fashion sense. I say Tony France had more style in his little finger!

1980

Singles

John Foxx: 'Underpass'
Siouxsie & The Banshees: 'Happy House', 'Christine', 'Israel'.
Mötorhead : 'Ace of Spades'.
Simple Minds: 'I Travel'
U2: '11 o'clock Tick Tock', 'I Will Follow'.
The Psychedelic Furs: 'Sister Europe'.
The Cramps: 'Drug Train'
Joy Division: 'Love Will Tear Us Apart', 'Atmosphere'.
David Bowie: 'Ashes to Ashes'
The Jam: 'Going Underground'
The Specials: 'Too Much Too Young'
Adam and The Ants: 'Cartrouble', 'Kings of the Wild Frontier'.
Bauhaus: 'Dark Entries'

Factory Fairy Tales

Theatre of Hate: 'Original Sin'
AC/DC: 'You Shook me all Night Long'
Killing Joke: 'Wardance', 'Change'
Magazine: 'A Song From Under the Floorboards'
The Fall: 'Fiery Jack', 'Totally Wired'

EPs

Human League: *Holiday 80*
Mötorhead: *Beer Drinkers and Hell Raisers*
Magazine: *Sweetheart Contract.*

Albums

Killing Joke: *Killing Joke*
Siouxsie & The Banshees: *Kaleidoscope*
Echo and The Bunnymen: *Crocodiles*
John Foxx: *Metamatic*
Mötorhead : *Ace of Spades*
Magazine: *The Correct Use of Soap*
Human League: *Travelogue*
Joy Division: *Closer*
Bauhaus: *In the Flat Field*
Teardrop Explodes: *Kilimanjaro*
U2: *Boy*
The Jam: *Sound Affects*
The Cramps: *Songs the Lord Taught Us*
The Ramones: *End of the Century*
Dexys Midnight Runners: *Searching for the Young Soul Rebels*
Peter Gabriel: *Peter Gabriel 3 Melt*
Adam and the Ants: *Kings of the Wild Frontier*
AC/DC: *Back in Black*
Iggy Pop: *Solder*
David Bowie: *Scary Monsters and Super Creeps*
Bruce Springsteen: *The River*

Ged Duffy

Bob Marley: *Uprising*
The Damned: *The Black Album*
The Psychedelic Furs: *The Psychedelic Furs*
Suicide: *Alan Vega and Martin Rev*

13: Advice to Barney, don't fuck with Slim

On the afternoon of 4 January New Order's road crew, Terry and Dave, came to Shan's house to collect our gear. Once the van was loaded, we jumped in the back with Slim and we were off to play The Fan Club in Leeds with Foreign Press and New Order. Slim could skin up in the dark so we were okay for the journey. When we got there, Slim and I met the stage crew who we had worked with at the Futurama Festival, and we had a good laugh with them all evening.

New Order arrived and Rob introduced us and they started to do their sound check. It took for ever for them to finally be happy with the sound. Foreign Press did their sound check, and they took a long time as well. The doors opened and we had no time to do a sound check but just enough to get our stuff set up on stage. The club was full by the time we went on and we played seven songs including two new ones written since Christmas - 'Catch me in Confusion', 'Reflected in Violence', 'Future', 'Resurrection', 'James', 'Copulation' and 'We are Nation'. We got a warm reception from the crowd. It felt great playing on a proper stage, with a proper PA and having stage monitors. We were so excited afterwards and we felt that it had gone well. Rob congratulated us and told us that he had some more gigs coming up for us. He also asked us to do a demo as he wanted to hear what we would sound like in a studio.

New Order came on and played a short set, maybe seven or eight songs and they had improved a lot since I saw them at the Squat, and had written some more songs. Gillian fitted in with the sound and it was great to see them develop. Afterwards we helped them strip everything down and load it into the van, said goodbye to the Leeds stage crew and jumped into the back of the van. Slim skinned up and we were still excited about what we had achieved that evening. The lads dropped us off at Shan's around 3am and Tony, Slim and I walked home to Burnage as there wasn't an all night bus but we were buzzing. We had to go back to Shan's the following afternoon as Terry was coming round to drop our gear off and we would be needed to carry it all upstairs into the loft.

A few days after the Leeds gig, we went to Frank the Hippy's

Ged Duffy

place in Didsbury to record our second demo which included 'Future', 'Copulation' and a song we had just written called 'Fairy Tales'. All three songs sounded good to us and we could see the marked improvement from our first demo. I called Rob to tell him that we had done a demo and he asked me to drop it in at Factory's Offices in Didsbury. The next day Slim and I called in at 86 Palatine Road. The offices were based in Alan Erasmus's flat on the first floor, and when we went in we met Lesley. She told us that Rob had said that we would be calling. We had a chat and she told us that she was Rob's girlfriend and that they lived in a flat in Chorlton. She showed us the room where they stored all the records. There were a couple of shelving racks and boxes on the floor all full of records. She told us that Rob said we could take whatever we wanted. Happy days.

Over the next couple of years whenever I went into Factory I'd take records straight off the shelf. I also used to take the bag of cassettes that were sent in so I could listen to them or tape over them with John Peel. These cassettes were demos and they never got listened to. There were tapes from several bands that made it such as The Cure and Bauhaus. Killing Joke sent one in a with a note asking "How did you get the snare drum sound on 'She's Lost Control'?" Factory's policy was to only sign bands that someone inside the Factory Family knew. 'Sign' is possibly the wrong word as we never had a contract or anything tying us to Factory. Like the fool I am, I taped over all these tapes with *The John Peel Show*.

Following the boredom of Durutti Column the next gig was Depeche Mode at Rafters. Their first single hadn't come out yet and the gig wasn't full. They looked like little kids hiding behind their synthesisers, but you could tell they were going to be big. They played some great Pop songs that night and were a great bunch of lads. We spent a lot of time backstage with them. The next band that Alan Wise booked to play was The Fall at Rafters – a full house and a great gig. Great bass and drums on every song. I talked to Mark E Smith for a while before the show, a true Salfordian Legend.

22 January: New Order 'Ceremony' (FAC 33) is released. An absolute classic single with a brilliant B Side 'In a Lonely Place' with a brilliant Hooky bass line. Got it from Lesley on the day it was released. I played it non-stop for days as I couldn't get enough of it. When I lived in Burnage I would catch the 169 or 170 bus up to Palatine Road to see Lesley at Factory. If I was broke, I would walk. These were great

times as Slim, and I would call in to see Lesley and have a cup of tea whenever we were nearby. It was a good atmosphere in the office.

Towards the end of January U2 played the Poly. These early shows were full of energy and relied less on the big stage show and more on the songs. Altered Images supported them, and they were better than when I saw them at Futurama 2. When I say better, I mean, the Poly had great acoustics, so they sounded better. Clare Grogan was as beautiful as ever. Both bands put on a great show, and we were happy going home that night.

5 February: John Cooper Clarke and Blue Orchids at Rafters. Alan Wise was involved a bit with the promotion of John Cooper Clarke, and this was the first of three nights of him appearing at Rafters. Slim and I worked this first night, but we couldn't do the next two. Blue Orchids played and they were very good. They were formed by Martin Bramah and Una Baines who had both left The Fall after recording *Live at The Witch Trials*. They had a Fall vibe to them, and I really enjoyed them. John Cooper Clarke was brilliant: skinny, wild hair, black suit and he just rifled off poem after poem without a break. He had the audience in stitches with some of his poems. "And it's bad enough with another race, but fuck me, a monster from outer space," is one of the best lines I've ever heard live.

6 February: Stockholm Monsters played Comanche Students Union in Manchester with Foreign Press and New Order. This was part of Manchester Poly and as far as I'm aware this might be the only gig ever held there. It was put on by Howard Jones who was the head of the Student Entertainment Committee. Howard later became the manager of the Hacienda and manager of the early Stone Roses. It was the same deal as before; Terry and Dave picked our gear up and we piled in the back of the van. We helped to unload and set up when we got there. It was the same line up as the gig at the Fan Club, once again no sound check. Tony and I were both into The Doors and Jim Morrison. We had just read that he had once started a gig by screaming "Motherfuckers" at the crowd, so Tony did just that when we got on stage. No one in the crowd knew what the fuck he was on about, but it sounded good from where I was stood.

We played nine songs, which included the seven we had played at the Fan Club and two new songs 'MC' and 'Fairy Tales' which we had written over the past few days. Both of these came via Lita's electric

THE MONSTERS AT THE COMANCHE STUDENT UNION
Left to right: me, Tony (kneeling down), John Bidet and Lita.

organ, and she was now getting heavily involved in coming up with melodies for us. 'MC' was a great favourite of mine and it was about the life of the Hollywood actor Montgomery Clift. We went down well, and we had a lot of our mates there to see us like June, Bob the Burger Man, Mani, Lee, Derek, Kaiser, Beach Red, Deli Polo Club and MTI. New Order played a short set of about 30 minutes, but they went down well. This was a much better performance and reception than the last gig they did in Manchester at the Squat. At the end we loaded everything into the van, and we went to Deville's and got drunk. Great night.

The following morning we all met in Town to get the National Express coach to Northampton where we were going to support New Order. We had decided against travelling down in the back of their van as it was a long journey. Bob the Burger Man had decided to come down with us as he had a couple of days off. Bob was a real character and we loved him. He was a quiet guy with a wicked sense of humour until the demon drink hit him and then he became Bob the Destroyer

Factory Fairy Tales

and wanted to fight everyone. The coach journey was a laugh and we stopped for about 40 minutes in the Derbyshire town of Ashbourne. We went in a pub and quickly downed two pints. It was a quaint picturesque town whose beauty was wasted on us as we just wanted to get wasted. We found an off license and got some supplies, so the rest of the trip went along quite nicely.

When we reached Northampton we asked a couple of locals where the Roadmenders Club was and after walking round for a bit we found it. Once inside, we saw that the equipment was all set up, so we sat in the corner and waited for New Order to do their sound check. Section 25 went on to do their sound check. Last time I saw them had been at the Beach Club and I'd really liked them. Since then I'd acquired their single 'Girls Don't Count' (FAC 18) from the Factory office and liked it. Once they'd finished we set up our gear and actually managed a few minutes to sound check.

I really liked the club, it had a great sound system, and the DJ played some great music, a mixture of punk, Reggae and Killing Joke. On the way backstage a guy stopped me and asked if he and his mate could come backstage. It was Daniel Ash and David J from Bauhaus, so I took them backstage and left them there. I had a chat with Daniel later and he was so down to earth. He bought me a beer as well.

We played the same set as the night before and the on stage sound was great. Bob the Burger Man told us we sounded a lot better tonight, so the sound check must have worked. We went down well with the crowd. I remember Tony throwing his bongo drums into the crowd and then asking for them back because he realized he would have to buy a new set to replace them! Section 25 came on and they played a song called 'New Horizons' which stood out from the rest of the set. They were a tight band, and went down well.

New Order came on and did their normal 30 minute set which consisted of eight songs. They started off with 'In a Lonely Place', what a brilliant song to start with. Early New Order had it all; a great sound, cool as fuck on stage and a proper 'fuck you' attitude. The crowd loved them and in these early days whenever I saw them people weren't demanding encores, they were just happy to see them play. When it was all over Section 25 went back to Blackpool and we climbed into the back of New Order's van for the short trip to London. We were playing again on the Monday with New Order and Section 25 at Heaven, so it was agreed that we'd stay with New Order.

Ged Duffy

We got to the hotel in the early hours of the morning, I think it was in Kensington. Rob had booked a few rooms and there were four in our room: Slim, Tony, Bob and me. We spent all night smoking, and we had some speed with us. It was a good night. Next day we had a laugh with Hooky and Barney at breakfast and then we walked round the area for a bit, had something to eat, and had a couple of pints in a local pub. Later that afternoon Barney was complaining about needing something and Rob told him to take the car and get it himself. Rob asked me to go with him. Hooky wished me luck as I left. I soon found out why. Barney was a crazy driver, driving fast and braking at the last minute. On one road there were parked cars on each side of the road with cars coming the opposite way towards us and I felt that the gap was too small. He drove towards the cars, and I looked at him and I swear he had his fucking eyes shut! We got through and he opened his eyes and said, "that was close" and laughed, probably as much in relief as anything else!

Rob had a drink with me before dinner and told me that Factory wanted us to record 'Fairy Tales' as a single. Martin Hannett was going to produce it and it would be recorded in Strawberry Studios in Stockport in March. I told the rest of the band, and they were really excited. That Sunday evening Rob took us all out for a meal and a few beers in a pub near the hotel, and I finally got to say hello to both Stephen and Gillian. They were a nice couple and very quiet and reserved compared to the other two. The following morning New Order had to be somewhere, so we were left to our own devices exploring the surrounding area. We had to be back at the hotel around 4pm to jump in the van and head to Heaven.

Heaven was owned by Richard Branson, it was the premier gay club in London. It was underneath the railway arches in Charing Cross and tonight's gig was a 1,000 capacity sell out. When we got to the club New Order were already there and Martin Hannett was there as well. Rob introduced us all to Martin and he seemed okay… but we didn't know him yet. Hannett was there because they had decided to use a quadrophonic PA system and he was going to mix all three bands. A normal PA system has an equal stack of speakers on the left and on the right of the stage. This quadrophonic system had the same equal amount of speakers on the left and on the right at the front and at the rear of the hall.

I sat on the floor in the middle of the hall and listened to New Order sound checking and it didn't sound right to me. I looked at

Factory Fairy Tales

**FINAL SOLUTION PRESENT
NEW ORDER, SECTION 25
& STOCKHOLM MONSTERS
in Heaven 9.00PM-3.00AM
MON, FEBRUARY 9TH**

OVER 18's ONLY. HEAVEN IS UNDER THE ARCHES AT CHARING CROSS, WC2. ADMISSION £2.50 IN ADVANCE ONLY. FROM ROUGH TRADE, SMALL WONDER, HONKY TONK & BONAPARTE (KINGS X).

the hall and it wasn't square so the speakers at the rear weren't in line with the speakers at the front. This would fuck up the sound. They spent a lot longer sound checking than normal and I don't think that they were happy with the sound. I don't think Section 25 got a sound check either. The important thing about New Order's sound check was that they played six Joy Division songs without any vocals. This was the first time I had heard them play even a riff of Joy Division and it was amazing to see and the few people who were in the room were lucky to witness it. The club opened and filled up fast. Lee had come down from Manchester in a car with a couple of the Russell lads, so we took them backstage and had a spliff and started drinking. Bob the Burger Man was having a few beers and having a good time. The bar staff all looked like Freddie Mercury: big moustaches, leather waistcoats to show off their hairy chests, leather chaps and cowboy boots. It was like being at a Village People concert, but they were all up for a laugh and the banter was great. I noticed that they talked to Slim a lot - more about that later…

We went on and played the same set as the previous two shows and we were the guinea pigs that Hannett worked with to try and get a handle on this four-way stereo system. We weren't experts on how a stage sound should sound but it was very weird hearing yourself on stage, through the speaker stack nearest you and also hearing yourself coming back on yourself from the rear of the hall. We got a good response from the crowd. After we came off we talked to Hooky and asked him to mix for us. Section 25 had the same problems and they didn't sound that great out in the hall. The crowd gave them a good response as well.

New Order came on and it wasn't the best that I ever saw them. The sound was weird, but the crowd loved them, and they gave a good performance. We had really enjoyed ourselves playing these three gigs. Bob the Burger Man had been a great laugh and hadn't got himself into any dangerous situations, but it was apparent that John Bidet stood apart from all of us. He dressed differently, didn't try to join in with our banter and basically made no effort to become one of us. He was also still playing in lots of bands, so we had to fit in rehearsals when he was available. We climbed in the back of the van and the journey back was a long four and a half hours which we spent smoking so the time passed. Then it was the normal walk back to Burnage and back the next day to carry the gear upstairs to our loft. Within a couple of days of us returning it was decided that John Bidet had to go and to be honest he wasn't too bothered when we told him. So, we were now looking for a new guitarist. We were torn about letting Factory know or not, but we decided that I should tell Rob what we had done. Rob was annoyed but I explained to him that 'Fairy Tales' was a keyboard-based song and that it would all work out in the end. So, the single was still on.

A couple of weeks later we went to Strawberry Studios to record 'Fairy Tales'. The idea was for us to record both sides on the same day. We planned on doing 'James' as the B Side. The second day was for mixing. The day before going into the studio, we had been rehearsing and Jim from MTI was sat there with us, and we played both songs for him to listen to. Jim said that my bass line didn't suit 'Fairy Tales' at which point Lita said she agreed but hadn't wanted to tell me. Jim picked up my bass and played four notes and said, "play that".

My new bass line changed the tempo of the song and made it slightly faster. So my bass line was actually written by Jim from James, and if it had made any money then I would have sorted him out. Shan, Tony, Lita, and I got in Strawberry early and set up all the equipment and ran through the two songs and we sounded good, tight, and well-rehearsed. Martin Hannett strolled in about three hours later, never said a fucking word to any of us and spent the next hour lining up all his drugs on the mixing deck. We naively believed that he would want to hear us play both songs live so that he could get a feel for the song but no, he simply demanded that Shan dismantle his drum kit leaving only the bass drum. He then told us that he would be using a click track and poor old Shan had to record his drums bit by bit and it took a long time before they were done.

He heard Lita play her electric organ. He told her to use the Steinway grand piano that was in the studio. Lita was in her element playing on such a great piece of kit but the whole appeal of the song was the fairground organ sound and Hannett killed the song without even listening to it first. We tried to tell him that the organ *was* the song, but he was either too stoned or too fucking ignorant to listen to us. By close of play on the first day all of the drugs had gone from the mixing desk. The next day started with him getting there hours late again and then taking an hour placing his drugs in a row across the mixing desk before he was ready to start again. Hannett made me play my bass in the control room straight onto the mixing deck. I told him I wanted to play through my amp as I had it set it the way I liked it. I did one take and he said that's okay, you're done. We had no guitarist, so he asked if we had anything else to play on top of the track. Lita spotted a recorder on a shelf and went back in and played a melody on it which was perfect for the song. When we played the song live, Tony used to whistle on it. Hannett didn't want to know about that. Hannett then suggested hand claps which we all did along with Slim. He didn't want any of us in the control room with him whilst he was recording so we spent most of each day playing pool, smoking dope, and watching the film *Debbie Does Dallas*. By the end of two days, we had only finished the recording of 'Fairy Tales' and all of the drugs that had been laid out on the mixing deck had gone – what a complete and utter fiasco! Rob phoned me the next day to find out what had happened, and he was fuming after I told him. I told him we wanted Hooky to mix us moving forward - he agreed.

During the rest of February and early March we worked six gigs at Rafters and apart from Josef K and ACR, the gigs just bored us. They were Fatal Charm, UK Decay, The Cheaters, and The Troggs. Alan Wise was on a run of booking bad bands.

Cargo Studios was situated in Rochdale above a music shop called Tractor Music and a PA hire company who had provided the PA for the *Rock Against Racism* gig in 1978. In early March we went into Cargo to record the B Side of the single. Hooky was behind the

Ged Duffy

mixing desk, so we were happy. We planned to record 'James' but no matter how many times we tried it we just couldn't get it right. It had a definite stop and restart in the song but after multiple attempts we still couldn't get these two bits right. Hooky asked if there was another song that we wanted to do but we couldn't agree on one. Whilst sitting there, I started to play a bass-line that I had been working on and everyone turned round and asked, "what's that?" so 'Death is Slowly Coming' was created. Lita added a keyboard to it straight away and Hooky recorded us two as the backing for the song. I had some words written and I gave them to Tony, and he added a few lines, and the vocal was ready. The problem was that the song was really hard to drum to as it was in a weird time, so Shan added percussion and also some electronic drum bits on the keyboards. Lita came up with a riff on the synth and Shan played that as well. Amazingly Lita managed to spot a recorder lying around and she played a great melody on it. I wonder how many Factory bands have used a recorder on both sides of a single?

Back when I was at school there was a craze for buying long plastic open ended tubes which you swung above your head to make a whirling noise. I can't remember what they were called but all the toy shops sold them. We spotted one of these in the corner and someone swung it whilst Hooky had it miked up. That's the weird noise in the background. I think that it might be Slim who did this.

At 2.07 minutes into the song I made a massive mistake. I played the song on the D and G string playing both strings together but at this exact moment I hit the open A string at the same time. I wanted to remove it, but Hooky liked it and it stayed in. When the single came out I remember *Rolling Stone* magazine saying that "'Death is Slowly Coming' is probably the most psychedelic song ever written without using a guitar". That made my day.

One day I was in Discount Records and Mark Farrow walked in. He was the graphic designer that I have mentioned previously in this book. I told him that I was in a band and that we had a single planned with Factory and that we didn't want a Peter Saville sleeve. I asked him if he would be interested in coming up with a design and gave him the details of the songs and the band name and he said he would play around with some ideas and get back to me. A few days later I was over at the Factory office and Tony Wilson came in and I told him about Mark and asked him if it would be okay for him to come up with some ideas. Tony said yes but it would have to be good for

Factory Fairy Tales

him not to use Saville.

Towards the end of March: Theatre of Hate, Classic Nouveaux and Naked Lunch at Rotters. At last Alan Wise had managed to get a good gig set up. The smart arse manager of Classic Nouveaux recognized Slim and me and remarked that the smoke machine would be used tonight. Smoke machine or not, they were still shite. I had already seen Naked Lunch play at Futurama 2, and I thought they were okay. They played a nice set. Theatre of Hate were brilliant: Kirk Brandon could sing, Stan Stammers was a great bass player, and they wrote some powerful songs which suited Kirk's vocal style. They had only released one single 'Legion' by the time they played this gig but they filled Rotters, and I reckon the club held about 1,000. It was a great gig and we got to speak to Stan and Kirk in the afternoon. This was followed by another great gig, a couple of days later, Orange Juice at Rafters. A brilliant gig by a brilliant band: Edwyn Collins was a nice guy, and he was sound all day with us. They played a great set of guitar-based Pop. You couldn't help but like them.

8 April: New Order and Minny Pops at Rock City, Nottingham. Slim and I decided that morning to go to Nottingham. After a good breakfast in the Magnet Café we caught the National Express bus over. When we got there we saw that the PA was Oz PA, so we went over to say hello to Oz, Eddie, and Diane. They had supplied the PA for lots of gigs at the Russell. They told me that they had been taken on by Rob to provide the PA at all future New Order gigs. Oz was also going to be mixing the sound at all their gigs.

We got in just before New Order did their sound check, so we watched it. They sounded really tight. After they finished Slim went to the toilet and I saw Barney follow him in there. A couple of minutes later Barney ran out laughing followed by a soaking wet Slim who looked like he was in the mood for killing someone. It turned out that Barney had found a fire bucket full of water in the toilet and had gone in the cubicle next to Slim, climbed on the toilet seat and poured the whole bucket onto Slim who was sat down on the bog. Slim plotted revenge - he found Barney's Melodica in an open box at the side of the stage, and ran off with it. He went to the toilet where he wiped his arse on the mouth piece, and put it back in its box.

Later, when New Order came on, the fourth song was 'Truth' and as soon as Barney put his melodica to his mouth you could immediately see his face change. He knew something was wrong but couldn't tell what. After a couple of moments he looked at Slim and Slim pointed to the melodica and then pointed to his arse and started laughing. Barney nearly choked. Revenge was sweet.

During the afternoon Will Sergeant, Les Pattinson, and Pete de Freitas from Echo and the Bunnymen turned up. They had all purchased new motorbikes and decided to go out on a run and see New Order and we spent the afternoon with them. They stayed and watched both bands and then left after New Order finished. Great lads, great band, RIP Pete. At the end of the gig, we helped Terry and Dave drop the gear down and load it in the van and we jumped in the back and were well stoned by the time they dropped us off in Manchester.

15 April: We played the Cyprus Tavern and I think that we played with MTI who now had Jennie as vocalist. Danny had been kicked out after too many fights. They had really developed and had some good songs. The jerky beat that is a trademark of James was now very evident. We lined up with Tony on guitar and vocals, Shan, Lita, and me. This was the first gig that Hooky mixed the live sound for us. We played 'Resurrection', 'Future', 'Catch me in Confusion', 'Soft Babies', 'James', 'Fairy Tales', 'Monastery', and 'Death is Slowly Coming'. The place was full of all our mates, and we really enjoyed it. Tony did a decent job of singing and playing the guitar, but we decided afterwards that we would try and get someone else in to play guitar. Rob was there that night and he phoned me the next day and told me to let him know when we were ready for some gigs with New Order.

14. A scrap with Bauhaus

We played Rafters on 16th May supporting Steve Garvey's band Motivation. We had been in contact with a guitarist called Mark, but everyone knew him as 'Eddie' because he looked like Eddie Munster. It was arranged that we would meet him for the first time at Rafters and then he could actually see us play. The Revilles were due to headline but cancelled so ex-Buzzcock Steve Garvey played instead. Maybe this is why there's some confusion about us supporting the Revilles.

Eddie turned up and we liked him. He had a bit of style about him, and it seemed that he would fit in. He was backstage having a spliff with us and I was playing a bass and he was playing along on Tony's guitar. Alan Wise told us to go on, and Eddie stood up to give the guitar to Tony who looked at him and said, "You're on with us mate, just watch where Ged's fingers are on his bass". Eddie shat himself, came on and played and he was just brilliant. He fitted in so he was now a Monster. We played 'James', 'Future', 'Soft Babies', 'Catch me in Confusion', 'Fairy Tales', 'Something's Got to Give' and 'Monastery'.

When we came off Eddie went and got a drink. He had never played on stage before, had no idea that he would have broken that duck that night and was totally made up that he had done it. There was a small crowd in that night, but they were all there to see us: Dr Filth, MTI, Beach Red, Deli Polo Club, June, Bob the Burger Man and Lee. Hooky was in Hamburg with New Order, so the guy whose PA it was mixed for us. Eddie didn't believe that we were mates with New Order, and that Hooky would normally do the live sound for us.

Tony was going out with a girl then who we called 'Happy Ever After'. She was petite, pretty, shy, and unfortunately she was backstage when Slim decided he needed a piss! Most people would go to the toilet but Slim decided to piss in the ice-making machine which was backstage in front of Tony and her. A couple of minutes later, the barman came in and filled his bucket with ice and Slim grinned as he returned to the bar. The relationship finished shortly after... As one relationship was folding another was about to start. Well not

Ged Duffy

Monsters at Rafters: Eddie, me and Lita

immediately. Mark the Ted introduced me to a girl from Old Trafford called Lesley Barber. We got on great and went out a couple of times over the next few weeks but nothing serious. We would see each other at gigs and clubs and occasionally spend the night together. She would play a big role in my life but not yet.

That month Echo and The Bunnymen released *Heaven Up Here*, it's an absolute classic and I loved it from the first listen. Great bass playing by Les, Will played some great guitar parts and McCulloch's vocals were superb. Not a bad song on the album. This was followed by Psychedelic Furs *Talk Talk Talk*, another brilliant album by a great band, with no bad songs on it, it's such a tuneful wall of noise with great vocals. 'Pretty in Pink' became a monster hit a few years later after a film of that name was released in 1986. Both of these two albums should be in your collection. Both are timeless classics.

At the beginning of June Department S played Rafters. I enjoyed this gig. It was a full house, and they played a great set of punky pop. I don't know if Vic turned up or not, but a lot of people kept shouting about his whereabouts! Popular guy, this Vic chap.

The following day Siouxsie & The Banshees released *JuJu*. In my opinion this is one of the greatest albums ever written. John McGeoch played the guitar of his life on this record. Budgie was one

Factory Fairy Tales

of the most underrated drummers. Every song is great, especially the darkness and intensity of 'Voodoo Dolly' and the beautiful pop of 'Arabian Knights'.

In the middle of June, we recorded 'James' as a demo at Frank the Hippie's in Didsbury. We wanted to get a tape to Rob so he could hear us with Eddie and then give us some more gigs with New Order.

20 June: Killing Joke at the Poly. We met up in the Salisbury and got hammered before we went to the gig. Once inside we had a couple of lines of speed and that straightened us out. We were buzzing and ready for another night of aural carnage. Around this time a Killing Joke gig was a special event. You knew what you were going to get, and they never disappointed. I don't think I have ever walked away from a Killing Joke gig disappointed. Youth and Geordie were both on top form that night. My ears were ringing for a couple of days. Killing Joke released *What's This For* a few days later – this was too much for me to take in as this made it four classic albums all coming out within weeks of each other. I loved the other three albums that I had bought from Discount, and this album joined the ranks as a classic. 'Follow The Leaders' was a great single and that song has a greater meaning to me, but that story is for later.

26 June: We played Deville's. I can't remember who we played with. I think it might have been MTI or Beach Red. We did the gig so Eddie would have played a planned gig before any New Order dates would arise. The place was full of our mates again and it was a good night. Rob turned up to see how we had changed since John Bidet had left us. He was impressed. Hooky was back behind the mixing desk.

Alongside the usual set list we had added 'Endless You' – the first song that Eddie had written with us. It had a bit of Bauhaus feel about it with his guitar style and that, coupled with Lita's organ playing, really worked well. The future was looking promising.

The next gig we worked was Monochrone Set at Rafters. Another good gig. I really liked this band, and they were really good on the night, another band that should have been massive.

In the middle of July Eddie and I went into Strawberry Studios so he could record his guitar part on 'Fairy Tales'. Thankfully Hannett wasn't there, or we would have been there for hours. Chris Nagle, the resident Sound Engineer at Strawberry, set everything up for Eddie. It

Ged Duffy

was done in one take. Now we just needed it mixing.

Towards the end of July Alan Wise started promoting gigs at Deville's again, as well as Rafters, so we were working when Frantic Elevators played. I'd seen them a few times and I thought that they were a band that could make it. 'Holding Back The Years' was their fourth and last single before Mick Hucknall left. They played a good set of pop and rock and I enjoyed them. This was followed up by Josef K at Deville's. They had played at Rafters back in February and they were good. Same again tonight, choppy guitar and fractured beats, great sound, the place was full.

August started off with Depeche Mode at Rafters supported by Ludus. Two shows – the first show was for kids. They'd had two singles out since their gig at Rafters back in January. Both singles had charted but one of them 'New Life' had got near the Top Ten so both shows were full. They had changed since the last gig; they had got more confident on stage and the PA was better. We had some good banter with them all during the evening. Within a few weeks 'Just Can't Get Enough' charted and the rest is history. This was followed by Siouxsie & The Banshees at the Apollo. They played 'Israel', 'Night Shift', 'Voodoo Dolly', 'Arabian Knights', 'Happy House' and finished with 'Love in a Void'. They were brilliant and John McGeoch was amazing. It was packed and there were no fights with the bouncers as far as I can recall although there were the Perry Boys outside again and there were a few fights. Then it was Aztec Camera at Deville's. Roddy Frame was a really nice guy. Got to know him better the following year when it turned out that he was mates with Mikey Eastwood who would become the other bassist with me in Lavolta Lakota. Mikey was at this gig, but I didn't know him yet. Roddy wrote some wonderful songs. It would be nearly another two years before his debut album *High Land, Hard Rain* was released. This was a good night. We got stoned with Roddy and we were very happy bunnies.

11 September: New Order release 'Procession' (FAC 33) - a classic single, great bass line. Another trip to see Lesley at the office. This was a really good follow up to 'Ceremony' and another rocking song to listen to. I played it for about a week and I loved the B Side 'Everything's Gone Green' as well.

Throughout the last two months we had been rehearsing and had ditched 'Catch Me in Confusion', 'Future', and 'Monastery' from

Factory Fairy Tales

the set. 'MC' had been resurrected and Eddie came up with a great guitar lick that he played in the verse along with power chords on the chorus and the song had a new lease of life. Rob gave us two gigs: we were to headline a Factory Night at Heaven with The Wake. There would be Factory music played all night and there would also be a Factory film, then we would play at Sheffield Poly with Section 25 and New Order a couple of weeks later.

Hooky hired a van and on the morning of 14 September we set off for London to play at Heaven with The Wake. We had a couple of mates come down with us in the van and I think Bob the Burger Man might have been one of them. Slim skinned up all the way down and we were stoned by the time we got there. When we got in we saw that it was Oz PA, and we set up our equipment. We were nearly finished sound checking when The Wake walked in. This was the first time that I had met them, and straight away it was clear that their singer, Caesar, was a good lad. I told him that I recognised him as the guitarist in Altered Images from the Futurama 2 gig in Leeds the previous year. Their bass player was a cool guy and we got on well and he used my amp for the gig because it was better than his. His name was Bobby Gillespie, later to find fame with Primal Scream. In between The Wake and Primal Scream, Bobby drummed for The Jesus and Mary Chain.. By the time The Wake came on there was a large crowd in. They were good, I enjoyed their set of atmospheric pop and I liked Caesar's voice.

Our new set was 'Something's Got to Give', 'Fairy Tales', 'James', 'Soft Babies', 'MC', 'Endless You', and 'Death is Slowly Coming'. Eddie played guitar on the first six songs, but he didn't think that 'Death is Slowly Coming' needed any guitar on it, so he sat it out.

Just before the club opened a couple of the bar staff came over and said that they remembered us from when we were there a couple of months previously, or should I say that they remembered Slim. They asked me if Slim was straight and quick as a flash I replied, "He swings both ways". Well, that was it, Slim spent the whole night running away from the bar staff and every time he came up to us he said, "I can't understand why these lot are following me". We fell about laughing. When we were travelling back I had to put him out of his misery - he was fuming. We were pissing ourselves. I was so pleased that there was a line of equipment between us.

A few days later we were rehearsing, and Eddie walked in with a little case which he said contained a trumpet. "What the fuck are you doing with a trumpet" we asked and as we came to 'Death is Slowly Coming' he got it out and played along. It sounded okay. We'd use that from now on. When we got to 'MC' he put his guitar down and we all stopped and said, "No Eddie, your guitar part's great on this song". He smiled and said, "Trust me". We started playing and Eddie played this slow lament on the trumpet, and it was amazing. It worked perfectly with the mood of the song. Eddie also came in with a great riff that he had written and after a couple of rehearsals it had become *Lafayette*. We should have played it at Sheffield, but we didn't for some reason.

23 September: Sheffield University with New Order and Section 25. Terry and Dave picked us up in the afternoon and took us to Sheffield. Within a few minutes of us arriving Mani the Mod, Kaiser, and some of Beach Red arrived. They had travelled over in a car, and we had a good night drinking and smoking with them. That night we played the best gig that we had done so far. We did the same set as the gig at Heaven and Tony introduced 'MC' as "This is a song for Sad Young Men". Eddie stole the show with his trumpet and afterwards Mani said that the hairs on his neck stood up during 'MC'. New Order were brilliant, they started the set with an instrumental version of 'Temptation' and did a great version of 'Everything's Gone Green' and 'Procession'. Whilst the rest of the Monsters and Mani's guys all went backstage to drink and smoke, Slim and I helped Terry and Dave take down the gear and load the van. After we'd finished we sat down and had a beer and shared a spliff. Then it was back in the van. It was a very interesting experience, being driven over the Snake Pass whilst sat in the back of a van in complete darkness apart from the light of a spliff. This was probably the first time that I was happy to get out of the van and Tony, Slim and I walked home to Burnage.

48 hours later, Slim and I were back at work for former Velvet Underground legend Nico at Rafters. She had been living in London but after this gig she decided to stay in Manchester. Alan Wise started to manage her, and she started to tour again. Tony Wilson, Rob Gretton, Hooky and Barney were all there to see her. She was still beautiful, despite the years of heroin abuse and she still had that Germanic voice. She played a couple of Velvet Underground songs 'Femme Fatale', 'All Tomorrow's Parties' and 'I'm Waiting for the Man'.

Factory Fairy Tales

According to Nigel Bagley, Alan Wise's business partner, they had been trying to book acts when they got a call telling him Nico was in a pub in London and she was broke. Nigel offered £200 for her to play. She said £200 and a bag of heroin. He agreed so she travelled up with her harmonium. Afterwards they put her up in a Bed and Breakfast and then got her a flat in Prestwich and she ended up living in Manchester for years. She loved the place. She could be seen many times riding her bicycle round North Manchester. I think that she ended up living with Alan a few years later.

The month came to a close with The Fall at Fagins. This was the first gig that The Fall did with two drummers and the sound was amazing. They were playing their own warped style of Rockabilly and it was so good. They filled Fagins and it was a great show. I remember that they started off with 'Fiery Jack' which was such a great single. Slim and I got a great view of the band and experienced the power of the drummers up close as we spent the entire gig kneeling down holding the stage monitors. The stage floor was pounding with the bass and the two bass drums.

Sometime in September I failed my driving test. Dad had paid for me to have lessons and had taken me out in his car every Sunday for a couple of hours. I failed on a stupid decision that I made. When Dad got home from work, he handed me the keys to his Escort van and said, "It's yours". I had to tell him what had happened, and he told me to book another test straight away and he would help me with the lessons. I didn't. I was so pissed off with what happened, I just left it.

1 October: We played the Gallery with MTI. Jenny and Tim were both singing for them at this point. I had only seen them three times this year, as they had spent most of the year rehearsing and getting it all together to become James a couple of months later. They were brilliant again on the night. The place was full with our mates, it was a great night. The Gallery was on Peter Street, just down the road from the Free Trade Hall. It was a small venue with 200 to 300 capacity. It had a great sound. I'm sure it had an upper tier, hence the name.

The following night, Rip, Rig and Panic play Rafters. They were fucking shite - pretentious art school wankers. Slim got into a disagreement with the band and their road crew which was to spill over the next time they met and have consequences for the Monsters. That's another story.

Ged Duffy

A couple of days, after the gig at The Gallery Eddie told us that he was leaving. He didn't want to be in a band anymore as he didn't like playing on stage. I think he was going back to college. We were gutted as not only was he a top bloke, but he was also a good guitarist. He could play lots of styles and we would have developed into a rockier band if he had stayed.

To be honest my heart started going out of the band once Eddie left. He was a proper indie guitarist who played what was needed on each song. No flashy solos, no trying to take over any of the keyboard driven songs, just played the amount needed per song. Not too little and not too much. He also kept coming up with some great riffs and I think we would have been a great band if he had stayed. A few days later we had a band meeting and agreed that Tony's youngest brother Karl would join us as a guitarist. My biggest concern was that he was only 16 and still at school. The dynamic of the band was about to change.

8 October. Joy Division release *Still* (FACT 40), an album of unreleased songs and a live recording, a tying up of all the loose ends. My copy had the cloth cover and the ribbon and is highly sought after now - another trip for a cup of tea with Lesley. This was a nice way to finish off Joy Division and concentrate on New Order.

26 October: New Order and Beach Red at the Ritz. Rob asked me if we were ready to play and I told him no, but I suggested that he approach Beach Red instead. Rob knew them from playing with us and also coming to a few New Order gigs when we were playing with them. Dr Filth were another of our mates that we introduced to Rob, and they played a few gigs with New Order as well. Slim and I also introduced James to him as well.

The band promoted the gig themselves and Slim and I were working as stage hands. The PA was huge and I'm sure it was Oz PA that did it. We set everything up and New Order did their sound check, and it didn't sound right. The PA was too loud for the venue. They had hired The Event Group to entertain people round the venue. They were a performance artist group, and they were running round the place basically annoying the shit out of people. There was a bloke locked in a cage screaming at everyone who walked past him. Beach Red came on and they were as great as ever. They were a proper band and they should have made it or at least recorded something for Factory.

Factory Fairy Tales

The place was full with 2,000 in when New Order came on. They came on about 45 minutes late, and the atmosphere was getting tense. I can honestly say that this was the worst time that I had seen them so far. Everything was either out of tune or out of time during the gig and I remember some people booing them. This was the first gig that I remember Barney being totally pissed before going on. Afterwards we took the gear down and loaded the vans and had a spliff. We had been drinking all day from the band's rider but since we were both speeding off our tits we couldn't get drunk.

The Ritz was a great venue. The dance floor was sprung which made watching a band great as the floor moved with you. It was renowned for its "Grab a Granny" nights and it was just down the same block from the Hacienda and is now a Grade II Listed building.

28 October: Bauhaus at Fagins. This was due to be played at Rafters, but the amount of tickets sold meant that it moved upstairs. I loved doing the stage at Fagins as it was on the ground level, so we had no stairs to carry gear up. When Bauhaus came in Daniel Ash recognised Slim and me from the New Order gig in Northampton. Fagins was a cabaret club, and the stage was low so cabaret singers could actually touch the crowd and vice versa. So when bands played Fagins our job was to kneel in front of the stage and hold the stage monitors secure when fans pushed against them. Bauhaus came on and the stage was completely covered in smoke. I could see Pete Murphy kicking his feet up in the air as he was dancing. I turned away for a few seconds to hold one of the monitors when I felt a kick hit me under my chin and throw me into the crowd.

I got up and knelt in front of the stage to carry on holding the monitors and when the smoke lifted I saw Pete Murphy flat on his back lying on the stage. He looked like he was knocked out and then I twigged what had happened, as I could see Slim stood up in front of the monitors, looking around the front of the stage as if he were searching for someone. Two roadies came on and pulled Pete Murphy off the stage, and the band carried on playing as the smoke machine kicked in again. After a couple of minutes the smoke cleared, and Pete Murphy was back on stage, and started to sing the first song 'The Passion of Lovers'. When the song finished he knelt down next to me and asked, "What happened?".

I pointed at Slim and said, "You kicked me in the face when you were dancing. I know it was an accident but see him over there,

Slim (bottom left) keeping an eye on Pete Murphy at Fagins

he doesn't. He saw me hit the deck and he punched whatever was moving in the smoke"

Pete said, "I'm sorry. I didn't mean to hit you".

I said, "No problem but you need to talk to him".

They started the next song which was 'In The Flat Field' and at the end of it he went over to talk to Slim, and peace was restored. They played a brilliant set and Pete was very careful where he danced. For the encore they played the Velvet Underground song 'I'm Waiting for My Man' and Nico came on stage and sang it with them.

We still hadn't mixed the single yet, and it was decided that sometime in early November we would mix both sides of the single on the same night at Strawberry and at Cargo. I lost the toss and had to go and sit with Hannett to do 'Fairy Tales' at Strawberry and the rest of the band went to Cargo to mix 'Death is Slowly Coming' with Hooky. Slim came with me to Strawberry, and as usual Hannett was late, so we had to sit round for a couple of hours. When he finally arrived he had to spread all of his drugs out before he could start. As soon as he was ready, he told us two to get out as we were not allowed in the mixing room. Slim told him to fuck off and that we were staying, and he was willing to discuss it further with him if he wanted. He didn't and we were allowed to stay. We just sat there, and whenever we suggested something he just blanked us. I don't like to speak ill of the dead, but he was an obnoxious, ignorant fucker.

In my opinion 'Fairy Tales' was a great song and for years Tony Wilson used to say that it was his favourite Factory single, but Hannett ruined any chance the song had of being good. We came out of Strawberry disappointed and hoped that the rest of the band had better fortune with Hooky. They did - Hooky did a great production job on 'Death is Slowly Coming'.

November started with Depeche Mode and Blancmange at Fagins. I was really looking forward to this gig. I couldn't get their single 'Just Can't Get Enough' out of my head. They had a lot more gear to bring in this time compared to the previous gigs at Rafters. Blancmange came on, they were a two piece - a singer and a guy on the synthesiser. They were great and I started buying their material as it came out. They had a great reception from the audience. Slim and I were on monitor duty at the front of the stage, and it was a much more civilised audience than at the Bauhaus gig, so we had no trouble.

The place was packed by the time Depeche Mode came on and they were greeted like heroes when they came on. They were more confident than the previous times I had seen them, and you could just tell that they were going to be a stadium band. They had already started the audience involvement bit. This gig was followed a few days later by Psychedelic Furs at Rotters. This was originally due to be played at Rafters, but they sold so many tickets it got moved. Fagins must have been booked up or otherwise it would just have moved upstairs. This was a great gig and they played songs off both albums. The place was packed, and Alan Wise probably oversold the number of tickets.

13 November: New Order release *Movement* (FACT 50). I went to see Lesley and got a copy. I played it for about a week solid and it was okay. Having heard all of the songs live on several occasions, it didn't sound as powerful on vinyl. I still play it occasionally nowadays. Beneath that Hannett mix there's a great set of songs just dying to be

released.

Later that evening Fad Gadget played Rafters. The gig was filmed and the cameramen needed the room on the stage, so we stood in the crowd and watched him. He had a really good band with him featuring a violinist, drummer, keyboard player, guitarist and a guy playing a weird cut away stand-up bass. The show was very good. Rafters was full.

The Birthday Party at Rafters – they started with 'Nick The Stripper' and played 'She's Hit' and 'Release The Bats' - crazy band, wild show. They were crazy Aussies - Tracey Pew was amazing, he played his bass like he was fucking it with crotch thrusts etc. I fell in love with the Birthday Party after this bought their albums at Discount the next day. I already had the single 'Release the Bats'. They became a favourite of mine and then I followed Nick Cave's career all the way till this day.

A few days later Gretton called me to say that they were planning on putting out a video showcasing the bands. It was going to be called *A Factory Video* and so we would have to do a video. But firstly, we would have to go into the studio and record a song for it.

7 December. We went into Cargo with Hooky to record the song for the video. We ended finishing two songs 'Something's Got To Give' and 'Soft Babies'. This was the first music recorded by this version of the band. We were now Shan, Lita, Tony, Karl, and I. We did it all in one day, with a normal person behind the mixing desk and not a prima donna.

9 December. We played The Hunting Lodge with Beach Red and MTI. Beach Red were as good as always and MTI were great on the night. I never saw them, or James, play a bad gig. This was the first gig Karl played with us, and we played two new songs 'All the Days of Her Life' and 'Happy Ever After'. It was a really good night. After the gig we decided to get a trumpet player since 'MC' didn't have the same feel to it as when Eddie played on it.

19 December: New Order release A 12 inch single of 'Everything's Gone Green' on Factory Benelux (FBN 8). This had already been released as the other side of 'Procession', but it now had two songs on the B Side 'Cries and Whispers' and 'Mesh'. I went round to see Lesley at Factory and got my copy. Around this time we got four acetates of 'Fairy Tales' to listen to and make sure that we were happy

with it. We confirmed it was ok. A couple of days later we got five white label copies of the single and I gave mine away to someone.

A few days before Christmas Malcolm Whitehead came to do the video with us. Malcolm was in charge of Ikon, the Factory Video Department, and he operated out of the cellar of Tony Wilson's house in Didsbury. We decided to go with 'Soft Babies' which ran for one minute and ten seconds. Later on we discovered that Tony Wilson was mad about this as it buggered up the running time of the video and as a result they had to use a longer live song off someone else to make up the time. We were doing the video in Shan and Lita's house and their parents were out for the day. It had snowed so we had a snowball fight in the front garden. It was good fun making it and we had a good day. I had been up for five days straight, speeding when we did the video and that's my excuse for looking like a wally.

On Christmas Eve we worked The Distractions and The Things at Rafters. The Things were great with Rocking Dave Holmes on lead guitar; great party music to get you started for Crimbo. Dave was in three bands at the same time - Dr Filth, The Renegades and The Things. Each band was a proper good time rock 'n' roll band. Rocking Dave is now Dr Dave as he has taught Psychology for over 30 years at Manchester University. He can be seen regularly on Sky News whenever a bad murder occurs discussing the mental state of the suspect. He has also been on various murder documentaries. He's a top bloke and still plays on the pub circuit.

Had a nice Xmas with Mum and Dad and then two days later I was 21. Slim and I went somewhere in town, I got very drunk and stoned, must have been a good night as I have no recollection of it. I have spent hours on the internet trying to find more gigs at Rafters and the above are all I can find. I know that I worked at Rafters at least once a week all this year and at Deville's several times more than I have written about.

For about the previous six months I had lapsed into a routine. I would speed for five days running and then come down for two. This meant I was doing lines of speed all day, and then staying up all night in my bedroom reading books or listening to music on my headphones. My Dad would be up at 5am so I would turn off my light until he left the house at around 6am. Looking back on it now I was stupid. Speed stopped me sleeping, stopped me eating, gave me spots, made me paranoid and basically killed my sex drive. The only good thing it did was enable me to drink whatever I wanted and not get drunk.

1981

Singles

New Order: 'Ceremony', 'Procession'
Siouxsie & The Banshees: 'Spellbound', 'Arabian Knights'
Birthday Party: 'Release The Bats'
Simple Minds: 'Love Song'
Echo and The Bunnymen: 'A Promise'
The Psychedelic Furs: 'Pretty in Pink'
The Names: 'Night Shift'
Blondie: 'Rapture'
Ultravox: 'Vienna'
The Jam: 'That's Entertainment'
The Specials: 'Ghost Town'
Rolling Stones: 'Start Me Up'
Bauhaus: 'The Passion of Lovers'
Theatre of Hate: 'Rebel without a Brain', 'Nero'
Public Image Limited: 'Flowers Of Romance'.
Killing Joke: 'Follow The Leaders'
Soft Cell: 'Bedsitter'
The Fall: 'Lie Dream of a Casino Soul'
Teardrop Explodes: 'Reward', 'Treason'.
OMD: 'Joan of Arc'
Gang of Four: 'To Hell With Poverty'.

EPs.

The Damned: *Friday the 13th*
The Fall: *Slates*
Buzzcocks: *Parts 1-3 EP*

Albums

Killing Joke: *What's This For*

Factory Fairy Tales

Siouxsie & The Banshees: *JuJu*
Echo and The Bunnymen: *Heaven Up Here*
New Order: *Movement*
Birthday Party: *Prayers on Fire*
Magazine: *Magic, Murder and The Weather*
Human League: *Dare*
Joy Division: *Still*
Bauhaus: *Mask*
Teardrop Explodes: *Wilder*
U2: *October*
Rolling Stones: *Tattoo You*
Gen X: *Kiss Me Deadly*
The Ramones: *Pleasant Dreams*
Public Image Limited: *Flowers of Romance*
Simple Minds: *Sons and Fascination*
Soft Cell: *Non Stop Erotic Cabaret*
Gang of Four: *Solid Gold*
The Gun Club: *Fire Of Love*
Fire Engines: *Lubricate Your Living Room*
The Scars: *Author! Author!*
Wah Heat: *Nah=Poo-The Art of The Bluff*
The Cure: *Faith*
The Psychedelic Furs: *Talk, Talk, Talk*
OMD: *Architecture & Morality*

15. Scooter in the sky

At the beginning of January Shan told us that he had found a trumpet player who was a friend of his from college - her name was Lindsay Anderson. She came along to a rehearsal, and we played her a cassette of what Eddie had played and she just played it straight away. So she was in. I had got some money off Dad for my birthday and Christmas so I went and bought a new bass. I had a short scale bass so now I went to the complete opposite extreme and got myself a Vox which had 24 frets on it so I could now play a lot more high notes.

4 January: New Order play 'Temptation' and 'Hurt' live on *The Riverside Show* on BBC 2. They came across really well on screen. Rob had asked me if I wanted to come down with them, but I couldn't be bothered, should have gone.

In the second week in January, 'Fairy Tales' was finally released, almost a year after we had recorded it. It was given the catalogue number (FAC 41). The sleeve came in two colours, green and burgundy. There were 5,000 of each made in the first press. Rob had taken Slim and I down to the factory to collect them. It was great to

Factory Fairy Tales

see how they made a record, and we were blown away by the cover.

Mark Farrow had designed the sleeve and in my humble opinion he made a superb job of it. Speaking to Tony Wilson after its release, he told me that he thought it was wonderful. The single sold out the first press but to be honest even if it had sold a bucket load we would not have made a penny from it. The recording costs were massive thanks to Mr Hannett and his fucking about, but the sleeve costs were astronomical as well. Mark based the design on an old book of Fairy Tales, so he used paper that was as close as possible to leather parchment, and the lettering as close as possible to gold leaf. For all I know it might be gold leaf. Who knows with Factory? He did the two colours and asked Tony which one to use, to which Tony replied, "Use both my dear", so he did.

The price of a single in the shops was around £1.10p.

Factory would sell a single to a record distributor for around 70p.

Our sleeve alone cost over £1 per single to produce, then add the recording and manufacturing costs, so you can see that the single lost a lot of money, but it fucking looked good and that was all that mattered!

My friend Colin Gibbins, the Factory collector, told me that later represses used a different quality paper with no embossed lettering so Factory might have got a bit of money back. Looking back on it all, I don't know what gave me the most pleasure – holding a copy of both sleeves in my hands to actually show people that I was in a band and not just a Billy Liar or the shock of hearing it being played on John Peel for the first time and hear him call it "a nice pop ditty"? He played it five or six times over the next few weeks. That made my day. It actually made it to Number 43 in the UK independent record chart.

20 January: Pigbag & 21 January: Orange Juice. Two great gigs which were both at Rafters. Two good bands. Two good nights. Pigbag had the best rhythm section I had heard in a long time, and they were great to watch. Orange Juice had some brilliant Pop songs to play. Edwin Collins was a star in the making.

Sometime early in 1982 Jim and Paul were over at Shan's when we were rehearsing, and they were looking for a name for their band. Having dropped 'International' from their original name they were initially re-christened Model Team but then faced legal action because there was a model agency of that name. We had a song called 'James', which was Paul's favourite of ours (it was Hooky's as well), and they asked us if we would mind if they used it as the name for their band. When I read *Folklore* by Stuart Maconie, the official history of James, this was not the version given by the band as to how they got their name. All I can say is that with the amount of drugs taken it's easy to forget what happened but mine is definitely the correct story!

22 January. We played North London Poly with New Order. Terry and Dave were doing something so they couldn't collect our gear and take us down to London. We hired a van, and I can't remember who drove us down there. Mani and Kaiser came down with us and we had a right laugh. Slim was skinning up all the way down and we were pretty stoned when we got there.

We managed to get a sound check which was unusual and much appreciated. 'All the Days of her Life' and 'Love is a Dose' were two new songs we played that night. Tony had heard me playing 'Love is a Ghost' by Theatre of Hate and he thought that Kirk Brandon was singing 'Love is a Dose'. When I explained that he was wrong, we had a song title. We went down really well with the crowd and it was the best gig that we had done so far but the gig got off to a bad start. We started with an atmospheric version of 'Death is Slowly Coming' with Shan and Lita on the keyboards and it sounded great from where I was stood on the stage but when the song finished not one person in the place clapped. They just stood there open mouthed. It was so fucking weird. The crowd made up for that start as they applauded every song that we played afterwards but it was an unnerving experience. Mani and Kaiser were raving about how good we'd been. There was a writer called Mark Johnson who was at the gig, and he also turned up in Birmingham the following day. He was writing a book about Joy Division and New Order called *An Ideal For Living* and it turned out to be really good and I bought a copy when it came out. I'm listed in the credits, but he forgot to credit Slim. He was an American and he followed everyone round all day and asked some unbelievably dumb questions, so he was pissing the band off. He interviewed Slim and me about working in the Russell and the times we had seen Joy Division, so some of the facts that you find in the book about the Russell, Apollo, Mayflower, Electric Circus, and Osbourne gigs came from us. We also told him about the New Order gigs we had seen as well, and the bit about the six instrumental Joy Division songs in the Heaven sound check came from us.

Factory Fairy Tales

Just before New Order came on Rob asked us two to play a jape on Mark and he would give us a tenner each. We accepted the deal. We went outside and found Mark's scooter. It was a Vespa and my mod mates Mani and Kaiser had always told me that the only proper scooter was a Lambretta. We noticed that the building had a ledge, about eight foot off the ground, which went round the outside of the building, and it was wide enough to put a scooter on. Next door there was guy driving a forklift, so a couple of minutes later, you can guess where the scooter ended up.

New Order were great, they started with 'Dreams Never End' and ended with 'Ceremony' and 'Temptation'. It was a great gig. There were some dicks near the front, and they started trouble in front of Hooky near the end of the set. Kaiser, Mani, Slim, Tony, Karl, and I steamed into them and sorted them out in a couple of minutes. As New Order finished Hooky tried to get involved and since we had sorted it out, we tried to stop him from joining in, but he still ended up decking someone who got too close to him.

This was the first gig that I noticed Barney used Ian Curtis's famous white Vox guitar on one of the songs, sorry I can't remember which song. As soon as they had finished we took Rob outside and he was well impressed and paid us both. Afterwards we were sat backstage and we had a few beers and a couple of spliffs before we all went outside to see Mark's reaction to his scooter being eight foot off the ground. Mark couldn't understand where his scooter was until someone pointed it out to him. Rob, Barney, and Hooky fell about laughing. New Order had started doing the odd jape on us, nothing bad but they were testing us so last thing we did before we climbed in the back of the van for the long journey back to God's Country was to let down all four tyres on New Order's car. I bet that stopped them laughing.

The next day we made our way to the Imperial Cinema, Birmingham where we were supporting New Order. Mani and Kaiser came with us again. Alan Wise was promoting this gig and when we got there he was panicking as he had forgotten to buy the booze for New Order's rider. For the benefit of people who don't know what a rider is, it's the food and drink a band requests backstage and it's usually part of the contract between the band and the promoter. I told Alan not to worry as I had seen an off license that was open just round the corner. He gave Slim and me a wad of cash. We noticed that the area was full of Asians and when we entered the off license, we got most of the stuff we needed, and joined the queue. We planned to get Barney's Pernod from behind the till. The shop was run by an Asian, and when we reached the counter he just blanked us and served the person behind. He did this a few more times before we started shouting at him. He told us that he didn't serve people like us. We left the place after I had convinced Slim not to tip over the racks and fight everyone. We went back to the venue, found Shan and he got served. This is the only time that I have ever had to face racism like this in my lifetime. I mean I've been in the Nile or Reno in Moss Side with the Rastas calling me Honky but this was serious.

New Order started their sound check and during it the three lads from Echo and The Bunnymen, Les, Will, and Pete walked in and sat with us. They were out on a ride on their motorbikes again and had decided to come to Birmingham. We did our sound check and went upstairs in the balcony with the three Bunnymen and sat there smoking until the place opened. The place was packed by the time we went on. We played the same nine songs we played the previous evening but in a different order. We went down really well with the crowd, it was a great gig. A couple of coaches had come from Manchester to the gig and there were a few of our mates scattered about the venue.

The Factory Video guy, Malcolm Whitehead, was there to tape New Order and he taped our show as well. I watched it the other day for the first time in about 15 years – brought back some great times. New Order came on and started with 'Temptation' and finished with 'Ceremony'. There was no encore. They went down great, and it was a good set. Afterwards we sat and drank with New Order and The Bunnymen and then we made our way back to Manchester. Mark the writer was there, and he was quiet and didn't ask as many stupid questions. He kept nipping out during the gig probably to keep an eye on his scooter! Nothing was said about the tyres.

31 January: Rip, Rig & Panic play Fagins. We hated them last time they played but for some unknown reason they were now in Fagins. Once again we were on monitor duty, and it was crazy trying to stop the fans from knocking them. We pushed and moved so many people during their set. We had not been getting along with the band at all during the day. They had an attitude towards us both, as did their road crew. Maybe they were pissed off that we had to keep pushing their fans back but whatever it was we knew that it was going to kick off.

Factory Fairy Tales

When we were taking the gear out with their road crew, a row developed between them and Slim. I was on stage taking the PA stack down and I heard the commotion, so I ran out to help Slim. Three or four of them were punching and kicking him. I managed to break it up and got Slim away from them. One of the people who had joined in kicking him was band member Gareth Sager. Slim swore revenge and told them that if he ever saw any of them again he would batter them. It wouldn't be long before he got his chance.

At the beginning of February, Rob rang me and told me that they wanted another single. At the next rehearsal, and after a long discussion, we came to the conclusion that we would rather do an album, so I called Rob and arranged a meeting. A couple of days later, I had a meeting with Rob and Tony at Tony's house in Didsbury. They told me that they wanted us to do a single, and I said that we wanted to do an album.

I told them that we had ten songs and we wanted to rerecord 'Fairy Tales' to make it sound like it was supposed to, and that we would have a couple of new songs written by the time the recording session started. There were also three old songs that we could resurrect and use as B Sides. I also recommended 'MC' as the next single, with the original slow version of 'MC' with an extra verse as the B Side and maybe do 'Catch me in Confusion' as a throw away third song and release it as a 12 inch single. They pitched their idea to me, and I pitched our idea to them. The result of the meeting was that they now wanted to do an album, and I wanted to do a single. So we did a single!

I should have agreed to an album and got the dates booked in Strawberry. If this had happened then I wouldn't have left in April. I would have stayed to see how the album turned out. This is still a massive regret of mine - another stupid decision.

After working a couple of nondescript gigs it was the turn of the big one - Killing Joke and Dead or Alive gig at Rotters on 21 February. Our mate Bernie was over from Liverpool with Pete Burns. We spent the early afternoon in the Salisbury, and we were stoned when we got to Rotters to start setting up the stage. Dead or Alive seemed a strange choice of support for a Killing Joke crowd but they went down well. I reckon Pete Burns scared the shit out of them! Killing Joke were fucking brilliant. Slim and I went and stood in amongst the chaos in front of the stage and had a wild time. The Joke never let you down.

Ged Duffy

A couple of days later Slim and I were in Discount Records when Rob Gretton walked in and suggested we went for a beer. We suggested the Salisbury, but he took us to the City Road Inn which we had never been in before. After a couple, he asked us if we would like to go and look at a new club that Factory were opening, so he took us over the road to The Hacienda. It was still being built but it looked amazing. He told us that the plan was for the stage to be at the far end and the bar to be on the right side, in the middle of the club. That made sense to us as it gave maximum viewing potential to the club. The only concern we told him was that the roof was too high and made of glass and this might affect the sound. He said that would be sorted before it opened, and we would be doing the stage if we wanted. We said yes.

The following day, 24 February, we went into Strawberry Studios in Stockport to record our second single 'Happy Ever After'. We had the studio booked for two days and this time there was no Hannett. Everything went really smoothly with Hooky mixing. There was no stripping down of the drum kit. We recorded most of the song live. Then Lita overdubbed the grand piano again, but the main melody of the song was her electric organ. Karl added a bit more guitar. Tony added the drum synth bit for the chorus. We all sang backing vocals on the chorus.

For the B side we re-recorded 'Soft Babies' and played it live. Hooky came up with the idea of making it longer, so we played it until he told us to stop. He then cut most of the instruments out of the middle section and got us all to go in and just said any shit that came to our heads during this section. Shan added more percussion and Karl played a few notes on the guitar in the third section of the song. Lita added grand piano on the middle section and Lindsay added some trumpet as well. We all sang backing vocals.

Both songs were recorded on the first day, and the second day was spent mixing. Unlike Hannett, not only were we allowed in the room, but everything was discussed and agreed with us and Hooky before anything got done. It was so different than being in the studio with Hannett. We ended up with three different mixes of 'Happy Ever After' and one mix of 'Soft Babies'. Hooky then did three different dub mixes of 'Soft Babies'. I had given Mark Farrow the other picture of Montgomery Clift that I had found in a book. It was a black and white picture, and he was telling me that he was going to colour in bits of it and it would be a gate-fold sleeve. It sounded great and I was looking forward to seeing it.

Next gig we worked at was Bauhaus at Rotters. When they arrived Pete Murphy recognized Slim and me from the Fagins gig and he came over to say hello. He said that he had no plans to kick either of us that night. Bauhaus came on to play 'Rose Garden of Sores' which has an offbeat, fractured rhythm and, in conjunction with the light show, it was a spectacular entrance. This was followed by 'Passion of Lovers' which is classic Bauhaus. They then played a lot of album tracks which ruined the atmosphere for a while, and it took them doing 'In the Flat Field' and 'Dark Entries' to get it back. I loved Bauhaus and this was another great gig. Sometime in February Theatre Of Hate release *Do You Believe In The West World* album. Another classic album from a very underrated band.

3 March: We played the Blue Note Club in Derby with New Order. Rob had phoned me a couple of days before to tell me that we might as well use their equipment and we only had to bring our guitars and keyboards. Terry and Dave picked us up and we got in the back of the van and Slim started skinning up. Familiar pattern developing eh? New Order sound checked and were then followed by us. I had a good nosey round Hooky's bass set up. He had an amp (a Hi Watt, if my memory serves me well) on top of a 2 x 18 inch speaker cabinet which was also attached to another 2 x 18 inch cabinet. Next to these two speakers he had a cabinet which was his effects box. This looked amazing as it had so many switches, controls, dials, and faders. Terry told me that I was never allowed to touch that. This box was the secret to the magical sounds that came from Mr Hook.

We were sat around when Mani, Kaiser and a couple of the North Manchester lot turned up. It was then that we noticed that there was a small gap at the bottom of the bar's shutters and Barney reckoned that Karl was thin enough to get under. He could, and once behind it, he became our bar man. We started drinking, and after we'd had a couple of drinks, the manager of the club turned up and had a fit. Rob calmed him down and told him to deduct it out of the fee.

Before we went on, Barney had noticed the state of the guitar that Karl was playing. He gave him his black Shergold guitar to keep. Rob deducted £50 later for the guitar, but Karl now had a good guitar to play. The place was full when we went on. Shan and I were buzzing about using Hooky and Stephen's equipment. Maybe this made us sound better on the night. It was like standing in front of a PA system being in front of those massive speakers. The Blue Note was a very

Ged Duffy

small club, and the stage was about six inches off the main floor, so the crowd was right up close and personal when we were on stage.

New Order came on and started with a new song 'Ultraviolence' and the crowd were dancing wildly at the front. During the third song 'Ceremony' the crowd's wild dancing was pushing back the stage monitors and Eddie the monitor guy came forward and pushed them back. At the end of the song, Terry was asking the crowd to move back so as not to harm the equipment. I think the crowd pushed New Order on as this was one of the best versions of 'Temptation' that I ever heard them play live. It was a brilliant gig. Mani told me a story that prior to us coming on he had left an old portable cassette recorder on the mixing desk and Hooky had a go at him about taping New Order to which Mani replied, "I'm here for the Monsters not you lot". Classic Mani, no bullshit.

Afterwards we sat round drinking and smoking before we got in the dark van again for the trip home. We came back via Buxton, so we had a load of winding roads to content with. I was glad to get out of the van when we arrived back in Didsbury.

The next day we had a band meeting, and it was decided that we were going to try and talk to Rough Trade Records to see if they would release 'Happy Ever After'. This decision was made after Tony Wilson's statement that the single would sell fuck all on Factory. I had a meeting with Rob to tell him what we were planning, and he assured me that nothing would change between us if we moved to Rough Trade. He would still carry on acting as an unpaid manager for us and would still do everything jointly with me.

After a few phone calls I finally managed to talk to Geoff Travis, boss of Rough Trade, and he agreed to see us in his office on 25 March so the day before Slim, Tony, Shan, and I took the National Express coach to London. It was a fun trip down and we drank a bit. We didn't smoke as people on the coach might have complained. When we got to London we got the tube across to Kings Road and had a walk around the shops. We were going to stay with a guy who lived in a squat on Fulham Road. Later that night we went to a couple of pubs on Kings Road including the Phene Arms which was George Best's local.

The following day we went to Rough Trade with a cassette of the single mixes. On the way we were walking past a TV studio and Jeremy Beadle suddenly appeared, walking towards us. At this point Slim looks at us three and says, "Thanks a bunch, you bastards" and runs off down a side street! Jeremy Beadle presented a show on Saturday nights called *Game For A Laugh* which was a show where people were set up for practical jokes – it was a huge hit at the time. Just as the 'victim' had been suckered in, Jeremy would step out and tell them they'd been had. So Slim thought we had set him up! It took us ages to try and find him and convince him it was just coincidence before we set off to Rough Trade.

Geoff Travis listened to our cassette a couple of times and told us that he was interested. We explained the way Factory worked as in there was no contract between us and them, and Rough Trade could have the single, just by paying the recording costs which, thanks to Hooky's involvement, were not massive. While all this was going on Slim was sat in the reception area and we heard the door open and shout "Oh it's you, you fucking bastard" followed by a cry of pain. We ran out to find that Slim was sat on top of someone hitting them. It was Gareth Sagar out of Rip Rig and Panic!

Geoff looked at me and said, "Is that with you", to which I replied "Yes". He handed the cassette tape back to me and told us to leave. So Slim cost us joining Rough Trade but in his defence Gareth Sagar needed a kicking for what he and his mates had done to Slim outside Fagins.

We decided to stay another night in London because The Fall and Birthday Party were playing that night at Hammersmith Palais. We got there early and just walked in and saw the sound check. The lads from The Fall said that we didn't have to pay. I then noticed that my old flat mate Lee was working as a roadie for The Fall. He did a few tours with them. We spent most of the evening with Lee and went backstage for a while.

I was so happy at seeing a gig at the Hammersmith Palais as one of my favourite songs from The Clash was the magnificent 'White Man In Hammersmith Palais'. Slim and I sat down with a spliff and sang a few words from the song, totally out of tune as neither of us could sing but we had to do it. The Birthday Party came on and blew me away. This was the best that I had seen them so far. Barry Adamson out of Magazine was playing bass for them that night as Tracey Pew was now in prison back in Australia. It seemed that he had been arrested on a recent tour of Australia and got sent down so Barry played a few gigs with them until he returned. The Fall, now with the two drummers totally integrated into the sound, were magnificent on the night. This was the best I had seen them.

16. Into Europe with New Order

After we got back from London, I met Rob to tell him what had happened and that the single would be coming out on Factory. He was glad and told me that we were going to Europe as the support act to New Order in a series of gigs in Holland, Belgium, and France in April. Rob had some concerns about Karl as he was only 16 and still at school. He was worried about what would happen if we got stopped at UK customs and they wanted to see proof of a legal absence from school. There was also the issue of him being inside licensed venues in the three countries – as it turned out Karl just played truant for the two weeks.

I told the rest of the band, and they were so made up with the prospect of playing in these three countries. We spent the next few days rehearsing every day and getting our One Year Travel Passes sorted out as most of us didn't have a passport. Slim was coming with us on the condition that he also worked as a New Order roadie on these dates as well. We managed to write a new song 'National Pastime' before we set off to Holland. I also changed my bass line to 'Fairy Tales' so that I was now following Lita's melody note for note on the middle eight section. At the last rehearsal Karl played me a couple of bass chords that he had worked out. I played them and added a third one to it and then we packed up the gear.

Wednesday 7 April 1982: Terry and Dave came to the house to pick up our gear. We loaded it in the van and about 20 minutes later New Order turned up in their hired mini bus. We all got in, and Tony and I ended up in the front seat alongside a mate of Rob's who was driving. As soon as we set off a map was thrust into my hands with the instructions, "get us to Harwich". I had never read a map in my life before and Tony and I were absolutely stumped. We gave directions as best we could, whilst at the same time smoking the joints that were being passed round.

After a couple of hours Rob stirred and asked "where the fuck are we? That sign said Norwich". We'd fucked up and after pulling into the services the proper route was planned. We got to the ferry with minutes to spare. Terry and Dave missed it and had to wait for the next one. This was the one and only time Tony or I were put in the front.

Ged Duffy

We immediately went to the bar. Nobody had any drugs on them, as they were all used before we got to the customs at the port, so it was time to get drunk instead. We sat round and drank and basically took the piss out of each other for the next six and a half hours until we were allowed back downstairs to the minibus. Slim and I got out on the deck for a few minutes during the crossing.

From the Hook of Holland we drove the short distance to the hotel in Rotterdam. I was sharing with Slim, Tony and Karl were sharing, and Lita and Lindsey were together, I don't know who Shan was in with, Steve and Gillian were together and then Hooky, and Barney shared a room. Rob, Hooky, Barney, Slim, Tony and I found a small bar round the corner from the hotel and camped ourselves in there.

I can't remember anything about coming back to the hotel at all. I remember waking up next morning on the corridor of the floor below my room so I must have got off the lift at the wrong floor, tried a door with my key and decided to fall asleep where I fell. Tony had fallen asleep outside in the bushes at the front of the hotel. He had been woken by a gardener picking up leaves with one of those sticks with points on the end of them. He must have prodded Tony with it who immediately woke up and was ready to fight him. Rob had to calm the hotel manager down who wanted Tony arrested.

When we came downstairs for breakfast we saw that Oz, Eddie, and Diane had arrived with their PA. They were followed a few minutes later by the lighting guy, Pete, from Light, Sound, Design. Dave and Terry had arrived overnight after getting the next ferry and the windscreen on their van had cracked on the journey. The whole crew was now here.

We had a few hours to kill before we had to get to the venue so Slim, Pete, and I went for a walk round. It was a port city, and you could tell that it was a rough and ready place. We walked for a while and realized that the only tourist places to see were museums, so we found a bar instead and had a couple of drinks.

8 April: The Glazenzaal, Rotterdam. It looked like a large venue outside, but when we got in it was a hall which held about 600 people with a stage at one end. Oz and Pete set their desks up at the rear of the hall. Slim and I stayed out front and helped set everything up whilst all the rest went backstage. Once everything was ready New Order came on for their sound check. As usual it took a long time. The

Factory Fairy Tales

MOJO CONCERTS presenteert
NEW ORDER
+ STOCKHOLM MONSTERS
DONDERDAGAVOND 8 APRIL, 20.00 UUR
GLAZENZAAL VAN AHOY TE ROTTERDAM
ENTREE f. 17,50   * 535

beauty of being the only support band was that we got to do a sound check every night. We played one or two songs so that Hooky could get the sound right for us and then we spent about ten minutes working on an idea that Karl had given me. Lita immediately came up with a keyboard bit and Shan with a drumbeat. I had an idea for the change and by the end of the sound check we had most of the song written.

We went off to find a bar, and when we came back to the venue there was a major shock waiting for everyone. Unbeknown to us, the wall behind the mixing deck was false and it was now open, so the hall was now doubled in size and held about 1200 people. This would cause issues with the PA and we'd have to resolve them during our set. I remember Barney and Hooky were really annoyed that the venue had done this.

We had rehearsed 11 songs to play, 'Fairy Tales', 'Death is Slowly Coming', 'Happy Ever After', 'Soft Babies', 'Something's Got to Give', 'James', 'MC', 'Lafayette', 'National Pastime', 'All the Days of Her Life', and 'Love is a Dose'. We planned on doing ten songs per gig and we were all going to take turns in choosing what order to play them in. When we came on the place was full. It was a weird crowd made up of punks, skinheads, mohawks, Hippies and normal people, definitely not your standard New Order audience. I don't think I saw one sad young man in a raincoat in the crowd! We went down great with the crowd as we had a few songs which were fast, they were dancing and bouncing into each other. New Order came on and played for just under 30 minutes and walked off. They never said hello or goodbye. The set was good but not great. The crowd demanded an encore and started booing. This carried on for a couple of minutes. The house lights came on and they still stood there screaming for an encore.

In Hooky's great book *Substance* he wrote that every Dutch guy at the gig was tall. Several years after this gig I worked for a Dutch company and had to go to Holland a couple of times a year for meetings and he's right, the average height of the guys I used to meet was about 6 foot 2. The crowd stood there booing and screaming at the stage and no one was leaving the venue. Slim and I had been away with United enough to realize that this was going to get nasty. We had been in the hall watching New Order, so we now decided to get back on stage just in case the crowd decided to take their anger out on Terry and Dave who were starting to take New Order's gear down. There were two or three mohawks near the front of the crowd who were the most vocal and one of them threw a pint pot at the stage which smashed. We all jumped out of the way and Slim went to the edge of the stage and shouted, "Come on then, I'll fuck the lot of you". Slim, Tony, Karl, Rob, and I grabbed whatever we could and jumped off stage straight into the middle of them. I had two of Stephen's drumsticks in each hand and was smacking them into the faces of everyone nearby.

After a few minutes it calmed down and we had taken control of the situation, mainly due to the fact that Slim had taken care of the fucker who had thrown the pint pot. Stephen's drum sticks had got smashed and had gone to drum stick heaven. Should have kept them as there's definitely a New Order fan out there who would have paid a fortune for them. Oz started taking down the microphones and he noticed a big skinhead with a bottle in his hand, just before he launched it at his head. He managed to duck and avoid the bottle which smashed on the stage behind him. Oz jumped into the crowd and started to batter the skinhead. He had him on the floor and was pounding him with his fists when four or five more skinheads joined in and started kicking Oz. Hooky had come from backstage to see what was going on and when he saw Oz getting attacked he jumped off the stage and ran towards him but a bunch of mohawks and skinheads jumped him, and Hooky was knocked clean out. This had all happened in a matter of seconds, and we didn't know who to try and help so Tony, Eddie and I went to help Oz, whilst Dave jumped off and went to Hooky. Slim found a metal rubbish bin at the side of the stage which was about four feet tall, and he jumped off stage and held the bin at head height and ran towards Hooky. I saw Slim out of the corner of my eye as we were fighting to get Oz out twat person after person with the bin. He was like a human bowling ball. By this stage, we had got Oz and our side of the hall had stopped fighting as we were all now watching Slim.

This big skinhead stood in front of Slim and didn't move. Slim didn't stop. The bin hit and split the skinhead's nose and blood went everywhere. As he went down Slim carried on running straight over him and got to Hooky and got him backstage. The fighting stopped.

Factory Fairy Tales

Slim One Rotterdam Nil.

It was only then that the one security guard at the venue showed his face and was screaming at us lot like we were to blame. Fucking wanker. When we got back to the hotel Hooky, Rob, Barney, Tony, and I went back to the bar and stayed there drinking. We found out afterwards that despite all the shit that had gone down, one of the crew had copped off with an American girl and she had entertained three or four of them back at the hotel. Next morning I got up and went downstairs for breakfast. Rob was having a heated meeting with the tour promoter, Wilhelm, as they discussed the previous night's events. The riot had made the front page of the local Rotterdam morning newspaper. Wilhelm was prepared to cancel the tour unless things changed.

It was agreed that New Order would play a longer set of nine songs as opposed to the eight that they played at every gig I had seen until now. Wilhelm was also going to get leaflets printed off for each gig explaining that New Order play a very short set, don't do encores, and don't talk to the crowd, that way people could get their money back if they decided not to come to the gigs. None of the four remaining gigs in Holland would be full. Wilhelm then went and made a phone call to confirm that the Amsterdam gig would go ahead, and he repeated this action every morning. We left to drive to Amsterdam, and this was where we could restock our empty drug cupboard.

As we approached the Red Light district Rob stopped the minibus. One of our party had spent the majority of the previous night in Rotterdam chatting up the ladies with no success so Rob took him out of the bus so he could pick a lady from the window displays. He choose "Miss Moonlight" and Rob paid for him. As he came back out to huge applause from everyone inside the bus, Barney had an idea. Rob and Barney went back into see "Miss Moonlight" and came out a couple of minutes later. They had offered "Miss Moonlight" a lot of money to fuck Slim and allow them to film it. She said yes but her pimp said no. Barney said that they would have used bits of it in upcoming New Order videos. Needless to say Slim was up for it.

As we pulled up outside our hotel there was a guy waiting in the car park. He was a drug dealer and we all stocked up from him. Slim and I got some speed and some weed. What a city! You check in with your drug dealer as soon as you arrive. We checked in our hotel with the same sleeping arrangements as before. Slim and I would not sleep again until we got back to Manchester.

9 April: Theater de Meervaart Amsterdam. The venue was a multi-purpose complex with exhibition rooms, a theatre, and a hall for gigs. The hall we were playing in held about 1000. There were no surprises lurking around the corner tonight as this hall couldn't be made bigger, but I noticed Oz having a walk round the perimeter of the hall just to make sure. He did this at all of the rest of the gigs.

During our sound check we worked on the new song with Lindsey playing the synthesiser alongside Lita on the organ. Tony had written some words that worked. I remember the line "little boys will play their games" which was probably a reference to the previous night in Rotterdam. We decided to play it that night. It's title was 'Miss Moonlight'. Had to be didn't it?

We played ten songs including, 'Miss Moonlight' and went down great, this was the best gig that we had played to date. The audience were the same make up as Rotterdam, and they were bouncing along with us as we played.

New Order came on and played nine songs. They went down well with the audience who didn't demand an encore as they had all read the leaflet from Wilhelm. There were about 700 in on the night. I helped the guys strip the gear down afterwards and then we went back to the hotel. Slim and I were speeding and had no intention of sleeping so we joined the usual suspects at a bar near the hotel that was open late. We had no time at all really to explore Amsterdam, but once we got to the hotel in Arnhem around noon the next day, we could see a bit of that city. Once we checked in Slim, Pete and I went round to see some of the sights. It had an old and new section of the city centre. It was an interesting place. We found a bar and had a few beers before meeting up again at the hotel.

10 April: Stockvishal, Arnhem: I was looking forward to playing here as it was one of the few venues that Sex Pistols had played in 1977. It was a proper old style punk venue. It was covered in graffiti and old posters. The toilets were a disgrace. The stage was at chest height in Holland which since they were all tall fuckers equated to head height in the UK. It was perfect, so if someone gave you shit then you could kick them in the chest. There was no heating in the place, and it was freezing. I doubt it even had running water. The bouncers were all mohawks covered in tattoos. The only time we were warm was under the lights when we were on stage.

There was a large, seated area outside the venue so Slim and I got a beer and sat there watching the people roll up for the gig. It was warmer outside than it was inside. Once again it was a weird gathering of fans. Pete asked me for a set list as he had gotten to know some of the songs, and he wanted to provide us with a better light show. This got better every night as well. We played another good set. It sounded great up on stage and I was getting used to that monster bass rig behind me. The audience loved us and were dancing again. 'Miss Moonlight' got played again tonight and it sounded better tonight. A few people even shouted for an encore after we had done our ten songs.

New Order played their nine songs and once again put on a great show before they went off with no encore. There were no problems. 'Procession' and 'Temptation' went down well with the punks – same script after the show, the usual suspects but in a different bar. Afterwards Rob came back to our room as we had some more beer in there which we had removed from the venue. We were sitting down, and I saw the football results on Dutch TV – City 0 Liverpool 5. Now I hate the Bin Dippers, but I couldn't let this opportunity pass to take the piss out of a blue. So I gave it Gretton with both barrels and do you know what he did. He took his glasses off and jumped on me and we were rolling round on the floor fighting each other. Slim stopped it and we sat down, had a beer, shook hands, and moved on.

11 April: Muziekcentrum Vredenburg, Utrecht: Another hotel and another city to have a quick look round. Years later I spent a couple of nights in Utrecht, and it was a nice city.

I can't remember anything about this venue: the promoter was still handing out his leaflets and the crowd was about 30% down each night. Sometimes when you're speeding you can get paranoid. I had never experienced that until tonight. I thought everyone was out to get me and I played the whole gig with my back to the audience. A couple of hours later it passed, and I was back to normal.

We played a great set again and went down really well with the punks. Afterwards I was sat in a bar with Rob, and he told me that he had been really impressed with the way we had performed so far on the tour. Wilhelm was impressed as well, so much so that he wanted us to come back in a couple of months and play Holland, Belgium, France, and Germany. Rob suggested that The Wake came over with us as a Factory Road Tour. He also told me that John Peel had enquired about us doing a session for him, but I wasn't to tell the rest of the band about any of these two plans until he finalized them both on our return.

The next morning we were off to Maastricht and like the previous four cities we had been to, it was also built around a river. The other thing common amongst the four was that they were full of cyclists who have the right of way on the footpaths. The amount of times we nearly got into fights because we didn't know that you were not allowed to walk down these cycle paths or because we didn't check the pavement for cyclists before we crossed the road.

12 April Staargebouw, Maastricht: This place looked like the Mayflower – what a dump! It held about 1000 or so and about 700 were in again. Once again we played a good set and the punks and mohawks liked us, they were dancing again. It was a good gig. Our last six songs we played were 'Love is a Dose', 'MC', 'Something's got to Give', 'National Pastime', 'Lafayette', and we finished with 'Happy Ever After'. All fast-paced songs which were played faster since most of the band were speeding. New Order went down well again, and I was enjoying seeing them play every day. They were great on this tour, and I loved them up till about 1990 when they went more machine-based, they were much better when they were Hooky and Stephen based. If you've got a brilliant bass player and a brilliant drummer why do you need machines to do their job? Just use the fucking real thing - just my opinion.

Same folks, different bar after the show. The next morning we said goodbye to the land of the giants and headed to Brussels, the home of the grey raincoat, a proper Factory city. By now the windscreen on the van had cracked and gone so Terry put a sheet of plastic across the windscreen and cut holes to see out of. It was raining, and we were driving against the wind, so they were going to get wet.

Tony, Slim and I sat at the back of the bus, smoking all the way. As soon as we approached the Belgium/ Holland border everyone in front passed all their gear down to us three at the back. I don't know what they had in mind - was it that we get caught with it all and they get away? So being proper Mancs we split it into three and swallowed everything. We didn't get stopped at the border, so all eyes were on us to return everything. We just looked at them and started laughing. We laughed for a while and there was some muttering going on in front of us. When we reached the France border, a few days later, I noticed that nothing was passed back to us...

We arrived at the hotel in Brussels where we were booked in to stay for three nights. It was the best so far and within a few minutes we had found a dealer and had restocked our supplies. Brussels must be one of the most boring cities in the world. It houses the European Parliament and as far as I could see there was nothing else in the city worth seeing. We found a few bars and sat in a few squares. We got back to the hotel around 6pm as we were going out as a guest of the Belgium promoter for dinner. Even though I was speeding I ate my steak as I hadn't had one for a while. There were plenty of drinks and plenty of laughs. Oz's crew: Pete, Terry, and Dave, all came with us. I think that there were a couple of people from Factory Benelux out with us that night as well.

Then most of us went to a bar later on and spent a few hours in there. The following morning Slim, Pete and I had a walk round Brussels and got back to the hotel just after lunch. We had to drive to Leuven which was about an hour away for the gig.

14 April: Lido, Leuven. This was a decent-sized venue which held about 800. After New Order sound checked we played 'Miss Moonlight' a few times and we now had it sounding right with everyone knowing when the changes happened.

When we came on the place was full of sad young men in raincoats. It was a Factory homecoming! They cheered and clapped through our set, and we went down well again. New Order played ten songs and it was like a triumphant homecoming. The audience lapped up everything they played and there was no moaning when an encore didn't happen. When we reached the hotel the usual crew went off for a beer. Next morning Stephen came downstairs and told Rob that there was a problem with the TV set in his room. It didn't work properly so he had taken it apart screw by screw and then couldn't work out how to put it back together, so it was in bits on the floor in his room. Rob paid for a new TV.

15 April: L'Ancienne Belgique. Brussels: This was a large venue which held 2,000 people and it was sold out. It had an upper tier which stretched round three sides of the venue. By the time we came on it was packed. Once again it was a Factory crowd. We played our best set and we had a great reception off the crowd. When we came off Rob came and told us that we were great. New Order played ten songs, went off and did 'Temptation' for an encore. They were on stage for about an hour. It was a brilliant gig by them. Slim and I were in the middle of the crowd watching them and they sounded great from where we were stood. Whilst we were stood there a pretty little girl came up and asked me if I was in the support band to which I replied yes. We talked for a while, and she came back to the hotel with us. She was called Nicky – I had got my first groupie. Thankfully the speed didn't affect anything, and we had a great night together. She left the next morning and we set off for Paris.

It was a long drive to Paris, and we were smoking in the bus all the way, so we were a bit stoned when we got there. Nothing happened at the French border, and we reached the hotel in Paris by about 2pm. We checked in and Slim, Pete, and I went off exploring. We went to the Eiffel Tower, walked along the Seine, and then decided to have a walk round the red light district in the Quartier Pigalle. Rob took us all out that night for a meal and then a few of us ended up in a local bar again into the wee small hours. Next day after breakfast, Slim, Pete, and I hit the streets again. We went to the Left Bank of the Seine to see all the artists and got back to the hotel around 4pm to get the bus to the gig.

Just before I left England I'd read in the *NME* that Spandau Ballet had become the first band to appear at La Palace and tonight was the second ever gig there. It was supposed to be a chic gay club. When we got there it was a dump, just a four-walled room with nothing special about it. I was disappointed.

17 April: Le Palace, Paris: The place held about 800, and we had to be completely finished and out of the venue by 11pm as the club would reopen at midnight. The doors opened at 7pm and New Order would be off by 10pm at the latest. Stephen had been messing about with his video camera during the whole trip so I asked him if Slim could tape us using his camera. He said no but he would tape us in return for me taping New Order – deal done. We did an interview with a French fanzine as 'Fairy Tales' had become a minor hit in France.

When we came on the place was packed with loads of punks and mohawks, so we started with six of the faster songs and they fucking loved us. They were dancing and some were pogoing at the end. This was probably the best crowd reaction of the tour. The stage was really small so we were just in front of the audience, and it was great as

Factory Fairy Tales

we could touch them if we wanted to. We played the usual set and after we finished 'Happy Ever After' a punk started to climb the PA stack on my side of the stage and Hooky was heard shouting "Get down, you thick French cunt". He didn't so Oz put pure feedback through that stack and the punk was clinging on until he gave up and got down. As we walked off I was still undecided at that moment, but I had played my last note as a Stockholm Monster.

New Order came on and played nine songs with no encore. I videotaped them for Stephen as agreed. When they finished bottles were thrown at the stage but security stopped it before anything could get out of hand. Once the crowd was gone, it was panic stations as we had about 40 minutes to pack everything away so the club could become a club again. As we were outside loading the van, the queue for the club stretched round the block as it was due to open at midnight till 4. A few of the party went back to the hotel and we stayed upstairs in the dressing room drinking until the club opened.

When we came downstairs, the transformation was unbelievable; the walls had false panels in them which when turned around made a new designer wall, so all the walls were different, Chandeliers now hung from the ceiling, the stage had gone, there were lights everywhere and a large area was now carpeted. It was amazing.

The music was all disco - Donna Summer 'I Feel Love', Sylvester 'You Make Me Feel Mighty Real' and Anita Ward 'Ring my Bell'. It made such a change to hear a whole night of stuff like this. A pint of beer in Manchester was about 80p whilst a bottle of beer here was about £2.50 so we kept nipping upstairs to get supplies from the dressing room. The club was 100% male so Slim kept his wits about him especially after his experience in Heaven. Slim and I had the party room during the tour and most people ended up in it at some point during the tour apart from Gillian and Stephen. In Paris Slim fulfilled his dream, he threw a TV set out of our window and watched it smash on the pavement below. Rob paid for a new one. Think I nodded to Gillian a couple of times over the whole trip, and I never got to talk to her at all.

The highlight of the tour was playing some great gigs. The low point of the tour was seeing a naked Hooky in our room using our

Rob gets close and personal with Lita and Lindsey whilst Stephen ponders the meaning of life... and drums

shower since his was broken and then to be followed a few minutes later by a naked Barney doing the same. Some New Order fans would pay to have been there to see that but it gave me nightmares for weeks! Next day we departed for Calais. As we were dropped off at Shan's we said our goodbyes, Terry turned up with the equipment and we carried it upstairs. This would be the last time I would be at our rehearsal room as a Monster. The next time would be to take my gear away and say goodbye.

17: Leaving a band by mistake

I got home, said hello to Mum, dumped my bag of laundry and went to bed for about two days. By the time I was alive again she had done my laundry for me and was pleased to see me. I did a lot of soul searching about the band and I came to the conclusion it was time to leave. Things had changed between Tony and me. At the start we were so thick as mates and, in my opinion, we were the heart and soul of the band, but since Karl had joined the dynamic had changed, Tony had to play the part of big brother.

Shan and Lita were twins and Lindsey was a mate of Shan's, so I was feeling more and more isolated in the makeup of the band. I don't know whether I felt this way because of the paranoia caused by speeding too much or not but something just didn't feel right, and it definitely wasn't the way it used to be. In Europe I spent so much time with Slim and away from them. I wanted us to be louder and faster and funnily enough a few years later when I heard Inspiral Carpets for the first time they were doing what I wanted us to do – less poppy and less trumpet. We were starting to veer towards Teardrop Explodes and I'd like us to veer towards Echo and The Bunnymen.

The problem started when Eddie left. He had written two songs for us, and they were both the direction I wanted us to go. We should have advertised for a guitarist after he left and waited until we got someone who played guitar like Billy Duffy or Johnny Marr. There were lots of good guitarists around at the time and the annoying thing is I found the perfect one two years later – bad timing once again, the story of my life.

I had the feeling that my relationship with Rob caused a bit of friction in the band. I wasn't the manager, I was just the guy that had the relationship with Factory, Tony Wilson, and Rob so I was always going to be the one that they dealt with, and I think that this caused some jealousy.

I went round to Tony Wilson's house and told him and Rob that I was leaving. They both asked me to take a couple of days to reconsider. Rob said that he had about ten gigs lined up that we could support them on, and he had started planning the tour of Europe with The Wake and the Peel session was a goer. Wilson was talking about doing

Ged Duffy

an album in the summer. I told them that I was sorry, but I had made my mind up.

I can't remember at all how I told the band that I was leaving. I have no recollection at all so I can't say whether they tried to change my mind or not. I have a complete mental block and maybe that suggests that it didn't go well. When I look back on it all now, some thirty-nine years later, I think to myself what a complete knobhead I was at twenty-one.

1. We were on the coolest record label in the world.
2. Tony had some great lyrics.
3. Tony had the image well before Morrissey.
4. We were the scally band before Happy Mondays had even formed.
5. We would have played more gigs with New Order, done another European tour, done a John Peel session, recorded an album and possibly another single in 1982 if I had stayed with them. I don't mean to sound big headed, but I think that we had a better set of songs to put on an album than the ones that they put on *Alma Mater*.

I should have given it to the end of the year and saw how the album had turned out. If I still decided to leave then at least I would have had a complete record of all the songs that we had written. When I left, the chance for the Monsters to succeed had gone by the time they finally replaced me, I had blown it for them as well as for me. Another bad decision.

To use Tony's words from the last song that this version of the Monsters wrote 'Miss Moonlight', "It's too late now to start looking back".

17 April: New Order release 'Temptation' (FAC 63). I went round to see Lesley and got a copy of both the 7 inch and 12 inch. Picked up a copy of Tunnel Vision 'Watching The Hydroplanes' (FAC 39) which I think was the first Factory release on coloured vinyl. Also got The Names 'Night Shift' (FAC 29) and Minny Pops 'Dolphin Spurt' (FAC 31). 'Temptation' was, is and will ever be a classic. I used to love the song live but the record was just as good. It was so catchy... *oh, you've got green eyes, you've got blue eyes.* 'Night Shift' should have been a hit as it was such a lush pop song. I loved it.

As soon as I got back home to Burnage I decided that I had to live somewhere else as it would be very awkward bumping into Tony and Karl all the time. I first met Andy Robinson at either the Cyprus

Factory Fairy Tales

Tavern or the Poly. He was a student and desperate to get in with the folks at Factory Records, so he got in with our circle of friends. We would see him and his girlfriend, Amanda out and about. Andy heard that I was looking to move and suggested I move in with him and Amanda. I was wary at first as they were totally different people than me. Andy was very well spoken and a bit posh. I think his family came from Oxford or somewhere near there. Amanda was definitely born with a silver spoon in her mouth. She was mega posh, and I was definitely beneath her class level. She was also a student. Amanda was pretty with a nice figure, and I could imagine her out riding her horse every morning wearing figure hugging jodhpurs and then demanding that the stable boy services her before breakfast. You can guess the type I mean. I thought that they were clever university types slumming it up North to see how the peasants lived.

Arnesby Walk was an eight storey tower block situated on Princess Road opposite Moss Side Centre. It backed onto the McEwan Brewery and the air smelt of hops. I moved in and the flat was great. We were on the top floor and the view over Hulme and into Manchester was brilliant. Over the next 12 months we were attacked by mice, cockroaches, and some sort of weird ant. The mice got sorted with mouse traps, but the rest were always an issue. Andy was sound to live with but Amanda barely spoke to me for the first few weeks. The lift seldom worked but we were fit in those days. Eight flights of stairs now would put me in hospital for about a week!

At the beginning of May I met Stephen Morris at the office in Didsbury and he gave me a copy of the Paris gig video which he had recorded. I took it home and played it and realized that we had been good on the night - we were a tight band. I was starting to realize that I had made a massive mistake leaving the Monsters and I was missing them all. I was missing writing songs and playing live. I should have swallowed my pride and gone round to tell them that I wanted back in. But I didn't. If I had I think that we might have had a chance of making it with what Rob had planned for us. But then the other side of me said that if they were missing me, they would have tried to make contact with me and they hadn't so it was time to move on…

10 May: The Birthday Party's *Junkyard* is released. It was, is, and will always be a classic album to me. Even the sleeve was great to look at. 'Dead Joe', 'She's Hit' and 'Hamlet (Pow, Pow, Pow)' were songs I

constantly played. This was followed, four days later, by The Clash *Combat Rock*. Normally when a Clash record came out I was excited but after the disaster that was *Sandinista*, I approached this album with caution. My fears were unfounded as it was another classic. 'Know Your Rights', 'Should I Stay or Should I Go', 'Rock The Casbah', and 'Straight to Hell 'were all great Clash songs.

21 May: the Hacienda (FAC 51) opens its doors. Terry Mason, Slim, 'Rocking' Dave Holmes and I were the first stage crew and we got there in the afternoon to set up for an all-female band from New York called ESG. First thing we noticed was that they had changed the design totally from what Rob Gretton had told us when he had been taken round a few months ago. The stage was now in the middle of the club on the right hand side. We noticed that the stage had a low ceiling which meant that most bands would not be able to use their own lighting rig when they played here. It also stopped bigger bands from using their own backdrops as they wouldn't fit. It was a terrible design.

The DJ Booth was tucked away in the corner of the stage, and they couldn't see anything that was happening in the club, and no one could approach them to request a song. A few weeks later it was relocated to the middle of the balcony, which was a great spot.

The area in front of the stage where the crowd would stand had walls and bollards round it so it was enclosed, and it had a step to get onto it which you would not see in the dark. Health and Safety would have made them change this design and make the floor open. The way it was designed drastically cut down the number of people who could see a band.

The ceiling was the same as before, mega high with a glass roof. This would bugger up the sound and in the summer months, bring daylight into the club. You want a dark club, not a sunlit one. When you came through the doors and turned into the club it looked amazing, but as a venue to see a band it was dreadful.

The dressing room was massive, clean, had working plug sockets, was well lit, and even had flowers set up in there. It was nothing like the shitholes that we had been in at all of the clubs we worked or played. The Russell was nothing like this.

We set up the stage and it was Oz doing the PA and then waited for the place to open. The club had to be "Members Only" to obtain the drinks license so Terry, Slim, Dave and I were given Honorary

Factory Fairy Tales

Membership Cards with our names embossed into them, but Peter Saville hadn't delivered them yet. We got them about a week later. The cost of a membership was £5.25. This membership guaranteed a free ticket to see New Order and a free ticket to see ACR. They sold 3,000 memberships and most of them never got to see New Order.

On this first night the audience were made up of a lot of press who came up from London and important movers and shakers from Manchester, so it was a free bar. We noticed that there was a token machine next to the bar which you took a token from, and you would get served when your number came up. They used this system for the first two months and finally realized that a club audience waiting for a drink act differently than Mrs Jones waiting for her bacon in Asda, so they scrapped it.

We went downstairs and discovered a small cocktail bar called The Gay Traitor with a list of cocktails from A to Z. Slim and I tried everyone in order and then stuck with a Zum Zum which was double vodka, double gin, and fresh orange juice. It took us a few weeks to get to this decision but then we would start each night in there with one of these.

Halfway down these stairs there was a seating area and most times Rob, Wilson, and the Factory lot could be found there. Slim and I used to spend time sitting there with them when we weren't busy. There was also a restaurant area with tables and chairs where we introduced ourselves to the chef and Suzanne the waitress. I can't remember the name of the chef and he would only be there for two months. Opposite the stage there were American Diner style seating: long, padded bench seats with a table separating them. These cubicles were all along the side of the wall and at each end there were stairs going up to the balcony. There were more tables and chairs set upstairs there.

After it opened we went outside to see how large the queue was, and it went round the corner of the street. Paul Weller from The Jam turned up and walked past the whole queue and tried to get in. He didn't have a membership and wasn't on the guest list, so he got turned away. He used the "Do you know who I am" line but it didn't work. He turned round and walked off and took some abuse off the waiting queue. At this time, The Jam were probably the biggest band on the planet, but he wasn't welcome at the Hac.

The club was opened by Bernard Manning, a famous blue Manchester comedian and when he came out on stage he got heckled by the crowd. He took one look at the place, turned to Tony Wilson, and said, "Worse fucking club I've ever played in", walked off, didn't accept his fee and went home.

ESG were three sisters from New York who played a set of bass heavy funk which frankly bored me to tears. This would become the norm for Slim and I as Mike Pickering booked some utter dross over the next few months. Once they had gone off Vinny Reilly from Durutti Column played a Grand Piano on stage while Tony Wilson joined with him to sing a bit and play a bit. We had so much fucking fun getting that stupid grand piano on and off the stage. It was impossible to hear anything as the acoustics of the place were awful due to the amount of open space the sound could travel. To be honest I don't think the audience missed much by not hearing it.

When the DJ played his records the sound was dreadful too as everything he played just went Boom, Boom, Boom Rob Gretton said that the sound system had cost £30,000 to be installed and I told him that they must have seen him coming as it sounded wank. He agreed with me - it would be upgraded in a couple of months. The new sound system improved the sound from the DJ, but the stage sound was still awful. A few months later they installed large solid plastic strips hanging from the ceiling to the floor which acted as a barrier to the main area of the club. You would come in to the club and then push open these strips to enter the stage and bar area. They were like a giant fly screens that you would find in cafés and shops. They looked awful and didn't match the décor of the club, but they improved the live sound of the bands and helped to get rid of some of the echo. I also think that they should have installed a false ceiling as this would have helped as well.

The club was open seven nights a week and at lunchtime on a Saturday and Sunday. They did this for the first six months and then dropped the Saturday lunchtime and completely closed on a Sunday. There was a giant video screen at either side of the stage, and they hired a video guy called Claude to control these screens. He would mix lots of images and just play them when the DJ was playing his records. So you could see an image of Hitler giving a speech followed by Mickey Mouse eating an ice cream. Every band that played there got filmed by Malcolm Whitehead and would be given a copy of their gig before they left free of charge.

The following night Cabaret Voltaire played to a crowd of about 70 people all bunched together on the dancefloor. This would turn out to be the norm. Slim and I went along on each night of the first week and there were about ten people in each night. We got free food off the chef, free cocktails downstairs, and free beer at the bar. This would become our routine.

Next up was Teardrop Explodes who played a secret word-of-mouth gig and only seven people turn up. There were more staff than customers. Fair play to the band who put on a proper show, but it was a very informal gig, and they were followed by 23 Skidoo who also play in front of a small crowd again. I enjoyed them. The Hac had bands on three or four nights a week and 90% of these shows were empty so I'm only going to list special gigs. If you are interested in knowing who these other bands are, I suggest you read Peter Hook's *The Hacienda. How not to run a club*, as he lists every gig that took place at the Hac. It's a great read.

Slim and I got into a routine. During the day we would meet in town and most nights we would go the Hac, get free food and drinks, and then go on somewhere else. The place was always empty, and due to its design and colour scheme, it always gave you the impression that you were cold. We would go to the Cyprus Tavern on a Sunday, the Ritz disco on a Tuesday, Deville's on a Wednesday, Legends on a Thursday, Poly disco on a Friday, and University disco or the Hac on a Saturday. This was a typical week and only changed if there was a decent gig on or United were at home.

Legends was an amazing cellar club on Princess Street opposite the Cyprus Tavern. It had the most expensive lighting rig of any club in Manchester and mirrored ceiling supports. Many a time I would be totally stoned and would stop to let someone pass me when it was actually my reflection walking towards myself in the pillar! Anyone who went to Legends and claims they didn't do that at least once is a liar.

As you left Legends the staff would give you a "£1 off a drink" ticket to be used next time you went there. I befriended the bouncers, and we would all club together and raise £5 which I would give to the bouncers for a wad of these tickets. We used to a drink a Red Witch which was half a cider, Pernod, and Blackcurrant which cost £1.09 so we would pay 9p per drink. We be able to have about four or five each with the tickets.

On gig days, once we had set everything up, we would go and have a few drinks with Rob Gretton and Mike Pickering in the

Ged Duffy

City Road Inn or Britons Protection. Lee Pickering and other mates would meet us in there before going over to the club. Once inside we would have a cocktail downstairs and then it would be time to work the stage. There would usually be a crate of Breaker or Pils lager left on the stage for us. Then we would watch whoever was playing that night.

Culture Club played at the Hac to a full house. We were stood on the stage when they walked in and Boy George pointed at Slim, who was stood on the stage, and said, "Is that the stage?" to which Slim replied, "No! This is Slim. Behind me is the stage!" The two of them hit it off and they were taking the piss out of each other for the whole night. It was a fun night. It was nice to finally see a full house in the club.

Around this time Slim and I spoke to Mike Pickering and suggested he stop booking shite trendy bands and book some proper bands. We gave him a list of The Birthday Party, Bauhaus, The Fall, Killing Joke, B52's, The Cramps, The Gun Club, and Psychedelic Furs. He took the list off us.

26 June: New Order play to a full house. The place was bouncing. It was great to see Hooky and Barney again and I spent a lot of time in their dressing room. I stood on the stage next to Hooky the whole gig. The power that came out of that bass stack was immense. They came on to a hero's welcome and they started with 'Dreams Never End'. Halfway through the second song 'Ultraviolence' they blew the club's power. The stage was in total darkness until someone changed the fuse some 20 minutes later. They played a great set and finished with a trio of 'Everything's Gone Green', 'Temptation' and 'In a Lonely Place'. I saw Tony France that night, the James boys, Beach Red, Bob the Burger Man and his sister June. I think June came back home with me. This gig was free to members and their guests and was the Hacienda's first complete sell out. The place held 1,600 and since each member could bring a friend for free, only 800 got to see New Order. The other 2,200 were well pissed off.

One Saturday night Slim and I dropped acid again. The Hac was empty apart from a few sat round and it was great seeing the lights and the video screen. I swear Mickey Mouse walked from screen to screen and then we opened the side door and sat outside by the side of the canal and watched the water flow for hours. It was an enjoyable

The Hacienda in the early 80s

time, and we came back to the flat and sat looking at the lights of Manchester for hours.

Every few weeks we would stay in one night and drop acid. One time Andy, Amanda and I were sat in the living room happily tripping listening to some music, and we realized that we hadn't seen Slim for hours. We called him and he came in and said, "Manchester's on fire". We followed him back into my bedroom which had a great view over the city and indeed there was a wild fire raging on the north side of town and the sky was thick with smoke. We watched it for hours and it never went out. We found out later that it was a tyre yard and it took a couple of days to put it out.

The other major thing that happened to me living in Arnesby Walk was that Andy taught me how to do hot knives and blowbacks. Hot knives is a method of having hash without having to use any tobacco. Basically you would heat up two knives over the cooker until the tips are red hot, add a piece of leb, black leb, or Moroccan onto one of the knives and cover it with the other knife. This would generate smoke which you would inhale using a bottle with the bottom cut off. This gave you an instant pure hit of hash and it got you stoned a lot quicker. A blowback is when you place the lighted end of the joint in your mouth, and you blow the smoke into someone else's mouth giving them a direct hit of hash.

Ged Duffy

The thing about the Hac was that there were always lots of females in there. It was a safe place for single women and groups of girls to meet as there were very few fights whereas the Russell had several fights a night. Even during the week, when it had maybe 30 or 40 people in and it was freezing, there would be single girls in there.

Since speed was killing my sex drive, I decided to cut my intake down to one or two days a week. Overnight my luck with women changed. There was a girl called Sarah who used to go to the Hac two or three times a week. I used to notice that she always came in on her own but always left with a different guy. She was good looking with long brown hair and looked like she had a good body under the baggy clothes she used to wear. One evening I was sat in one of cubicles opposite the stage and she sat next to me. We talked for about 30 minutes until a guy walked up and she said to me ,"sorry I'm with him tonight but write your address down for me". I wrote it on a napkin and handed it to her. As she left she asked, "do you work?" to which I replied "no". I thought nothing of it, and when Slim turned up a few minutes later, we had egg and chips courtesy of the chef, a couple of free pints from the bar and off we went into town for a night out.

A couple of days later I was in bed when there was a knock at the door, it was Sarah. She walked in and asked me which room was mine. I pointed to it, and she walked in dropped her clothes and got into bed! I didn't make it to town or to the Hac that night. I was right, she had an amazing body. I saw her a few more times in the Hac, and we chatted, and she would always be with someone different. Then at closing time one night, I was leaving on my own as Slim hadn't come out that night, she came up to me and asked me if I wanted to take her home. I enquired about the guy I had seen her with that evening, and she told me that he was a dickhead and she had decided that it was no entry for him. It turned out to be an unexpected great night!

On another occasion about two or three months later on a Saturday I was walking back from the Hac and I had just reached the entrance to my block when I saw Sarah sitting there. She came up to the flat and told me that she had been in a cab with a guy going back to his place and they had argued. She saw that the cab was near the brewery, so she had jumped out at the lights, and came to see if I could help her. She had forgotten the number of my flat so she had knocked on a few doors with no luck. Another unexpected fun night occurred. She stopped coming in the Hac and I never saw her again.

Factory Fairy Tales

Same thing happened with another girl, let's call her CM, who used to leave with a different guy every night. One night I was waiting for Slim to turn up and the place was deserted as ever and she came over. We spoke for about 30 minutes and then Slim turned up. She left us alone and I didn't see her again until closing time. Slim had left to get the bus back to Burnage and I went outside. CM was stood there and she walked up to me and asked if I wanted to take her home. Another unexpected good night. She came round the flat a couple more times over the next few weeks. There were a lot of accommodating pretty ladies in the Hac.

July started with the release of *Revelations* by Killing Joke. 'The Hum' - what a fucking tune. Another brilliant album by the band, this stayed on my turntable for a few weeks, and I still play it now. This was followed a few days later by Echo and The Bunnymen playing at the Hac. Our mate Bernie was over from Liverpool and Les, Pete, and Will came over asking me about the Monsters and I told them I had left. We spent most of the evening backstage with them. Ian is a great lad and we had an interesting conversation about Liverpool and United. They played a good set despite the sound issues with around 600 in to see them.

Next up were Simple Minds. When they came in they were pissed off that they couldn't use their lighting rig due to the height restriction of the stage. They managed to use some of it by putting lights behind the band. I can't remember if their backdrop fitted or not. We had a great chat with them backstage. They all ironed their own stage pants and shirts before going on. I thought that was very rock 'n' roll. Their PA was too large for the place, so it stopped any echo, and they sounded good. There were about 800 in on the night and the area in front of the stage were dancing throughout. Jim Kerr told me how their PA had been used for the Pope's tour of the UK. It had been arranged about a year earlier and they gave it to the Pontiff free of charge. When he discovered this gesture the Pope rang Jim and thanked him and finished the phone call with the message "I promise you a miracle". The next day he wrote the lyrics and Charlie came in with a guitar riff and the song was born - true or not I liked it, being a good Catholic boy!

A couple of days later it was the turn of Blancmange. This was a brilliant gig and it was well attended. Then it was The Birthday Party. At last Mike Pickering had booked a band that we had suggested. I

Ged Duffy

remember Malcolm, the video guy, coming up to me afterwards to tell me that they had been the best live band that had played there. They put on a great show and the 900 strong audience went wild. Nick Cave was prowling the stage and interacting with the audience but to me Tracey Pew slamming his bass into his crotch stole the show, a truly great bass player. Backstage they were wild, drinking, and doing drugs. We spent a lot of time in there talking to them. They were really approachable.

25 July: The Rolling Stones at Roundhay Park, Leeds. Slim and I were so excited as we were going to see living legends and we discussed what songs we hoped that they would play as we made our way over to Hooky's house in Moston. We got there earlier than arranged in the hope that his wife, Iris, would feed us. She did, she made a great egg and chips! This was something that Mikey and I would take advantage of the following year, we would drop into see Hooky sometimes on the off chance of a meal. We always got one!

Hooky drove us to Leeds. I think he got hold of the tickets off a promoter he knew. When we got there we made our way in just as The Rolling Stones came on. They started off with 'Under My Thumb' and they were brilliant. They finished with 'Miss You', 'Honky Tonk Woman', 'Brown Sugar', 'Start Me Up', 'Jumping Jack Flash', and 'Satisfaction'. What an amazing six songs to finish a gig with! There were over 120,000 in the park and the mood was brilliant, really mellow.

Around this time, the chef in the Hac left and was replaced by a guy called Henry. He became great mates of ours and he later moved into Hulme Walk with Big Stuart and Dave Hicks, so we saw him a lot away from work as well.

8 August: *A Factory Video* (FACT 56) was released. The video for 'Soft Babies' was on this tape (see above). It turned out well - I liked it. I went over to see Lesley at Factory to pick up my copy. A few days later I was back to see Lesley again as 'Happy Ever After' was released with the catalogue number (FAC 58). I had not seen any preview of the sleeve and it took my

Factory Fairy Tales

breath away it. Mark Farrow had excelled again – what a great design. I was very pleased with how the single turned out but because of Factory's stupid non-promotion policy the single sold fuck all. Deep down inside I had hoped that someone in the Monsters would have given me a white label to listen to or an idea of how the cover looked. They knew where to find me. They didn't fucking bother. That pissed me off.

Bauhaus played the Hac, and this was another of our suggestions to play here. They played a long set and went down great with the crowd. It was half-full again so about 800 in. Backstage they didn't seem the same as they always had been, and it came as no surprise that they broke up a month after this gig. Slim and Pete Murphy got on great backstage and had a few drinks together. The next gig at the Hac were our friends Rip, Rig and Panic. They played their usual set of pretentious art school shite. Slim spent the whole gig growling at Gareth Sagar. Gareth spent the whole gig shitting himself. I'll never forget his face when he walked in so full of himself and then saw Slim and the arse dropped out of his world.

The following day the Joy Division video *Here Are The Young Men* (FACT 37) came out. It featured songs from the two gigs at the Apollo supporting Buzzcocks. It was a great snapshot of an amazing band. It meant a lot to me as I had been at both gigs. Once again, I got it from Lesley.

For Bow Wow Wow, the Hac was packed. We spent a while

backstage talking to the three guys about The Ants as they were the original Ants and had played on every record up to 'Cartrouble' in early 1980. They were three of the coolest guys that ever walked on stage. Annabella was beautiful up close, and she joined in all the banter in the dressing room. Great set and I was amazed at how well she could sing. They were cool as fuck. They had some fans with them from London and they got in a fight with Slim and Hooky backstage afterwards.

One day we went into Record Peddler on Swan Street opposite The Band On The Wall. Mark and Craig were the new owners, and the shop was full of punk and New Wave records. It had a large collection of second hand vinyl as well. This shop now became part of our daily routine but we always felt a little bit guilty buying off them because of our close association with Discount Records.

At the start of September Lee Pickering and I went to Paris for a few days. We got the Magic Bus from town, and it took us all the way to Place de la Concorde in the centre of Paris. We found a hotel in Quartier Pigalle which was cheap and spent the next few days seeing all the sights, walking round the red light district, walking along the Seine. I think we went to see the Mona Lisa in the Louvre. We drank a lot and smoked a lot. It was a great break. Lee was always a great bloke to go places with as he was easy to get along with.

On our return, I met a guy called Mikey in Record Peddler. He was the brother of Mark, one of the co-owners. Mikey was a cool dude, totally stoned, laid back, and reminded me of Shaggy off Scooby Doo. He was tall, wore drainpipe jeans, a denim jacket, and a white t shirt. He had spiky ginger hair shaved along the back and sides. He liked Stockholm Monsters and he told me that he was a guitarist looking to join a band. It set my mind ticking. Around this time, I dug my old leather jacket out of the wardrobe and ditched the sad young man clothes. Got myself a pair of Chelsea boots and started rocking again.

18: Several scouse bands with stupid names

One Saturday morning Nigel Baguley picked Slim and I up from my flat, we had been out at the Poly disco the previous evening and were pretty wrecked. The festival was being held at Deeside Leisure Centre in Queensferry, North Wales. The venue was an ice rink which had padded mats laid over it, so the audience was actually standing on ice. It was fucking freezing in there. It was really dark inside compared to the bright sunlight outside. It was basically a big shed with a stage built at one end.

When we got in the PA was already set up, so we went and had a cup of tea and a couple of lines of speed which pepped us both up and we were now ready for two days of non-stop bands. After an hour or so we heard the familiar sound of Terry and Dave pull up outside with New Order's gear, so we carried everything in and then the band came, and sound checked. We had a catch up with Hooky, Barney and Rob and I think that they stayed there all day. I'm pretty sure I saw Rob and Hooky a few times during the day whilst we were moving gear.

Once again the stage was split in two by a curtain and the bands played a 30 minute set and the bigger bands had a 45 minute set. There was a time gap between each band of around 10 minutes and 20 minutes with the later bands.

The first band came on at 1pm in the following order:

Sleeping Figures: They used slides and backing tapes and were really depressing.

Disco Students: Poppy dance band. Cheered the crowd up after the dour previous offering.

The Cherry Boys: Pop band from Liverpool. Sat and had a spliff. Easy listening and nothing to write home about.

Vince Berkeley: Time to have another joint and a beer.

Blue Poland: another scouse band. Sounded like a poppy version of Gang of Four with two singers. Liked them.

3D A Fish in a Sea: another scouse pop band. They sounded like so many other bands from Liverpool.

The Icicle Works: The most well-known band of the day so far. Was

Ged Duffy

FUTURAMA · 4
QUEENSFERRY — NORTH WALES
Leisure Centre — Deeside 82
Saturday ——————— Sunday
SEPTEMBER 11th – 12th SEPTEMBER
noon onwards ———— noon onwards

NEW ORDER
THE DAMNED
BLANCMANGE
dead or alive
KING TRIGGER
CHINA CRISIS
Southern Death Cult
THE DANSE SOCIETY
DURUTTI COLUMN
and introducing BRILLIANT!
sex gang children
the ROOM
The Decorators
dolebiloveyou
Dislocation Dance
Icicle Works
the fARmERS
the boys
STOCKHOLM MONSTERS
THREE COURGETTES
Gene loves Jezebel
THE MARCH VIOLETS
NAAFI SANDWICH
BLUE POLAND
PUNCHING HOLES
with Brian Bond
JO:A Fish In Sea
Cook the Books
THE CHERRY BOYS
The Alarm
the Membranes
ZANTI MISFITZ
ORCHESTRA JAZIRA
Vendino Pact
Hooray!
VINCE BERKELEY
DISCOBOLISK
special guests from Germany-
WORKFORCE
with special guests:
Ideal
NICO

looking forward to seeing them and they were pretty good. 'Nirvana' was a good song. They played atmospheric pop. Another scouse band.

Dislocation Dance: Had seen them several times in Manchester so we sat backstage and had a spliff.

The Alarm: This was the first time that I had ever heard the name "The Alarm" but just by their appearance I knew I would like them. They played an acoustic set with three guitarists and no bass player. The songs were powerful, and the three singers worked well. I followed this band until they called it a day in 1991. Best act of the day so far. Had a chat with Dave the guitarist, he came from Salford.

Naafi Sandwich: very unusual for a scouse band as they weren't poppy. They were pretentious shite to be honest.

Three Courgettes: These were the surprise package of the day playing a set of 1950s Doo-wop, gospel, rock 'n' roll. They were a guitarist, a female vocalist and a guy playing bongos. Absolutely brilliant and they livened up the atmosphere and mood in the place.

Factory Fairy Tales

The Wake: What a mood killer! Not poppy enough for the scouse majority in the crowd but I thought they were great. Had a good chat with Caesar and Bobby Gillespie afterwards – great guys.

Dalek I Love You: another scouse pop band. Didn't like them.

Durutti Column: Spliff time but to be honest I have to say probably the best crowd reaction so far. They must have all been stoned.

Brilliant: Was really looking forward to seeing this band. This was Youth from Killing Joke's new band and they had two bass players. We stood on Youth's side of the stage, and it was great listening to him, another top bass monster. They didn't go down well with the crowd and to be honest if Youth hadn't been in them I wouldn't have watched.

New Order: Blancmange hadn't turned up, but they had been in contact to say they had problems with their transport and would get there so New Order went on. I stood on Hooky's side of the stage, and it was amazing to watch him at close quarters. The whole floor near me was vibrating from the power of his bass. They played for over an hour and started with 'Ultraviolence'. They also played 'Procession', and a really powerful atmospheric version of 'In a Lonely Place'. The last three songs were 'Everything's Gone Green', 'Temptation', and 'Age of Consent'. When they came back on for the encore, Barney introduced '586' with "This is only because you have been here as long as we have".

Blancmange: they finally turned up and went on to headline the show. Once New Order had finished, a lot of the day ticket people left and didn't get to see Blancmange. They had a guitarist now so there were three of them on stage. The guitar changed the sound of some of the songs and I thought it was a clever addition. Once again a brilliant set from them but it's impossible to follow New Order. After Blancmange went off more people left the hall.

Cook The Books: another scouse band. They had missed their slot earlier in the day, so they were allowed to go on now. They were a poppy band who were okay. Not ok enough to buy any of their records but okay enough to kill some time until the next day.

Some of the crowd went to sleep in the sports hall, which was next door, but we were staying in the ice rink. We were pissed off that Alan Wise hadn't supplied somewhere for us to sleep, like the coach at Leeds in 1981. We met some folks from Manchester and sat with them for a while. After a few minutes sitting down, the cold from the ice was starting to come up through the floor mats and it was fucking freezing, so we decided to go and sit on the empty stage. There was no way we would sleep with the speed we had taken so we sat on the stage, smoked, and drank all night, and just watched what the people were doing out in the hall. There was some shagging going on under sleeping bags, lots of drinking and drug taking and impromptu singalongs. It was a good vibe. I seem to recall that Hooky stayed overnight with us as he was due back the next day to mix the live sound for Stockholm Monsters. I think that he helped us with the stage the next day as well. Hooky was a top bloke!

Next morning we were ready to do it all again. The Damned's road crew turned up and we helped set them up. When the band came in they came over to talk to Slim and me as we knew them from the Russell and from The Grants Arms pub, so we had a laugh with them. They did their sound check and sounded great.

Zant Misfits and **Vending Pact** were first on, and I have no recollection of anything about them.

The Membranes: Bang average post punk band. Didn't like them that day and never got into them afterwards. Made a lot of albums though so some people liked them, each to their own.

Discobolisk: Heard the first song. Went and had a spliff.

Black: Wasn't on the bill but played; really good voice, another scouser. He played with a backing tape. Didn't get a good reception from the audience but I liked him.

Gene loves Jezebel: Didn't like them. I watched the whole set, but they didn't float my boat. Too much time spent on image and less spent on writing.

The March Violets: The Sisters of Mercy did it first and better.

The Decorators: They were a bit of light relief after the Goth bands, but their intimate pop was just not right for this size of venue.

Punching Holes: The singer had just left Punishment of Luxury and he was trying to do his usual theatrics, didn't quite work in this venue.

The Room: Another scouse band that played guitar pop. They were okay.

Stockholm Monsters: It was really strange standing at the side of the stage watching them play without me. This was the only time I

Factory Fairy Tales

ever saw them play. Paul Kershaw aka Kersh was on bass playing what I wrote. Had a good laugh with Tony and Kersh. I can't remember having much dialogue with the rest of them. Kersh was one of our old crew at the Russell so I was happy for him. I have no view on whether they were good or not.

Within a few months of playing at the Futurama Kersh sadly passed away due to a drug overdose. He was a heroin addict. RIP mate, you were a fucking legend, one of our Russell crew. He was replaced in the Monsters by another of the Russell crew John Rhodes, who also sadly passed away a few years ago. RIP John.

Sex Gang Children: they had the venue turn the lights off leaving just the stage lit up as dancers wearing special black body suits with painted on skeletons danced round it. The lights reflected onto the skeletons, and it looked weird. They also had a fire eater who was prowling the edge of the stage trying to look menacing but unfortunately for him, his wig caught fire and he had to run off, Slim and I pissed ourselves. I liked them but the singer tried to act like Jaz from Killing Joke and there's only one Jaz. Musically it was a good set. Some of their crew were the guys that had trouble with Slim and Hooky at the Bow Wow Wow gig at the Hac. Slim had a word with one or two of them to remind them of their manners.

The Danse Society: Much better than their set at Futurama 2 but still a second division Goth band.

Orchestra Jazira: Why? Wrong time, wrong place.

Southern Death Cult: Absolutely brilliant. They had the hall rocking. Ian was a great front-man. We had a chat with him afterwards.

Nico: She brought the atmosphere right down again but because she's an icon everybody listened. She was backed by The Invisible Girls for the majority of the set. She played a couple of songs solo with just her harmonium, which is a keyboard instrument in which the notes are produced by air driven through metal reeds by foot-operated bellows. She played 'All Tomorrow's Parties', 'Femme Fatale', and 'I'm Waiting for My Man', and the audience loved her. She was great.

Dead or Alive: Pete Burns was a top lad. We'd met him a couple of times in the past and his group were just starting to get rid of the Goth side and move to the disco side that would make them a big band. This was a good set and the audience liked them.

Ged Duffy

The Damned: Went into the crowd to see them and was down the front in amongst the normal mayhem. They played 'Disco Man', 'Just Can't be Happy Today', 'Dozen Girls', 'Love Song', and finished off with 'Neat, Neat, Neat' and 'New Rose'. They came back on and did 'Happy Talk' and 'Smash It Up'. They finished and the crowd were screaming for more, so they came back on and did a wild version of 'Looking at You' the MC5 number and then they were gone.

We started to take down their gear and the PA stacks. After about an hour we were done, and Nigel Baguley was waiting to run us home. It had been a great weekend despite the fact that half of the bands were shit pop acts from Liverpool but The Damned more than made up for it. I have a memory in my head that C.P. Lee, formerly of Alberto Y Lost Trios Paranoias, played a short set on one of the days. I can't find any record of it so maybe the drugs put the memory in my head. One question I have never got the answer to is why does every band from Liverpool (apart from The Farm, The Coral and The La's) have a stupid sounding name? Just a thought. Is it a prerequisite that every scouse band has to have one and also play jangly pop?

20 September: Yazoo at the Hac. Played 'Don't Go', 'Only You', and 'Situation'. The one man backing band of Vince Clarke and the powerful blues voice of Alison Moyet deserved better than the audience reaction they received, which was cold and reserved although it was pretty full. I thought that they were brilliant on the night. My God can she sing, and she made the Hac sound like a proper venue. I would have loved to see her front a proper blues rock band – that would have been amazing.

Sometime during September Andy went to visit his family for a few days. I was dreading being alone with Amanda as she never talked to me and looked down on me as far as I was concerned. Andy left on the Saturday, and I was out all day and came home in the early hours of Sunday morning and so never saw her.

I got up on Sunday and had no plans, so I sat in the living room and put some music on. She came in, sat down with me, and started talking. We started drinking, smoking, did some hot knives and a couple of blow backs. The more stoned she got, the more she opened up and she actually turned out to be a funny girl. We stayed there for hours and then she got up and said, "it's late. I'm off to bed. Do you want to come with me?" So I did. We had a great night. I suppose I was her bit of rough. We never did it again, it was our little secret, and our relationship changed for the better in the flat from then on. I can confirm to you that Andy was a very lucky guy!

19: Hooky gave me a speaker cab so I had to play again

William S Burroughs did a reading at the Hac and we had to set chairs up all over the dance floor as the sparse audience would be sitting when he performed. Most people sat but some people sat cross-legged on the floor. The bar had to shut when he was on as he wanted silence. The following night saw Jah Wobble and the Invaders of the Heart, another one of my bass heroes. He blew his bass amp during the sound check and I dashed back to the flat for my H/H Amp so he used that for the gig. When he was finishing the last song my amp blew. He was mortified afterwards and kept apologising. He took my address and said that he would send me some money to cover the cost of the repair. About three days later a cheque for £100 arrived in the post. It cost me 10p to repair as it was a fuse that had blown. Tidy profit. Top bloke. Shame no fucker was there to see him play!

Next up were Psychedelic Furs and Sisters of Mercy. This was the type of double bill that Mike Pickering should have been putting together from the start. Both bands were our suggestions and the place was full. The Sisters of Mercy were perfect for the Hac as they used a lot of echo in their sound. They played a great set and went down well with the large crowd. The Furs were just magnificent and played a couple of songs off their forthcoming album *Mirror Moves*. This was a great night for the Hac, and it was followed up a couple of days later by Blancmange. Great songs. Great gig. Full house. They were getting better every time I saw them. They are still a band that I play today.

The following week it was Bauhaus and Southern Death Cult at Salford University. Dave Hicks was a flatmate of Big Stuart and introduced us to Ian Astbury, their front-man. Dave knew him because of their joint interest in all things Red Indian. We had already met him at the Futurama Festival but now we became mates with him. Southern Death Cult played a short set and sounded different to anything that was around at that moment and Ian was a great front man. Bauhaus started with 'Bela Lugosi's Dead' and played 'Passion of Lovers', 'Hollow Hills' and 'Ziggy Stardust' among others. For the encore Nico came on stage with them and they played 'I'm Waiting for My Man' but she was that out of it that Pete Murphy had to hold her up all the way through.

Big Stuart had finished his degree at UMIST and decided to go and live in London. He left Hulme Walk around this time. He would figure greater in my story soon again. His place at 97 Hulme Walk was taken by his younger brother Guy Parker. Guy was in Manchester going to University, he was a top bloke and who had two best friends – Mike Joyce (who became the drummer in The Smiths) and a lad called Roy. Roy came from Welshpool and had never lived in a big city before. He arrived in Manchester as a student and on his first night out in the city he got mugged, went to a club, copped off with a girl, had his first ever blow job, got shagged and caught a dose. Welcome to Manchester, Roy!

27 October: Killing Joke at the Poly. We got drunk beforehand and went to worship at the church of Killing Joke. They started off with a belter of a song 'The Hum' and played 'Pssyche', 'We Have Joy', and finished with 'Wardance' and 'Birds of a Feather'. The one thing that you were sure about a Killing Joke gig was that you would come out absolutely knackered and covered in sweat as it was impossible to stand still and watch. Youth had left them by now and Raven played bass at this gig. I was upset when I had heard that Youth had left but Raven was just as good and the sound didn't change.

I was sat in the flat in Hulme Walk one night with Slim, Henry the Chef, Dave Hicks, Ian Astbury and a lad called Glenn. Ian was talking about leaving Southern Death Cult and he told Dave that he should be in a band. Dave said that he wanted to be a singer and Ian turned round to look at me and said, "You and Dave should get a band together". Dave looked at me and said, "We should". My mind started ticking again

Since the Hac had opened Slim and I had been pressuring Mike Pickering to give a support slot to James and finally he relented and gave them a spot with Big Country. Slim and I spoke to Wilson and Gretton and suggested that they come along and watch them and as a result they offered them a single deal. We were so pleased – both of us loved James and felt that they deserved a chance. The rest is history and I have followed James ever since and they remain one of my favourites to this day. We never told any of the guys from James what we had done, and it really pisses me off that I see Mike Pickering always mentioned as the man who gave James their chance. If it were left up to him they would never

Ged Duffy

have played the Hac.

17 November: Big Country played with James. We spent most of the time in the dressing room with the lads from James. Jim had a Westone bass, and I had a play along on it, it felt great and easy to play. We also spoke to Stuart Adamson again and he went back to Stretford to collect some of his family after the sound check. James were magnificent and they had got so tight since the last time that I had seen them. They had written some new songs as well and they went down well with the crowd. Big Country were great as well: big songs, big riffs, big guitars. It was great to see them have so much chart success as a guitar band. Orange Juice were the next band to play the Hac and it was another great night with about 700 in. Another great guitar based band. They had some great tunes.

One Saturday Slim and I had been to see United, and we went out with Big Stuart to the Salisbury and then onto the Hac. The Hac was dead and since Slim was going home I decided to go back to the flat early. When I got back I could hear talking coming from the living room. I popped my head in and saw Andy and Amanda with a Goth guy and two Goth girls. I thought that they must be student mates so I poked my head in, said hello and turned to go to my room but Andy invited me in. He introduced them and I could see that the guy was with one of the girls but the other one, Julie, was very pretty with long dark hair. There was no room to sit so I sat on the floor, started drinking and smoking and it was an enjoyable evening.

After a while Julie got up to go to the bathroom and I noticed that she was wearing multiple layers of clothing with a long floor length dress, she had long crimped dark hair. When she came back in she sat on the floor next to me and started talking to me. A little bit later, her friends got up to leave and asked her if she was coming with them to which she replied no. We had another spliff and Andy and Amanda left and went to bed. Julie got up and asked me to take her to my room. She got in and started to take off her clothes. She had great tits, cute ass and long legs with stockings and suspenders on. I then noticed that she had a pieced tongue and I had one of the best nights of my life with her. The next morning she got up and said 'thanks'. I asked her what for? She told me that she was getting married the following weekend and I was her last fling. She said that she was going to get fucked that weekend no matter what, but they hadn't found anyone for her, and they ended up in the flat when I arrived, and decided that

Factory Fairy Tales

she was going to have me. Her future husband was one hell of a lucky guy. I walked her to the bus stop, kissed her goodbye and wished her a happy marriage.

A few weeks later I was in the Salisbury waiting for Slim to turn up when I went into A1 Music next door and spotted a two-tone wood effect Westone Thunder bass and took it off the wall and started to play it. I fell in love with it. I put a deposit on it and came back the next day to buy it. I was back in the game. Slim was happy when I told that I was going to ask Mikey and Dave Hicks to form a band with me, he said that they were good choices. Dave dressed in leather and looked like a cross between early Adam Ant, before he became a pirate, and a young Jim Morrison with his long locks. He was the perfect front man. I now needed to set up a meeting with Dave and Mikey, but I also needed a speaker for my amp. I talked to Hooky a couple of days later, and he told me that he had just upgraded his set up and I could have one of his 2 x 18 speaker cabinets off him. He didn't want money for it. A couple of weeks later Dad took me to New Order's rehearsal unit behind Marks & Spencer in Prestwich village to collect the speaker. Guess what? It had New Order painted on the rear and people remarked on this fact.

Dave, Mikey, and I met and agreed to form a band. We would rehearse in the cellar under Record Peddler. Dave knew a drummer and we would start rehearsing as soon as he had sorted him out. Mikey went to buy a guitar and came back with a gold and white, semi acoustic, Gibson bass. He had fallen in love with it and named it Daddy. Dave and I were a bit confused, but Mikey was so excited – looks like we were having two basses now. Dave could play guitar, so he was okay with it. Mikey put flat wound strings on his to deaden the sound and he would mainly play E and A strings. I would play higher up the neck mainly on D and G strings. I had round wound strings. I would play lead bass and he would play a backbeat. I would use a pick and he would use his fingers and slap the bass as well sometimes. It sounded like it could work. I had already decided to change my way of playing, no more Hooky type melodies, no more bass chords, it was to be rock bass and I was going to wear it as low as I could go. When I saw how cool Paul Simonon, Sid Vicious and Hooky looked playing, I wanted some of that.

December started with the Hac hosting two gigs by Reggae superstars Gregory Isaacs and Dillinger five days apart. Both gigs attracted large crowds and there were a lot of Rastas in on both nights. Two brilliant gigs with amazing bass and drums which made the sound in the Hac sound reasonable for once, I enjoyed them both. Then U2 and The Alarm played at the Apollo. I went to this by myself - U2 started with 'Out of Control' and played 'Sunday Bloody Sunday', 'New Year's Day', and finished with 'I Will Follow'. The Alarm were great as well, they were so full of energy with the three-pronged attack of two guitars and a bass. They reminded me of The Clash with their great stage presence, and they all had massive hair which impressed me as well. I became a fan on that night, and I have got every record they ever released. This was the *War* tour and U2 were just about to hit their peak over the next couple of years as the first album *Boy* was a classic whereas the second album *October* was pretty bland, and it was important for them to get back on track.

Then it was the turn of The Jam at the Apollo on their farewell tour - they were outstanding on the night. They played 25 songs starting with 'Start' then all the big hits. I don't think Slim came to this. I was sad that The Jam were calling it a day and that this would be the last time I ever saw them play live.

Next up at the Hac was Grandmaster Flash, it was an interesting night watching this guy work. I really enjoyed it. Decent crowd as well. I had first heard his name when Blondie namechecked him in Debbie Harry's rap section in 'Rapture'. I started to pay a bit of attention to him after this gig. Then it was the turn of Blancmange, their third appearance at The Hac that year and their best appearance. It was a sell out. 'Living on the Ceiling' had charted and was a big hit, so they were massive now. I had already got their debut album Happy Families and I knew most of the songs they played. The year finished with ACR at the Xmas Party. Got stoned and dropped a tab. Interesting gig and light show. Great music to listen to whilst tripping. That was a good night.

1982

Singles

New Order: 'Temptation'
Killing Joke: 'Birds Of A Feather'
Birthday Party: 'Dead Joe'
Simple Minds: 'Promised You A Miracle', 'Someone Somewhere

Factory Fairy Tales

In Summertime'
Echo and The Bunnymen: 'The Back Of Love'
Psychedelic Furs: 'Love My Way'
Iron Maiden: 'Run To The Hills'
Frantic Elevators: 'Holding Back The Years'
Wah Heat: 'The Story Of The Blues'
Blancmange: 'Living On The Ceiling'
The Clash: 'Rock The Casbah', 'Should I Stay Or Should I Go'
David Bowie: 'Cat People (Putting Out Fire)'
Bauhaus: 'Spirit'
Theatre of Hate: 'Do You Believe In The Westworld', 'The Hop'
Sisters Of Mercy: 'Alice'
Soft Cell: 'Say Hello, Wave Goodbye', 'Torch'
Southern Death Cult: 'Moya / Fatman'
Yazoo: 'Only You', 'Don't Go'.
OMD: 'Maid of Orleans'.
Dexy's Midnight Runners: 'Come On Eileen'

Albums

Killing Joke: *Revelations*
Siouxsie & The Banshees: *A Kiss In The Dreamhouse*
The Damned: *Strawberries*
Theatre Of Hate: *Do You Believe In The West World*
Birthday Party: *Junkyard*
The Fall: *Hex Enduction Hour*
Iron Maiden: *Number Of The Beast*
Blancmange: *Happy Families*
The Clash: *Combat Rock*
Judas Priest: *Screaming For Vengeance*
Yazoo: *Upstairs at Eric's*
The Jam: *The Gift*
Roxy Music: *Avalon*
Bruce Springsteen: *Nebraska*

Ged Duffy

Fun Boy Three: *Fun Boy Three*
Simple Minds: *New Gold Dream*
Dexys Midnight Runners: *Too-Rye-Ay*
Grandmaster Flash And The Furious Five: *The Message*
The Gun Club: *Miami*
Kate Bush: *The Dreaming*
Billy Idol: *Billy Idol*
Cabaret Voltaire: *2x45*
Lou Reed: *The Blue Mask*
The Psychedelic Furs: *Forever Now*
The Cure: *Pornography*

20: Lavolta Lakota - what a shit name!

A few things of note occurred at the start of January 1983. Hooky and Tony France joined our stage crew at the Hac, Lee Pickering moved into the third bedroom at Arnesby Walk, and Lavolta Lakota were formed. It was so funny watching bands arrive at the Hac to discover that Hooky was carrying their gear in. You could see them thinking, is that Peter Hook? No, it can't be, can it? We would wait to see how long it would be before they nominated one of them to come forward and ask the question.

Every weekend there would be a few staying over and Henry the Chef was round a lot. It was a party zone and if it wasn't at our place, then it would be at Hulme Walk. Glenn was now part of our crowd and he started bringing round cocaine most weekends so we would have a line or two. What a character – he came from Bolton and his family were well known criminals. He robbed handbags from clubs and was involved in lots of dodgy deals. He was a punk with a blond mohawk and besides his dodgy way of making money he was a great bloke. He got involved with some heavy duty criminals around the end of the 1980s and just disappeared overnight. He's probably buried under a car park in Manchester!

Dave Hicks had found a drummer, Pete Flanagan, so we had our first rehearsal in the cellar under Record Peddler. Pete was a solid drummer and the first song we wrote ended up being the only single we recorded, 'A Prayer'. I had been listening to 'Psyche' by Killing Joke and I wrote an intro, verse, and chorus riff to sound like that song. Well it sounded like it in my head anyway. I came to the rehearsal with that riff and by the time we had finished, the song was nearly finished.

Near the end of January New Order played the Hac. It was good fun seeing them and Terry and Dave were on form as we took the piss out of each other as we set the gear up. It was great seeing Oz, Eddie and Diane again. New Order started with 'Your Silent Face', and finished with 'Temptation', 'Ceremony', 'Age of Consent' and 'Blue Monday'. It was a great gig. The Hac was packed, and the crowd loved them.

Throughout January, we rehearsed a lot and by the end of the month we had written five songs: 'Nightmare', 'A Prayer', 'Vision Quest', 'Old Rockers', and 'Mitawin'. Dave had come up with the riff for 'Old Rockers' and 'Mitawin'. The other three had come from my bass. Dave came up with the name, Lavolta Lakota, which I hated; it was more Red Indian shit. It's supposed to mean "All the Tribes Together" or some shit like that.

On 8 February we loaded all of the gear into the back of Dave's car, a Morris Oxford or an Austin Cambridge I'm not sure which - Slim and him drove to Spirit Studios whilst the rest of us set off walking. About 15 minutes later we met and went up to record a live demo. Spirit was a 16 track studio near the Mancunian Way. We played four songs live with Dave singing along so we could hear what we sounded like. The songs we recorded were 'Nightmare', 'Old Rockers', 'A Prayer' and 'Vision Quest'. We used to wind Hooky up no end telling him that 'Old Rockers' was written about him. Dave used to dedicate it to him at most gigs.

The following week Divine played at the Hac, I was really looking forward to seeing her. The place was nearly full. There was a large turnout from Manchester's gay community which brightened up the cold interior of the Hac. Harris Glenn Milstead was a great bloke who spent most of the afternoon chatting to Slim and I in the dressing room. He was a pleasant, polite guy who was easy to talk too but as soon as he put the costume on, he switched into the foul mouthed Divine. It was fascinating to see the transformation.

Immediately she started telling Slim and me to fuck off if we weren't going to fuck her. We were pissing ourselves. She was dressed in an off-the-shoulder sparkly dress and sang to a backing tape and did seven songs including 'Shoot Your Shot'. She spoke to the crowd between each song about sex. Afterwards she switched back into plain old Harris and was normal again. We asked Divine if she had eaten real dog poo in 'Pink Flamingos' and of course she said yes and said she'd enjoyed it. When I asked the same question to Harris he said no.

18 February: Lavolta Lakota's first ever gig at Lancaster University. Dave had arranged it through some students that he knew who ran the entertainment committee there. We were playing with a couple of local bands, and it was agreed that we would be using their equipment. The four of us and Slim packed the guitars in the boot of Dave's car

Factory Fairy Tales

Top: The Crescents in Hulme with John Nash on the left, (middle) a friendly Hulme welcome for the boys in blue, (bottom) The White Horse, a great pub with John Nash behind it.

and went to the gig. We played the five songs that we had written and it went down well. It was a nice gig to get started with and I really enjoyed it. Afterwards we all stayed at a student's flat and got drunk and stoned. The following morning, Pete, Slim and I decided to get the train back to Manchester during which Pete told me that he was leaving. I think he was going back to college or something. So we had played our first gig and lost our drummer at the same time. That's a great start.

We had a couple of interesting gigs coming up which took my mind off the drumming situation for a short while. First up was Richard Hell and The Smiths at Rafters. This was the first time we had worked for Alan Wise in a while as he had been concentrating on managing Nico. After both bands had done their sound check Alan asked Slim and me to carry about 30 chairs down from Fagins and set them up in front of the stage. When the audience started coming in we had to keep them away from the chairs. Just before The Smiths went on the seats were occupied by family members of the band. Parents and grandparents were all there. Once The Smiths were on Slim and I had to stand behind the chairs so that no one banged into the people sitting there. It was so strange as comments were being passed from the families to the stage and back from the stage to the families. "Oh Stephen, that was wonderful" or "John, I never knew you could play like that", that kind of thing. It was like a private concert for the family. Very fucking strange, I must say. Despite that The Smiths sounded good again and when they finished we had to get all the chairs back upstairs to Fagins. I had never seen anyone do this at a gig before. Richard Hell was really good. The crowd liked him, and we spent a bit of time backstage with him - top bloke.

The next gig we worked was The Birthday Party back at the Hac. They had impressed everyone so much the last time they played that they were asked back. Malcolm Whitehead taped this gig and released both gigs on *Pleasure Heads Must Burn* (IKON 7), then a few days later we went to see Southern Death Cult at the Poly. This turned out to be their last gig as Ian Astbury left them soon after. They were good on the night, but Ian definitely made the right decision. Ian stayed in Hulme Walk that evening with Slim, Glenn and I. We had a great night listening to music, drinking and getting stoned. We had spent some brilliant nights in Hulme Walk over the past few months so a couple of days later I moved into Hulme Walk with Henry the Chef moving in the opposite direction. I liked living in Arnesby Walk but I wanted

Factory Fairy Tales

to be nearer Hulme Centre, as it was a long walk home up Princess Road after a few beers in the White Horse or a proper dope session in someone's flat in one of the Crescents. Hulme Walk was where the action was, and it didn't have eight flights of stairs to climb, just one if I remember correctly. The only downside about living there was that Hicks used to rob everyone's food out of the fridge and deny it.

After Pete left us we didn't see any point in rehearsing until we found a drummer. After a couple of weeks we were sat down in Hulme Walk and Slim was looking for some music to play and he put on the Dr Filth single 'Slaughterhouse', and I was looking at the sleeve and it gave me an idea. I went to see Mark the Ted in Didsbury and I asked him if he knew how to get hold of Guy Ainsworth. Mark gave me his parent's number and I contacted him. He came down to a rehearsal and joined in. Now we could rehearse again. He was a fucking brilliant drummer; he could hammer the toms on a tribal song and give you a proper rock beat on another song.

February ended with the release of U2's third album, *War*. This was a classic return to form from the boys with songs like 'Sunday Bloody Sunday', 'Two Hearts Beat as One', 'New Years Day' and the atmospheric '40' which featured The Edge on Bass. It was loud bass, loud drums, loud guitar and loud vocals and great driving rock songs.

The Eurythmics. Their tour manager was annoying us whilst we were trying to get the gear set up. He kept telling us what we had to do or telling us that we weren't doing things the way Annie Lennox liked. It was winding us up so Slim took him to one side, opened the side door of the Hac which backed onto the canal and politely told him that if he opened his mouth again he would throw him in. He left us alone after that. They were really good on the night, and Annie Lennox can really sing. The place was pretty full.

7 March: New Order release 'Blue Monday' (FAC 73). I went to collect it from Lesley and played it to death. What a song. Unique. I hadn't seen her for a while, so I had a cup of tea and a catchup.

Next up was a gig by a living legend from The Velvet Underground. The place had to be full didn't it? Everyone liked The Velvet Underground. John Cale turned up, talked to Slim and me, played a great set of songs for nearly two hours on piano and acoustic guitar and only 40 people showed up in a club with a 1,650 capacity! The night after John Cale it was the turn of Spear of Destiny, I loved them but again it was only half full. Great lads, they spent a lot of time talking to Slim and me and we had a beer in the dressing room with them.

Slim, Glenn, Mikey and I went to see the Sisters of Mercy at The Gallery. It was packed. They were amazing and did an unbelievable version of the Dolly Parton standard 'Jolene'. They never released this song on record. Shame because they did it justice. The Undertones closed the month off with an electrifying performance at The Hac. During 'Teenage Kicks', the electricity went off and Feargal Sharkey carried on singing with the crowd. It was great. Guess the electrics weren't used to having a two guitar band play there. It was pretty full as well. Sometime this month, Hanoi Rocks played at The Gallery; a proper rock 'n' roll gig - twin guitars, big drums, and long hair.

One night Slim and I were eating egg and chips in the Hac restaurant and the place was empty with maybe 30 or so in when three students went up to the restaurant counter and started to be rude and obnoxious with Suzanne the waitress. We could see she was getting upset about something, but we kept out of it for the moment. Finally Henry the Chef came out of the kitchen to find out what was going on. One of the students started giving some verbals to Henry, leaned over the counter and pushed him and Henry twatted the guy in the face. The three of them threatened to batter Henry until Slim tapped one of them on the shoulder and advised them that they should go before anything serious happened to them. They left. About an hour later two Police Officers walked in and arrested Henry!

Life in Hulme Walk was crazier than ever. It was party central most nights with people staying over all the time, some for days on end. Slim, Glenn, Mikey, Guy, Mike Joyce, Roy, Billy Duffy, and Ian Astbury were all regulars. Glenn ended up staying that often he moved in. I don't think any of us actually told him that he could. He just kept bringing a bag with him each time that he would leave in someone's room and then one day he was in. Late one night, after seeing a gig at the Poly, Ian and Billy came back with me and we stayed up smoking and drinking. They were telling me that they were starting up a band called Death Cult and they were looking for a drummer and a bass player. They asked me if Guy and I would be interested in joining them. If I had known how good Billy was on the guitar then I would have said yes, but I was thinking that they would be Southern Death Cult Mark II. I don't know whether to count this as a bad decision or not as I was never sure if they actually meant it or not. I have

Factory Fairy Tales

always told myself that they were joking so as to make the pain of that decision not seem as bad as it was when they formed The Cult but now, thinking back on it, what the fuck was I doing to say no to The Cult! What a fucking wally! This was the chance of a lifetime. Anyway keep reading for more fuck ups...

April kicked off with Orange Juice, followed by Big Country who had around 1,200 or so in. Then it was the turn of The Gun Club and The Sisters of Mercy. This was a proper line up for a gig. I absolutely loved The Gun Club and I thought that Jeffrey Lee Pierce was a great song writer. They were brilliant on the night as were The Sisters of Mercy. We had a good time backstage with both bands and shared a few beers and spliffs, again it was about half full.

We had rehearsed a lot and we now had two new songs making it seven songs in total. The new songs were 'Circles Beat Squares' and 'The Violation Of'. I had come with the riff for 'Circles Beat Squares' and Dave and I had each put a riff into 'The Violation Of'. Guy's drums on both were amazing. So sometime this month we played our first gig with Guy at The Gallery, I think. I just can't remember. It might even be Deville's. 1983 was a bit of a massive drug taking year and most of it is a blur.

Hulme Walk had Dave, Guy, Glenn, Ian, and I living there, and it was completely overcrowded so Slim, Glenn and I decided to get a place of our own. We went to the Council Office in Hulme and asked about getting a flat. The guy said that we could get keys for flats in any of the Crescents and move in straight away. He gave us the keys for a couple of flats, which we went and looked at, and we decided to move into 325 John Nash Crescent.

Hulme was split into two areas either side of Princess Parkway. Hulme Walk was the side nearest the Poly and University and was mostly two storey maisonettes. To get to the other side of Hulme you had to walk across Hulme Walk Bridge which was affectionately nicknamed "Death Bridge" on account of all the students that would get mugged crossing it.

Once across the bridge you walked past some more maisonettes until you reached Royce Road. The Grants Arms pub was to your right and the Russell Club was directly in front of you, but it was now known as the PSV Club. Behind the PSV were four blocks of flats known as the Crescents.

Ged Duffy

They started building the Crescents in the late 1960s and they were finally completed in 1972. They were based on the same design as the famous Crescents in Bath. Once built it was the largest council housing development in Europe encompassing 3,284 deck-access flats with accommodation available for over 13,000 people. There were four south-facing blocks, each seven storeys high, with flats ranging from one bedroom to five, and each flat had its own private balcony. The kitchen and dining rooms were the only rooms that looked onto the walkway at the front of the flat. The walkways and the adjoining walkways to other Crescents were wide enough so the milkman could drive his milk float along them. The four Crescents were named after famous architects: John Nash (Buckingham Palace), William Kent (Treasury buildings in Whitehall), Charles Barry (Houses of Parliament), and Robert Adam (Harewood House). These four eminent architects would have turned in their graves if they saw what monstrosities ended up bearing their names, from neoclassical design to brutalist concrete blocks. By the early 1980s most families had moved out as the design hadn't been thought through – families wanted proper gardens for their kids while pensioners felt isolated stuck on the seventh floor. There was a large grassed area behind each block and at the back of John Nash there was Hulme Centre with shops, a library, and the White Horse pub. You could get the most amazing beef patties from one of the shops there. We spent many an hour sat on the grass drinking, eating and smoking. It didn't matter what time of day or night you sat there, you could hear a band rehearsing in one of the flats, heavy dub coming out of somewhere, there was always something happening as some of the flats had been turned into illegal drinking dens (shebeens), punk venues or discos. The only thing that I never saw when I lived there was a brothel but there must have been a few. Sometimes we would have a game of football on the grass but mostly just lie there getting stoned or drop a tab of acid and watch the world go by – great times.

Hulme was a 'no go' area for police unless they came in mob handed. The majority of people there were either drug dealers, thieves, muggers, pimps, hookers, rent boys, musicians, DJs, writers, poets, film makers, photographers, unemployed or students – it was the heart and soul of Manchester's creative community and would lead to the boom in the city over the next decade. It was a great place to live. However the lifts stunk of piss and sick, and never worked and when they did you stood the risk of finding some bloke getting his cock sucked by a hooker when the doors opened. It was that kind of place. If you stood on the green in front of The Eagle pub for a couple of minutes you could score whatever drugs you wanted. Go in most of the pubs and you could buy anything from cars to guitars, all knocked off. When we moved in we met the twins, Sue and Judy, who lived next door. They came from Cumbria and were both hairdressers. Judy and I started going out. We were never really a couple, just shagging buddies. We were definitely not faithful to each other, but it was fun while it lasted, and my hair always looked good.

A typical day would involve getting up late afternoon, then off to the Hac by 7pm. We'd eat and have a few drinks, all free of charge, then go on somewhere else for the night. Most nights Glenn would have coke with him. We would do a few lines and drink a lot. Back home we would smoke, do more coke, and go to bed around 6. Sometimes Slim, Glenn and I would go up on the roof of John Nash and sit there smoking and watching the world wake up. One night we dropped a tab of acid and sat up there on the roof watching the sunrise. It was amazing. We were really mellow until this black guy with ginger hair started jogging round the edge of the roof. If that wasn't weird enough, especially if you're tripping, he ran round for about an hour. We kept looking at him and then at each other, as the three of us were checking to see if we all saw this person or he was our own private hallucination.

Finally Slim asked "Do you see him?"

We both said "yes".

We found out later that this guy ran round the roof most mornings.

At about this time Hooky went into Strawberry Studios and recorded the instrumental 'Theme' and gave it to us to be used as our intro music. It was a great piece of electronic percussion, and it was played before every gig we played. I think that he had some time left over from a session he had done to create a few seconds of music for one of Tony Wilson's TV shows. Tony had already paid for the time, so Hooky made use of it. It was issued on the *Cool as Ice* compilation on LTM Records under the name of Be Music, but it was just Hooky on his own. We then asked him to be our record producer, live sound guy and van driver. He was happy to say yes.

2 May: New Order release *Power, Corruption & Lies* (FACT 75), my favourite New Order album. I loved it from day one. Check out the bass on 'Age of Consent', it's fucking awesome. Great start to an

Ged Duffy

album. This is probably the New Order album that I play the most nowadays as I think some of songs on their later ones sound a little dated. Another trip for Slim and me to Didsbury to see Lesley.

One night I was in Hulme Walk and Ian Ashbury told me that he had something to give me and handed me a full size confederate flag which I hung over my amp and speaker at every Lavolta gig from then on. Ian had been given it by a Red Indian Chief he had met. Nowadays I would have thought twice about it but back in 1983 it had no political baggage in the UK apart from being an art statement. It was a whole different time to live in, there was no political correctness and if somebody got offended at something, they just fucked off. Of course it's a lot different now with social media and I'd probably would have gone 'viral'!

13 May: We played at The Dortminder Bier Keller in Leeds with Death Cult. I think this was their first gig. We hired a van and Hooky drove us over. We played well and went down well with the crowd. It was full, as Southern Death Cult came from Bradford. I didn't like Death Cult musically at all as they were still doing Red Indian shite but that changed when they became The Cult and Billy Duffy became an axe hero. We met their manager, Ian Stewart, who also managed Play Dead and used to manage The Stranglers. He introduced us to something that he called The Rommel. I was the first to try it. He made me stand against a door and he gave me a blowback. I closed my mouth, held my nose, and couched down and stood up very quickly ten times, opened my mouth and nose and walked away. It was amazing. My head said I'm ok whilst my legs went fuck off, we're going nowhere. It was crazy, I had no control of my legs. This became our drug game of choice. We played six or seven gigs with Death Cult during the rest of May. I can't remember where or when. Blame it on The Rommel.

Do you remember when Henry the Chef got arrested a few weeks earlier? Slim and I had gone to Henry's legal team and given statements. The Hac had booked a lawyer for him as they knew he was innocent. He was charged with assault with intent to injure. The student and his mates had said that Henry had attacked them without warning and that they had done nothing to provoke the trouble. Suzanne, Slim, and I were all down to be called as witnesses. On the morning of the trial we met up in Hulme and went together to court along with Glenn.

Factory Fairy Tales

The student and his mates came in and since the area was full, the only seats available were directly opposite us. As they sat down Slim started staring directly at the guy that Henry had punched. The guy was feeling uncomfortable and kept looking away. Slim then started rocking backwards and forwards in his seat, like a demented person, never taking his eyes off the guy. Then he started growling like a dog, whilst still rocking backwards and forwards, without taking his eyes off the guy. The guy looked even more uncomfortable and when his legal team arrived, he got up and ran over to them. A few moments later, Henry's lawyer came over and told us that the other side had dropped the charges and he was free to go. We went to the Salisbury and got absolutely shitfaced.

Towards the end of May, we went into Strawberry studios for two days to record 'Nightmare' and 'Vision Quest'. Tony Wilson had asked Hooky to record a 30 second piece of music that he could use in one of TV shows. Hooky told him to pay for two days at Strawberry Studios so he could do it. Hooky did it in about an hour and we had the rest of the time free of charge to do the demo. Thank you Granada TV.

Hooky had New Order's drum machine and their Emulator with him, so Guy and him wrote a drum machine pattern for 'Nightmare' and we recorded the song to the drum machine. Guy went in and added drums and extra percussion. Hooky added some sounds from the Emulator and got Dave to play extra guitar which he then played in reverse. It sounded nothing like Lavolta Lakota. Hooky did a couple of mixes of 'Nightmare'. We then played 'Vision Quest', which was a song that Mikey played guitar on, and so it had only one bass on it. Hooky added some percussion to the track and some more weird sounds from the Emulator. Unfortunately we didn't have time to mix the song. This was a really good demo as it sounded nothing like us. I took the cassette to Legends the following Thursday and the DJ played 'Nightmare' and several people danced to it. He also had a few people approach him to see what he had just played. He played it for the next four Thursdays, and it got a great response each time.

21: Follow the leaf

Glenn, Slim, Mikey, Ash, and I decided to have a couple of days in London. We stayed with Big Stuart, Mark, Martin, Robert, and Big Dave at their squat on Fulham Palace Road. That first night we went to the Chelsea Potter pub near the squat and went to bed early as the lads had to be up for work but once the lads had all gone out we went for a mooch round London. Breakfast in a café on the King's Road was followed by the tube to Oxford Street and we went round a few shops and a couple of bars and got back to the squat around 6pm. Around 7pm we left to go to Leicester Square, as we planned to go to The Batcave. On the tube we saw Kirk Brandon and Stan Stammers from Spear of Destiny and of course Glenn had to give them a blast of Theatre Of Hate's biggest hit, 'Do You Believe in The West World' on the journey. Once we got off the tube, we had a couple of beers in a pub.

The Batcave was famous as a Goth Club and we saw some beautiful women walking towards it from our window seats in the pub. We were all hoping that they might fancy a bit of northern rough for the night. As soon as I got in I noticed there was a US Army Jeep parked next to the bar for some reason. Couldn't work that one out. Glenn went to the toilet and was gone for a few minutes. I was holding his drink so it wouldn't get robbed or spilled. After a few minutes, he came back with a tab of acid for each of us. Only Glenn could find a dealer within five minutes of going somewhere. So we all dropped a tab and waited for things to develop.

After an hour or so, nothing had happened so Slim and Glenn went to find the dealer. They returned with another (free) tab for everyone after Slim and the dealer had come to an arrangement. We all dropped this second tab and you can guess what happened next… Within about five minutes of having this second tab the first one kicked in. Any ideas of finding romance with a beautiful Goth girl went out the window with this first rush.

We had a great night in The Batcave tripping off our heads; the lights, dry ice, and the music seemed amazing to me. I was so glad that I had clocked the Jeep earlier on, or that might have freaked me out. Some of the Goths looked like The Addams Family and I was greatly

Big Stuart

amused by them. I saw a lot of Morticias that night and unfortunately a few Uncle Festers and that was just the women! I guess I must have seen The Thing as well.

We left the club at 2am, and Glenn spotted some ants on the pavement so the ten of us got on our hands and knees and started crawling round Leicester Square, people were having to walk round us, or climb over us, as we pursued our little friends on their journey. We were singing 'Ant Music' as we did this. Anyone that got in our way was politely told to fucking move by Slim. This pursuit of our little friends was very important to us at that moment.

It was decided that we should walk back to the squat, about a 90 minute from Leicester Square. We walked for about four hours. We kept stopping to look at things along the way. Then Glenn pulled a massive leaf off a tree and started to sing "Follow The Leaf" to the tune of the Killing Joke song 'Follow The Leaders'. That was it. Anyone passing must have thought that we had escaped from a mental hospital or something as we marched in line behind Glenn who was holding the leaf above his head, singing the song as we marched.

Around 6 we found two couples playing mixed doubles tennis in a park and we stood there for about an hour cheering them on and singing songs, they must have been terrified. Fancy going out that early in the morning to play tennis and seeing a load of lunatics converge on you. After a bit I think they realised that we meant them no harm, so their energy levels went up with each cheer from us. It was amazing watching the ball change shape and colour every time it was hit backwards and forwards between the four people. I could have watched it for hours.

When they finished they waved to us and left so we started walking again. We got back into Leaf mode and carried on singing our ode to Killing Joke. Just as we were getting within about 100 yards of the squat, we decided to stop for a rest and sat on a couple of benches right outside the tube station when someone suggested going in and travelling somewhere. By now it was rush hour and we sat there looking at all the businessmen in their bowler hats and pin stripe suits and started singing 'Smithers Jones' by The Jam. We stayed on The Circle Line for a complete loop of the track and then decided to stay on again. I've always been a people watcher, and I like nothing more than to sit in a bar and just observe people's behaviour. It's amazing people watching, while you are tripping. Some of the businessmen had moustaches that moved and danced, some of the men blended into the person sat next to them, some of them had shapes growing out of their heads, some of the sexy secretary's had their tongues out wanting to lick me, some were wagging their fingers at me, some were just coloured shapes flickering in front of me. This was my trip and I was loving it.

During this second loop of The Circle Line Mark, Martin, and Big Dave all got off at different stations and the rest of us stayed on the tube. During the third loop we saw the guys at the stations they had got off at. They were all sitting on the platforms by themselves. By now, we should be coming down from the trip, but the second rush came.

We got back to the squat and started smoking dope to bring us down. Over the next couple of hours Big Dave, Martin, and Mark made their way back to the squat. We were all still tripping. We had planned on going home that evening, but since we were still so out of it, we stayed another night. Robert decided to take his car out and ended up crashing it in the West End. We went to a bar that night and stayed there until closing, went back to the squat, and smoked all night to try and bring us down while the lads stayed up all night then went to work next morning. We got the train back and even the next day I was seeing shadows and flickering colours in my peripheral vision. It was a night to remember. When I met up with Big Stuart a couple of years ago, after not seeing him since his wedding in 1989 , the first thing we spoke about was the 'Night of the Leaf'.

22. Playing the Hacienda at last

We played about ten gigs with Death Cult in June, I can't remember where and when to be honest. This was followed by about another ten gigs with Play Dead. Slim and I introduced Steve O'Donnell and Andy Robinson to the stage crew at the Hac so they could take our places when we weren't able to work as we were playing a lot of gigs. Steve was an old mate from Burnage, and he met his future wife Carol at the Hac as she worked behind the bar.

It was great living with Glenn. He used to cop off all the time and whenever the girl had a friend with them I managed to get off with them most of the time. One night he came back from Deville's with two girls. Slim and I had been somewhere else and when we arrived the girl that Glenn was with, told her friend to go with me and she agreed. Just before we went to bed, Judy the Twin knocked on the door and came in and went to bed with me. Glenn rescued me by having a threesome with the two girls. He had the biggest grin on his face the next morning, and he told me that it had been the night of his life. The following week, we bumped into the girls again at the Poly disco and they came back with us, so I got to spend the night with her anyway. A couple of weeks later we saw them again and when they came back with us they suggested that we swapped so we did, and I had the other one.

In June Ian Stewart asked us if we wanted to have a song released on *The Angels Are Coming*. He told us that it was going to be a compilation released on cassette later in the year. We said okay.

6 July. We supported The Smiths at the Hac. We had done several gigs with Death Cult and Play Dead in small venues. This was the first large venue that we played. We had a right laugh with Mike Joyce and Johnny Marr, but Morrissey was up his own arse. Malcolm Whitehead videoed us and when I watched it a few days later I was shocked that we didn't sound that bad. We were just missing a good guitarist as Dave was a good front man. Hooky was away with New Order in Canada so I think the guy who owned the PA did the sound for us.

Ged Duffy

Morrissey used to wear flowers sticking out of the arse pocket of his jeans and would throw some out into the crowd. The box of flowers was sat at the side of the stage, so Glenn cut all the heads off them. There were no flowers visible when they went on. During our set Glenn got some Tampax, dipped them in red wine and threw them into the crowd. I announced, "we can't afford flowers like The Smiths, so please accept these gifts". The audience moved back as quickly as they could, I thought it was funny but I guess we were too rock 'n' roll for the serious indie crowd.

After the gig Glenn told Slim that we were missing a guitar tuner and that The Smiths road crew must have taken it. Slim lost it and took matters into his own hand. He had two of their road crew up against the wall with a hand round the neck of each of them whilst the third one was frantically searching for the tuner. Glenn put his hand in his pocket and pulled out the tuner saying, "I've found it". Slim growled at all three of them and walked off. It was Glenn's idea of a joke. Slim would have hammered them if Glenn hadn't come clean. Loads of our mates including Mani were there that night and we got a good reception from them. Tony France had a heated argument with Morrissey at the bar before we went on. I think a few home truths about his image and The Smiths record sleeve designs were discussed between the two.

15 July. We supported Play Dead at The Gallery. Hooky was back behind the desk for this one and then the following night again in Coventry - both good gigs. Play Dead sounded like a poor man's Killing Joke. We played loads of gigs with them, and I don't think that I ever spoke to any of the band.

20 July: New Order; they started off with 'Blue Monday', and 'Age of Consent' and finished off with 'Temptation', 'Thieves Like Us', 'In a Lonely Place', and 'Everything's Gone Green'. Brilliant gig, a sold out crowd - a great night. I stood on Hooky's side of the stage, and it was great watching the swaying crowd in the Hac. They were Manchester legends now.

A couple of days later it was The Fall. Another great gig and the Hac was full. Around this time Big Stuart came back from London and moved back into Hulme Walk. He became our main driver alongside Hooky. We also moved out of the cellar in Record Peddler and into a

Factory Fairy Tales

room above Johnny Roadhouse on Oxford Road. We actually only rehearsed there about four times over the next few months and when we did we just ran through the usual set. No jamming, no new ideas, nothing.

Lavolta Lakota were playing four, five or six nights some weeks so Hooky and Dave Hicks collected the money from the promoters (any trouble Slim collected it), and then they hired the van out of this kitty. Sometimes we would hire it for a couple of days and sometimes it was cheaper to have it for a week or 10 days. I saw Killing Joke play somewhere in Manchester in late July or early August, I can't remember where the gig was. The Poly or Salford University spring to mind. I know we played somewhere the following night with either Play Dead or Death Cult and we didn't have a gig planned for the night after that and having discovered that Killing Joke were playing in Preston so about 20 of us went there in the van. We played somewhere the night after.

Another time about 15 or 20 of us jumped in the van and went for a day out in Alderley Edge which is a very posh area in Cheshire where a lot of footballers live now. The actual Edge is a strip of land separating a narrow and short valley from the higher ground of southeast Cheshire. It is a public access woodland area, and the area is riddled with the old Alderley Edge Mines. We all dropped a tab of acid and spent hours chasing each other round playing cowboys and Indians. It was so much fun. A great day.

One Friday in early August Slim, Glenn and I were in the Poly when Glenn came up and told us to follow him to the toilets. He had bought some heroin off a dealer. Glenn had got some foil, so he put some powder on it, and then heated it from below with his lighter, whilst one of us inhaled the smoke. This is called "Chasing The Dragon". The three of us did it and it was an amazing high. We were so out of it the rest of the night. We did the same for the next two Fridays and then we were playing so we didn't get there again for a few weeks. Without these gigs we would have become smack heads. I'm so glad we didn't.

Tony Wilson told me that we were going to do a single for Factory Benelux. I asked him why we couldn't be on Factory. He told me, "You're too rock 'n' roll for Factory, darling" so in August we spent two nights at Strawberry Studios to record 'A Prayer' and 'Mitawin'. Hooky has already told a story about this session in the foreword. I suggested that we mix 'Nightmare' and 'Vision Quest' as they would make a great 12 inch single. Dave said that we had already agreed to release 'Nightmare' on *The Angels Are Coming* compilation and we shouldn't release it again. I replied "no fucker will buy the cassette and we're wasting a great song".

So we did 'A Prayer' and 'Mitawin'...

'Mitawin' was the best guitar that Dave ever played, and it was too good a song to be put on a B Side. Listen to the drums on this song, they're great. Hooky did a great job with mixing it. 'A Prayer' had brilliant drums again, the way Guy smashes those toms. All the background noises were played by Hooky on New Order's Emulator. We all sang backing vocals. The session went well, and Hooky also did three remixes of 'A Prayer', including a dub one which sounded great, and we should have used one of them on a 12 inch single. So all you New Order fanatics out there, I bet you didn't know that Hooky played on this single. You're going to have to try and find a copy of it now to complete your collection!

23: Mark E Smith doesn't share his beer

Around this time Glenn came home with a girl and she had a mate with her. I knew that I would end up with the other one, but I couldn't work out which girl Glenn was with as he was talking to both of them. One of them was a large stocky girl who looked a bit rough and the other had a real pretty face with her hair shaved at the side and then spiked and crimped on top. Obviously I preferred girl number two but as a 'wingman' I had to help Glenn so whoever I ended up with I had to be nice to them so that they don't grab their friend and go home. We sat talking for a while and when Glenn and the stocky girl went off to his room I was so pleased. The pretty girl stood up and I saw that she was about five foot seven, had large tits and long legs which were barely covered by the tiny dress she was wearing. I watched her walk into my room, and I thought this one's nice. When we were in bed together something felt different this time, I felt an attraction towards her. It was more than just casual sex. The following morning I walked her to the bus stop, and she gave me her number. Normally I would have thrown it away, but I didn't as I wanted to see her again. We met again the following weekend and we ended up going out. She came from Wythenshawe, and I can't tell you her name. After we split she got involved with a Christian Prayer Group and turned her life over to Jesus. According to her new religion, her life only began when she was baptised. She has asked me to keep her name out of this book so she will be known as 'my partner' for the rest of this story.

In September we went out on tour with Death Cult followed by a tour with Play Dead followed by Death Cult again. In between these gigs we played a mini tour with The Fall, and some dates with Cabaret Voltaire. The first time we played with The Fall Slim and I went in the dressing room and took a can of beer each from the rider. Mark E Smith shouted over "Support bands don't take our beer", to which Slim replied, "Fuck off Smith or I'll knock you out" - Mark started laughing and told us to take whatever we wanted. He got on great with us moving forward. He even watched us a couple of times and told us that we were pretty good and different. He liked different.

We supported Death Cult at Glasgow Night Moves because Caesar

FUTURAMA·5
Queens Hall ~ Leeds '83
SATURDAY 17th SEPTEMBER

The BAY CITY ROLLERS
HOWARD DEVOTO
*COMSAT ANGELS
CLOCK DVA
the Smiths

GINA X — (from Germany)
SILENT RUNNING (from Ireland)
THE CHAMELEONS
DANIELLE DAX
THE CHEVALIER BROS.
RED LORRY YELLOW LORRY
A POPULAR HISTORY OF SIGNS
RED GUITARS
SEX BEAT
EDWARD'S VOICE
MASQUE OF BIZARRO
REAL FOO FOO
MUA
COLENSO PARADE (from n.Ireland)
CURIA VERITAS
THE LOST BOYS
plus special guests
John COOPER-CLARKE
compere: Mr TRASH   AND CURIOUS YELLOWS

SUNDAY 18th SEPTEMBER

KILLING JOKE
Death Cult
the ARMOURY SHOW
with Richard Jobson (Skids)
and John McGeoch (Siouxsie/Magazine)
special U.S.A. guests:
BRYAN GREGORY (ex-Cramps)
with BEAST
and...JAYNE COUNTY
LIGOTAGE with Becky Bondage
POISON GIRLS
THE MEKONS
PLAY DEAD
THE 3 JOHNS
THE BOX 2
NEW MODEL ARMY
UNDER TWO FLAGS
HOLY TOY (from Norway)
FLESH FOR LULU
PLEASURE AND THE BEAST
ACTION PACT
GROUND ZERO
LAVOLTA LAKOTA
BONE ORCHARD
SPECIAL guests: JOOLZ (poet)
Mark Miwurds (comedian)
and the EKOME AFRICAN DANCERS

TICKETS:£7.50 (per day) - £12.00 (both days) from:
Or from ticket agencies:- John Keenan, P.O. Box HH9, LEEDS 8, LS8 1AN.

LEEDS:Cheap Thrills(Boar Lane).Advent Records(Woodhouse Lane).Project(Roundhay).
Merrion Centre Badge Shop.MANCHESTER:Piccadilly Records.Virgin.SHEFFIELD:Virgin.
WAKEFIELD:J.A.T.HULL:Shakespeare's.HALIFAX:Bradley's.BRADFORD:NEW.YORK:Red Rhino
LIVERPOOL:Probe.Penny Lane.STOKE-ON-TRENT:Mike Lloyd.STAFFORD:Lotus.
DERBY:A.E.COSH.NOTTINGHAM:Selectadisc.BIRMINGHAM:Cyclops.SOUTHPORT:Town Records
BLACKPOOL:Graffiti.NEWCASTLE: LONDON:Virgin Megastore.Rough Trade.
There may be an extra charge of 15p per ticket at most outlets. (Booking fee)

and Bobby Gillespie, from The Wake, came to see us and we stayed at Caesar's flat in The Gorbals afterwards. Hooky stayed with us as well. We were drinking, smoking, and having some coke all night. The next day we played Whitby Bay Playhouse which was an old cinema/theatre with amazing dressing rooms. We had our own dressing room, and it had a massive mirror with light-bulbs all round the outside of it. Glenn emptied both dressing rooms of light-bulbs so we would never have to buy one again for our flat! After we played our set a girl came down to the front of the stage selling ice creams. Whitley Bay was still set in the 1960s.

When Death Cult came on to do their encore we decided to go on stage with them. Mikey stood behind Jamie, Guy sat down next to the drum kit, Dave went and stood to the side of Ian, and I stood behind Billy. They started playing and we mimicked their every move and pose. Ian started laughing and grabbed hold of Dave and danced with him and shared the mic with him. It was a good laugh. The next two nights we played at The Warehouse in Leeds and at The Limit

Factory Fairy Tales

Club in Sheffield both local crowds for Ian, so they were great nights. *The Face* did a multi-page spread on Death Cult and wrote a bit about us coming on stage with them in Whitley Bay. It was the only press coverage that we ever got!

16 September was Slim's 21st birthday and we arranged to meet with a few mates in The White Horse at 6pm. We ate at The Magnet Café in the day and went for a beer in the Salisbury. My partner turned up and she was out for the night with us. By the time we got to the White Horse, we'd had a few but the serious drinking would soon begin. We had a couple of lines in the toilets and the rest of the crew arrived. A few of the lads from Hulme turned up and when we left to walk to the Poly there was about 20 of us.

En route we stopped off for a couple at Clynes Wine Bar in Hulme. Once inside the Poly we met a lot more people including Muppet, Lee, Derek, the twins, and some of the old Russell crew. We started smoking and had a few more lines. By about 11pm Slim had passed out so we put a few chairs together and stretched him out on them. People were still buying him drinks, coming up to him, opening his mouth and pouring the drinks down his throat. In the end we had to stop them doing that.

By the time the Poly closed all his 'great mates' had fucked off and left Glenn, Big Stuart, Mikey, Guy, Guy Parker, Roy, and me to work out how to get him home. We tried to walk with him but that didn't work so we carried him holding a leg and an arm each. We had to keep stopping to have a rest because he wasn't slim. Eventually we decided to drop him off at Hulme Walk. Glenn and I went home. Guy was staying with us that night.

The next morning we had to be at Hulme Walk at around 10 as Hooky was picking us up as we were playing with Death Cult and Sex Gang Children at Brixton Ace in London. When he arrived he took one look at us all and couldn't believe how rough we were. Slim was like a zombie and still wearing the same clothes from the night before. The only one who looked okay was Dave, but he hadn't been out with us. We got in the van and started smoking. Slim, Glenn and Mikey were all skinning up and it was constant spliffs all the way down to London. Things were that bad Hooky had to wind his window down so he wouldn't get stoned. When Hooky opened the back doors of the van outside the venue, a massive cloud of smoke escaped and we all fell out. If you were standing at the back of the van when the doors

Ged Duffy

```
**************  PNLSU ENTS PRESENTS  **************
                ▅▅▅▅▅▅▅▅▅▅▅▅▅▅
                        O N
                Friday 30th September, 1983

                ******************************
                        T H E    F A L L
                                +                LAVOLTA
                T H E   M O D I S T S           LAKOTA
                ******************************

The Theatre                                          £2.75p
The Polytechnic of North London    Doors Open: 7.30 p.m.
Holloway Road
London N7 8DB                                Ticket Number
Nearest Underground: Holloway Road              000288
**********************************************************
```

opened, you would have got stoned just by breathing.

Big Dave, Mark and Martin were there to see us, and we hit the beers backstage and carried on smoking. I have no recollection of even playing that night. I remember asking Big Dave, "What time are we on?" to which he replied, "You've been on, and you were fucking good". It was a wild night. Slim got in some bother with Sex Gang Children and things weren't pleasant, but I was so out of it I only found out about it the next day.

We got back to Hulme at around 6 am and Hooky picked us up again at 11 as we were playing Day 2 of Futurama 5 at The Queens Hall, Leeds. I was looking forward to it. We were fourth band on, and when Hooky reversed the van up to the doors we saw that it was the same stage crew that we'd worked with on the previous festivals. We set up and played. There were a lot of Death Cult and Play Dead fans there that had seen us several times before, so we were one of the few early bands to have a crowd in front of us dancing. It was a great gig and after we packed up Hooky pulled the van round to the end of the car park, and we went back inside to watch some of the bands. We spent some time in Death Cult's dressing room and Ian Stewart took us into see Killing Joke and we stayed there a bit. I think Hooky spent a lot of time in there.

The first band I went into the hall to see was New Model Army and they played a great set, they're a very underrated band. Then I watched Play Dead and they sounded as good as they always did, very professional but all the songs sounded the same. The Mekons were brilliant. Death Cult were magnificent and probably the best that I had seen them play so far. They had the crowd eating out of their hand

Factory Fairy Tales

and I was thinking that I had definitely made a mistake staying with Lavolta Lakota. Killing Joke came on to a hero's welcome and were on fire that night. They started off with 'The Fall of Because' they also played 'Pssyche', 'Sun Goes Down', 'We Have Joy', 'Requiem', 'Empire Song', 'Wardance', and 'Change' among others. We had a great day sitting in different band's dressing rooms, watching bands, smoking, speeding, and having a couple of Rommels as well.

A few days after playing Futurama we were off doing dates with The Fall. I loved this band, so I was really looking forward to playing with them again and the first gig was at Hellfire in Wakefield followed by Nottingham Rock City, North London Poly, The Boys Club in Bedford, and The Mayfair Ballroom in Glasgow. We stayed with Caesar again as we were playing the following day at Buster Browns in Edinburgh. After we'd finished sound checking in Wrexham we went into a nearby pub. It was your typical North Wales pub where everyone was talking in English until they hear your accent, and then all the conversation turns to Welsh. This has happened to me so many times in North Wales, they hate the English but without our tourism they would be broke… anyway, back to the story. There's four sat at the bar, and we could tell that they were taking the piss out of us. Then totally out of the blue Dave speaks to them in Welsh. The look on their faces was a picture. The look on our faces was a picture as well. They had been talking about Slim and he asked Dave to tell him what they had said. When Slim found out he challenged them to say it to his face. They drank up, said sorry and left. It turned out that Dave was born in Cornwall and learnt Cornish and Welsh growing up – all Celts together. I have found out that nowadays he calls himself Davyth and he works in a language department of the European Union.

Then it was off with Play Dead to play Liverpool College, Retford Porterhouse, Tiffany Dungeon Club in Leeds, and then Jilly's Rock World in Manchester before we had a night off where we went to see John Foxx at the Hacienda. He was magnificent and put on a great atmospheric set. The following day it was supporting Play Dead at Birmingham Golden Eagle, and Coventry Poly before more gigs with The Fall at Huddersfield Poly and Sheffield University.

24: Moving out of Hulme by mistake

My partner suggested we get a flat together, so I suggested we go to the Council Office and get a flat in one of the crescents but she wanted a clean break, so we moved to Fallowfield and rented a bedsit in a house in Granville Road. This was the start of me losing contact with a lot of my friends in Hulme and at the Hac, but I didn't know that yet. Should never have left Hulme, all of my life was there and definitely not in Fallowfield. This was another bad decision.

The bedsit was awful - dark, damp and uninviting. The landlord was doing building work all the time we were there. We woke up one morning to find a worker at the end of our bed staring at us. He had come into our flat by mistake. The landlord was a twat and didn't give a fuck about his tenants. He only accepted the unemployed so he could charge whatever he wanted in rent as the Social Security would pay it.

One of the first things I did when we moved in was to get a tape done of the four songs we had recorded with Hooky. I sent a copy of this tape, along with a letter, to various record labels including Situation 2, Small Wonder, Beggars Banquet, 4AD, Mute and Rough Trade. From the start of the band I had kept a back seat whilst Dave controlled things. I had asked Hooky to come on board as our producer, sound guy and part time van driver and my relationship with Tony Wilson and Rob Gretton had got us the single deal with Factory Benelux but everything else that had happened with the band was all due to Dave.

We had six more gigs with Death Cult planned for the year starting with The New Gatsby in Liverpool, Nottingham Rock City, Fagin's, Sheffield University, The Tin Can Club in Birmingham, and London Empire. Then it was the Hacienda with The Gun Club followed by London Klub Foot with Play Dead.

This last gig was due to be on 8 December and after speaking to Ian Stewart I discovered that there were no more gigs planned until the end of January. I was not happy with the fact that we never rehearsed or jammed any ideas for new songs, so I intended to have a band meeting after the Klub Foot gig as I wanted us to get a guitarist

Factory Fairy Tales

in so that Dave could just be a front-man. To be honest he wasn't a great guitarist and if you have two bass players and a brilliant drummer, then you need a strong guitar to create the melody and in my opinion Dave was not that man. I had already decided to nominate Ash as our new guitarist. I knew that this wouldn't have caused a big issue as all of us liked him. He was a lad who used to knock about with us, at the Hac and he'd started going out with Judy the twin. He used to run a fish stall at the Arndale Market, so he had a bit of smell issue (only kidding). He would have fitted in perfectly.

Mikey was also a good guitarist, and I was going to suggest that we get a synthesiser and then he could switch between synthesiser, bass, and guitar on different songs. I had no doubt that he had the ability to pick up the synthesiser. We had to do something to break up the monotony of the sound. It wouldn't have cost us much to get one, just a trip to a few pubs in Hulme and we would find one. I also wanted to drop all of the Red Indian shite because Southern Death Cult and Death Cult had already done that, and they had done it much better than we could. I'm a Mancunian born and bred so what the fuck has Red Indian culture got to do with my life? So the name would have to change or be shortened to Lavolta. I was going to suggest that we rehearse four times a week for the rest of December and the whole of January and in that time we would have written at least another six or seven songs and we would have a good set of songs to choose from moving forward back into gigs from February onwards. I also wanted us to get a manager and I was going to suggest Ian Stewart or Rob Gretton. Either would have done a great job for us on a part time basis.

Before then we played four gigs with Death Cult without much hassle apart from Mikey being caught smoking a joint by coppers outside the venue in Liverpool. They let him off with a warning. Then it was onto The Tin Can Club in Birmingham which was above the Sunset Strip Club in Digbeth. We didn't go in the strip club as it was full of Hells Angels who were all outside giving us grief as we carried the gear upstairs. I think that, at some time, the venue had been part of the strip club with the velvet curtains backstage and heart shaped mirror in the dressing room, or it might have been a knocking shop. Nothing seemed any different tonight from any of the gigs we had played over the last six months. We did our sound check, Hooky was mixing the sound, Big Stuart had driven the van, Glenn and Slim were there to help set up the gear. The club was full by the time we went on, and I spotted a few of the regulars who were following Death Cult around at the front of the stage. They had recently started dancing to us at every gig and knew the songs. Not difficult really, as we only had seven. They had seen us several times over the previous six months.

I can't remember which song it was, but I think that it was during 'Vision Quest' that a guy got on stage and started doing some weird dance. I looked at Slim, who came over and pushed him off. I noticed that Dave was looking angry and was shouting at Slim. Not a wise move. Slim told him to fuck off. A few minutes later the same cunt got back on stage and started dancing in front of me. I put my foot through his arse and sent him packing into the crowd and with that Dave stormed off stage. I didn't have a clue what was up with him. We finished the song; I told the crowd that we had finished and off we went.

It turned out that the guy dancing was a Red Indian Chief from America and had come to see Dave. He was dancing a good luck dance for us. Well, guess what, it never fucking worked. We had a massive bust up and I told Dave that I had enough of all the Red Indian shite, and I was done. He said, "ok, no worries". Guy then said, "If Ged's out, then I'm out", and he quit as well. We all got stoned in the back of the van whilst Dave sat up front with Big Stuart and Hooky. I got them to drop my gear off in Fallowfield and my time with Lavolta Lakota was over.

As soon as I left I should have started a band immediately with Guy, my partner and Ash before Lavolta Lakota got him. Between us all we could have found a singer round Hulme and moved on. I walked away with no regrets. We lacked leadership, ambition, creativity and drive; we would never have made it. Dave was an arrogant man who looked down on us, and thought he was better than any of us whereas in reality he was the weak link in the band. He had the image but he wasn't a great guitarist, and he definitely wasn't a great singer, just my own personal opinion. I never saw Lavolta Lakota play live again and believe it or not I never ran into Dave Hicks again.

LAVOLTA LIVE:
November: 25th Birmingham Tin Can
29th London Empire Rooms
December: 7th Haçienda
8th London Klub Foot

Top left: A Prayer single cover, (top Right) gig flyer, (middle) letter sent to record companies, (bottom) 1983 Hacienda Xmas card listing Lavolta Lakota.

benelux single due for January release

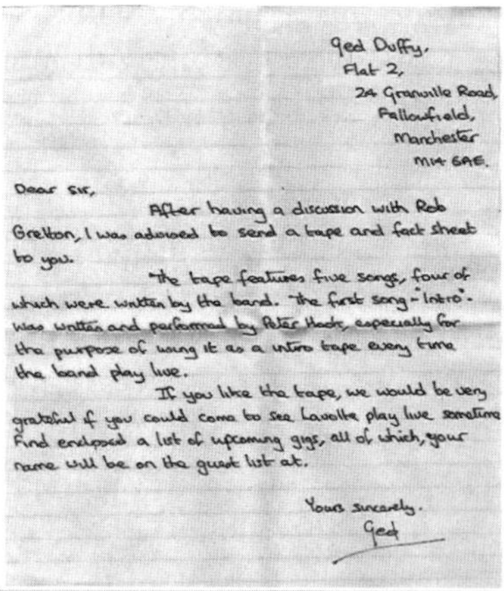

Ged Duffy,
Flat 2,
24 Granville Road,
Fallowfield,
Manchester
M14 6AE.

Dear sir,

After having a discussion with Rob Gretton, I was advised to send a tape and fact sheet to you.

The tape features five songs, four of which were written by the band. The first song - Intro - was written and performed by Peter Hode, especially for the purpose of using it as a intro tape every time the band play live.

If you like the tape, we would be very grateful if you could come to see Lavolta play live sometime. Find enclosed a list of upcoming gigs, all of which, your name will be on the guest list at.

Yours sincerely,
Ged

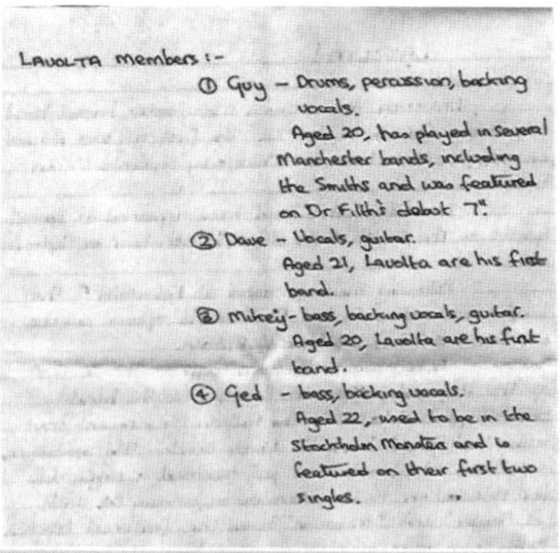

LAVOLTA members:-

① Guy - Drums, percussion, backing vocals.
Aged 20, has played in several Manchester bands, including the Smiths and was featured on Dr Filth's debut 7".

② Dave - vocals, guitar.
Aged 21, Lavolta are his first band.

③ Mikey - bass, backing vocals, guitar.
Aged 20, Lavolta are his first band.

④ Ged - bass, backing vocals.
Aged 22, used to be in the Stockholm Monsters and is featured on their first two singles.

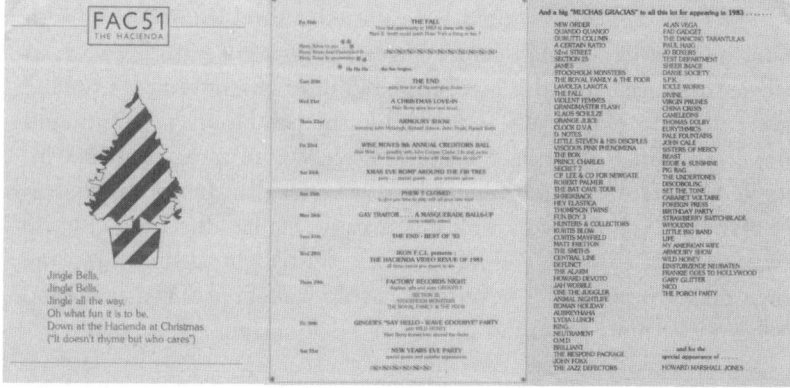

FAC 51
THE HACIENDA

Jingle Bells,
Jingle Bells,
Jingle all the way.
Oh what fun it is to be,
Down at the Hacienda at Christmas.
("It doesn't rhyme but who cares")

And a big "MUCHAS GRACIAS" to all this list for appearing in 1983 . . . . .

NEW ORDER — ALAN VEGA
QUANDO QUANGO — FAD GADGET
DURUTTI COLUMN — THE DANCING TARANTULAS
A CERTAIN RATIO — PAUL HAIG
52nd STREET — JO BOXERS
SECTION 25 — TEST DEPARTMENT
JAMES — SHEER BLISS
STOCKHOLM MONSTERS — DANSE SOCIETY
THE ROYAL FAMILY & THE POOR — S.P.K.
LAVOLTA LAKOTA — ICICLE WORKS
THE FALL — DIVINE
VIOLENT FEMMES — VIRGIN PRUNES
GRANDMASTER FLASH — CHINA CRISIS
KLAUS SCHULZE — GAMELEONS
ORANGE JUICE — THOMAS DOLBY
CLOCK D.V.A. — EURYTHMICS
51 NOTES — PALE FOUNTAINS
LITTLE STEVEN & HIS DISCIPLES — JOHN CALE
VISCIOUS PINK PHENOMENA — SISTERS OF MERCY
THE FIX — BEAST
PRINCE CHARLES — EDDIE & SUNSHINE
SECRET 7 — PIG BAG
CP LEE & CO FOR NEWGATE — THE UNDERTONES
ROBERT PALMER — DISCOBOLISC
THE BAT CAVE TOUR — SET THE TONE
SHRIEKBACK — CABARET VOLTAIRE
HEY ELASTICA — FOREIGN PRESS
THOMPSON TWINS — BIRTHDAY PARTY
FUN BOY 3 — STRAWBERRY SWITCHBLADE
HUNTERS & COLLECTORS — WYGGEN
KURTIS BLOW — LITTLE BIG BAND
CURTIS MAYFIELD — LIFE
NATY HATTON — MY AMERICAN WIFE
THE SMITHS — ARMOURY SHOW
CENTRAL LINE — WILD HONEY
DEFUNCT — EINSTURZENDE NEUBATEN
THE ALARM — FRANKIE GOES TO HOLLYWOOD
HOWARD DEVOTO — GARY GLITTER
JAH WOBBLE — NICO
ONE THE JUGGLER — THE PORCH PEOPLE
ANIMAL NIGHTLIFE
ROMAN HOLIDAY
AUDIOPHANS
LYDIA LUNCH
KING
NEUTRAMENT
OMD
BRILLANT
THE BESPOKE PACKAGE   and for the
JOHN FOXX   special appearance of...
THE JAZZ DEFECTORS   HOWARD MARSHALL JONES

244

Ged Duffy

7 December: James at Jilly's Rock World. I still called it Rafters as I had so many memories there. James were awesome every time I saw them. They had now developed into a really tight professional band and the songs were getting better.

I didn't go to see The Gun Club, and I'm still mad that I didn't. Guy and I decided to stay away so there would be no issues with Lavolta Lakota. We knew that they were playing without us, and we felt that it wouldn't be fair to them if we were there. The day after Lavolta Lakota played at The Hac, several people got in touch with me to tell me that Dave Hicks had talked about Guy and me in a very derogatory manner when he introduced the band on stage. I wasn't there so I can't confirm that he did, but if he did, then there was no need for him to do so. The only thing I do know is that he definitely wouldn't have said anything like that if Guy or I were there that night. Billy Duffy and Shan Hira stepped in to replace Guy and me. They played in London the following night as well. At least both of these audiences saw a brilliant guitarist play, and that was a first for a Lavolta Lakota gig.

14 December: Killing Joke. Brilliant night and a full house. Even the shit sound in the Hac couldn't ruin a Joke gathering. The following night was Spear of Destiny, another great night, another big crowd. This was followed 24 hours later by The Fall making three classic nights on the trot. This proved to be the last gig that I worked at the Hac. It was a ball ache getting home to Fallowfield on the night bus and I couldn't stay in Hulme as my partner didn't want to be alone all night. Maybe she was concerned that I might have become Glenn's wingman again when he chatted up girls. Who knows?

I have only mentioned the gigs that I remember, and the only one with Cabaret Voltaire I can recall is the one we did in Bournemouth. I know that we did about ten gigs with these guys. They were great as it was a completely different audience to play in front of and we were always listened to by their crowd since we were nothing like them, we generally got a good reception from their crowd. The lads in the Cabs were great guys and Slim and I knew them from the Russell and early Hac days, so we had a lot of time for them. They were just down to earth Sheffield lads who supported shit Yorkshire football teams and liked a drink. They were also putting on a great show every time we played with them as they now had a drummer and some great songs to play like 'Fascination'.

Factory Fairy Tales

It was great fun going round the country playing so many gigs and I'm so glad that I was part of it. We got into so many scrapes especially in London when there would always be some member of a band that had caused issues with Slim at the Hacienda present who felt the urge to remind him. It usually didn't end up well for them! We nearly got arrested for vandalism in Leeds after we got stuck in an underground car park when the gate stuck. The owner was not very happy with our attempts to remove it and the boys in blue gave us a lecture. Hooky fell asleep once in the back of the van and we put Immac on his beard. He was so pissed off with us when he woke up but his beard must be glued to his face as no hair fell out.

THE ANGELS ARE COMING

The Angels are Coming came out on Pleasantly Surprised sometime in the last three months of the year. Bauhaus, The Alarm, Stockholm Monsters, Blue Orchids, and Nico were all on it but guess what, Play Dead or Death Cult weren't on it, and it sold fuck all…

1983

Singles

New Order: 'Blue Monday'
U2: 'New Year's Day', 'Sunday Bloody Sunday'
The Fall: 'The Man whose Head Expanded'
Public Image Limited: 'This is Not a Love Song'
Blancmange: 'Blind Vision'
Aztec Camera: 'Oblivious', 'Walk Out to Winter'
Tears For Fears: 'Mad World'

Ged Duffy

The Alarm: 'The Stand'; '68 Guns'
Simple Minds: 'Waterfront'
David Bowie: 'Let's Dance', 'China Girl'
Sisters Of Mercy: 'Temple of Love'
The Smiths: 'Hand in Glove', 'This Charming Man'
Bauhaus: 'She's in Parties'
Funboy Three: 'Our Lips Are Sealed'
Big Country: 'Fields of Fire', 'In a Big Country'
Spear Of Destiny: 'Flying Scotsman', 'The Wheel'
REM: 'Radio Free Europe'
Cabaret Voltaire: 'Just Fascination'

EPs

Sisters Of Mercy: *Alice*; *The Reptile House*
James: *Jimone*
The Alarm: *The Alarm*
Death Cult: *Death Cult*
The Birthday Party: *Bad Seeds*; *Mutiny*
The Cure: *The Walk*
The Gun Club: *Death Party*

Albums

New Order: *Power, Corruption and Lies*
Killing Joke: *Fire Dances*
Echo and The Bunnymen: *Porcupine*
U2: *War; Under a Blood Red Sky*
Soft Cell: *The Art of Falling Apart*
Aztec Camera: *High Land, Hard Rain*
Tears for Fears: *The Hurting*
Iron Maiden: *Piece Of Mind*
The Waterboys: *The Waterboys*
Yazoo: *You and Me Both*
The Fall: *Perverted by Language*

Factory Fairy Tales

Rolling Stones: *Undercover*
Big Country: *The Crossing*
The Ramones: *Subterranean Jungle*
The Stranglers: *Feline*
Spear Of Destiny: *Grapes Of Wrath*
ZZ Top: *Eliminator*
REM: *Murmur*
Talking Heads: *Speaking In Tongues*
David Bowie: *Let's Dance*
Pete Shelley: *XLi*
Cabaret Voltaire: *The Crackdown*
Billy Idol: *Rebel Yell*
Yello: *You Gotta Say Yes to Another Excess*

25. How hard can it be to find a fucking drummer!

Life in Fallowfield was still taking some getting used to after the party time existence that I had enjoyed in Hulme. If we wanted to go anywhere we had to get the bus whereas we walked everywhere in Hulme. Fallowfield was a nice area, bordering Withington and was about a 20 minute walk through Ladybarn to Burnage. It was three miles south of town and full of students as it was a short walk from some parts of the university complex. Nearby was Platt Fields, a beautiful park with a large boating lake which has an island in the middle, a Labyrinth, picnic area, two children's play areas and an area set aside for concerts. I would love to live there now as I would walk round the park on a daily basis, but we never went there as we were more concerned about getting the next wrap of speed, next lump of dope or the next three litre bottle of cider. Nowadays it's full of wine bars, coffee shops, restaurants, and has a Bohemian vibe but it was nothing like this in 1984.

Most days we would get up late afternoon then stay in getting stoned, drinking cheap wine, cider and Cinzano, watching videos, and listening to music. Once a fortnight I would go to town and see some of the usual crew, Slim, Glenn, and Mikey, when I had to sign on at Aytoun Street.

I was still going to as many home games as possible and would get the bus to the Poly and meet Big Stuart, Slim, and the lads in the White Horse in Hulme. Sometimes I would go out with them afterwards and my partner would meet us in the Salisbury to join us for the night. We would normally end up in the University disco, Devilles or the Hac. My partner and I would stay with Slim and Glenn and then get the bus home the next day. Sometimes I would see Mani and Kaiser out and about but it was around this time that I started to lose track of most of them.

In February, The Alarm released their debut album *Declaration,* and it was one of the most powerful debuts I had heard in a long time. The songs were so well-written and so easy to sing along to as every song had a big chorus. The singles '68 Guns' and 'Where Were You Hiding When the Storm Broke' both became massive hits. I had followed this band since Futurama 4 when they were one of the first bands on.

Factory Fairy Tales

The first gig we went to in 1984 was James at The Venue in March. They were still a four piece at this stage with Paul still playing guitar. A few days later our landlord asked us to move out of the flat, so we had no option but to go and live with my partner's parents in Newall Green, Wythenshawe.

I had no money coming in since I had stopped working at the Hac when we left Hulme, so getting another flat wasn't going to happen. We should have moved back to Hulme and got our own flat in one of the crescents. My mates were there and I would have worked at the Hac again, so we would have had some money. I should have been more forceful and dug my heels in. Hulme was the answer to our problems, moving to Wythenshawe just ended up alienating us from everyone. There would be little room at my partner's parents' house so my 2 x 18 speaker cabinet had to go. The lad downstairs was learning to play bass and I gave it to him. He was out the day we left so I left it at the back of the house, under shelter out of the rain, and put a note though his door telling him where it was. I should have left it in Dad's garage. I have often wondered how much I would have got for that speaker, previously owned by Hooky with 'New Order' painted on the back. You can see a pattern developing here with me regarding sensible decisions.

Wythenshawe is about ten miles from town and is an 11 square mile council estate. At that time it was the largest council estate in Europe with over 18,000 council properties. We moved in with her parents and they were okay. Her Mum drank like a fish and was drunk every night and her Dad would have a few glasses of whisky every evening so we started to drink even more and cut down on the drugs as her parents wouldn't approve. Her Dad would rent films from the video shop, and we would watch one every night and sometimes two. We settled into a routine of us being alone most days in the house and then we would be a family in the evenings.

21 March: I met Big Stuart, Slim and the guys in the White Horse and went to Old Trafford to see United play Barcelona in the return game in the Cup Winners' Cup. United had to win by three clear goals to knock Barcelona out, and the Catalans had Diego Maradona in their team, who was the greatest footballer in the world at that time. I still think that he's the greatest of all time. In the first half, United had a corner, which was turned in by Bryan Robson and Robbo pounced on a goalkeeping mistake early in the second half before

Ged Duffy

Frank Stapleton hammered another into to make it 3-0 on the night. The referee had to ask Paul McGrath to open his pocket midway through the second half to allow Diego Maradona out so he could be substituted. When the final whistle blew United had gone through to the next round, and some of the fans invaded the pitch and carried Bryan Robson off on their shoulders. It was the best atmosphere I ever witnessed at Old Trafford only to be matched by a couple of games in 1993 against Sheffield Wednesday, when Steve Bruce headed in two goals in seven minutes added on time to basically guarantee United the Premier League title, and Blackburn Rovers when Steve Bruce and Bryan Robson lifted the Premier League Trophy.

I went home as usual every Sunday to see Mum and Dad, and one Sunday, in April, Mum told me that Rob Gretton had rang a few days earlier and had asked me to call him back. I called Rob and he explained that New Order now had enough money to take on two more full time roadies. They had a European tour, an American tour and another European tour booked till the end of the year. He wanted to employ Slim and me, but I explained that I had just moved into my partner's parents' house, and it wouldn't look good if I was disappearing away so much. I recommended that he gave the job to Andy Robinson, my old flat mate from Arnesby Walk. Andy went on to form a band called Life, who ended up doing some records for Factory. After several years, he went on to become New Order's Joint Manager, so he did all right for himself. Like I said, when I first met him you could tell he was desperate to get in with the Factory crowd and fair play to him, he succeeded. Had I accepted Rob's offer then it could well have been me becoming their manager as my relationship with the band was very good.

Looking back on this decision now; we were living with my partner's parents so this would have been an ideal scenario as I could have gone away and worked, whilst she stayed at home and had money coming in every week. I said no for love and look where love got me in the end! I could have seen the world for the next ten years and got paid for doing so. What a wasted opportunity!

What a fucking knob I was in those days. It was definitely a massive mistake on my part.

In April New Order's 'Thieves Like Us' (FAC 103) is released. I got my copy from Lesley at Factory. I think this is one of the best singles they did, I love it. The synthesiser pattern at the start is great and it reminds me of the Human League. It was a perfect pop song with a magnificent Hooky bass line.

At the beginning of May Echo and the Bunnymen released their album *Ocean Rain*. This was their best album, in my opinion, and it featured 'The Killing Moon'. Having listened to it again, all nine songs are beautifully put together and the whole album flows. The sleeve photo was outstanding as well. This is another album that I have played to death.

A couple of weeks later I was so excited as we were going to see The Cramps at the Hac. At last we had enough money to go out. When we got there the bar staff treated me like I was still working there and gave us free drinks all night, happy days. I soon realized how much I had missed Zum Zum's. The Cramps were as powerful as ever, great gig, full as well and great to see Glenn, Slim, Big Stuart and the gang again.

Sometime in July, the Lavolta Lakota 7 inch single was released on Factory Benelux with the catalogue number (FBN 34). The two songs 'A Prayer' and 'Mitawin' turned out okay, but the single cover was fucking awful - more Red Indian shite!

August turned out to be a good month as we moved into a new flat and I passed my driving test. Dad paid for lessons for me, and he was also teaching me when I went home on a Sunday. My partner's Dad worked for Manchester City Council in a managerial capacity and pulled a few strings and got us a two bedroom flat in Baguley. Between friends and family we managed to furnish the place. One of the bedrooms and the living room were above a walkway, and since nobody lived under these two rooms, we set the bedroom up as a rehearsal space. I got on okay with my partner's parents, but it was nice to be in a place of our own again. It was great to be able to smoke dope again as over the last few months I had only been able to do so wherever I was back in Hulme or out with Slim.

Sometime around this period Stockholm Monsters released their only album *Alma Mater* (FACT 80). I jumped on the bus and went to see Lesley to get my copy. I really liked it. 'Something's Got To Give' was the only song left since my days in the band and for some unknown reason they only played the first verse instead of the whole song. It was a strong album, but I think that if we had done one back in 1982 it would have been stronger.

In October U2 released their classic album *Unforgettable Fire* which was produced by Brian Eno and had been partly recorded at Slane Castle and Windmill Studios in Dublin. This was a change of direction by U2 as the songs were so melodic and featured a lot of synthesiser and guitar treatments done by Eno. 'Pride (In The Name Of Love)' and 'Bad' were stand out tracks. Later that month Lloyd Cole and the Commotions released their brilliant debut album *Rattlesnakes* and The Pogues released their debut *Red Roses for Me*. Both of these became favourites of mine.

We managed to get to the Hac a couple more times to see The Cult in September where we spent a lot of time backstage with Ian and Billy, Gun Club in October and Spear of Destiny in December. We also ended up in the Hac a couple of times after United home games for a drink. We spent the rest of 1984 and the beginning of 1985 soundproofing the bedroom and advertising for other people to join the band.

In early January we finally got a response to our advert. A singer called Steve and a guitarist called John came along to meet us at the flat. We got on like a house on fire and decided to start a band called The Shop. We agreed to advertise for a drummer, but started rehearsing and writing songs whilst waiting to find one. Over the next few weeks we wrote four songs, but we still didn't have a drummer. I reached out to Mark the Ted to try and get hold of Guy Ainsworth but he didn't know where he was. John had a basic drum machine and so we used that instead.

In March we did a demo at Frank the Hippy's, he was still a complete stoner. We recorded all four songs, they sounded great. A couple of days later I took a copy round to Tony Wilson's house, and he listened to it. He liked it and told me to get a drummer, play a gig, and he would sign us. I left a copy with Lesley to take home to Rob. He contacted me via my Mum and promised me some gigs with New Order if we could just get a drummer or a proper drum machine.

At this point John decided to leave, he would have been the perfect guitarist to replace Eddie when he left Stockholm Monsters. John and Steve came as a pair, and we were so pleased that Steve decided to stay with us. He told us that he could play guitar a bit and he brought one to the next rehearsal. He was a basic guitarist, but it fitted in with our sound, so we carried on rehearsing. We were still looking for a drummer and we would now look for a guitarist as well.

At the beginning of May we did a demo at Kev's. He was Steve's mate, and he owned a four track. We went there and recorded two songs and taped another that we had just made up whilst we were there. They sounded good and a lot different than the previous demo two months ago.

Later that month New Order 'The Perfect Kiss' (FAC 123) was released, I got my copy from Lesley. What a brilliant single! I saw the video on TV and there's Slim and Andy Robinson stood behind the glass looking at the band as they play. It should have been me standing there… and a few days later they released their new album *Low-Life* (FACT 100). It starts with one of my favourite New Order songs 'Love Vigilantes' with a great melodica, guitar and bass riffs which all work so well together. This song is classic New Order. 'This Time of Night' proves that Barney's electronic bits can work really well with a classic Hooky lead bass riff. 'Sunrise' is a classic Hooky-driven New Order song. This is a great album, and I really liked the sleeve with the photos of the four band members with the semi-transparent piece of paper with New Order printed on it so you could choose whose face was the cover. It was Hooky for me which shouldn't be a surprise to anyone reading this.

We had now written six songs but still hadn't found a drummer. We wanted to play a gig or two, so we decided to make a backing tape. I had seen several bands playing with backing tapes so why not. At the start of June we went back to Kev's to make a backing tape. He had a good drum machine, so he wrote the drum pattern for each song, and guitar, synthesiser, and noise effects were all added to the tape. The tape was made so that there would be no gaps in the live sound as the gaps between songs were filled in with noises. Then we got Kev to tape us playing along to the backing tape. It sounded good.

24 June: We played our first gig at The Venue, a small basement club on the same block as the Hac. It was difficult to play to a backing tape as it was a cassette played through the PA system and it was always slightly behind what we were playing. It was awful, especially if some engineer decided to put some echo on it as it then totally put everything out of time. We played the six songs to a small audience. I didn't invite any of the old crew, so it was mainly strangers watching us. We went down okay. My partner's Dad was there to see us. He was our biggest cheerleader, and took photos of us. He was an amateur photographer and had converted the box bedroom into a dark room. He also took us places so he could photograph us. The Venue shut down when The Hacienda Apartments were getting built when it was filled with concrete to form part of the foundations of the building.

A few weeks later, we decided to get a proper demo made so went to Twilight Studios. It was a 16 track studio based in Salford. The engineer listened to our backing tape and told us not to use it on the demo. He listened to both songs that we were going to record and wrote a new drum pattern on his drum machine. Both songs turned out well and they were both played on Piccadilly Radio by Tony 'The Greek' Michaelides on his evening show. I gave a copy of the tape to both Wilson and Gretton and got the same response again "get a drummer".

Saturday 13 July 1985 is a day where the majority of the western world sat down and watched Live Aid from Wembley Stadium and then from John F Kennedy Stadium in Philadelphia. This whole event had been put together by Bob Geldof, singer of Boomtown Rats, and Midge Ure, singer of Ultravox, to raise money for the starving people of Africa. It started at noon in London with Status Quo playing 'Rocking all over the World'. The main stars of the show were Queen and U2 who both put in amazing performances. David Bowie did an amazing version of 'Heroes'. U2 planned to do three songs but during the second song 'Bad', Bono went into the crowd and pulled a girl out who was getting crushed and danced with her on stage, so they played the song for 12 minutes and ran out of time to play the third. Paul McCartney finished it all with a brilliant version of 'Let It Be'. The UK bit finished at 10pm and then we had six hours of the USA side to watch. To be honest the whole USA section was wank but it was great to be able to stay up late and watch it.

16 July. New Order at the Hac. Great gig. Absolutely packed. They had crash barriers set up round the stage and Big Stuart was sat behind them all night stopping people climbing over. Saw Slim and the rest of the guys. The place was full, and it was bouncing, brilliant atmosphere. We stood in the audience, and it was great to see the reaction that they had to certain songs.

31 July. The Gallery. Our second gig. Went down okay. Over the next couple of months we played at The Town Hall Tavern, The Venue, and The Boardwalk. All were okay. We were still looking for a drummer, but we couldn't find one.

On 24 October 1985 my lovely Mum passed away. She had been in Manchester Royal Infirmary hospital for a routine hip replacement and caught a blood infection. She was kept in for a few days, got worse and transferred to St Ann's Hospice in Heald Green, which was a couple of miles up Kingsway from our house. She was 66 and she drifted away as I held her hand and whispered in her ear that I loved her. Margaret and Dad were there in the room, and she went very peacefully. Dad was a broken man so I arranged the funeral. We took her back to Lacken where she was laid to rest in the most beautiful surroundings. The church played 'Abide With Me' as we carried the coffin up the hill to the cemetery. The song kept drifting out to sea and back. It was so atmospheric and to this day I can't hear this hymn without crying. When they play it at the FA Cup Final I have to get up and walk out of the room.

My Dad had been estranged from his step brother Joe for many years and I forced the pair to meet, shake hands and make up at the wake for Mum. It was great to see them bury the hatchet after many years. Mum was such a lovely, gentle lady who never had a bad word to say about anyone and I miss her greatly. My partner's Mum wouldn't come over for the funeral as her whole family disliked Irish people and the only one that I think accepted me into the family was her Dad who was a decent bloke and died far too young.

When we got home we carried on rehearsing and had written another six songs, but we couldn't play them live as they weren't on the backing tape. There was no flexibility in our gigs, it was the same six songs or no songs, and after playing further gigs at The Gallery and The Boardwalk, Steve decided to leave. He was an amazing singer and the best that I ever played with. He had a great range and his lyrics were outstanding. Over the last few months he had got in with a Christian prayer group, they changed his life completely and most of the lyrics he wanted to write moving forward would be in line with their views. Maybe it was time for him to move on. These were the same people that my partner later got in with.

3 December. New Order played two shows at the Hac - a matinee and a late night. Happy Mondays supported at both, we went to both. The matinee had lots of adults at it, mates of the bands and Hac members so some of the kids were let in to the later show. I think that they came on about 11pm. They played two different sets. Saw Rob and the guys, great night.

The only exciting thing that happened to us in Wythenshawe was getting broken into - these lads had moved in upstairs and burglaries suddenly started at the same time. I was pissed and I lost it. I ran upstairs and started kicking at their door. The guy who lived opposite came out and asked me what I was doing and I told him and he told me to follow him. He kicked the door in and I followed him into the flat. There were six lads in the flat and he knocked five of them out and told the last one standing that if my stuff wasn't back in my flat there would be problems for them all. On the way out he told me that he was a self-defence instructor for Greater Manchester Police. The next day there was a knock at the door, and everything had been returned. They moved out a couple of weeks later. I would have my own run in with this guy later but that's another story.

We were getting nowhere with the band, so we decided to exchange our flat with a couple from London. He had got a job in Manchester and the idea was they came to Wythenshawe, and we went to White City in West London. It fell through so we decided to give the band one last chance. We soon got a replacement guitarist – Mike was originally from Cumbria, and had a distinctive Lake District accent. He was brilliant and had played in a band in Cumbria with Mark Knopfler before he formed Dire Straits. He was married, had a mortgage and worked so he was nothing like us. We started rehearsing and he had a lot of ideas. The new songs sounded good and the old ones sounded better. We met a couple of drummers who came round to practise with us but they were already in bands so nothing happened.

In July, I went to Aytoun Street to sign on as usual and they called me into an office for a chat. They told me that since I had signed on in April 1980 I had never applied for a job so they suggested I start looking for a job or they would suspend my money. As instructed, I went next door to the Job Centre and registered. To my horror they found me a job as a driver/warehouseman at a Plumbing and Heating Merchant in Sale. Before I could take all this in they had called the company and arranged an interview so I got on the bus and went to Sale. I tried everything possible to fuck it up but the manager, Dave Riley, offered me the job, there and then and I started the following Monday.

I went round to see Dad to tell him. He was made up for me. I wasn't. I asked him to lend me some money so I could buy a bike so I could cycle to work. He rang Irish Pat, the mechanic, and asked him if he had any second hand cars and an hour later I was the owner of a lime green Ford Fiesta Mk 1. Dad insured it for me. I was ready to

Ged Duffy

start working. My partner was amazed that we had got a car, and we went on road trips most evenings and most weekends. At least it got us out of the flat. I started work on the Monday at Labone Plumbers Merchant who were part of the BSS Group. My job was to work in the warehouse, serve on the counter and sometimes do deliveries.

In late July James released their debut album *Stutter*. Out of the four of us: Stockholm Monsters, Beach Red, Deli Polo Club and MTI it was the Model Team lads who actually made it. I was so pleased for Jim and Gavan when it came out. I felt gutted for Paul as he was the original driving force of the band and no longer part of it. I loved this album and I kept playing it for ever. I have stuck with these guys from 1980 in Cyprus Tavern.

During September, I dropped into see Lesley so that I could pick up New Order 'State Of The Nation' (FAC 153) and *Brotherhood* (FACT 150) which had both just been released. Both were great. 'State of The Nation' was a definite improvement on the last couple of single releases. This side of the single was definitely Hooky's version as it's a rockier song than the other side 'Shame of The Nation' which was Barney's take. I played the A Side a lot and didn't play the B side much at all. *Brotherhood* had some good songs on it like 'Weirdo', 'As It Is When It Was', 'Broken Promise' and 'Way of Life'. There are some great Hooky bass lines on this album.

Then a miracle happened, we found a drummer and a singer, Mike and Robert, and we had a couple of rehearsals. We sounded great as a proper band, and we soon polished off five songs. We had about another ten to introduce to the new guys. We changed the band name to Blue Moves. My mind was whirring: a couple of weeks practice and then we can play live and get Tony and Rob down to see us and get a single deal with Factory. Happy days. Then the fucking drummer leaves! Back to fucking square one again!

13 October: New Order at the Hac. Another great gig, saw Rob, Hooky and everyone. My partner and I stayed with Slim, Glenn and Mikey in Hulme - it was a great night.

In November we went into Twilight Studios to do a demo. We played both songs live with a guide vocal. Then we spent hours redoing both songs and adding percussion and extra synthesisers and guitars. The engineer had come up with a great pattern on the drum machine for both songs. Then it was time for Robert to sing. When he got in the Vocal Booth he completely froze. He couldn't do it, no matter what we said to him. He couldn't sing, couldn't even talk. We packed up and agreed that the vocal could be done when we were coming back to mix it all at the end of the month.

5 November. New Order 'Bizarre Love Triangle' (FAC 163) was released. Back to see Lesley at Factory. Great bass line from Hooky. Nice vocal line from Barney.

A few days before we were due back to Twilight Studios, Robert told us that he was leaving. He realized that he could sing in front of people but couldn't do it in a studio. It was a massive shame as he was a great singer, with a great vocal range and also wrote some intelligent lyrics. Now we had a problem. We were due back at the studio, and we didn't have a singer. If we didn't go we would still owe the money so Mike said that he would sing, and my partner would sing backing vocals. So we went back to Twilight Studios and Mike sings on both songs, he had a great voice. You could pick out the Lancashire dialect on some words. The demo turned out great and I think that it was the best that I had ever been involved with in the studio. I took it to both Wilson and Gretton. They both said it was really good, but they wanted to see us live so the same old problem again, we need a drummer.

We started 1987 still trying searching for that elusive drummer. I was working and we were rehearsing maybe once a week and it was going nowhere. A few weeks into the year Mike came one day and told us that he had found a drummer, so we arranged a rehearsal. He came round and started to play – it was going great when all of a sudden a guy ran into the room and kicked the drum-kit over. We were totally confused and couldn't understand what was happening. He had been knocking at the door and when we didn't open it, he decided to kick the front door in. All he had to do was to be patient, wait about a minute and we would have finished the song, heard him knocking and then answered the door.

It was the guy who lived upstairs, remember him, the one that trained Greater Manchester Police in unarmed combat. We calmed him down, he apologised and he left. We decided not to contact the Police as they would have started making things difficult for us as he was one of their own. The drummer packed his stuff, departed, and rang Mike later that evening to say that he wasn't interested in joining us. We carried on for a few more weeks but still couldn't find a drummer.

In March U2 released the magnificent *The Joshua Tree* album which was stunning even down to the fantastic sleeve photos taken by Anton Corbijn. The first single off it 'With or Without You' is one of the best atmospheric songs that I have ever heard, and I put it up there with 'Atmosphere' by Joy Division. It has such a simple melody which just carries you along with a superb vocal line by Bono. Every song on the album is good and the whole album just flows along. 'I Still Haven't Found What I'm Looking For', 'Where The Street Have No Name', 'Bullet The Blue Sky' and 'In God's Country' are all great songs as well.

Sometime in April we decided to call it a day with the band and spoke to Mike. He agreed that it was not meant to be. In the meantime, my contract with the heating company was coming to an end and I managed to get a job working at Manchester Airport as an aircraft cleaner. I would be working 12 hour shifts: two days 7am to 7pm and then two nights 7pm to 7am on a four on/four off shift pattern. We decided to sell all the equipment, so I took it all to the music shop in Cheadle.

My partner and I decided to spend the money by going to Ireland for a week camping. It was great as we went to Lacken, Galway, Cork, Killarney, Kerry, and Dublin. It was a great break. During this break I did a lot of thinking and as soon as we came back, I split up with my partner and she moved out of the flat; I stopped doing drugs, I cut down on the drink, I grew up and moved on with my life.

During the next few months I kept hearing that our old singer Steve had been seeing my partner a lot and telling her all about his prayer group. She started going with him to attend their meetings and it changed her life drastically. She became a member of the Jesus Squad, and now lives her life in a totally different way than I live mine.

Working at Manchester Airport was great, I was earning a good wage and living alone so I only had to make decisions for myself. I felt so much better without being stoned all the time and it was great to be able to sleep again. I started to go out again to the Hac, Poly disco and to Hulme and I was spending some time with Slim, Glenn, and

Factory Fairy Tales

Big Stuart. I was working four days on and four days off, but I was doing at least two days overtime per week so I was limited to how often I could go out. I had found a blue who worked the alternate shift pattern to mine, and we swapped shifts so we could both go to see our respective teams.

10 June 1987: New Order at The Hac, a great gig and they finished with a great version of 'Temptation'. Bumped into June again and discovered that she had moved into a flat in Sedgley Park near Prestwich and I visited her a couple of times. We would meet in the George in Prestwich, and chat to Mark E Smith out of The Fall whenever we were there as that was one of his watering holes. June and I were so right for each other. It's a shame that it never happened. She lives with a guy now and is really happy. I haven't spoken to her in a few years now. I'm pleased for her.

About a couple of months after my split, I was in the Poly disco one Friday night when I met Lesley Barber who was there on her own. We talked, spent the night together and since she was with no one we decided to start going out. She was fun to be with, never stopped talking and was full of life. She came from a family of United fans which was great, but she wasn't keen on most of the music that I liked but we overcame that.

20 July 1987. New Order release 'True Faith' (FAC 183), a great single with a great Hooky bass line and one of Barney's best vocals. The B Side '1963' was a brilliant song and one of the best songs that they ever wrote in my opinion. It came completely out of the blue as it is nothing like anything they were writing round this period. I went to see Lesley at the office to get it.

Lesley Barber and I started going out seriously and she would be round my flat in Wythenshawe whenever I wasn't working. She wasn't keen on live music, so we would go to the Hac, Poly, Legends, Deville's, Cyprus Tavern, University or the Conti. She wasn't into drugs at all, and I don't think she ever touched any in her life, and she stopped me taking any. We would see Slim and Glenn most times we went out. She introduced me to her Mum and Dad, Ann and Frank and they were really nice people.

Ged Duffy

Albums 1984-1987

New Order: *Low Life*; *Brotherhood*

U2: *Unforgettable Fire*; *The Joshua Tree*

Lloyd Cole and the Commotions: *Rattlesnakes*; *Easy Pieces*; *Mainstream*

Public Image Limited: *This Is What You Want*; *Album*; *Happy*

Blancmange: *Mange Tout*

ZZ Top: *Afterburner*

James: *Stutter*

The Alarm: *Declaration*; *Strength*; *Eye of the Hurricane*

Simple Minds: *Once upon a Time*; *Sparkle in the Rain*

David Bowie: *Tonight*; *Never Let Me Down*

Sisters Of Mercy: *First and Last and Always*; *Floodland*

The Smiths: *The Smiths*; *Meat Is Murder*; *The Queen is Dead*; *Strangeways, Here We Come*.

The Cult: *Dreamtime*; *Love*; *Electric*

The Cure: *Kiss Me, Kiss Me, Kiss Me*

Echo and The Bunnymen: *Ocean Rain*

Spear Of Destiny: *One Eyed Jacks*; *World Service*; *Outland*

REM: *Document*

The Pogues: *Red Roses for Me*; *Rum, Sodomy & The Lash*

The Waterboys: *A Pagan Place*; *This is The Sea*

Killing Joke: *Night Time*; *Brighter Than A Thousand Suns*.

New Model Army: *Vengeance*; *No Rest for the Wicked*; *The Ghost of Cain*

The Psychedelic Furs: *Mirror Moves*; *Midnight to Midnight*

The Gun Club: *The Las Vegas Story*; *Mother Juno*

Happy Mondays: *G-Men*

The Damned: *Phantasmagoria*; *Anything*

EPs.

Sisters Of Mercy: *Body and Soul*

James: *James II*; *Village Fire*

Factory Fairy Tales

New Model Army: *Better Than Them*; *The Price*
U2: *Wide Await in America*

26. Love and marriage

Things were going great with Lesley (that's her on the opposite page) we had been going out for a while and so in early 1988 I asked her to marry me. She said yes... well she didn't. I took her to an Italian restaurant and I got down on one knee and asked her to marry me to which she replied 'no'. I was shocked and started to get up and she burst out laughing and said, "Course I'll marry you, you idiot". We set the wedding for June 1989 and decided to start looking for a house as she didn't want to move into my flat. Now I had a wedding to save for so I was working more overtime at the airport, and we would go out maybe once every 10 days or so for a meal or a drink.

I spent all of the summer of 1988 (the second summer of love) working six days a week and we went a lot of days with Ann and Frank for country walks followed by a pub lunch. I used to look forward to them. We found a house in Woodhouse Park which pleased me as it was nearer to the airport than my flat and if we needed to save money then we could sell my car as I could walk it. Lesley didn't really want to live there but with me doing shifts it made more sense, so she agreed. After about four months of being fucked around by the woman who was selling the house we withdrew our offer and walked away.

One of Lesley's friends lived in North Manchester and told her about a house that was for sale in Blackley. We went to view it and both fell in love with it. The house was high up off the road and you had to climb up steps to get to the front door. It was big with two reception rooms, kitchen, three bedrooms and a bathroom and it had large front and back gardens. There was an Indian restaurant six doors down one way and an off license six doors down the other - I was sold. The bus stop was about 100 yards away and it was a straight road some three miles or so into the centre of town. I would go there most Saturday mornings to check out the new records released. It cost £27,500 and after paying our 5% deposit we were now officially mortgage holders.

In October U2 released their film *Rattle and Hum* and the album of the same name. I went to the cinema to see the film and I loved

Factory Fairy Tales

it. I like fly on the wall documentaries and this one didn't disappoint. The album was good as well but some notable songs 'Desire', 'Angel of Harlem' and 'When Love Comes to Town'. I loved the version of 'I Still Haven't Found What I'm Looking For' which was preformed with the Harlem New Voices of Freedom Gospel Choir. 'Desire' was U2's first ever number 1.

17 December 1988: New Order and Happy Mondays at G-Mex. This was my first ever time here at what used to be the old Central Railway Station with a capacity of around 12,500. It was great to be at a gig again as I'd spent so much time working. Both bands were great on the night. I saw Slim again, I hadn't seen him in months. Lesley and I stayed in the crowd, and it was great to see so many people there to see New Order. I remember they played 'Ceremony', 'Age of Consent' and 'Temptation'.

We got the keys to the house on 6 January 1989 and I moved in and started to decorate. Lesley would come and stay over but she didn't move in until our wedding day. This suited me as the house was a tip until I finished everything. The house had high ceilings and there was a massive stone fireplace in the living room. This was the feature that sold the house to me. The only downside was that the kitchen was very small but it suited us. Over the next few months Frank and I re-turfed the gardens and Dad and I put up a new fence at the rear and at the side of the house.

At the end of January New Order released *Technique* and I went to get it off Lesley at Factory. I fell in love with it and it's such a great album. The way the electronics, guitar and Hooky are merged together is brilliant. There wasn't a bad song on it and my highlights were 'All The Way', 'Love Less' and 'Run'.

11 February 1989: Big Stuart married Tracey. Slim and Glenn were there and a lot of the Hulme crowd. That was the last time I saw Stuart until 2019. Within a couple of days Tracey and him moved to the US to start a new life. Stuart had been offered a job over there that was too good to turn down. They still live over there near Boston.

A couple of weeks later in February, I went to the Hac to see The Stone Roses play in front of a large crowd and had a chat with Tony Wilson, Mani and a couple of the stage hands but besides them, I didn't know anyone else there. I was so pleased for Mani when the Roses became massive. It couldn't have happened to a nicer bloke, a proper Manc Legend. The Hac was putting on very few gigs now, from 1988 until its closure in 1997 it was a club venue known all around the world. People came from everywhere to queue up and experience the vibe. When Tony Wilson opened it he wanted it to become as famous as Studio 54 and he finally had his wish. This was the last time that I ever went to the Hac and the last time that I ever saw Tony. It was also the last time I spoke to Mani until researching this book.

This was the start of *Madchester* when everyone in the world knew the city – Stone Roses, Inspiral Carpets, Happy Mondays and James provided the music. The drug Ecstasy made it famous and the Acid House scene took over the city and spread all over the country. I was more interested in the music, I have tried several drugs in my life but I've never had an E, so I don't know what it does to you. I do know that I loved those four bands and still do - it was a great time.

Since Big Stuart had left and Slim was away a lot with New Order, I started going to the game with my future father-in-law, Frank. We had to move to the Scoreboard Paddock section as the United Road section was getting seated. Now all stadiums were going all seater. In the 70s and the 80s the atmosphere at Old Trafford had been brilliant, the Stretford End would be swaying most games and when a goal was scored people went nuts. The United Road would be offering out the away fans and K Stand would fight anyone. All seater stadiums killed the vibe. We used to meet people in the stands but now it was becoming season tickets, sitting in the same seat, with no control of who was sat round you. The singing stopped as the singers in the

Factory Fairy Tales

Stretford End were all moved round the stadium. It also priced out the working man who liked a pint, a cig and the game.

With work being so busy gig activity was minimal, but I was still buying records and in May Stone Roses debut album was released. It was an absolute classic. One of the best debut albums ever released. From 'I Wanna be Adored' to the epic 'Resurrection' it just flowed as an album with some great bass playing by Mani.

Lesley and I were married at St Alphonsus RC Church, in Old Trafford, in June 1989. It was a gloriously hot day and Lesley must have found it difficult to move around in her dress. I remember how proud dad looked that night. All of my Aunts and Uncles were over from Ireland. Big Dave had come up from London the night before and we had gone out and got hammered. When Lesley stood next to me at the altar I whispered to her that she looked beautiful to which she replied, "what the hell have you done to your hair". Slim couldn't come as he was in the US with New Order. We flew out to Paris for our honeymoon the next day. What a great city. I love it there.

12 August 1989. I finished work around 7pm and drove to Blackpool to see The Stone Roses play at The Empress Ballroom. I got in about 20 minutes before they came on. They started off with 'Elephant Stone', 'Waterfall', 'She Bangs The Drum's and finished with' I Am The Resurrection'. What a great gig. Think I was the only person in there not wearing flares, my days of wearing flares stopped in 1977.

Due to the Hillsborough Disaster the government had announced plans to start making football stadiums all seaters. The Stretford End needed to be demolished and rebuilt to accommodate seats and Martin Edwards (the owner) didn't have the funds to do so. He agreed to sell the club to Michael Knighton for £10 million pounds therefore putting into motion the strangest sequence of events I have seen on

Ged Duffy

a football pitch. The opening game of the season was a home match against Arsenal. Prior to kick off Knighton ran onto the pitch wearing a United tracksuit top, shorts and socks. He did keepie-uppies before smashing it into the net at the Stretford End. After doing this he waved to the Stretford End before leaving the pitch to massive applause – no one knew what was going on; was this our latest signing? He looked a bit old. Arsenal were league champions but as if to add to the bizarre nature of the day United hammered them 4-1 with new signing Neil Webb playing like Michel Platini. Unfortunately over the next few weeks it transpired that Mr Knighton didn't have sufficient funds to buy the club and the sale fell through and with it went United's form…

We started this new season as proud owners of two season tickets in F Stand in line with the penalty line. We were sat next to an Indian girl called Sal and her boyfriend from Birmingham. Within a year the boyfriend had gone but I would sit next to Sal for the next 14 years and she became a great friend.

On 23 September 1989 Frank and I went to Maine Road for the derby. We got tickets from a friend that worked at the City Ticket Office for the North Stand. We were sat on Row 11 and prior to kick off the whole block of 10 rows in front of us stood up, turned round to face the crowd and started chanting "United" before jumping forward into the blues (and us). I grabbed Frank and pulled him to one side as the stand erupted into a full scale brawl. The game kicked off and had to be abandoned after five minutes as the fighting spread onto the pitch. After a few minutes, the Police came into the stand and restored order. Once it was calm again they marched the whole block of United fans out onto the pitch and across to the Platt Lane Stand. I told Frank that we should go with them, but he didn't want to, so we ended up sitting in the empty block by ourselves. Within minutes of the restart City were two goals up and playing us off the pitch. City won 5-1 and we had to clap all five goals! Mark Hughes scored an amazing flying volley right in front of us and we couldn't celebrate it.

Sometime in 1989 the Underground Market closed. They concreted over the entrances and bricked up the entrance where Discount Records used to be on Norfolk Street. A couple of years ago I saw a post on Facebook where a builder had to repair a wall on Norfolk Street. When he removed a few bricks he put his phone through the hole and took photos. The steps down to the stalls are still there. The stalls are still there, and I could see Discount Records with

Factory Fairy Tales

its shutter pulled down on the right hand aisle. Everything is frozen in time down there. Why don't the council reopen it? It was a magical place.

In April, Lesley and I took Dad over to Ireland for a week. He let me do all of the driving in his car. He had decided to stop as his reactions were slowing down. When we got to his house he gave me his two door red Escort Mark II, a beautiful car. It was 12 years old and had only done 27,000 miles. So I was now the proud owner of a lovely car and we set off to get the ferry from Holyhead to Dun Laoghaire. We had a great week staying in CastleLacken. Dad showed Lesley the house where he was born, where he grew up, where he went to school, and his mother and father's graves. It was great as he had never told me any of this and I was learning it all now. We went to see all my uncles and other people in the village. It was like he was saying goodbye to everyone.

27 May 1990: Big Dave and his two mates, Charlie and John, came up from London and stayed with us for the weekend. Lesley dropped us off at Spike Island so we could go and see The Stone Roses. Spike Island is an artificial Island situated between the Sankey Canal and the estuary of the River Mersey in Widnes. It was completely surrounded by chemical works and the Shell Oil Refinery, so the air stank of chemicals, which were being pushed out of all of the massive chimneys situated nearby.

The whole area was fenced in, and when we got to the gate our crate of lager was confiscated by the fucking Bin Dippers doing security. I reckon house parties in the Mersey Swamp were well stocked with beer for weeks after the gig. Years later I told Mani and he told me that they were not supposed to take anything off anyone at the gate. Robbing scouse bastards, well it's in their blood, I suppose.

The whole gig was awful, apart from The Stone Roses. There were a couple of beer tents, and it took about an hour to get served, so every time we went to it we got two pints each, to last us a while. The toilets were awful. The PA was terrible so you couldn't hear any of the DJ's that played and even Jah Wobble just drifted away across the banks of The Mersey.

The Stone Roses were fucking amazing, despite the lousy sound. They came on at around 9pm with Mani playing the familiar bass line to 'I Wanna Be Adored' and Ian Brown holding a giant inflatable globe. They played 'Elephant Stone', 'She Bangs The Drums', 'Shoot

You Down', 'One Love', 'Sally Cinnamon', 'Sugar Spun Sister', 'Standing Here', 'Fools Gold', 'Where Angels Play', 'Waterfall', 'Don't Stop', 'Something's Burning', 'Made of Stone', 'Elizabeth, My Dear' and finished with 'I Am The Resurrection'. The 30,000 crowd lapped them up and sang along to every song. When they went off, the DJ played Bob Marley's 'Redemption Song' whist a massive firework display exploded in the Cheshire night sky. It was amazing and what a great gig by The Stone Roses. We walked about a mile and Lesley was waiting for us to take us home. The lads went back to London the next day.

The following day New Order 'World in Motion' (FAC 293) was released. I went and got it from Lesley at Factory. This would be my last ever visit to the office on Palatine Road, but I didn't know this at the time. This song was recorded with some of the England Football team as their song for the upcoming World Cup. It was a great tune, and the highlight was the rap section done by England winger John Barnes. It was class. This was my favourite football single until 1996 when The Lightning Seeds released 'Football's Coming Home' with David Baddiel and Frank Skinner. As an aside in 2018 or early 2019 pre-Covid, Peter Hook and The Light played in Boston, USA and Big Stuart went along to see Hooky. When Hooky played 'World in Motion' he got Big Stuart to come on stage and sing the John Barnes bit. When he finished the song Hooky told the crowd "Now you know why Stuart isn't a singer".

A few days later James released their album *Gold Mother*. This was

Big Dave and me having a beer or three

an absolute classic album with 'Come Home', 'Lose Control', and later presses had 'Sit Down' on it. 'Sit Down' had been out a few months as a single but it was reissued and reached number 2 in the charts. It is a brilliant single, I love this whole album.

In July I went to see The Rolling Stones at Maine Road and they were absolutely brilliant. They started off with the classic Keith Richard riff driven monster of a song 'Start Me Up' and they played another 24 classics - it was a memorable gig. This was followed the next day by Inspiral Carpets and The La's at G-Mex - another great gig. The Inspirals were how the Monsters should have sounded, that fairground keyboard with powerful bass, guitar, and drums. They started with 'Real Thing', 'Directing Traffic' and then played 'This is How it Feels', 'Sackville', 'She Comes in The Fall', 'Commercial Rain', and 'Joe'. The place was full and there was a great atmosphere at the gig.

27: Twat*

At the end of July that year Dad took ill and was rushed to Manchester Infirmary Hospital where he was kept in for a few days. He was having trouble breathing and they had him attached to an oxygen machine. He was discharged a few days later after I had made some changes to his house. His bed was now downstairs, and the hospital provided him with a commode and a portable oxygen machine. They arranged for a home help and meals on wheels to visit every day. He was not allowed to go upstairs, and he would have to wear the oxygen machine every night in bed. Margaret and I took turns staying with him each night and then one night he told me to go home as he wanted some peace and quiet. I didn't want to, but he insisted and got angry with me, so I got up to leave and he hugged me and told me that he loved me, and this was very strange behaviour for Dad as he didn't like to show his emotions. That night, 5 August 1990, Dad passed away on his own with no fuss or bother. He was a shy, unassuming and quiet man and that's how he wanted to go. I think he knew what was coming and he didn't want me to see it. He died from asbestosis due to 40 years of exposure to it. His lungs were shot, and he never smoked a cigarette in his life.

A few days before he passed he asked me to get a lawyer round to the house so he could make his will. He left the house to Margaret which was worth £60,000 and he had some money in an off shore bank account with the Bank of Ireland set up at the Ballina branch which was worth just over £60,000 and this was for me. This account was a joint one with my Uncle Mick. He had about £17,000 in cash under the floor boards which was to be used for the funeral and then split between Margaret and me. This cash was not in the will. I phoned Mick to tell him about Dad's passing and since he was over in Ireland he said that he would tell the rest of the family.

There would be a few people travelling by boat or plane to the funeral and these would all need accommodation. I was to pay for all the funeral costs, travel arrangements, accommodation, and meals out of the underfloor money. We had a lovely mass for Dad at St Bernard's RC Church in Burnage and as Dad was driven away to Manchester

---
* *John Cooper Clark summed my uncle up in one word*

Factory Fairy Tales

Airport we left the church and a crowd of us went in Slim's old pub the Victoria and had a couple of drinks. We then drove to Holyhead in a convoy of four or five cars to catch the 3.15am ferry. The following morning we landed at Dun Laoghaire Port and drove to the north side of Dublin to the airport to meet the coffin. All of my uncles were waiting for us there with the hearse. Dad was loaded into the hearse and correct protocol would be for close family to follow the hearse so Lesley, Ann, Frank and I were in dad's old car so we should be the first with Margaret and her husband Tommy in the car behind but no… Mick jumped in first and we set off. As soon as we cleared Dublin we were doing 70 miles an hour and I found this totally disrespectful, so I overtook Mick and the hearse and pulled in at the front and stopped. I got out and went apeshit with the driver of the hearse and he told me that Mick had told him that we had to be down in Lacken at a certain time as he had something to do. I told the driver that I was paying his fucking bill and he would drive at 40 miles per hour and show some respect to my Dad. I then knocked on Mick's car and told him what was happening and to get behind Margaret's car and show some respect. If I could have guessed what happened next I'd have punched the twat's face in.

When we got to CastleLacken Dad was carried into the church and we all went to Mick's house where his wife Margaret had put on a spread for everyone, and all of the village were there. It was great remembering all the things that Dad had done. The following day it was the funeral and we buried him with Mum. It was another beautiful ceremony, and they are both laid to rest in a beautiful corner of the world. He was 75 years old. He was such a great man, strict but fair and always ready to help anyone. I miss him a lot. I miss his flat cap.

That night we went to the local pub and had dad's wake. Mick and his wife Margaret hated drinking with a passion so not much was consumed the previous day, but we made up for it that night. Over there, as soon as someone finishes their drink they go and order another round and if you aren't paying attention you can end up with several drinks lined up in front of you. The Guiness was lined up on the bar with each one at a different level, as it is a long-winded process to get a pint of the black stuff ready.

The following day Lesley and I went to see the bank manager to discuss Dad's account. He claimed that he had no record of any account even though I had a bank statement giving all the details.

Ged Duffy

There was nothing we could do. We drove back to Lacken and I went to see Uncle Mick who told me straight to my face that he didn't have a clue what I was talking about as he didn't have any accounts with Dad even though I showed him the statement in joint names. He told me that Dad mustn't have been of sound mind when he had told me about the account or that I misunderstood what Dad had said. Dad knew exactly how much was in the account and the only mistake he made was to trust that snake and it cost me £60,000 in the end. I knew that the twat was lying but there was nothing I could do about it as Irish law was in the dark ages in those days. Years later the bank manager was arrested for embezzling funds and sentenced to 10 years, when I found out this news I contacted the Head Office of the Bank of Ireland in Dublin, and they could do nothing to help me as they said the money had been taken either by the bank manager or the other joint account holder, ie. Mick. I could never prove it, but I know who took it, or at least split it, with the bank manager.

A couple of days later I was so down knowing that a member of my family had shafted me that Lesley suggested I took Ann, Frank and her to Castlebar which is a big market town. Lesley and Ann went off shopping whilst Frank and I went for a pint. We went in a bar and about five minutes later a guy walked in with a piano accordion and started playing. Within about 20 minutes there were a large group assembled playing Irish songs. It was great and when Lesley and Ann turned up they stayed to listen. We were there well over three hours, and the craic was epic. We stopped at Pontoon Lake for a meal on the way back. It was a great day.

Before we left Mick invited us to his house where he presented me with a bill for the spread that Margaret had put on. The man was a millionaire, claimed to be Dad's best mate and he demanded money for something that I had not even asked for. His house would have been the last place to take people to as they couldn't drink and the Irish drink at Wakes. I couldn't handle the bare face cheek of the twat! When we got back to Manchester there was a letter from the solicitor regarding the will. After contacting Social Security for Dad's last week of pension due, they asked for proof of the value of the estate. On discovering that there was an undisclosed bank account they demanded over £9,000 in money paid to Mum when she was alive which she was not entitled to so I had to pay that. I had paid everything for my Dad which he would have been proud of, and I walked away with nothing. Margaret had her own house in Levenshulme, and she and

Factory Fairy Tales

her eight kids, Kevin, Emma, Marie, Lisa, Louise, Mary, Thomas and John all moved into the house on Mauldeth Road. I asked her to sell her old house and give me £4,500 to cover half of the cost of the Social Security Bill. I thought that this was fair, she didn't, and we didn't have much contact for the following eight years or so except for family functions where I was pleasant to her. If the roles had been reversed I would have sold the house in Burnage and split the money 50/50 with her so that we could both have had a new start in life but she didn't and I got nothing from the estate whereas she got a house worth £60,000 and the money from the sale of her old house a few years later. Dad left me all of his tools which were in the garage and a couple of months later Mick returned to Didsbury and told Margaret that Dad had told him he could have them, so he cleared the garage out - another kick in the teeth. In the word made famous by John Cooper Clarke my Uncle Mick really was a TWAT.

28: Daddy Duffy goes to Rotterdam and this time it's 2-1

On 18 August 1990: I went to London and stayed at Big Dave's flat and we went out on the Friday night and got drunk. The following day we went to Wembley for the Charity Shield against champions Liverpool. Who could have known that Bin Dippers would not be league champions again for another 30 years and that United would win 13 before they would win their next one. I left most of my money in Dave's flat as I knew that there would be a few pickpockets about with the Dippers being in Town. Crap game. Finished 1-1. Went back to Big Dave's to find that his flat had been broken into and my money had gone - so much for my forward planning eh? Thoughtfully they had taken my train ticket out of my wallet and left it on the bed for me so at least I could get home the next day. There was some serious fighting inside and outside of the Wembley Park Tube Station between Reds and Scousers. This happened before the game. I didn't see anything after the game. What happened before was wild.

December 1990: James played two nights at G-Mex. Went to both nights. They were brilliant as ever. Both gigs full. The version of 'Sit Down' was amazing on both nights and one of them has been released as a 12 inch single. This was the first time that I had seen James where the crowd joined in the singing, now it's common practice at a James gig. They had made it massive, I was so pleased for Jim.

In January I started looking for a new job. I loved working at Manchester Airport, but Lesley didn't like being alone in the house whilst I was working nights. I was looking at the Jobs Vacant section in the *Manchester Evening News* one day and saw a job for a warehouse person at Labone, so I rang Dave Riley the next day, went to see him and got offered the job. They had moved from Sale to Weaste in Salford. This job was working Monday to Friday and paid a lot less than what I was earning at the Airport. I did a lot of overtime at the Airport and there was no possibility of doing that this new job so we would be financially worse off. I tried to get her to change her mind, but she wanted me home with her. We had to tighten our belts a lot after this decision.

My world changed for ever on 25th April 1991 as I became a

Factory Fairy Tales

father. Our first son, Jack Francis Duffy was named after Lesley's Dad and my Dad. Overnight I had responsibilities and had to grow up. I was at work when I got the phone call from Lesley to tell me that she was starting to get labour pains, so I drove home like a lunatic and took her to North Manchester General. I was so excited. Lesley was being checked by the midwives and they said that she would be hours before she was ready. After about 40 to 50 minutes I found a midwife who basically called me an idiot, told me not to panic, and Lesley was not due for a few hours yet. I persisted that much that she came in, examined her and immediately rushed her into delivery room number seven (Bryan Robson's number) and Lesley went into labour and delivered Jack within minutes - it was so quick that she had no time to take any pain relief. It was an amazing experience to see Jack being born and to cut his umbilical cord. I respect women so much as if it were left to men, the human race would never have got going. I sat there for hours with this bundle of life in my arms as he stared into my eyes. I was so proud. We soon got into the routine of feeding and changing nappies. I was so pleased to do my share and I loved it. This was the most important thing in my life now but I was gutted that Dad hadn't been around to see him.

When we took Jack home we had to learn how to look after him. He would sleep in his cot in our bedroom for the first few weeks while I converted the box room into his nursery. I painted the walls yellow, hung some posters up, got a bookcase and filled it with story books to read to him. I got a large mobile to hang from the ceiling which when lit would display lots of different animals all over the ceiling and walls. Lesley decided not to breast feed and we took it in turns to make up his bottles to feed him.

United made it to the Cup Winner's Cup Final that year so Graham Knapp, a colleague at work, and I went to Rotterdam. We got the coach at 10pm from Old Trafford, and there were around 300 coaches in the car park opposite the ground. The coaches left in groups of five or six and drove in a convoy to Dover. At Dover Docks, the car parks were empty except for United coaches and there were no wagons around as they were held back in a holding pen until all of the coaches had departed.

United fans were playing a game of football in one of the car parks with about 1,000 shirts playing against 1,000 skins. Once 20 coaches had been loaded, the ferry would pull out and the next one would pull in to get the next 20 coaches. After a couple of hours our coach boarded and we were en route. Since this was the first year that English clubs had been allowed back into European football following the Heysel Stadium disaster, there was a blanket alcohol ban. We sat in one of the lounges and watched TV. The coaches all went to a location outside Rotterdam and parked up. There was a compound set up for fans with food trucks, toilet facilities and a stage which featured Mancunian and local Dutch bands playing. There was a heavy police presence as German and Polish skinheads had threatened to come to Rotterdam to fight the United fans.

The police were all wearing United hats and scarves and at one stage, there was about 5,000 United fans doing the Conga round the park with police officers joining in. The atmosphere was like a carnival. When we got back on our coach we were issued with our match tickets and given a police motorbike escort direct to the stadium. All the roads were closed to allow us fast access to the ground. Every motorbike had a United flag tied to its aerial. We found out later that the Barcelona fans had been treated the same way. It had rained all day and it was very heavy by the time we got to the stadium. We were in the bottom tier of the Zuid-Zijde Stand behind one of the goals. The seats were wooden benches with no seat numbers, so we sat near the back because we were out of the rain. Looking around we could see the Barcelona fans at the other end of the ground and the two sides round the pitch were completely full of United. It was like a home game as we sang for 90 minutes. It was a good game with Mark Hughes scoring two, including a thunderbolt from an impossible angle before Ronald Koeman pulled one back with a great free kick. The last ten minutes were tense, but we all celebrated when Bryan Robson lifted the trophy high in the Rotterdam night. The journey back, went without any issues and we arrived back the following afternoon. The whole thing had been organized brilliantly by the Dutch, and there was no trouble

Now I was earning a lot less, we realised that it would be very difficult to afford holidays with a young child, so we bought a caravan. I went to Glossop Caravans and looked at all the new models and they cost a fortune. I asked about second hand ones and they still cost a lot of money. They took me to the Clearance Area at the back of the yard and I bought a four berth one for £60. It was due to be taken apart for spare parts and they told me that I wouldn't be able to tow it a lot as it was on its last legs and just about road worthy I towed it to a camp site in Caerwys in North Wales and left it there.

Factory Fairy Tales

For the next few years, between Easter and the end of October, we would drive down most weekends (when United were playing away) and spend two weeks there in the summer. The site had a shower block, launderette, and a shop. It was great for kids. I have so many memories of the caravan, Jack learnt to ride a bike there, Jack and Tom out playing in the field for hours playing football, running and playing on the swings and the slide. They loved it there.

Inspiral Carpets played at G-Mex later that year, another great gig by a great band. Lesley actually came to this one with me since she loved 'This Is How It Feels'. Funny thing is, and this shocked me, she told me afterwards that Stockholm Monsters should have sounded like the Inspiral Carpets. She was right. They were supported by The High and The Railway Children if my memory serves me right. The place looked about half full as I don't think people liked the second album *The Beast Inside* as much as their classic debut *Life*.

In September, the music world changed overnight with the release of *Never Mind* by Nirvana. This was proper loud distorted guitar music and the world accepted it and made them famous virtually overnight. It was the end of the laid back baggy E scene and grunge was here and I loved it. I got into other bands like Alice in Chains, Pearl Jam, and Soundgarden.

Lesley was a Local Intelligence Officer for Greater Manchester Police, and she was stationed at Longsight Police Station. She worked from 7am to 3pm one week and then 3pm to 11pm the following so we would have to arrange child care for Jack when she returned to work that October. We found a lovely Irish woman called Dympna in Blackley and she took Jack every morning, and we would take turns picking him up.

In November 1991 Factory Records release the boxset *Palatine* (FACT 400). This compilation consisted of 49 tracks spread over four albums. Stockholm Monsters had 'Happy Ever After' released on the *Tears In Their Eyes* album. I went to see Lesley at the Factory office to get a copy and there was no answer when I rang the bell. One of the neighbours told me that Factory had moved out the previous year. I went to town and got a CD copy in HMV. Years later I found a cassette version at a car boot sale and I swapped both for a vinyl copy off Dave at Music For The Soul Records in Urmston in 2018. In the booklet which came with *Palatine*, Tony Wilson wrote the following: "Walking into Warner Brothers, Burbank, in the mid 80s Kevin Laffy of A&R asked me, "What happened to the Stockholm Monsters, they were great". I hugged the man: knowledge shared by few. The fairground melodies, the exhilaration: scallies before Liverpool even. I loved them and couldn't sell them".

Lovely words from Mr Wilson but if he had promoted us properly then I think the first two singles 'Fairy Tales' and 'Happy Ever After' would have had a chance of being big pop singles. He also wasted similar opportunities with OMD and James who both could have had big careers on Factory instead of making money elsewhere. When they decided to start promoting bands both Happy Mondays and Northside made it big. We just came along at the wrong time.

We had a great Christmas round at Ann and Frank's. Jack was spoiled rotten. It was great to have a family and I didn't miss the wild world of Hulme anymore, although that too had disappeared as the crescents were demolished along with the Spinners, White Horse and Russell Club – a great part of my life had been erased and I lost track of Glenn and Slim when this happened.

When I went back to work after the Christmas break I was asked to come and work in the office and given their two biggest customers to look after - this new level of responsibility came with a nice pay rise. Things were looking up. In June I went to see Guns N Roses at Maine Road. They were supported by Faith No More and Soundgarden all were great on the day.

29. Champions at last

The Premier League started in August 1992 with a big fanfare and United started the new season with a hangover after throwing away the league the previous season, losing at Anfield of all places. After losing away at Sheffield United (2-1) and Everton (3-0) at home, we managed a 1-1 draw at home to Ipswich to get our first point of the season and then our summer signing Dion Dublin scored the last minute winner in a 1-0 win at Southampton. Dion then went and broke his leg in the next game and missed the rest of the season.

So without his new striker, Fergie was under pressure to buy David Hirst from Sheffield Wednesday and I was hoping it wasn't true as he was just a poor man's Mark Hughes. We needed someone different, someone exciting, someone with charisma and a few months later we found the perfect guy as on 26 November 1992 Eric Cantona signed – it proved to the final piece in the jigsaw. Eric walked in like he owned the place and he hit form straight away, United were eighth in the league when he joined but by New Year's Day we were third and rising. No one in the world, and I include Fergie in this, could have foreseen the impact he had both on and off the pitch and he only cost £1 million. The deal came completely out of the blue and was announced around 10 pm at night. *News at Ten* on ITV broke the news with a simple sentence at the end of the show. No wall to wall Sky Sports News in those days!

The same month as Eric Cantona signed to become a Manchester icon Factory Records went bust. I was in shock when this happened. How could a record label have been run so badly? They could have made a lot of money if they had just promoted like every other label. Opening the Hac was a good idea but then not designing it to be live band friendly and having a booking guy who went for trendy instead of solid bands were not great business decisions but the club should have made loads of money from the Acid House craze but then drug gangs got involved and it was forced to shut. Happy Mondays were massive but then drugs got to them too and their last album had been a disaster. All of this is covered by Hooky in his book on the club, it really is incredible.

In May 1993 New Order released *Republic* on London Records, the name of the label itself was all wrong! I wasn't really keen on it but 'Regret' was a great single. To be honest, I think that apart from releasing 'Regret' as a single New Order should have called it a day as I can't think of anything that they released after leaving Factory that was on a par with their early stuff.

Also that month United finally won the league for the first time in 26 years. Two games that stood out were Sheffield Wednesday and Blackburn Rovers at home. The referee had got injured during the Sheffield Wednesday game and had to be replaced. United were losing 1-0 as the game went into injury time and in that seven minutes Steve Bruce scored two goals to win us the game 2-1. The roar was that loud, I thought that the roof would come off Old Trafford while rival fans muttered darkly about 'Fergie Time'.

The day before the Blackburn Rovers game we were at the caravan in Wales. The only team that could stop United winning the league was Aston Villa and they were playing Oldham Athletic. If Villa lost, United would be champions. Every United fan at the site was listening to the game on the radio, whilst the Scouse families were playing outside. Villa lost 1-0 and all the Mancunians ran out screaming with joy whilst the scousers retreated back into their vans. The woman who owned the camp site set up a BBQ with beers and we all got smashed out of our heads while the Mickey's stayed out of the way. It was fucking brilliant. That Sunday and into the next day was a carnival atmosphere at Old Trafford, some people never went to bed – the whole stadium was singing non-stop and to cap it all we got a free kick at the end of the match. Gary Pallister had been the only outfield player who hadn't scored a goal that season, and he scored. It brought the whole house down. United won 3-1 and there were tears of joy when Bryan Robson and Steve Bruce lifted the trophy together.

A couple of weeks later Lesley, Jack and I went to Ireland. Jack was about two. We stayed with my Uncle Paul and during this trip Uncle Paddy made me milk a cow so that Lesley could see me do it. She was pissing herself as I had forgotten to tie the tail and you can guess what happened. Even though I was covered in shit I milked her. During this trip we left Jack with Aunty Cathleen who was dying to get her hands on him, and went to a pub in Killala. Whilst we were there this farmer walked in and he had a big round red face and looked like a typical Irishman. Paul called him over to me and I found out that he was my cousin Noel, Uncle Joe's son. Joe was my Dad's half-brother. Two days later we went round to meet Joe and his family at their farm, and it was nice to finally meet them.

Brit Pop started in 1994 with Oasis, Blur and Pulp - three great bands, three different bands, three different sounds. Oasis issued their debut *Definitely Maybe* and it was a classic. Guitar songs in 4/4 time with no frills, big choruses and music to stomp your feet to. Their second album (*What's The Story) Morning Glory* had the beautiful song 'Wonderwall' on it. Blur wrote more quirky songs with a touch of The Kinks to them. They also put keyboards on some of the songs, but they were a great band as well. Pulp wrote some of the best songs that I have heard in years on two albums: *His n Hers* and *Different Class*. I love these albums. I loved all three bands but if I had to pick one then it would be Oasis as they came from Burnage.

After seeing United win the league and cup double in 1994 we had a great summer at the caravan, and I noticed that a few of the scouse families hadn't come back to the site. We had a great time driving round North Wales and went to Anglesey and Carnarvon Castle as well. We went over to Dublin on a day trip as well which was amazing, and I had a pint of Guinness in Temple Bar. After returning from the caravan, my car was stolen. We couldn't afford a second, so I had to buy a bike and cycle the 12 mile round trip each day to Weaste and back. This broke my heart as the car was the only thing of my Dad's that I had so it's theft was like erasing his memory.

30. Double trouble at home

Money was tight so I got a really well-paid job making tea bags at Brooke Bond in Trafford Park. I would work a week at 6am to 2pm and then a week from 2pm till 10pm. The only downside was that I would have 22 mile daily round trip cycle. During the summer we spent time in the caravan and then Lesley asked me to take Jack away for a few days as she needed some rest due to being six months pregnant. I decided to take Jack to Ireland, so we went over on the coach from Chorlton Street Bus Station to Holyhead where we boarded the boat. The next morning the coach took us to the main bus station in the centre of Dublin where we boarded the coach to Ballina. It was exciting doing this with just Jack and me and he kept me occupied with his questions and cheerful smiling face. Uncle Paul picked us up in Ballina and we stayed with him and Cathleen. They had a mad Jack Russell dog called Russell, which if you put your hand over him and started turning it in a circular motion, he would start to chase his tail for ever. He was so funny to watch. We would walk down to the Strand every day and play there. It was so quiet and peaceful unless a cow started mooing. I was civil towards Uncle Mick and on the last night Paul asked me what was wrong between us. I explained about Dad's money and that's when he told me about taking Mick to the bank a few minutes after I rang to say that Dad had passed away. He told me that Dad had told him about the joint account with Mick and he believed that Mick and the bank manager shared my £60,000. There was nothing I could do. When we came back Lesley was well rested, and we waited for the new arrival to arrive.

Our second son, Thomas Patrick Duffy, was born 20 September 1995. He was named after two of my favourite uncles. Lesley wanted to call him Felix. I wanted to call him Cantona. We agreed on Felix Cantona Duffy and then both got cold feet. I think we both made the right decision in the end. It was amazing to see the way Jack bonded with him immediately and these two have been inseparable ever since. It's a joy to watch them together and it fills my heart with pride how they have turned out. It was entirely different with Tom who was five days late and we had a prearranged appointment to come in to North Manchester General to induce Lesley. We ended up in room seven again, our lucky room. They gave Lesley some drugs to start the

Factory Fairy Tales

process up and I told them that when it happens, it would be quick. The nurses looked at me as if I were talking in a strange language and told me to settle in, it would be hours. About 40 minutes later I went to find a nurse and I had to practically scream at her to examine Lesley. When she examined Lesley her face changed, and Thomas was born about 10 minutes later. At least she apologized afterwards for not believing me. I saw Thomas being born and it was another moving moment and once again I got to cut the umbilical cord. For the first few hours of his life he just lay in my arms looking up at me. Now I had double trouble in my life. Things would never be the same again but in a good way.

I had a full week off at Christmas as the factory shut down completely. I hated the job as it was so boring but some of the folks on my shift were sound. I operated one production line making square-shaped Brooke Bond PG Tips tea bags. The one plus side of the job was that cycling 22 miles per day had made me fit. I used to love cycling home at 10pm as I would come down Deansgate past the Fantasy Bar. This was the first lap dancing club in England at 140 Deansgate which used to be the Magnet Café. Sometimes there would be a girl or two in tiny coats outside smoking as I cycled past. I was sat at the traffic lights one night and I was looking at one of the girls and she asked me if I had seen enough to which I replied, "no your coat is hiding everything". She burst out laughing and opened her coat and showed me what she got, I nearly fell off my bike!

George Best was 50 on 22 May that year and to celebrate his life BBC2 had a whole evening dedicated to him on 19 May. I taped the whole evening on a six-hour long video tape and a couple of weeks later Lesley and I settled in to watch it all with a few glasses of wine. During one of the shows, I paused the tape to go and get a drink. When I came back into the room Lesley was on the floor with her face pressed up against the TV screen. I asked her what she was doing, and she said that I was on the telly. I looked at the still paused image and it was the photograph of my school trip in 1968 to Old Trafford and I was there in black and white. The following Monday I phoned the BBC and a few days later I got a phone call from the producer and I explained about the photo. He took my address and a few weeks later a laminated copy of the photo was sent to me from the nun that had arranged the trip. She was now living in Dublin. How lucky was that, I happened to pause the tape at that exact spot!

One day I was cutting our front lawn when I felt the grass move and heard an enormous bang followed by a long loud hum. Rochdale Road was one of the main routes into Manchester and the house was exactly three miles from town and there was a massive cloud of smoke over the City. I ran inside, turned the TV on and discovered that the IRA had set a massive bomb off in the city. Thankfully, no one was killed. It was an awful thing to happen but the one good thing to come out of it was that part of the Arndale Centre had to be rebuilt and Europe's biggest toilet was no more!

At the end of August Uncle Paul passed away so I went over on my own for the funeral. Paul was 72 years old and was a beautiful man with not a mean bone in his body. I carried his coffin and was honoured to do so. The wake was an event as everybody knew Paul. He was the local taxi driver, plumber, joiner, roofer, builder, car mechanic, and engineer. The whole village mourned his loss. Paul had built Mick's house and as a payment Mick gave him a piece of land next door where Paul built his house. Mick hadn't signed the land over to Paul and once he had passed, Mick started a campaign trying to force his widow Cathleen out. He never succeeded thankfully. I never spoke to Mick or his bitch wife once during this trip. When I think back, Mick's wife Margaret was the only person that Mum never liked. She had been a schoolmistress and always looked down on people as if they were beneath her. Somehow she had got in with the priest and was part of his circle, so the local farmers respected her. I fucking hated her with a passion even before she and her husband robbed me.

In October 1997 we went back to the caravan to lock it up for the winter. A couple of days later the camp site called to tell me that when their tractor started to tow our van into the yard for the winter the top part of it followed the tractor, but the axle and wheels stayed behind. They got £30 scrap for me. That van had provided us with holidays and weekends away for five years. Well worth £60!

That New Years Eve Lesley and I went to the Embassy Club to see Bernard Manning. I had phoned to get tickets and the answer machine told me to contact a mobile number which I did, and Bernard answered it which shocked me. He said, "come to the Embassy, son, you'll love it, I can guarantee you a great night". He then started telling a joke and he got to the punchline, stopped and said, "if you want to hear the punchline you'll have to come to the club". He was a right character. We went along and as we were queuing outside we noticed that some people were getting taken from the queue and were going in. These people were picked to sit at the front, so Bernard had people to take the piss out of. If you were an old guy, he would ask you if it was cold in the ground this morning and don't forget to pass on his regards to Roy Orbison when you return to the ground tonight. He came on and did a turn for about 20 minutes, then he introduced a group who were awful, a juggler, and a mime artist. Bernard came on and did an hour and at 11 o'clock he left to see in the New Year with his mum. I saw him five or six times over the years, and he wasn't racist as people claimed. He used to say in interviews that on stage he hated everyone: old, fat, skinny, ginger, black, white, Chinese, he didn't care. If he could get a laugh by insulting you he would, and you knew what might happen before you went to see him. If he insulted you then a round of drinks would appear at your table as a thank you from him. He did at least two or three shows a week free of charge for charity and he dedicated a lot of his life to raising money for charity.

Sometime in 1997 the Hacienda finally shut its doors for the final time. What a massive opportunity lost. I hadn't been there in years, and it was an Acid House club for the last few years of its life. Another great Manchester landmark lost to private landlords.

31: Devastating news

In February I started a new job as a salesman for Potterton Boilers. Lesley pushed me into accepting it as I thought I was too quiet to be a sales rep and to be honest I thought that 80% of the reps that I knew were complete tossers. The only really interesting one was a real eccentric called Clifford Morris who was chauffeured around in a car. He used to wear a three piece suit with a dicky bow and a bowler hat, he was Stephen Morris's dad. Lesley told me to be myself and I did. I now had a company car, a Citroen Xantia, so no more cycling. My days of becoming a fat bastard were about to begin.

16 July 1998: New Order at the Apollo. Absolutely brilliant gig. They started off with 'Regret' and played 'Isolation', 'Ceremony', 'Atmosphere', 'Heart And Soul', 'True Faith', 'Temptation' and finished with 'Blue Monday'. They came on for an encore and played 'Run', 'Love Will Tear Us Apart' and 'In a Lonely Place'. Finally, I was at a gig again and Lesley came with me, and we went backstage and met the guys. This was the last time that I ever saw Rob Gretton.

Sometime in the late 1990s I decided to sell all of my vinyl records. I had been buying CD's for a few years and it was impossible to get a new stylus for my record player, so they took up a lot of space. I should have packed them away and put them in the loft. I had over 1,500 singles, both 7 inch and 12 inch and over 1,200 albums. Reading my story, you will have seen some of the records that I had from the day of release. I also had lots of Factory memorabilia posters: Flexi Discs, badges, leaflets, Hacienda Xmas Cards, and my Hacienda Honorary Membership card. I sold all of this stuff as well. I never dreamed that any of it would become collectable years later. An example of one record that I had is Joy Division's first press of 'An Ideal for Living' 7 inch single which now sells for over £6,000 on E Bay. I got it from Discount Records for 70p. Put this down as another stupid decision.

Our world was about to come crashing down as towards the end of 1998 Lesley found a lump at the side of her breast. She showed it me and asked me to feel it. It was large and solid. I asked her how long she had felt it and I was shocked at her reply. She had found it when it was the size of a pea and she had shown it to a nurse at a Well Woman clinic who had told her that it was probably a bra strap rubbing on her and to get her bra sized properly. That was about six months earlier and the only reason she had told me now about the lump was because it had got so hard. I had private medical insurance through my work, so we arranged for her to see a Consultant. He sent her for a scan, and they did a biopsy. A few days later, we got the news that we didn't want to hear as she was diagnosed with Breast Cancer. Within a couple of days she was in for surgery to remove the lump and some tissue round it under her armpits. The surgery went well, and they sent everything away to be analysed. It came back as being an aggressive form of cancer.

In late January 1999, Uncle Paddy passed away at the age of 81. Lesley was well enough to travel so we left the lads with Ann and Frank, and I contacted Margaret for the first time since 1995. The only contact we had since I was robbed of my money was for Jack's and Tom's Christenings. We went over and stayed in a guest house just outside the village as I didn't want to stay with Mick and Margaret. Paddy's funeral passed well, and I was proud to carry him and speak at the Mass. It annoyed me no end that Mick's wife Margaret was arranging the funeral and I had to tell her that I was reading at Paddy's mass, and I couldn't give a fuck about her arrangements. I knew Paddy had always hated her, I had spent so many holidays working as Paddy's assistant I was very close to him. At the funeral Mick approached me and asked if Margaret and I could visit him that evening on our own.

I asked Tommy to come with us, Lesley was happy to stay in the guest house as she didn't need any hassle. When we got to Mick's he told us a story that Paddy hadn't made a will and it had been his intention to give the house to him so that Margaret's sister could move over from England and live there. I kept quiet. Mick then produced a legal document drawn up by a solicitor which he asked us both to sign. This document stated that we gave up any claim to Paddy's estate. I told Mick to go fuck himself and told him that Paddy hated Margaret's sister and if he had done a will he would have left the house to either my nephew Kevin or me due to time spent with him. We left the house and went back to the guest house, collected Lesley and went to the pub to discuss what had just happened.

Under Irish law Uncle Johnny, Uncle Mick and the children of Mary Murray (Margaret and me) were all entitled to a share. Uncle Paul's wife Cathleen was not entitled to anything. So Margaret and

Ged Duffy

I were entitled to a sixth each. Mick appointed himself executor of the estate without permission from the rest of us. The estate consisted of the house and land and also a quarry that we owned up in the mountains. My Cousin John had been using the quarry for years, with the permission of Paddy, to build walls and houses for people. Mick decided that the house and land was worth about £30,000 and made an offer to the three of us which we refused. In retaliation, he locked the gates of the quarry and threw John off the land and put him out of business.

By this time all of Uncle Johnny's children - John, Moira, Ann and Margaret were involved fighting their Dad's corner and we paid for an independent valuation of the house and land, and it came back as £100,000. Mick had the quarry valued at around £75,000 whereas the guy we hired came back with £400,000 minimum and he had someone interested in buying it as a going concern. Mick said it wasn't for sale. We were prepared to go to court, and Moira was very well off as she had sold off the jewellery stores she owned in London and her husband was a big property player so they could face Mick off. He had to succumb in the end and the house and land were sold at auction for 175,000. Mick paid all of his legal fees out of this and there was nothing we could do as he was the Executor of the Estate. The guy who bought the house planned to modernise it, build two extensions at the rear of the house underground into the slope of the field so that from the road the property looked the same. He would give the house as a wedding present to his daughter. His problem was that he told Mick of his plans at the auction. Mick's wife Margaret then applied to join the Planning Committee and was accepted and she immediately blocked the plans. Their plan was to sit tight, let the guy do a couple of appeals and then approach him with a lower offer to take it off his hands. The guy who got the house was very rich and some 22 years later the house is still empty and in ruin, all because of Mick's greed.

After selling the house nearly a year earlier Mick finally decided to settle the estate and pay us all. After paying the legal fees at the time of the auction we were shocked to see all of the deductions that he somehow managed to invent in this final invoice. Margaret and I both got £10,000.

Mick left the quarry alone for a couple of years and it ended up being flooded and unworkable and he got a valuation of around 40,000 and sold it. Our share was £7,000 each and this time I got

Factory Fairy Tales

Dad's solicitor to take care of our claim so that when all of the money came in he deducted £4,500 off Margaret's claim and gave it to me. He also deducted all of the legal costs that I had paid for the house to be put in her name plus 50% of the other legal costs. Her debt to me was paid and we resumed contact again. Thanks to the messing round done by Mick and his devious ways I got just over £17,000 on an estate that even allowing for 20% in fees should have paid Margaret and me £65,000 each. I'm sure that the estate's accounts were inflated massively to stop anyone but him getting any decent money out of it. If he had been honest then we would have walked away with a nice sum, but he was a twat who wanted to feather his own nest.

During all this legal wrangling Uncle Johnny died of a broken heart. He was torn in two due to the behaviour of his younger brother Mick. Once again I was over for his funeral, and he was buried in Lacken Cemetery near the rest of his family. I have a funny story about Johnny's wake. They held an open casket wake in their house. Johnny was over six foot eight inches and wore size 14 shoes. He was the original gentle giant and was the nicest man I have ever met. His kids clubbed together and got him a solid oak coffin. When it was time to move his body to the hearse it was decided that eight of us would carry him. We lifted the coffin and carried it towards the window of the farmhouse, and we passed it through the window with people going outside to balance it until the eight of us put it in the hearse. We carried it into the church and by the time we came out of the church it was raining. It was decided that due to the weather and the weight of the coffin, the hearse would drive into the cemetery and get as close as possible to the grave. When we got near the grave Cousin John slipped and the funeral directors had to jump in to balance the coffin as it looked like the eight of us were going to end up in the hole with Johnny! Mick was shunned by the whole family, and he wasn't allowed to see Johnny's body or to sit with the family at the church. The whole village blanked him and his wife. I had an indentation shaped like the corner of the coffin dug into my right shoulder for several weeks after carrying the coffin.

In early 1999 Lesley started a six-week course of radiotherapy. When this was finished, they did another scan on her, and it looked like the cancer hadn't got bigger and there was no sign of it in her lymph nodes. This was positive news, so they decided to send her for chemotherapy to hopefully kill it. This treatment was rough as chemotherapy is basically poisoning your body – it is a savage, unforgiving treatment. She would have the chemotherapy once every three weeks, for a total of six doses. She would come home from Christie Hospital and spend the next week in bed throwing up. This would be followed by a week of being physically unable to do anything, and a week of being normal. As soon as she had got used to being normal again it was time for the cycle to start again.

People living in Manchester are very lucky to have Christie Hospital. It is one of the leading cancer treatment facilities in Europe. The first time I went there I was in tears as people were there with holes in their faces, children had tubes sticking out of them and everyone looked in a bad way. As time went on I stopped noticing and everyone blurred into the background. It's a sad fact of life that if you see something like this every day then it just becomes the norm.

Lesley loved her hair, and after the second dose of treatment her hair started to fall out, so we had a tear-filled evening with me cutting it off. We were both crying our eyes out, and it was one of the worst things that I have ever had to do in my life. The following day, I took her to a place that provided wigs for cancer patients, and she got a couple of wigs that she liked. She finished the treatment and was discharged until the end of the year, when she would come back and have another scan, so she started to go back to work on a part time basis. It was now around May 1999.

On 15 May 1999 Rob Gretton passed away in his sleep. I didn't find out until a few weeks later so I didn't go to his funeral. I have been to his grave and paid my respects. He was a top bloke and I have nothing but respect for him. RIP Rob. One of the soundest blokes that I have ever known. Top Man, Legend, Genius, Bitter Blue. Miss you mate.

32: 1999 and all that

Manchester United had dominated domestic football in the 1990s, it truly was a great time to be alive. After signing Eric Cantona United won the league 4 times out of 5 and then Eric retired. The last couple of titles had seen the rise of a bunch of young players now referred to as 'The Class of '92' – players such as Ryan Giggs and David Beckham - and these were the players that now propelled United to ever greater heights. The one thing Alex Ferguson hadn't yet cracked was success in the European Cup, so dear to United fans because of Munich. The 1998-99 season would change all that.

I had complained to my Sales Director, Paul Massey, about the fact that all of the other salesmen played golf and did a lot of corporate entertaining whereas since I didn't play golf, I never got the opportunity to do anything. He asked me what I had in mind, and I told him that I could get hold of two tickets for the Champions League Final, so he agreed to pay all the costs for one customer and me to travel to Barcelona. This was all agreed at 3am at the annual company conference at the Scarisbrick Hotel in Southport on 4 January whilst both of us were pissed. Great! All United had to do was to get to the Final.

3 March: Inter Milan at home in the Quarter Final of the Champions League. Two great crosses from David Beckham onto the head of Dwight Yorke gave United a 2-0 lead which was preserved by an amazing overhead goal line clearance from Henning Berg.

17 March: The return leg at the San Siro, Inter went ahead early in the game. United held on and Paul Scholes scored late on to make it 1-1 on the night and we go through to the Semi Final.

7 April: We played Juventus at home in the Semi Final. Juventus take the lead with a goal from their skipper Antonio Conte. United really struggle in the game, but in injury time Ryan Giggs smashes one in the roof of the net in front of the Stretford End. The final score is 1-1 so we have to win or get a score draw of 2-2 or higher in Turin. I thought the roof was going to come off the stadium as the ball hit

the back of the net.

21 April: At the Stadio Delle Alpi in Turin, Juventus start off like a house on fire and go 2-0 up within the first 11 minutes thanks to two goals from Filippo Inzaghi. Then Roy Keane took over and played the game of his life and started to control the game. A corner from Beckham and Keane scored a great header. A few minutes later Dwight Yorke scored to bring the tie level just before half time. In the second half United took total control as Juventus faded away. Denis Irwin hit both posts with shots from the edge of the penalty area before Dwight Yorke broke away and rounded the goal keeper only to be brought down the referee plays advantage as the ball went to Cole who puts it into the empty net to make it 2-3 to United. United are through to the Champions League Final - Full speed Ahead Barcelona.

Lesley and I were going mental at home when the final whistle went but then reality set in. How am I going to remind my boss what he had said in a drunken stupor some five months earlier? He won't remember, will he? At that moment the phone rang and a familiar cockney voice asked me "Well, who are you taking then?" I was pleased that he had remembered.

The treble was definitely on, and it was all decided in ten days in May. United played Spurs in their final league game to decide the winners of the Premier League and won 2-1 after falling behind and six days later Frank and I were at Wembley to watch United play Newcastle in the FA Cup Final. It was a weird atmosphere for a cup final as we knew that we would win, and we did so at a stroll with no danger caused by Newcastle at all, goals by Teddy Sheringham and Paul Scholes giving us a 2-0 win. I have never felt as relaxed at a game as I was that afternoon, Newcastle were never going to bother us. Afterwards the celebrations were muted as if everyone was saving themselves for the big one on Wednesday in Barcelona, even though we'd just completed our third League and Cup double in five seasons, which is mad when you think about it. I remember walking back to the train station and Newcastle fans were screaming at United fans to celebrate. It was a very strange situation. They were all singing and shouting and if you didn't know you would think that they had won it.

Four days later I picked up Jimmy Ogden from his house in Horwich near Bolton and we went to Manchester Airport. Once

Factory Fairy Tales

inside we discovered that one of the three terminals had been allocated to Manchester United. On the departure screen there was a plane leaving for Barcelona every ten minutes and there were dozens of jumbo jets parked on the tarmac and as one plane departed another one was towed into that bay.

When we landed in Barcelona, the captain wouldn't let us off the plane until we all started singing 'Glory, Glory Man United' so we obliged him. When we got off we saw that he had a Manchester United flag flying out of his window and he was wearing a United bobble hat on his head. When we got outside the airport there were free buses laid on to take us to the city centre. On the bus Jimmy told me that he would be paying for everything whilst in Barcelona. I told him that Paul Massey would want me to pay. He smiled and said "If you say no, Ged, I'll tell Paul that I had a rotten time here with you". I had to accept.

Once in the City Centre we decided to get on an open top bus which took us round half of the city and out into the mountains to see the Olympic Stadium which is home to Espanyol. On the way back we passed a massive park and there was a game of football going on between United fans and Munich fans, it looked like about 2,000 a side.

All along the route we saw United fans everywhere and when we got off the bus at La Ramblas it resembled Old Trafford on a match day. Every statue had a United hat, scarf and banner hanging from it. The market stalls had United flags hanging from their roofs, and even the police motorbikes had United scarves tied to their aerials. It was a great party atmosphere and despite all the warnings the bars were all open and doing great business. We went to a restaurant and had a lovely meal. It was full of Reds and Germans. It was a great atmosphere with no hint of trouble with plenty of beer-driven songs being sung. I felt sorry for the Germans as everyone of them was wearing a Bayern scarf, woolly hat and big coats and the temperature was in the 30s. After eating we got on the metro and everywhere was full of Reds and it looked like we outnumbered them by at least three to one.

When we got near the famous Camp Nou I was so disappointed as it resembled the outside of the Arndale Centre! The ground may have been a shithole outside but as soon as I got inside it took my breath away. You entered the stadium just below the top tier and then made your way down inside to the lower tier where we were sitting as most of the stadium is actually below ground level. When I got to ground level I went to the pitch side and stood there looking around at this magnificent cathedral of football. I could see all four sides from this position but when I got to Row 27 of Gol Nord 1 Gradeeria seat 20 I could only see the bottom bit of the opposite end and the bottom tier of the two sides. The view of the pitch was amazing.

The seats were rigid, and the base did not fold up but luckily there was enough room for two people between you and the seat in front which came in very handy as there were two people for every seat in our section as so many had got into the stadium without tickets, so we stood for the whole game.

Paul Scholes and Roy Keane were both suspended for this game, so Fergie had to make a couple of tactical changes. In the week leading up to the final Bayern Munich had appealed to UEFA to make the pitch narrower. Their argument was that the Camp Nou was the widest pitch in Europe and United had Giggs and Beckham on the wings. Amazingly UEFA agreed and the pitch had a couple of metres taken off both sides. The game started badly with Bayern scoring from a free kick right in front of our end within the first six minutes, they dominated the game and Munich also hit the woodwork twice during the game. With time running out things were looking desperate so Fergie changed things and we started to play a little bit. Just before the end of 90 minutes the Germans made a big show of taking off Lothar Matthaus and Stefan Effenberg to great applause from their fans. They had run the game and now they were looking to see out injury time. Some German fans set off flares behind the other goal to celebrate, United had barely had a shot on target.

The board went up showing three minutes to go. Shit! Just three minutes. Well, we've had a great day and maybe it's not meant to be. Shit! Only three minutes to go. Come on Boys. Please do something. Do anything. Hey, we've got a corner and Schmeichel's coming up for it. Make it good Becks, please make it count. Schmeichel's presence in the box is causing them a problem, the German machine could not compute a goalie in the box. Great corner, poor header out, poor shot from Giggs but the ball's come to Teddy who strokes it into the corner. Pandemonium. Utter fucking pandemonium breaks out round three quarters of the Camp Nou. I ended up about six or seven rows further down in the stand. I had to get back to my row. Great, made it. By the time I got back to my seat we had another corner. Everything goes in slow motion: great delivery, Teddy heads it on and the ball is in the air *And Solskjaer has won it*. Manchester

Factory Fairy Tales

United have won the Champions League and with it the Treble. It seems the noise and celebration for the first goal was just a rehearsal as the stadium erupts.

Once again I end up a few rows down as I see a guy fall from the tier above to luckily land on his back between two rows of seats. His fall was cushioned by a ruck sack on his back. He gets up and starts screaming that all his beer in the ruck sack has exploded and leaked. Two guys grab him and hoist him on their shoulders. There's beer dripping everywhere but he soon forgets his woes as he joins in the singing as seconds later the team are in front of our end of the stadium celebrating. I look above me and the whole tier above was shaking, and I mean shaking.

Outside the stadium there are Germans lying on the ground everywhere crying their eyes out, while delirious United fans walk past them singing songs about Hitler and his one testicle and politely asking them where they were in 1945, totally politically incorrect nowadays but not so in 1999.

Back in the airport there were rows of jumbo jets lined up, 500 fans would be counted onto a plane, and it would leave. Then the next plane would pull in and the next 500 would get on that plane. When I dropped Jimmy back at his house, he handed me all the receipts he had collected whilst in Barcelona and told me to claim the money back from the company. I said no, but he demanded that I accept them. When I asked why he was doing this he stated that he had never had a better football experience in his life, and he couldn't thank me enough.

Both City and Liverpool have had seasons where they won three trophies, but no one has ever won the three biggest trophies in three games over the space of ten days. This had never been done before and I guess it will never be done again.

The next day the Home Office announced that it had been the largest single movement of people out of the UK since the D-Day Landings. The Mayor of Barcelona estimated that there were over 60,000 United fans inside the stadium and at least between 50,000 and 65,000 more in the city without tickets. The next afternoon, I went to town to see the homecoming of the treble winners. All roads into the city were closed by lunchtime and the police issued warnings to stay away as town was packed to bursting point. Over 1,000,000 were there to see the parade and yet City fans still claim Manchester is Blue. No, my friends, Manchester is Red.

33: Worst Christmas imaginable

Lesley finished her course of chemotherapy and went back to work again, initially on a part time basis which would be steadily increased until she felt comfortable coming back full time. She was only working a few hours each day with no late shifts, and she soon settled back into the routine. All of her mates rallied round, and she was out having meals and drinks a couple of times a week. We would try and get out at a weekend, and go for walks with Frank, Ann and the lads. During the summer we went camping in France and that was an enjoyable trip. Lesley also took the lads on day trips out and about with her parents. Her Station decided to arrange a charity night for her. It was a great night and local football clubs, and businesses donated items and one of the sergeants, who owned a holiday home in Spain, donated a week in his home. The guy who won the auction for the holiday gave it to Lesley, so she went with the lads, and I think her sister Jo a few months later. Lesley had a scan towards the end of the year, and it looked okay. It seemed that the cancer had shrunk a little. The consultant hoped it would have made more progress, but it was positive news, so we looked forward to Christmas.

Sometime during the late 90s I went to four gigs at The Talk of The North in Eccles. This was a working man's cabaret club. They were called *An Evening with* and basically each artist would appear on their own, play some songs on an acoustic guitar and talk to the crowd about their career and how they wrote some of their best songs. I saw Pete Townsend (The Who), Ray Davies (The Kinks), Steve Harley (Cockney Rebel) and Ronnie Drew (The Dubliners). They were all great nights and each artist had to do two hours. Chicken and chips in a basket was thrown in with the ticket. Brilliant nights.

Lesley had another scan in early 2000 and the consultant was a little bit concerned about some small growths and started to monitor them. She had to go to several appointments and have lots of people poking about with her. She stayed cheerful and optimistic throughout it all. Her hair was slowly regrowing, but she still had to carry on wearing a wig. Around about this time they started pumping her full of steroids which made her gain weight. After this scan, she sat down and told me that she felt she didn't have much time left and wanted things to change. She said that she wanted to start going out, have a good time, party a little and it would be best if I moved out. Her other thought was that it would be good for the lads to get used to living alone with me as she wanted me to have them as much as possible. I disagreed but after talking it over we decided that it could work.

I looked at renting, but everything was really expensive and then I found a Mid Terrace in Nepaul Road, Blackley about five minutes' drive from our house for sale at £7,500. The deposit was only £375 so I bought it and moved in a few weeks later. The lads would stay with me every weekend and a couple of evenings during the week. On a matchday, they would come to Ann and Frank's with me and stay with their Nanna whilst I went to the game. I suppose in a way this helped them getting used to not having their Mum around. Lesley and I still saw each other a lot and I was round to help her with anything she needed doing round the house. We hadn't broken up; we were just living in different houses. She was going out a few nights a week and I started to go and see the odd gig as well.

Lesley and the kids went away with Ann and Frank for a summer holiday, and I think they went away with Jo as well sometime over that summer. She had stopped wearing her wig as her hair had grown a little bit. It was very short but at least it was hers. At her second scan, later in the year, the growths had started to grow again but they had not spread so it was agreed that she would do a six week course of radiotherapy again, just to be on the safe side. This treatment used to leave her sore as it basically burnt away at her body. She was tired a lot and work put her on extended sick leave again. I would do her shopping for her and take the lads out more so she could rest. We had Christmas as normal round at her parents, and we acted like everything was normal round the kids. They enjoyed having two houses I think.

By this point I had moved to a French boiler manufacturer called Chaffoteaux that had a dreadful reputation as cheap French shite and to be honest it was. Lesley and I had been invited to see the New Year in, in Paris. Chaffoteaux were taking all the UK Sales Team and their partners for a couple of days there. We flew over on the morning of 30 December and got a taxi from Charles de Gaulle to the hotel. I have never been scared in a car before but when we got near to the Arc de

Ged Duffy

Triomphe I could see that about 10 lanes of traffic were merging into four. The taxi driver just kept driving and God knows how we never got hit. We had a lovely afternoon shopping… Didn't enjoy paying for it! The following day we explored the sights and then we had the company party on a boat down the River Seine. It was amazing: wine, beer, food, music, and dancing. We stopped near the Eiffel Tower and watched it light up to say 2001 at midnight. The firework display was out of this world. Within a few weeks of returning from Paris I was headhunted by Ideal Boilers and decided to join them.

Lesley went for a follow-up scan, the small growths had got bigger, but the main concern was that there was another tumour, so she went through chemotherapy again. This was a more aggressive type of chemotherapy than before, and hit her hard. She would be bed bound a lot but after it was all done she had another scan and the chemotherapy had worked; the tumour was getting smaller. Lesley was going out a lot with her friends and enjoying life as much as she could. She was still wearing the wig as her hair had gone again following the last round of chemotherapy. She was a little concerned about something and so she was sent for another scan. This scan came back to show that the cancer had spread to her lungs and other vital organs. More treatment could be done but it might not work…

Sometime in 2001 TLM Records released three Stockholm Monsters CD's. TLM was run by a guy called James Nice and he had bought up the rights for the Monsters after the demise of Factory Records. *The Last One Back* was a mixture of demo tapes and live shows. I featured on nine of the tracks. The cover of the CD was the hotel that we stayed at in Paris in 1982. *All at Once* was a singles collection and I featured on four of the songs, but my bass-line was played by Karl on another three songs. I enjoyed listening to these CD's as they filled in a bit more from my days in the band. The third CD was the *Alma Mater* plus some more songs added on as extras. Karl played my bass-line on one of the extra songs.

At the beginning of December I went to see James at the MEN Arena. This gig was advertised as their Farewell Gig. It was an amazing emotional night with some sound issues but they were still great. When I came out I was sad as my favourite band were no more. They played a great set of hits including 'Say Something', 'Sometimes', 'Laid', 'Hymn from a Village', 'Johnny Yen', 'Getting Away With It All', 'She's a Star', 'Come Home' and of course the magnificent anthem 'Sit Down'. The MEN Arena had opened in 1995 and this was my first ever visit there. It was a great venue with really good acoustics, and it had a good seat layout. I would go there a lot more over the years.

On Christmas Eve 2001 Lesley had woken up to find that her ankles had completely swollen up, she called me and I was round a few minutes later and we knew it was near the end. We had seen this happen to other patients who had been in the same wards as Lesley when she had been having treatments and we knew that death would be within a few days. I called the Doctor and as soon as he saw her ankles, he arranged for an ambulance to take her to a Hospice in Bury. When I showed him out of the house I asked if she could stay here and die to which he replied, "Do you want your lads to walk in and find her dead, and then expect them to want to live in this house?" he was right. He told me that she should survive until Boxing Day at least.

We went to the Hospice with her, and Ann, Jo, and Frank came to see her. We all stayed there until we were thrown out later that evening and it was arranged with the staff that we would all come and have Christmas dinner in her room the next day. Ann would cook it at home and then Jo would bring it there. Jack and Tom stayed at my house that night and at 6am on Christmas Day I got a phone call from the Hospice asking us to come as the end was near. I had to wake up Jack and Tom on Christmas Morning, and explain to them that their Mum would probably pass away that very day.

We got there at the same time as Ann, Jo, and Frank. Three nurses were waiting for us at the entrance, and they told us that she had sadly passed away. After three years of chemotherapy, radiotherapy, operations, tears with hair loss, and constant hospital visits, she had gone. We never got a chance to say goodbye by her side.

I later found out that she had already passed away when they called me but that they never issue news like that over the phone. She was 37 years old. I was so glad that Ann, Jo and Frank were there as I broke down when I heard the news, and they could console Jack and Tom. The nurses were amazing as they hugged everyone and stayed with us in the car park until we were composed enough to see her body. I moved back into the house immediately to keep everything as normal as possible for the lads. As you can imagine Christmas was a nightmare as we had dinner and gave the presents out with no feeling of happiness. Lesley loved Christmas and that's why we decided to stay go through with it. Everywhere was shut over Christmas so I couldn't make any arrangements for the funeral until the new year. My mate Frank Roper came everywhere with me and without his support I don't know if I could have handled it all. Lesley had planned everything, so I just followed her wishes.

Jack was 11, and Thomas was six when their mum died and I'm so proud of the way they handled it. She would have been so proud of them at her funeral, wearing matching three piece suits, shirts and ties, and the way they handled themselves all through the day. The church was packed with Lesley's work colleagues and friends. She was loved by so many with her bubbly personality. I remember that Jack and Tom both held my hand the whole day and I could feel their hurt especially at the grave side in Blackley Cemetery. Christmas has never been the same again for us.

34: Single Parent

So at the start of 2002 I became a single parent with a job that took up a lot of my time and without the help of my in-laws, Ann, Frank and Jo and my sister Margaret doing overnight stays and babysitting, I would never have managed it.

For a long time after Lesley's death I was completely torn apart, but I had to keep it together in front of the lads. Ann and Jo came round and cleared all of her clothes and possession from the house as I couldn't bear to do it. Things got slightly better with time, but it was difficult working, coming home and becoming Mum and Dad to two great lads. I did my best.

The only escapes I had was United home games, which made me think about something else for a couple of hours, and some weekends when the boys would stay with Ann and Frank whilst I went out with my mate Frank Roper. I knew Frank from work, and we would meet up with another work mate, Dave Gaffey, and go drinking or have a curry in Oldham. Frank was in a band called Cosh Goblins and they used to play in pubs so I would watch them. It gave me hope to carry on. These two helped to drag me through everything over the next few years.

A few months into the year I decided to sell the little terrace. I went round one day to get the post and there was a leaflet offering to buy houses for cash. I rang the number and a couple of days later I was offered £9,000 which I accepted. Looking back on it now, I should have just rented the place and it would have made me a lot of money by now. Bad decision again...

I took Jack and Tom to Florida for their summer holiday. They absolutely loved it even though we had to be caked in Factor 50 as we are pale white-skinned Mancs with red hair. We went to all the sights, and I remember at Epcot there was an area with several fountains which would stop and then all suddenly explode again at the same moment soaking anyone nearby. Tom went and stood in the middle of them and wouldn't come out. He got soaked that much I had to go in a shop and buy him a whole new set of clothes, including underwear. It cost me an absolute fortune. The lads had a great time and it cheered them up for a couple of weeks. The only undies I could get was a pair of girl's Mickey Mouse ones and Jack and I ribbed him wicked. He threw them in the bin at the hotel when we got back. If I have embarrassed you Tom by writing this, I don't care cos you cost me a lot of money that afternoon.

I went to three gigs at Lancashire Cricket Club, in July 2002. I got five tickets for each day and took some customers. First night it was David Bowie on the *Heathen* tour supported by Suede, The Divine Comedy and The Pixies. It poured down all day and we got absolutely soaked so we had to compensate by drinking lots of beer, all on Ideal Boilers. The Pixies played a short set which sounded really good. I knew none of the songs, but I liked them. Wasn't that bothered about The Divine Comedy to be honest but I loved Suede. I already had their albums so I was really into them, and they played a great set with 'Trash', 'Animal Nitrate' and 'She's in Fashion'. The sun came out and the rain stopped just as Bowie came on. He started with *'Life on Mars'* and his set was made up of a few songs from his new *Heathen* album and some oldies. He played 'Ashes to Ashes', 'Starman', 'China Girl', 'Changes', 'Heroes', 'Let's Dance' and finished off with a great version of 'Ziggy Stardust'.

The second day was not as good as the first. The place was packed with young and old punks. The first band on was Less Than Jake who were a ska band and not my cup of tea. No Doubt were next on and I hated them. Just before Green Day came on the PA played 'YMCA' by the Village People and it was so funny seeing thousands of punks doing the actions to it. It was a great moment. Green Day were fucking brilliant even though I only knew five of their songs and they played these on the day: 'Maria,' 'When I Come Around', 'Time of Your Time', 'Minority' and 'Basket Case'. After they finished a song they announced the next one and asked if anyone could play it. They got three people up out of the crowd, and they played that song. At the end of it Billy Joe gave his guitar to the lad that had just played it.

The third day was the one I had been looking forward to as it was New Order supported by Echo & The Bunnymen, Doves, and Elbow. Doves and Elbow both played good sets and were appreciated by the crowd. I got into both of these bands after this gig. Echo were magnificent on the day. New Order came on and were sensational. They opened with a classic 'Love Vigilantes', 'Transmission', 'Regret', '60 Miles per Hour', 'Atmosphere', 'She's Lost Control', 'True Faith', 'Temptation', 'World In Motion', 'Digital', 'Love Will Tear Us Apart', and 'Blue Monday'. Keith Allen came on to sing on 'World In Motion' and Barney introduced him as "The Prince of Darkness". Hooky dedicated 'She's Lost Control' to the late great bassist of The Who John Entwistle. Hooky also dedicated 'Love Will Tear Us Apart' to "All of you, Manchester, because I'm fucking proud to live here". They played 'Can't Get You Out Of My Head' by Kylie Minogue as the intro and exit out of 'Blue Monday'. Three great gigs and they cheered me up no end. I didn't go to any gigs (apart from pub gigs with Frank Roper) the rest of 2002 or the majority of 2003 as I liked being at home with the boys.

As you can imagine it was a very low key Christmas and the lads agreed that we shouldn't put any decorations up but we had as good a time as we could considering. We went to the graveside on Christmas morning, and this is something that we've done every year since. I took Jack and Tom to Ireland for a break over Easter, went to see my folks down in Mayo, stayed in Salthill in Galway, Tralee in Kerry and Cork City before staying with my cousin in Dublin.

A few weeks after the following season finished my Father in Law Frank passed away suddenly. I was so upset as he was a great friend to me. We had been going to every United home game together since 1988. He was buried in Blackley Cemetery close to Lesley. This set me back again, as I loved Frank. Looking back on everything now, I should have got some help to get me through everything. I had been in a very deep depression for over two years, whilst still trying to function as a responsible parent. I know that I never grieved for Lesley properly and I think that with all the tears I have cried whilst writing this section of the book, this has finally happened some 20 years later. I finally feel at peace now.

I know that I snapped at Jack and Tom a few times, when I should have realized that they were going through the same shite as me and I should have shown more empathy towards them. For this I sincerely apologize and hope that I didn't ruin their childhood years. I hope that they can forgive their old Dad as I did the best I could. I spoke to United's Ticket Office, and they agreed to transfer Frank's season ticket over to Jack but we had to move into the Family Stand as he was 12. I agreed and now Jack was coming to the games with me.

In July 2003 we moved into a house in Urmston. Our old house in Blackley was full of memories and this was a new start. It was a great distraction with decorating and arranging things in the new house. My mood started to brighten little by little. Jack and Tom loved the new house, and both really enjoyed living round there. Tom went to a new school, and he made loads of friends straight away. I think moving was the best decision I ever made as even though they would never forget their mum, new surroundings meant that they weren't reminded of her every day.

I was so proud to go to the game with Jack. We had the best seats and with the executive boxes behind us, we would see a goal or an incident and immediately turn round and watch it through the window of the box. It was great. First game was Bolton at home opening day of the season. En route to the game we both had foot long hot dogs with tomato sauce, and I had onions as well. This became a ritual, and we did it before every game. United won 4-0 and Cristiano Ronaldo made his debut in the second half. He was described afterwards by the press as a circus act due to the amount of step-overs he did during his time on the pitch. Jack loved him immediately whereas I was a bit sceptical – I guess Jack was right!

I went to one proper gig towards the end of 2003, to see Killing Joke play at the Academy in Manchester. They were brilliant as ever, but the most important thing is I found Slim. He was Head of Security, and we had a chat. I told him about Lesley, and he was shocked and saddened. He had known her since the night I met her back in 1981 at Rafters.

35: American Woman

I was feeling down and lonely by now as my life was just work, being a single parent, watching United and the very occasional night out with Frank Roper for a beer, curry or the odd pub gig.

One bright spot was United winning the FA Cup in Cardiff beating Millwall 4-0. This was Jack's first cup final, and I was so proud to have him with me. We had a great day in Cardiff. I drove into North Wales and went through Snowdonia, so it was a scenic route. I parked up outside Cardiff and met a work colleague who lived down there, and he drove us to the stadium. It was a stroll in the park for United and Jack got to see us lift the FA Cup. He was so excited. Afterwards we met my mate again and he got us back to my car in quick time and we hit the mountain road back home.

In July I took some customers to Lancashire Cricket Ground to see Madness supported by The Stranglers and Ocean Colour Scene. The Stranglers came on all dressed in black, and I loved them. I made the customers stand in front of JJ Burnel the bass player. Their set was great, and they went down well with the crowd. They played 'Peaches', 'Skin Deep' and 'Golden Brown'. Then it was the turn of reggae star Jimmy Cliff who played a slow set with the main song being his classic 'The Harder They Fall'. He left the stage as quietly as he entered it. Ocean Colour Scene were on next, and they played really well. I didn't really like them musically, but I did like 'Day I Caught The Train'. Madness were amazing and as soon as they came on I lost one of my customers. We spotted him right at the front in the middle of about 200 fez wearing loons who were going mental to the nutty boys. When he came back he was totally shagged.

We were back the next day to see The Cure supported by Elbow and Keane. Keane were amazing on the night as they played a vibrant set which was full of emotion and their singer Tom could really sing. I loved them. Elbow were really good as well as they played songs off their two albums so I knew most of the set. They would go on to become a big festival band in the next few years. The Cure came on all dressed in black and played a set which included 'Fascination Street', 'Love Song', 'Inbetween Days', 'Just Like Heaven', 'Picture of You', 'Play For Today', 'A Forest 'and finished off with 'Boys Don't

Cry'. These two gigs helped, as the shadow hanging over me started to clear and I was starting to slowly look forward instead of looking back

I was having issues with my National Sales Manager at Ideal as in the fact he was a complete knobhead but thought that the sun shone out of his arse. I found it hard to bite my tongue, so I left and joined Ferroli Boilers. This was a really good decision for once made by me. My new boss Martin Youd was a top bloke. Ferroli's HQ was in a town called San Bonifacio near Verona in Italy. As part of my duties I took customers over to the factory in Italy and I usually did at least two trips per year. We would fly into Verona, Treviso, Venice or Milan and then we would stay in Soave or Verona. On these trips we would always have a day in Venice, an evening in Verona, a day at Lake Grada, and of course a morning doing a tour of the Ferroli factory. Sometimes we would visit Modena, the Ferrari museum and test track at Maranello or the beautiful town of Padua. Over the next four years I enjoyed working at Ferroli and I have some great memories of the trips. On one trip we were waiting to get the water taxi out of Venice back to the coach park and one of the installers wasn't paying attention as he boarded the boat. He missed the step and fell into the canal! When we stayed in Verona the hotel was built onto the end of a block of shops. We used to look at who the installers were and if they were quiet and reserved then we would turn left out of the hotel and take them to the Café bar as this was usually a safe well-behaved night. If they were rowdy then we would turn right and go to the strip club. I would explain to them in the hotel bar before we left what the club was like. My credit card would be at reception, and they could have as many dances as they liked. The girls would take them into a large room which held about 20 girls dancing at the same time and sit them on a chair, pull a curtain round all four sides. There would be no music and the girls would strip immediately and dance near to the guy. The guy could touch the girl and she would guide where his hands would go. One customer fell in love with a stripper from Romania, came back to see her a few times, divorced his wife, took her back home to UK and got married to her. She divorced him two years later and took him for everything.

One night we had major trouble at the strip club. We had a gang of installers over from Sunderland and they were all covered in tattoos and the strip club was too much for them. They were pissed from the moment they got on the plane in Newcastle until they got off the plane four days later. Anyway one of the lads took a girl for a dance and as soon as she stripped off, he pulled his cock out, grabbed her head and pulled her towards it. She pulled free and kicked him right in his bollocks with a six inch stiletto. The bouncers came in and I had to stop the two sides fighting each other. We didn't go back there again on that trip. Next day I had to take the offender to Verona Hospital as he was peeing blood.

Some of the memories that have stuck with me were witnessing a beautiful wedding in St Mark's Square, Venice with the service read in Latin. The bride looked beautiful and when the groom kissed her all of the installers stood up and applauded. The look on the installer's faces as the water taxi turns the corner and Venice comes into view was always a picture as they see how beautiful the city is. Being sat at a pavement bar in Verona next door to the Arena when an opera starts. The Arena is a Roman amphitheatre which holds concerts. The feeling you get when they first start to sing, I've seen hardened old installers shed a tear when they hear it. In Verona we would go to a beautiful restaurant with an open fire and the food was cooked in the middle of the room. At the end of the meal everyone would get a glass of Grappa which was a shot which was between 35% to 60% proof. Martin Youd would dip his finger in the glass and then set it on fire. I would be sat next to him, and I would dip my finger in my glass and light my finger off Martin's. We would go round the table getting everyone to do it. It was great looking at their faces when Martin first did it. Taking the installers to the city of Sirmione on Lake Grada and they see the beauty of the lake and then take them round the lake to another bar and sit and wait to see how long it would take. "She's got her tits out"," that ones showing her pussy" and "there's a bloke there with his cock out". Then the penny would drop as it was a nudist beach. The restaurant in Sirmione was built on the lake and had a glass floor. It was an amazing setting to have a meal. One day we were stuck for about 45 minutes on a five minute journey as we waited for Luciano Pavarotti's funeral procession to pass on his final journey to Modena. We had some great times in Italy.

Frank Roper used to always have a girlfriend and on his advice I joined an online dating site. My profile message read something like this "I always wanted to look like Keith Richard circa 1969 but I ended up looking like an extra from The Bill. Hey ho, that's life". Totally out of the blue I was messaged by a girl from Portland, Oregon. She thought that I came from Manchester, Massachusetts, and she was thinking of moving to Boston. When I told her that I came from Manchester, England she was still interested as she loved Joy Division and New Order. Her name was Janine Riggs.

I looked at her profile and it was full of professional photographs. It said that she worked in the Adult Entertainment industry under the name of Veronika as an actress, she was a glamour model and dancer and wanted to find someone that would take her out to the Pacific Coast and make love to her on the hood of his pickup truck under the moonlight. I really liked the idea of that but wasn't sure if she would want to do the same on the bonnet of my blue Citroen Xsara Picasso on Blackpool Prom! She had hundreds of guys following her, and I was intrigued as to why she messaged me. If you saw my profile photo you would have thought she was crazy. We started messaging, then it was phone calls at all hours of the day and then video messaging. First time she saw me on the screen she said, "I knew that you couldn't look as bad as your profile photo". First time I saw her on the screen I thought "what the fuck is she doing with me?".

We had so much in common, we got on so well and I fancied the pants off her. She had a figure to die for and she was way out of my league. She looked beautiful and had an incredibly sexy voice. She just turned me on. We agreed to meet, and I got everything sorted out my end. She paid her own flight. I was hoping that I could have a wild sex-filled few days with her. I was not disappointed!

Within a few weeks she flew into Heathrow, and I was so made up when she came through customs. She looked so cute wearing a bobble hat over her long ginger hair. She had a baggy top on and really tight sweat pants which showed off her figure, topped off with fur lined booties. I was in shock that this beautiful person had flown over 5,000 miles to meet me, I totally forgot where I was parked, and we had a good laugh walking round trying to find the car. That broke the ice between us, and the next few days were amazing. We spent that night in a hotel in Soho, went for a nice meal and had fun walking round the sex joints. Next day I had arranged a surprise for her as we took the Eurostar to Paris. Proper romantic me, I know how to treat a lady. We had a great day walking round Paris, including a trip to Pere-Lachaise Cemetery to see Jim Morrison's grave. It was a very emotional moment for me as I still worshipped him and it got me thinking about great days with my fellow Morrison devotee Tony France.

Factory Fairy Tales

We went round Paris again the next day and we flagged down a taxi driver who drove us round several sites, stopping at each to let us both out to see them properly. He dropped us off the hotel and as we got ready to go out that evening, Janine noticed that she had lost her purse and her passport was in it. When we went downstairs to go out, the girl on reception told us that the taxi driver had dropped her purse back. His next fare after us found it and handed to him. It was a nice ending to the day. The next day we went back to London, spent another night in a hotel and she flew off back home to Portland and I drove home. We had agreed that there was an intense spark between us, and we would see each other again soon.

We carried on talking and a few weeks later, she flew into Heathrow and got the shuttle plane up and I picked her up from Manchester Airport. She stayed for a week in our house in Urmston – she got on great with Jack and Tom. We went out a couple of times, the four of us, ten pin bowling and to the cinema, and the following month I flew over and stayed at her apartment in Portland, and I fell in love with the city. It was legal to smoke dope, there were trash metal stations, punk stations and classic rock stations on the radio, there was a strip club on every block and in a lot of bars. Bars sold real ale brewed locally as well as having Guinness, Bud, Coors and Boddingtons on draft. Manchester's finest was a basic in each bar. Janine worked as a stripper in a few Portland clubs. She had an amazing body so why not use it. I saw her dance a couple of times and she did some amazing tricks using the pole which earned her a lot of money. Whenever we went in a bar that had any strippers working we would sit at the side of the stage and drop a dollar every time they finished a dance. She never minded if I went off for a private dance with any of the girls. I loved it over there.

I came home and went back to work, but I couldn't stop thinking about being with her, so I returned again a few months later and we just clicked as we did the first time we met. It was great to see and feel her again. During this trip she took me sightseeing and we went to the Oregon coast to see the Pacific Ocean and then to the Columbia River Gorge and Mulnomah Falls. These are places of natural beauty. We climbed the path all the way up to the top of the Falls and looked out onto the Columbia River the other side of a six lane freeway. We went to visit her mother who lived in what can only be described as a shack out in the mountains of Washington State. She lived with a proper redneck who spent the whole time showing me his gun. There were a number of old cars left abandoned out in the field with the grass grown above them and there were two rabid dogs chained up to a fence. The house stank of cat piss and my clothes stank for days afterwards. Despite seeing what her mother was like, I was hooked!

On the way back from the house we stopped in to visit a bar in the local town. The whole of the outside wall was full of pick-up trucks, small ones, monster sized ones, long ones and short ones. We pulled into the only space left. We went in and it had a wooden floor covered in sawdust. It was the sort of place where Clint Eastwood would stand up and punch someone and the whole place would explode into a mass brawl. I clocked two empty seats at the bar, and hoped she didn't walk to them. Well, she walked the full length of the bar to get to the bar. She was wearing a skin tight top with no bra, a tiny skirt and her cowboy boots. I felt the eyes of the entire bar staring at this little lady's cute ass. We sat at the bar, and I ordered a beer and a shot times two. Next thing, the area round us went dark and a giant of a man stood behind us. His hands were bigger than my head. He was definitely a logger by the clothes he was wearing.

"Hi, little lady, how you doing?" he said

Janine whispered, "I'll put a bottle in his balls, and you put yours in his face".

"Ok" I gulped. If we were going down then we would swing the first blow.

He heard my voice and asked, "Are you from England?"

"Yes, Manchester" I replied tightening my grip on the bottle.

He then asked "United?" and Janine told him that I was a season ticket holder. It turned out that he was a member of the Washington State Manchester United Supporters Club, and they were having their monthly meeting. We spent the evening drinking and talking United with them. It was amazing! Reds really are here, there and everywhere.

We decided on this trip that we wanted to be together. I had the lads so I couldn't go over there so she was going to come over here. We decided to get engaged and applied for a fiancé Visa so she could come and live with us in Manchester. It was granted and I arranged to go over at Christmas and get everything sorted in Portland and she would come back with me.

I went over on 27 December 2004, my birthday, and unbeknown to me she had arranged a great surprise for me. The last time I had seen her dance I paid to have a private dance with another girl, and she had asked this girl to come round, so we could have a threesome as my birthday gift. This was to be my last fling before we got married.

Unfortunately my plane got delayed in Manchester by several hours and I missed my connection to Portland. I ended up spending the night in Washington DC, went on a taxi sightseeing tour of the city and spent several hours in an Irish bar whose best selling beers were Guinness and Manchester's finest Boddingtons. So I missed what would have been the best night of my life. The only consolation was that my flight to Portland was upgraded to First Class as an apology for the delay.

We spent New Year's Eve in Las Vegas - a mass of neon lights, slot machines and hookers. We went to the MGM Grand, and saw Tom Jones getting walked through the place to go to a private party. Then we saw this mass of blonde hair with an army of paparazzi in tow and it was Pamela Anderson. I wanted to see the lions, so we had a look at them in MGM and went to play the slots at Paris. As soon as I had put a quarter in the slot a waitress came up and gave me a bottle of beer. As long as you are playing they keep the beers coming for free, so we had a bit to drink in there. We went out on the Strip to see in the New Year, and it was a great night. The next day we flew back to Portland for a day. I flew back to Manchester and the following day Janine flew into Heathrow. Tom and I picked her up and she moved in with us and we were married at the end of the month. We got married at Sale Registry Office with Margaret and Frank Roper as the witnesses. Margaret's eldest girl Emma was there as well with Jack and Tom. She settled in well and three months later we hired a van and collected all of her belongings which had finally arrived at Liverpool Docks. We had a few teething problems at the start with the two different cultures. We both spoke English, but we spoke a

Janine as 'Veronika'

different language. If I called her a bitch, it would lead to a massive row as that was the equivalent of me calling her a cunt. She called me retarded and I would have to explain about what it meant in England.

Janine settled into life in Manchester. I got her a Fiat Barchetta left hand drive sports car so she could drive round. She was happy. I explained football to her, and she enjoyed it. She, in turn, explained American Football to me and I still watch it to this day. She already liked Joy Division, New Order, The Smiths and Echo and The Bunnymen. The ringtone she had for me was the Bunnymen song 'Lips Like Sugar'. I got her into Bauhaus, Killing Joke and a few more bands and in turn she got me into bands like Aerosmith and classic rock like Black Sabbath and Led Zeppelin. We liked the same films, books and music. She found it hard to understand things like *Only Fools and Horses* but loved *Father Ted* and *Phoenix Nights*.

We started going out most Sundays to what used to be the old Factory Dry Bar on Oldham Street in Town. £5 to get in and five or six local bands would play. It was a bit like an updated version of the Manchester Musicians' Collective which used to be at The Cyprus Tavern every Sunday.

I saw New Order for the last time on 14 November 2005. They were great on the night. They started off with 'Ceremony' and also played 'Love Vigilantes', 'Regret', 'Transmission', 'Love Will Tear Us Apart', 'Temptation' and finished with 'Blue Monday'. They came back on for an encore and played 'Shadowplay', 'Warsaw', 'She's Lost Control' and finished off with and amazing version of 'Atmosphere'. Janine was so pleased that she had finally seen them. After Hooky left New Order in 2007 I wouldn't dream of going to watch them live again, as New Order, without Hooky, is like the Rolling Stones without Keith Richard – a fake band.

During our time together, Janine and I went to see loads of gigs in Manchester including: The Dubliners, Nick Cave, The Stranglers, The Damned, Killing Joke, Echo and The Bunnymen, Bauhaus, The Killers, The Editors, REM, Feeder, Oasis, Black Rebel Motorcycle Club, and Placebo, and a few more that I can't remember. Some of these bands played at the Academy and we would find Slim and have a chat with him. Tom met Slim when we went to see The Damned there. We also went to see the WWE two years running when they turned up at the MEN Arena. Jack and Tom loved the wresting. Janine told them that she had got through all of the trials to become a WWE

Factory Fairy Tales

Diva. When she got down to the final selection she was injured in a match with another girl, so had to leave the programme. We didn't believe her until one of the male wrestlers, Big Show, spotted Janine in the crowd and came over to talk to her. He had been in the camp at the same time as her.

36: Another son

I tried to get tickets to see Simple Minds play in Manchester, but they were sold out instantly but I managed to get tickets to see them in Dublin at the end of January 2006. Janine was seven months pregnant, so we checked with the airline to make sure she could fly. So we flew to Dublin and I hired a car. We were staying at a hotel on Upper O'Connell Street, next door to the Ambassador Theatre. The receptionist told us that Simple Minds were staying in our hotel as well. We went to the gig, and they were amazing. It was great to be able to see them so close again, as they had been playing big arenas for years and this was a small building.

We went back to the hotel and sat at the bar. After a few minutes, a guy came up to me and said "Hello, Paul". I looked at him and said "I'm sorry, you must be mistaken. My name isn't Paul". He didn't believe me, so I went upstairs and got my passport. This guy was the Tour Manager for Simple Minds, and he thought that I was an Irish country singer called Paul Brady. He asked if we would help him play a joke on Jim Kerr, so I wrapped Janine's scarf round my mouth and sat there.

Jim Kerr and Charlie Burchill came in and sat down next to us. Jim put his hand out and said, "Hi Paul". I nodded shook his hand and Janine said that I had a bad throat infection, and I was under doctor's orders not to speak. They got us some drinks and they were talking away to the pair of us, with me nodding and smiling as a response. The Tour Manager was sat next to me pissing himself. In the end I spoke and told them who I was, and they had a laugh about it. I told them that I had worked the stage at the Russell, Rotters and the Hacienda when they had played. They remembered the stout lad, Slim. It was a great night.

Next morning, we nipped into HMV on O'Connell Street and Janine had me stand at the end of a rack, while she picked up Paul Brady CD's and compared the sleeves to me. She worked out that if you looked at me side on, then I looked like him.

I drove the 180 miles to Lacken, visited Mum and Dad's grave, had a walk on the beach and then drove to Achill Island. This is a beautiful part of the West of Ireland. The road signs are in Gaelic and most of the people who live there still speak Gaelic as well. We spent the night at an Inn and the following morning, we drove back to Dublin and flew home.

In March 2006 our son Liam Gerard Duffy was born at Trafford General Hospital and life was going fine. She had to have an emergency C Section due to him turning and it was very strange watching Liam being pulled from her belly. I was sat with him for hours and Ann turned up with Jack and Tom to meet him. Janine took a few weeks to get over the operation and she was okay once healed.

The 2006/07 season started with Janine coming to the games with us. To get her a ticket, Jack and I had to move out of the Family Stand and the three of us moved to the top tier of the North Stand. It was a climb up eight flights of stairs to get to the tier and I would enjoy a plastic bottle of warm weak beer before I took my seat. The view was great from up there as you could see the whole pitch and you could see the moves happening before they did. It just shows how great a player Paul Scholes was as he could see the moves at ground level. The stand was very steep, and it gave you a sense of vertigo with a pull forward sensation when you jumped to celebrate.

The season finished with United crowned champions again with a six-point gap to Chelsea who finished runner-up. Ronaldo came of age and was unplayable this season and all of the doubters had been silenced. This was the start of the Ronaldo that went on to become one of the best players in the world but more importantly after three long years United were back. I was so pleased that Jack had now experienced a league-winning champaign. It was great to see the joy on his face when we lifted the trophy.

Janine had severe post-natal depression to such␣as extent she couldn't stand seeing me holding Liam. This went untreated and, coupled with severe money issues, caused arguments and tension in the marriage. I never knew at the time what was wrong with her. I should have gone to see the doctor with her and got her some help because we were a perfect fit. She left me in July 2007 and took Liam back to America with her. I should have fought harder to keep them. If we couldn't be together then I should have refused to pay for her flight to the States and used the money to set her up in a flat somewhere in Manchester instead. She could have had a new life over here, and I could have seen Liam every weekend. This one was, without doubt, the *worst* decision I ever made as I never got to see my son grow up.

When Janine was with me, I could never understand how someone like me could have ended up with a woman like that. I was definitely punching well above my weight. When we used to go out men would hit on her when I went to the bar. If I left her for just a minute someone would be trying it on with her.

However Janine and I loved each other with a fierce passion and our relationship was very intense but we just couldn't live together. When I look back on it now we would argue over the most meaningless things which were mainly caused by cultural differences. We should have asked what they meant instead of the red mist descending and a row developing that went on for a couple of days. I feel that I should apologise to Jack and Tom for putting them through it. I hope that it didn't ruin your childhood. I also want to apologise to Liam as his parent's inability to communicate with each other robbed him of the chance of having a Dad and growing up with his step brothers. It stopped him living in Urmston, which is a leafy suburb of Manchester instead of living in a dodgy part of Portland with high gun crime.

We were hot-tempered red heads, and the relationship was passionate – we were either head over heels in love or at each other's throats, there was no middle ground. We spent the whole time either fucking, fighting or trying to make up. Neither of us would back down and it's a shame that it didn't work out. We tried but it was not meant to be.

On 10 August 2007 Mr Manchester, Tony Wilson passed away. I didn't go to the funeral as I knew that it would be packed. I have been to pay my respects at his grave. His headstone was designed by Peter Saville

Factory Fairy Tales

and Ben Kelly and his coffin was given the catalogue number (FAC 501). Manchester Town Hall flew their Union Flag at half-mast to honour his life. RIP Tony, you fucking legend.

In late November Sex Pistols played at the MEN Arena and I was so glad to have finally seen them. I know that they were 30 years older and didn't have the same shock value as in 1976 but it was the four original members playing the same songs that they had recorded together. The place was sold out and they put on a great show. I loved them. You can't get better than the guitar intro to 'Pretty Vacant' and the pounding beat of 'Holidays in The Sun'.

37. Moscow and Divorce

The next major event for me in April 2008 was James reforming and they released a new album *Hey Ma*. I loved it from the first listen. Jack, Tom and I went to see them at Liverpool University. James were great and Peter Kay (famous comic from Bolton) introduced them on the night. They played a lot of songs from *Hey Ma* and the crowd weren't very receptive and kept asking for the old stuff. Tim Booth told the crowd that the new songs would be classics soon so give them a chance. It was so good to see them back together again.

Jack and I flew out of Manchester on 21st May bound for Moscow and the Champions League Final. We wanted to see Red Square, but the police told us that unless there were about ten of us, we would get mugged on the tube so we spent the day in the Fan Zone outside the stadium. We had our zone and Chelsea had the same at the opposite end of the stadium. There was no way of getting out of the Fan Zone once you had gone in so there was no chance of any trouble between the fans.

After a couple of hours a group of about 600 Russians wearing blue scarves walked into our Fan Zone. They were all marching together and singing and there was a bit of tension as they matched towards us. No one was sure what was happening, and we were a bit wary. As they got nearer we could see they were carrying a massive banner with a picture of United centre half Nemanja Vidic and they were singing his name. It turned out that they were all fans of Spartak Moscow who Vidic used to play for. They hung around for a while, drinking with the United fans and swapping scarves. They were top guys. The game was being played at the Luzhniki Stadium and the pitch was miles away from the stands, as it had a massive running track going all round it. United went ahead with a brilliant header from Ronaldo and Frank Lampard equalized for Chelsea before half time. The second half was boring but then Drogba was sent off for slapping Nemanja Vidic four minutes from the end of extra time before it went to penalties. This slap probably cost Chelsea the cup as Drogba would have been one of the first penalty takers for Chelsea instead of John Terry – when Ronaldo missed his penalty Terry stepped up and I couldn't bear to watch it, so sat down. He slipped as he hit the ball and it hit the post. Our end of the ground erupted and the guy standing next to me pulled me up by my hair and both he and Jack were screaming in my face. We scored the next two penalties, which meant that Nicolas Anelka had to score to keep Chelsea in the tie. Edwin van der Sar saved and United were once again champions of Europe. We celebrated with the players as Ferdinand and Giggs lifted the trophy. The celebrations went on for a long time down at our end. It was 1.30am in Moscow. Getting home proved to be a nightmare – we were stuck at the airport for hours thanks to a bureaucratic fuck up and didn't get on our flight until 11.30 the next day!

During the summer I went back to Portland to see Liam and Janine. Tom didn't want to come with me this time. We argued a bit and she was more bitter toward me, and I thought that there was probably another man in her life. God knows, enough of them used to hit on her. I went there in hope and came home and accepted the reality that it was done. I dated another four or five off the dating site, but they didn't float my boat.

Due to financial issues I was unable to see Liam again until the summer of 2011. I lost over three years of his life. It's really hard having a child that you can't see because they are on the other side of the world. It has caused me so much pain over the years. As it turned out, I missed everything important about him growing up. First words, first steps, first day at school. My lads had their step brother taken away from them and they have never had a real relationship with him. I thought things couldn't get much worst but in December 2008 I was made redundant from my job at Ferroli Boilers.

It took me nearly nine months to find another job as there was a global recession taking place. Due to all of the home improvements that Janine and I had done to my house, I was in massive negative equity. I had to sign on again as unemployed and the social wouldn't pay my mortgage for the first three months and then they would only pay a certain percentage of it, so I was screwed. I tried to get a job, but I kept getting knocked back as "being over qualified".

Then I received a phone call from a barrister from Portland. He told me that Janine wanted a divorce, but she wanted him to talk to me. He explained that due to an agreement between the US and UK regarding absent fathers, he was entitled to take child benefit and alimony every month out of my salary. I told him that I was unemployed, and he explained that it would kick in once I was working again with the missed payments being collected first. He explained that the reason why he was calling me was to assure me that Janine did not want this to happen as we had already agreed a monthly payment for Liam, and she did not want alimony. He told me that his hands were tied and once the divorce started then legally he had to demand these payments and the only way he could ignore these payments would be if I was declared bankrupt. This would make his demands null and void. I had large credit card debts, one large loan, a huge mortgage and was running out of ideas. I was officially declared bankrupt in April 2009 and was discharged a few months later.

The bankruptcy solved most of my financial woes, but I was still not paying my mortgage and the mortgage company were not really helping. I had a few meetings with Shelter, the Homeless Charity, regarding the fact that I might be made homeless soon. They came to the bankruptcy hearing to make sure that no charge was put on my house. They also dealt with the mortgage company for me. In September, the week before I was due in court to have my home reprocessed, I got offered a new job. As a result the court date was cancelled. The mortgage company then spoke to me and after adding on all the missed payments with interest, my new payment would be £1250 interest only per month. I would still be in a major financial hole for a few years more until I sold the house in 2017 but at least I was not going to be homeless.

At the end of the 2009/10 season I had to give up my Season Ticket at United as the Glazers had finally priced me out of going to see them. I had enjoyed my time watching the Reds as after winning the league in 1993 Fergie got greedy and won it another 12 times. Throw in two Champions League, four FA Cups, three League Cups, and two World Club champions - it's been fun.

I got divorced in April 2010 on the grounds that Janine would go off the radar for weeks on end and not answer my calls, so I had no idea whether Liam was okay or not. It was totally frustrating for me, and I don't think that she ever understood how painful it was for me to have no contact with my son or if she did, she just didn't care. Thankfully, things are much better nowadays.

I read recently, that the top causes of depression are as follows: death of a loved one, marriage, divorce, loss of a job, moving home, birth of a child, and bankruptcy. Between the end of 2001 and the middle of 2010, I experienced all of these life changing events and I'm still standing!

Factory Fairy Tales

1988 – 2021

100 albums

New Order: *Technique*
U2: *Achtung Baby; All that You can't Leave Behind; How to Dismantle an Atomic Bomb; No Line on The Horizon; Songs of Innocence*
Stone Roses: *Stone Roses*
Public Image Limited: *This is PIL; What The World Needs Now*
Oasis: *Definitely Maybe; (What's the Story) Morning Glory*
Nirvana: *Never Mind*
James: *Gold Mother; Seven; Laid; Millionaires; Hey Ma; La Petite Mort; Living in Extraordinary Times*
The Alarm: *In The Poppyfields*
Inspiral Carpets: *Life; The Beast Inside*
David Bowie: *Heathen; The Next Day*
Blur: *Parklife*
Pulp: *His n Hers; Different Class*
Muse: *Absolution; Black Holes and Revelations*
The Cure: *Wish*
Echo and The Bunnymen: *Evergreen; Siberia*
Placebo: *Placebo; Without You I'm Nothing; Black Market Music; Sleeping with Ghosts; Meds*
REM: *Out of Time; Automatic for the People*
The Killers: *Hot Fuss; Sam's Town*
The Editors: *The Back Room; An End has a Start*
Killing Joke: *Killing Joke (2003); Absolute Dissent*
Iron Maiden: *Fear of the Dark; Brave New World*
Queens of the Stone Age: *Songs For The Deaf*
The Pretty Reckless: *Light Me Up*
Happy Mondays: *Bummed*
The Damned: *So Who's Paranoid; Evil Spirits.*
Nick Cave: *Murder Ballads; Dig Lazarus Dig; No More Shall We Want; Nocturama; Let Love In.*

Ged Duffy

Iggy Pop: *Post Pop Depression*
Artic Monkeys: *Whatever People Say I Am, That's What I'm Not.*
Black Sabbath: *13*
Johnny Cash: *American III; Solitary Man; American 1V The Man comes Around.*
The Charlatans: *Us and Us Only*
The Cranberries: *No Need to Argue.*
Green Day: *American Idiot*
Linkin Park: *Hybrid Theory; Meteora.*
Metallica: *Black Album; Load; Reload.*
Mötorhead : *1916.*
Lou Reed: *New York*
The Verve: *Urban Hymns*
Coldplay: *A Rush of Blood to the Head*
Radiohead: *OK Computer*
Sheryl Crow: *Sheryl Crow*
Bruce Springsteen: *High Hopes; Working on a Dream.*
Saw Doctors: *If This is Rock and Roll I want my Old Job Back; Same oul Town.*
Guns N Roses: *Appetite for Destruction; Use Your Illusion I; Use Your Illusion II*
Foo Fighters: *Sonic Highways*
Slow Readers Club: *Build a Tower*
PJ Harvey: *Stories from The City; Stories from The Sea; The Hope Six Demolition Project.*
Fountains of Wayne: *Welcome Interstate Managers*
Blondie: *No Exit*
Neil Young: *Chrome Dreams II*
Seasick Steve: *Hubcap Music*
Rolling Stones: *Voodoo Lounge*
Manic Street Preachers: *Gold Against The Soul; Everything Must Go.*
Noel Gallagher's High Flying Birds: *Noel Gallagher's High Flying Birds*

Factory Fairy Tales
Liam Gallagher: *Why Me? Why Not*
The Levellers: *Levelling The Land*
Northside: *Chicken Rhythms*
Psychedelic Furs: *World Outside; Book of Day*

A life spent making mistakes?

Janine and Liam came over to see me in 2011, 2012 and 2013. It was great to see how Liam had developed and actually go places with him. Janine and I had a few rows but nothing serious. I went over there in 2016 and then we met in Ireland later that year. One interesting thing happened on this trip when we went to a place called Ceide Fields which was in the next village over from Lacken and whilst there we saw some guys doing a dry stone wall demonstration. I asked them what stone they were using, and they told me that it was Lacken stone. This was the stone from our quarry, so I quizzed them further and discovered that my Uncle Mick had been the silent partner in the company that bought the quarry from him, as Executor of the Estate, several years ago. Once again, he had shafted the lot of us! The only thing I have left to say about this man is that he passed away a couple of years ago and his bitch of a wife passed away a couple of days before him. Both funerals were attended by their three sons who came over from Manchester and nobody from the village attended either funeral. They can rot in hell if there is one.

In 2017 I sold my house and cleared my debts, it had taken me nearly ten years to sort out the mess I had got myself into following the breakup of the marriage. Tom lives in a flat with his mate and Jack has his own house where he lives with his girl friend Nic.

Over the last few years I have seen Iron Maiden, AC/DC, The Specials, The Cult, Red Hot Chilli Peppers, The Pogues, Muse, Radiohead, The Editors, The Damned, The Stranglers, Killing Joke, and Linkin Park (Tom came to this with me and I will make a bold claim that it was the best ever gig that I have been to in my life. The fusion of rap, metal guitar, rock bass and drums and a great singer in Chester Bennington made it so memorable) to name a few. I still go and see James as often as I can and gigs that stand out are James at Manchester Central 2008, the Bridgewater Hall acoustic tour 2011 (where they played with a 22 piece Orchestra and a 16 person choir which was a mind-blowing experience), MEN Arena 2013 with Echo and The Bunnymen, Albert Hall 2017, MEN Arena in 2019 with The Charlatans, and Bingley Festival 2019 with Echo and The Bunnymen. James are the one band that Jack or Tom will come and see with their

Factory Fairy Tales

Dad and I'm so proud that they both like them. Around this time Frank moved to Lytham St Annes to live with a new woman, and we haven't had much contact since he moved.

Looking back on it all now I can definitely say that I have been blessed. I was born in the greatest city in the world and was fortunate to have been at the right age when punk kicked the doors down of the established British music industry and Johnny and his boys marched in. I had some great times, saw some amazing bands, worked at several great venues, formed my own bands, recorded singles for the coolest record label in the world, toured with New Order, The Fall, and Death Cult, did a few too many drugs, drank a lot, and met several lovely ladies along the way.

The Electric Circus, the Russell Club, the Mayflower, the Osbourne, Rotters, The Hulme Estate, Belle Vue, Arnesby Walk, and TJ Davidson's Rehearsal Studios, where Joy Division filmed the video to 'Love Will Tear Us Apart' have all been demolished. Rafters, Fagins and Deville's are now offices. The Hacienda had its front section demolished, rebuilt, and converted into apartments. They kept the large stage doors, which we used to load the band's equipment in, as part of the frontage of the building. The Cyprus Tavern is now a Greek restaurant.

I really feel that the council missed a massive trick with the Hacienda. Crosby Homes converted the building into apartments, and the council should have negotiated an area behind the stage doors where they could have displayed Hacienda artefacts and housed the Factory Records collection of Colin Gibbins. It would have been a fitting tribute to the legacy of both Factory Records and the Hacienda. It would have made Tony Wilson proud.

I was so fortunate to have found two of the most amazing women and married them both. Lesley was the calm rock that I needed at that stage in my life. She taught me how to live and behave in a normal relationship. She made sure that I never drifted back into the world of drugs again and ensured that I would live past the age of 30. Janine was the wild, sexually liberated girl that I needed to bring me out of the deep, dark depression that I was in, following the passing of Lesley. She gave me hope, and a whole new outlook on life. We fitted together perfectly.

When I go to a gig nowadays, I stay near the back because if you are anywhere near the stage you can't see the fucking band because every prick is holding their phone above their head filming the show. I would ban phones from gigs if I could.

I've managed to make contact with Slim, Karenne, Steve O'Donnell, Guy Ainsworth, June Fellowes, Deb Zee, Pete McKay, Danny O'Sullivan, Mark Hoyle, and Rocking Dave Holmes via Facebook. Big Stuart came back to Manchester for a visit pre-Covid and I met up with him, his brother Guy, skinhead Paul and Lee Pickering. Lee and I have met a few more times since. I have met up with Mani as well. I talk to Tony France and Hooky on the phone. Met Kaiser in The Old Nags Head in Town a couple of years ago and had a great chat over 10 pints of Guinness.

I've been to see my ex-partner as well a few times. She is 100% focused on her Christian beliefs and she scares me at times with her warnings that the Trumpets are sounding, the chosen will rise, the mark of the beast and the end of days.

Big Dave comes up from London every quarter with his job and he stays at Giggs and Neville's Hotel Football which is opposite Old Trafford. I meet up with him and we have a beer and a meal. We've been to a couple of games as well in the League Cup and Champions League whilst he's been up. I was speaking to Tony France recently and he told me that when I left the band, the heart went out of it and that he should have followed me out the door as it was never the same again.

Thanks to James Nice, from LTM Records, for sending me a vinyl album of Stockholm Monsters *All at Once* a few years ago, I ended up buying a turntable and my vinyl collection has now grown to about 600 albums. So I'm addicted to vinyl again and I love the hunt of searching out a great record.

If you're ever in Manchester, check out 'Reel Around The Fountain Records' in Stretford Arndale. You won't be disappointed. Tell Nigel that Ged's book sent you and he'll look after you! The other shop is 'Music For The Soul Records' in Urmston and once again, tell Dave that I sent you and he'll take care of you.

I now have a job that I enjoy doing and I work for a company called Hydroheat Underfloor Heating. I love it and my biggest disappointment is that this will be my last job. My two bosses, Tom and Lee, are top blokes. Jake and Daisy are both cool people and Charles pumps his techno out loud in the warehouse. I used to be constantly told that I'd never make it to the age of 30 but now I'm a grumpy, old, fat bastard, that's still got his own teeth and hair. Not bad for a 60 year

Top: Jack and me just after the birth of Tom, (middle) Liam on holiday in Ireland, (bottom) Nic, Jack and Tom.

Ged Duffy

I was honoured to meet Colin Gibbons and be photographed in front of his magnificent and complete Factory Records vinyl collection.

old. And do you know something? I'm fucking happy with my life.

This has been my account of growing up in Manchester and if it differs from your recollection of those times, then I'm sorry. I've written it as my 60 year-old brain remembers it. Most of the dates I have got off the internet, but I have to say I reckon that I must have been to at least 1,200 gigs over the years.

If anything in this book has offended you. Just get over it. Insults to my friends from Liverpool and Leeds are just football based as I love both of these cities and have friends from both . I pondered long and hard about putting so much football in the book but that's what Manchester is famous for, music and United (sorry my blue friends).

Hope you enjoyed it. As you will now be well aware I have made

Factory Fairy Tales

a lot of stupid decisions over the years and in my defence they felt right to me at the time, if only we had hindsight!

I found this quote which just about sums up my life:

> *"A life spent making mistakes is not only more honourable, but more useful than a life spent doing nothing"*
>
> George Bernard Shaw

Acknowledgements

Thanks to the following people for their help:

Peter Hook, Mani, Colin Gibbins, Lee Pickering, Iain Key, Nigel Young at Reel around the Fountain Record Store, James Nice, LTM Records, Janine Duffy, Deb Zee, June Fellowes, Tony France, Mick Middles, Big Dave Sands, Big Stuart Parker, Marc Jones, Karenne Wood, 'Rocking' Doctor Dave Holmes, Julie Adamson from Russell Club Facebook Group, Graham McPhail from the One Man Clapping Facebook Group, Rob Sonic Kerford, Guy Ainsworth, Steve Smith: webmaster@neworderdiscography.com, Kaiser, Dave Garland from Music for The Soul Record Shop, Andy Jenkins, Gabor@ Bauhaus Gig Guide, Margaret and John O Reilly.

Last of all, a special mention to a great mate Slim; without knowing you, most of this book would never have happened. You had my back for several years and got me in and out of several scrapes, and I'm forever grateful for knowing you.

Reference Materials

Colin Gibbins: *Manchester Music and M9 Kitz*. Buy it. It's a great book.

Peter Hook: *Unknown Pleasures*

Peter Hook: *Substance, Inside New Order*

Peter Hook: *The Hacienda, How not to Run a Club*

Mark Johnson: *An Ideal For Living*

James Nice: *Shadowplayers, The rise and fall of Factory Records*

Mick Middles: *Factory, The story of Factory Records*

Stuart Maconie: *Folklore, The Official history of James*

Gareth Ashton: *Manchester: It Never Rains*

Martin Ryan: *Friends of Mine: Punk in Manchester 1976-1978*

Photo credits

Russell Club photos: Deb Zee, Lee and Tony, Terry J Egan; Monsters at Rafters: Rob 'Sonic' Kerford; Bauhaus at Fagins: Mark Atkinson; Colin Gibbins and his collection: Leroy Caines; John F Keenan for the Futurama posters; Tony Barratt for the Commanche photo.